WORD

EFFECTIVE SENTENCES

PARAGRAPHS

44 GLOSSARY

THE MACMILLAN HANDBOOK OF ENGLISH

FOURTH EDITION

JOHN M. KIERZEK

and

WALKER GIBSON

THE MACMILLAN HANDBOOK OF ENGLISH

THE MACMILLAN COMPANY
New York

Second Printing 1960

Library of Congress catalog card number: 60-5258

The Macmillan Company, New York
Brett-Macmillan Ltd., Galt, Ontario

Printed in the United States of America

ACKNOWLEDGMENTS

The following British and Canadian publishers and authors' agents have kindly granted permission to reproduce material from the publications cited. All quotations granted by American publishers are credited in the places of their occurrence in the text.

George Allen & Unwin Ltd.: *On Education* by Bertrand Russell.

Edward Arnold Publishers Ltd.: *Two Cheers for Democracy* by E. M. Forster.

Jonathan Cape Ltd.: *In Our Time* by Ernest Hemingway, and *The Enormous Room* by E. E. Cummings.

Cassell & Company Ltd.: *Into Battle* by Winston Churchill.

Wm. Collins Sons & Co. Ltd.: *The Houses in Between* by Howard Spring.

J. M. Dent & Sons Ltd.: *Scenes and Portraits* by Van Wyck Brooks.

Eyre & Spottiswoode Ltd.: *Autumn Across America* by Edwin Way Teale.

Hamish Hamilton Ltd.: *The Big Change* by Frederick Lewis Allen, and *The Second Tree from the Corner* by E. B. White.

George G. Harrap & Co. Ltd.: *Mirror for Man* by Clyde Kluckhohn.

William Heinemann Ltd.: *Of Time and the River* by Thomas Wolfe, *Cannery Row* by John Steinbeck.

The Hogarth Press Ltd.: *The Death of a Moth and Other Essays* and *Between the Acts* by Virginia Woolf.

McClelland and Stewart Ltd.: *Blood, Sweat and Tears* by Winston Churchill.

Methuen & Co. Ltd.: *Hills and the Sea* by Hilaire Belloc.

William Morris Agency: *The Houses in Between* by Howard Spring.

Paul Reynolds & Son: *The Wind and the Rain* by Thomas Burke.

Ann Walkins, Inc.: *Up Front* by Bill Mauldin.

PREFACE

Those who have used earlier editions of *The Macmillan Handbook of English* are familiar with the general plan of this book. Like its predecessors, this edition is a rhetoric and handbook combined. It may be used as either or as both. Material that can be most profitably used in classroom instruction has been placed in the rhetoric. Material most useful in the marking and revision of papers has been placed in the handbook. Of course, one part supplements the other and enables the teacher to repeat instruction, when necessary, with new materials and a fresh approach. The first part of the book attempts to give the beginner the sort of helpful, common-sense advice about writing that he needs the most when he is a beginner. The student is introduced to the concept of English as a living and growing language. He is then taken through discussions of grammar as a tool of effective writing, of building good sentences and good paragraphs, to the process of planning and writing compositions of various kinds and lengths. The first section leads up to a discussion of a long paper based on the investigation of published material, the most elaborate and ambitious project that the student will undertake.

The chapter on the library paper has been entirely rewritten. Most of the material in it is new, including a new sample research paper. The system of documentation in footnotes and bibliography has been adapted to suit the needs of undergraduates from the revised *Style Sheet* of the Modern Language Association.

The material of the second part of the book—the handbook itself—is organized under forty-four divisions. A comprehensive index and a theme-correction chart help both the student and the teacher to find any section easily and quickly.

In a period when both linguistic research and pedagogical methods are in a state of rapid change, it is essential that a handbook for students of writing should present from time to time a new and fresh face. Old illustrations become dated; through long use, teaching devices lose their vitality. Profiting from experience, from new knowledge, and from the good advice of other teachers, we have tried to strengthen and enrich the teaching devices that proved useful and have discarded those that proved weak. Much of the illustrative material is new; all of the exercises have been rewritten. Most important of all, perhaps, the handbook has been simplified so that its forty-four divisions are more compact and convenient for teacher and student to use.

In the preparation of the fourth edition we have received advice and help from teachers throughout the country, and for that help we wish to express our deep gratitude. Special thanks go to Professor Oscar Cargill, New York University, for his valuable advice and for his help in seeing the book through the press.

We also wish to thank those whose student papers or outlines we have used as examples throughout the book: Hallie Ashton, Jeanne Ball, Alan Berman, Pat Caven, Shirley Haag, Janet McIntosh, Marilyn Manley, George R. Powers, Elizabeth Roosa, Michal Rubin, Pearl Swanson, and Audrey Wilsey.

John M. Kierzek
Walker Gibson

CONTENTS

Part 2: A HANDBOOK OF WRITING AND REVISION

Part 1

THE EXPRESSION AND COMMUNICATION OF THOUGHT

Chapter 1

THE ENGLISH LANGUAGE

"þyslīc mē is gesewen, þū cyning, þis andwearde līf manna on eorðan tō wiðmetenesse þǣre tīde þe ūs uncuð is, swylc swā þu æt swǣsendum sitte mid þīnum ealdormannum ǫnd þegnum on wintertīde, ǫnd sīe fȳr onǣled ǫnd þīn heall gewyrmed, ǫnd hit rīne, ǫnd snīwe, ǫnd styrme ūte; cume ān spearwa ǫnd hraedlīce þæt hūs þurhflēo, cume þurh ōþre duru in þurh ōþre ūt gewīte. Hwæt hē on þā tīd þe hē inne bið, ne bið hrinen mid þȳ storme þæs wintres; ac þæt bið ān ēagan bryhtm ǫnd þæt lǣsste fæc, ac hē sōna of wintra on þone winter eft cymeð. Swā þonne þis mǫnna līf tō medmiclum fæce ætȳweð; hwæt þǣr foregange, oððe hwæt þǣr æfterfylige, wē ne cunnan. For ðon gif þēos lār ōwiht cūðlīcre ǫnd gerisenlīcre brę̨nge, þæs weorþe is þæt wē þǣre fylgen."[1]

It is a long road that our English language has traveled since that day more than thirteen centuries ago when the old thane arose and, with the dignity of one good man speaking to another, said to his king, "Now, this is the way it looks to me. . . ." He spoke in the native tongue of the inhabitants of England, a language known by scholars as Anglo-Saxon or Old English. This, more than any other tongue, in spite of all the intermarriages and all the additions of new blood, is the one important great-ancestor of the English language which you and I speak and write.

The Family of Languages. The position of English in the family tree of Indo-European languages is shown by the table on page 8. English is one of a number of West Germanic languages. The Germanic group of languages is one of a number of groups,

[1] See page 17 for a free translation.

all descended from a hypothetical parent language, the Indo-European. All this is true yet highly misleading unless we remember that, although English is mainly Germanic in its original history and in the way it relates words in sentences, the words themselves come mostly from other languages. Less than a quarter of modern English words are Germanic in origin, whereas over half are derived from Latin. The rest of our English vocabulary has been borrowed from a whole range of miscellaneous languages: ancient Greek, Scandinavian, French, Spanish, Italian, German, Russian, Arabic, Persian, American Indian, and many others.

It was a very long time ago when families or tribes first broke away from the parent Indo-European group of people and, through separation, made inevitable the formation of separate languages. The facts about how this must have happened, and about the relationships among the various languages, have been dug up and pieced together comparatively recently, with a ratiocinative skill that makes a fictional detective look like an infant. No living man has ever heard or seen an actual Indo-European word. The idea that this language existed is a hypothesis—a particularly well-documented sort of guess—and yet, like most scientific hypotheses, it is almost as good as a proved fact. Very likely a parent Indo-European language did exist; scholars are even willing to place the home of those who spoke it as somewhere in central east Europe. A few clues, like the existence of words for animals and plants of a temperate European climate and the absence of any words relating to sea or ocean, gave the philologists their interesting lead.

And as to how language itself originated, your guess is as good as anybody else's. Nobody knows, and at present there does not seem to be any possibility that anybody ever will know. Scholars amuse themselves with ingenious guesses, but they do not pretend that their guesses are hypotheses.

Periods of Linguistic Change. Students of the English language have divided its historical growth into three main periods: the Old English Period, from 450 to 1100; the Middle English Period, from 1100 to 1500; and the Modern English Period, from 1500 to the present time. It must not be assumed, however, that in any one year the people of England stopped speaking one kind of language and began speaking another. The change was gradual, and yet there were definite historical events occurring at the times mentioned which caused a more rapid change in the language of the people of England. These events were the invasion of England by the Angles, Saxons, and Jutes in 449, the Norman Conquest in 1066, and the coming of the English Renaissance about 1500.

There were, of course, people in England before 450. The earliest known inhabitants of England were the Britons, a Celtic branch of the Indo-European family, with whom Caesar's Roman armies came into contact in the summer of 55 B.C. Almost a century later the Roman armies of Claudius returned to England and proceeded in earnest to conquer and enslave the native Britons. Four centuries of Roman rule left the natives so thoroughly Romanized and dependent upon their masters that when trouble at home forced the Romans to pull in their armies from their distant colonies, the Britons were helpless against the attacks of their northern neighbors.

According to a later historian, a native prince, Vortigern, called in some Saxon tribes from the mainland of Europe to fight the northern invaders. Unfortunately for the Britons, these liberators quickly took the entire country into protective custody and proved that spears and axes can be instruments of genocide as devastating as an atom bomb. What Britons survived the wars and massacres retreated westward and northward; a few must have remained, existing as best they could in unhappy servility. First Britons and then Britons and Romans occupied the English land for five hundred years of known history and left practically no trace upon our English language. The real history of our language begins with the Angles, the Saxons, and the Jutes.

The Old English Period. From 449, the legendary date of the first coming of the Saxons to England, to 1066, when William the Bastard defeated and killed the Saxon King Harold at the Battle of Hastings, is a period of 616 years—a time span almost four times as long as the present life span of the great American republic. Many things can happen in 616 years, and many things did happen. England became civilized, prosperous, and largely Christianized.

Under the influence of the Christian missionaries and the organized church, schools and monasteries were set up. Politically, the English land was divided up among four important kingdoms—Northumbria, Mercia, Wessex, and Kent—which at various times rose to temporal importance and then declined, as kingdoms do in a space of six hundred years. These kingdoms, too, were visited by trouble of the kind that they had brought upon the Britons. Another Germanic people, the Danes, descended upon the island in raids of growing magnitude over two centuries of time and came close to drawing the final curtain over the first scene of what was to become the great drama of the English-speaking peoples. The Danes and the Anglo-Saxons were, in a way, kinsfolk, and although kinship did not mellow the savagery of feud or war, it may have been one reason why the two people could arrange to live together at first in a sort of cold war and later in an armed friendship. Gradually the Danes were absorbed by the more stubborn and also more civilized breed, and although the Danes, like most invaders, wantonly pillaged libraries and burned books, enough of the written language of the Anglo-Saxons survived so that we know pretty well what sort of speech our ancestors used. The language remained predominantly Anglo-Saxon; it is estimated that the Norse additions amounted to less than five per cent of our present vocabulary. From the Danish we have such everyday words as the verbs *give*, *hit*, *raise*, *take*, *want;* the nouns *sky*, *sister*, *skirt;* the pronoun forms *they*, *their*, *them;* and hundreds of place names in the eastern part of England, which was once known as the Danelaw.

The Middle English Period. About a century and a half before the end of the Old English Period, another Scandinavian people, the Normans (Norsemen), landed on the Normandy beaches, took over the country, settled down, and adopted the language and culture of the French. In 1066, William, Duke of Normandy, after a tempestuous and unsavory career in his own country, laid claim to the English throne. The Norman Conquest followed his decisive victory at the Battle of Hastings. What eventually happened to the language of England can be better understood if one remembers that the Norman Conquest was not a mass migration of one people intent upon displacing another, but rather the personal adventure of a dictator grasping for more power and distinction. William the Conqueror proceeded to subdue Anglo-Saxon England from above, killing and replacing the native rulers, confiscating what property was worth taking and parceling it out to his followers, promulgating new laws and decrees. Meanwhile, life went on; the work was done, crops were grown, trade revived, and the common people continued to speak their native Anglo-Saxon speech. The language of the court and the upper classes was Norman French. The language of the church was Latin, the universal language of that day.

For a time England continued to be trilingual. In the course of time a number of things happened which tended to separate the English people from their neighbors across the Channel. For the rulers it became increasingly more important to be kings of England than to remain dukes of a small French province. Wars with France and Scotland, the Crusades, a break with the Church of Rome, the rise of the middle classes, all tended to foster a sense of national unity and importance. By the middle of the fourteenth century, English, not French or Latin, became the accepted language of the ruling classes, the law courts, and the church. More than that, one dialect of the three which had persisted since the earliest Anglo-Saxon times, the East Midland dialect of London and its governmental agencies, emerged as the leading language of England, a position which it has held to this day. The fact that Chaucer, a Londoner, wrote his popular stories in this dialect may have helped to establish it.

Naturally, the English that emerged was greatly enriched by additions of Norman French words. As one might expect, most of these words came out of the social, political, and economic life in which the Normans dominated. From the language of government we get such words as *parliament*, *crown*, *duke*, *sovereign;* from the law courts *judge, jury, justice, jail, plaintiff;* from feudal life and the life of the higher social classes *castle*, *count*, *baron*, *vassal*, *liege*, *war*, *prison*, *barber*, *grocer*, *tailor*, *mantle*, *labor*, *chamber*. And as an example of the fact that often two sets of names of the same object survived, there is the old joke that

Indo-European

- 1. Indo-Iranian
  - Indian
    - Sanskrit
    - Prakrit, etc.
    - Hindustani, etc.
    - Gypsy
  - Iranian
    - Old Persian
    - Zend
    - Modern Persian, etc.
- 2. Armenian
- 3. Hellenic
  - Ionic
  - Attic
  - Doric
  - Æolic
    - Modern Greek
- 4. Albanian
- 5. Italic
  - Oscan; Umbrian
  - Latin
    - French
    - Spanish
    - Italian
    - Portuguese
    - Roumanian
- 6. Germanic
  - Norse (North)
    - Icelandic
    - Danish
    - Swedish
    - Norwegian
  - Gothic (East)
  - West
    - High
      - German
      - Austrian
    - Low
      - Old Saxon
      - Dutch; Flemish
      - Frisian
      - Anglo-Saxon (English)
- 7. Balto-Slavic
  - Baltic
    - Prussian
    - Lithuanian, etc.
  - Slavic
    - Russian
    - Bulgarian
    - Czech
    - Polish
- 8. Celtic
  - Gallic (old Gaul)
  - Gaelic
    - Irish
    - Scotch-Gaelic
    - Manx
  - Cymric
    - Welsh
    - Cornish
    - Breton

whereas the Saxon knew his domestic animals on the hoof as *swine*, *sheep*, *cow*, *calf*, *ox*, and *deer* (all of Anglo-Saxon derivation), the Norman lord knew them on the table as *pork*, *mutton*, *beef*, *veal*, and *venison* (all of Norman derivation).

By the end of the fourteenth century the language had taken on a distinctly modern look. If we examine closely the following samples, the first in Anglo-Saxon, the second from the time of Chaucer, the third from the time of Shakespeare and King James I of Great Britain, and the last from the present, the whole thing begins to come into focus. The strange Anglo-Saxon words become less strange and puzzling, and we seem to be observing, in a fashion, the coming of age of our language.

And eft hē ongan hī æt þǣre sǣ lǣran. And him wæs mycel mę̄negu tō gegaderod, swā þæt hē on scip ēode, and on bǣre sǣ wæs; and eall sēo mę̄negu ymbe þā sǣ wæs on lande. And hē hī fela on bigspellum lǣrde, and him tō cwæð on his lāre, Gehȳrað: Ūt ēode sē sǣdere his sǣd tō sāwenne. And þā hē sēow, sum fēoll wið þone weg, and fugelas cōmon and hit frǣton. Sum fēoll ofer stānscyligean, þār hit næfde mycele eorðan, and sōna ūp ēode; and for þām hit næfde eorðan þiccnesse, þā hīt ūp ēode, sēo sunne hit forswǣlde, and hit forscranc, for þām hit wyrtruman næfde. And sum fēoll on þornas; þā stigon ðā þornas and forðrysmodon þæt, and hit wæstm ne bær. And sum fēoll on gōd land, and hit sealde ūppstīgendne and wexendne wæstm; and ān brōhte þrītigfealdne, sum syxtigfealdne, sum hundfealdne.

—From the Anglo-Saxon translation of the Gospels, about the year 1000.

And eft Jhesus bigan to teche at the see; and myche puple was gaderid to hym, so that he wente in to a boot, and sat in the see, and al the puple was aboute the see on the loond. And he taughte hem in parablis many thingis. And he seide to hem in his techyng, Here ye. Lo, a man sowynge goith out to sowe. And the while he sowith, summe seed felde aboute the weie, and briddis of heuene camen, and eeten it. Othere felde doun on stony places, where it had not myche erthe; and anoon it spronge vp, for it had not depnesse of erthe. And whanne the sunne roos vp, it welewide for heete, and it driede vp, for it hadde no roote. And othere felde doun in to thornes, and thornes sprongen vp, and strangliden it, and it yaf not fruyt. And other felde doun in to good loond, and yaf fruyt, springynge vp, and wexynge; and oon broughte thretti foold, and oon sixti fold, and oon an hundrid fold.

—From translation by John Wycliffe, about 1380, revised by John Purvey, about 1388.

And he began again to teach by the sea side: and there was gathered unto him a great multitude, so that he entered into a ship, and sat in the sea: and the whole multitude was by the sea on the land. And he taught them many things by parables, and said unto them in his doctrine, Hearken; Behold, there went out a sower to sow: And it came to pass, as he sowed, some fell by the way side, and the fowls of the air came and devoured it. And some fell on stony ground, where it had not much earth; and immediately it sprang up, because it had no depth of earth: But when the sun was up, it was scorched; and because it had no root it withered away. And some fell among thorns, and the thorns grew up, and choked it, and it yielded no fruit. And other fell on good ground, and did yield fruit that sprang up and increased, and brought forth, some thirty, and some sixty, and some a hundred.

—From King James Version of 1611.

Again he began to teach beside the sea. And a very large crowd gathered about him, so that he got into a boat and sat in it on the sea; and the whole crowd was beside the sea on the land. And he taught them many things in parables, and in his teaching he said to them: "Listen! A sower went out to sow. And as he sowed, some seed fell along the path, and the birds came and devoured it. Other seed fell on rocky ground, where it had not much soil, and immediately it sprang up, since it had no depth of soil; and when the sun rose it was scorched, and since it had no root it withered away. Other seed fell among thorns and the thorns grew up and choked it, and it yielded no grain. And other seeds fell into good soil and brought forth grain, growing up and increasing and yielding thirtyfold and sixtyfold and a hundredfold."

—From the Revised Standard Version of 1952. By permission of the National Council of Churches of Christ in the United States and Thomas Nelson & Sons.

Modern English. The year 1500 has been arbitrarily set for the beginning of the Modern English Period because near that time two events of superlative importance took place: William Caxton set up his printing press in England in 1476, and England began to feel the first impulses from the continental European Renaissance. The history of the English language since 1500 is one of gradual growth and enrichment, not of violent change, mainly because no foreign invader has again succeeded in setting foot on the tight little island. There have been, it is true, "movements," like the swinging of a pendulum, which hurried or retarded the change. The Elizabethan Age enriched the language in both flexibility of structure and added vocabulary. The Classical Period, which followed, stressed correctness, conciseness, and simplicity. In the Romantic Period the pendulum swung to the other extreme. In addition to this rhythmic swing from the liberal attitude to the conservative and back to the liberal, there were other influences at work. The simple dignity of the King James Bible of 1611 acted as a brake upon the exuberancy of both Romanticists and Latinists. From time to time some writer rediscovered the virtues of the speech of the common people. England became first a world empire and then the mother country of a world commonwealth of nations, and the speech of the people who inhabited one half of a little island became a world language.

Several other profound influences upon the course which the English language took must be mentioned here. One is the standardizing influence of the dictionaries, the grammars, and the printing houses, which beginning in the eighteenth century set up standards of correctness first in spelling, then in pronunciation and meaning, and more recently in good usage. Another is the elevating influence of almost universal education. A third, and now probably the most powerful influence, is that of television, radio, and motion pictures. The speech of the radio and television announcer and newscaster has emerged as the standard speech of the nation today—and tomorrow, it seems probable, of the whole English-speaking world. This standardizing influence is extremely powerful; regional differences in America, although they may always remain, tend to grow less prominent and less important. Two wars have done their bit to scramble dialects in this country, and, on the international scene, to mix Australians, Americans, and British; hence it need not be rash prophecy to assume that national differences in pronunciation and usage will in time become less noticeable.

Our Changing Language. When one looks back upon the fifteen hundred years which are the life span of the English language, he should be able to discern a number of significant truths. The history of our language has been a history of constant change —at times a slow, almost an imperceptible change, at other times a violent collision between two languages. Our language has always been a living, growing organism; it has never been static. Another significant truth which emerges from such a study is that language at all times has been the possession not of one class or group but of many. At one extreme it was the property of the common, ignorant folk, who used it in the daily business of their living, much as they used their animals or their kitchen pots and pans. At the other extreme it was the ward of those who respected it as an instrument and a sign of civilization, and who strove by writing it down to give it some permanence, order, dignity, and, if possible, a little beauty.

As we consider our changing language, we should note here two developments that are of special and immediate importance to us. One is that since the time of the Anglo-Saxons there has been an almost complete reversal of the different devices for showing the relationship of words in a sentence. Anglo-Saxon was a language of many inflections. Modern English has few inflections. We must now depend largely on word order and on function words to convey the meanings that the older language did by means of changes in the forms of words. Function words, you should understand, are words like prepositions, conjunctions, and a few others which are used primarily to show relationships among other words. A few inflections, however, have survived. And when some word inflections come in conflict with word order, there may be trouble for the users of the language, as we shall see later when we turn our attention to such matters as *who* or *whom* and *me* or *I*. The second fact we must consider is that as language itself changes, our attitudes toward language forms change also. The eighteenth century, for example, produced from various sources a tendency to fix the language into patterns not always in accord with the way people actually used it. At the present time there is a strong tendency to restudy and re-evaluate language practices in terms of the ways in which people write and speak.

Levels of Usage and Functional Varieties of English. It has been customary to divide the living language of the present into three main levels of usage, each characterized by certain distinctive practices and conventions. At the top is "formal" English; at the bottom is the spoken language of the uneducated—call it the "vulgate" or the vernacular. Between the two extremes is the level of informal writing and everyday speech. This classification, however, like most attempts to classify and formalize the complexities of human behavior, is too neat, too precise. The language habits of people somehow refuse to conform to these classifications, as they refused to conform to the rules of the eighteenth-century grammarians. The word "level" itself is none too felicitous here. One does not climb upstairs—culturally, that is—to write to his congressman, or descend to his cultural basement to gossip with the oil-burner repairman. In fact, in our unpredictable society, we might find that the repairman speaks beautiful English and reads Shakespeare on his weekends. One could readily distinguish thirty-three "levels" instead of three: below the "vulgate" one might place the profane, the vulgar, and the obscene, and one might also distinguish various important degrees of informality and formality. Furthermore, the classification is misleading because from it the student might infer that each level has its own exclusive vocabulary, inappropriate on the other levels. The truth is that the main word stock of each level is appropriate also at the other levels. Such words as *bread, meat, mother, church, prayer, dress, work, sleep,* and thousands of others are the property of all people speaking English at any level. And finally the classification is unfortunate because it tends to obscure the basic unity of standard English and to stress unduly the differences among its varieties.

You must understand that serious students of our language, like scientists in other fields, are constantly propounding new ideas, new hypotheses and generalizations. The "levels of usage" formula has been recently modified. One should speak of "levels" as "cultural levels": on the lower levels the language is characterized by carelessness, illiterate speech, excessive slang, profanity, and that sort of thing; on the higher levels we have the language of the educated, characterized to some degree by care, precision, order, and good taste. The newer formula is based not on culture but on functions, that is, differences due to place, situation, occasion, or purpose.[1]

Perhaps the most useful way for us to discriminate among various "occasions" when various "levels" of English are appropriate would be to ask ourselves just what is happening between the author and the reader. Is the author, by his choice of words, suggesting a relation between himself and his reader that is intimate, easy, friendly, or is he by a more formal use of language setting himself up as distant from his reader, detached and impersonal? We all know how in everyday conversation we can utter the same words in different ways and imply very different relations with the persons we are speaking to. For instance, we can say "Hello" in many different ways with different meanings everyone understands. We can stress the second syllable—"Hel-*lo*!"—and indicate we are glad to see the other person. We can stress the first syllable—"*Hel*-lo"—in such a way as to mean, "Oh Lord, you again?" We can even (using our eyebrows) say "Hel-lo-o-o" and mean "What a cute chick *you* are!" This is what is meant by *tone of voice,* and it is a basic method by which we demonstrate friendliness or hostility, interest or boredom, in the various occasions that confront us every day.

Words written on a page, of course, have no sound—and certainly no eyebrows. Yet they carry tone too; they imply a relation between the "voice" that is addressing the reader, and the reader who is being "spoken to." Let us consider two examples:

> It is often possible so to control one's employment of language that a precise relation between speaker and addressee becomes absolutely defined.

> You can often use words carefully enough so as to let your reader know whether you're being easy and informal with him, or formal and stiff; you can show him just where he stands with you.

[1] John S. Kenyon, "Cultural Levels and Functional Varieties of English," *College English,* pp. 31–36, October, 1948.

These two sentences *mean,* more or less, the same thing, but their *tone* is utterly different. In the first sentence we are being addressed formally by a writer whose whole air is very serious. Notice the relatively long words he uses; notice how carefully he avoids the split infinitive, "to so control," in order not to sound colloquial. In the second sentence, however, we are very close to the writer, and the whole relation is informal. Notice the simple vocabulary and the way the direct address in the second person supports a conversational manner.

In this connection we may quote from a little "pocket book" printed as early as 1831, under the title *The Universal Letter Writer and Complete Correspondent,* which expresses in a quaint but surprisingly modern manner the doctrine of "functional varieties":

> To lay down any particular rule for this sort of composition is incompatible with its nature; but as a letter is nothing more than a substitute for speech, so it should resemble in its style, as near as possible, the language we should use in discourse.
>
> In commands, our language would naturally be concise without arrogance; in requests, pleasing without cringing; in supplication, tender, moving, without servility; in narration, plain without much embellishment; in description, rich and glowing without exuberance; upon matters of importance, it should be dignified; in affliction, condoling; in mirth, light and jocose; in advice, serious without austerity.
>
> The style must also be adapted to the relative situation of the parties corresponding, thus—among friends and equals, it would be familiar; to our superiors, respectful; to our inferiors, courteous; to the aged, reverential; to the youthful, gay and joyous.
>
> It will be thus perceived that to lay down any particular style for this species of composition, is impossible. It will be almost as variable as our ideas on passions—every different thought requiring a variation in the manner of expression. Indeed, it must possess the versatile powers of Alcibiades, in adapting itself at all times, to all occasions, to all ages, and to every subject. It is not to be restrained within any particular limits, and, therefore, cannot be confined to one definite style; for, although, in general, its nature requires plainness and simplicity, yet there is, perhaps, no species of composition in which all the various styles, from the most plain and unadorned to the most rich and embellished, can be used with more propriety than in epistolary correspondence.

Let us see now what the differences in the varieties of standard English are and how they affect our choice of appropriate language to use in various situations.

Standard English. The differences between varieties of English have often been explained by likening language to clothes. For formal occasions we put on our formal clothes; for a tennis match we dress in sports clothes; for plowing corn or driving a tractor we put on overalls or dungarees. Similarly, we suit our language to the occasion, to the subject, and to our readers or listeners. So far the comparison is good. When we pause to analyze the analogy, however, we are trapped by the word "formal," which to most people means "tails and white tie," a costume which millions of Americans have never worn, or perhaps never seen worn except by actors on a motion-picture or television screen. And yet every American home which can afford a radio set or a newspaper has been exposed daily to both written and spoken formal English. We must amend our analogy by a further definition of terms, by extending the range of "formal" clothes to include the well-pressed business suit. It is misleading to try to confine the main current of our language to "the cold and lonely heights of formal and highly specialized scientific and scholarly language."[1] The language which we call "formal"—for want of a term with less unfortunate connotations—is far from cold and lonely. It has warmth, strength, beauty, and an infinite range and variety. It is not confined to a few scientific and scholarly treatises. The great body of our literature, from Shakespeare down to the latest book on the international crisis, is written in formal English. It is the language of most books of history, sociology, political science, botany, chemistry—every textbook that you use in college. It is the language of the professions, such as law, medicine, teaching. It is the language of all serious essays, of a good part of all novels and of poems, and of radio newscasts and commentaries. Most business letters are written in formal English. So are the news and editorial sections of many newspapers. As a matter of fact, a good share of the nation's private and public daily work is done with the help of formal English.

[1] Arthur G. Kennedy, *Current English,* p. 17.

What, then, are the distinguishing marks of standard English in its more serious and dignified uses? First, the restrictions upon vocabulary are so slight as to become almost negligible. In contrast to the incredibly vast riches of the "word hoard," as the Anglo-Saxons called it, the inappropriate or unacceptable words are few indeed. Slang and vulgarity, of course, are inappropriate. In more formal situations, most of the words which a modern unabridged dictionary labels as colloquial are inappropriate. There is a general feeling among students that formal English demands only "big" words, bookish words, words with a Latin ancestry. That is not true. The simple, homely, everyday words are as much a part of the vocabulary of formal English as the multisyllabic words. Notice carefully, for instance, the words used in each of the following excerpts—in most of these, words actually spoken on occasions as formal and solemn as any in the long and tragic history of mankind.

We the People of the United States, in Order to form a more perfect Union, establish Justice, insure domestic Tranquility, provide for the common defence, promote the general Welfare, and secure the Blessings of Liberty to ourselves and our Posterity, do ordain and establish this CONSTITUTION for the United States of America.

And then one of the older men, who agreed with the king, arose and spoke: "It seems to me, O King, that this present life of man, in comparison with that which is unknown to us, is as if you sat at the banquet table in the wintertime, with your chiefs and your men about you, and a fire burned and the hall was warm, while outside it rained and snowed and stormed. There came a sparrow and swiftly flew through the hall. It came in through one door, and it flew out through the other. Now, so long as he is inside he is not cuffed by the winter's storm, but that is for only a moment, the twinkling of an eye, and at once again he goes from winter back into winter. So this life of man appears but for a moment. What went before it or what comes after it, we do not know. Therefore if this new teaching brings anything more certain or fitting, it deserves to be followed."

—From the Anglo-Saxon version of Bede's *Ecclesiastical History.*

I went to the woods because I wished to live deliberately, to front only the essential facts of life, and see if I could not learn what it had to teach, and not, when I came to die, discover that I had not lived. I did not wish to live what was not life, living is so dear; nor did I wish to practise resignation, unless it was quite necessary. I wanted to live deep and suck out all the marrow of life, to live so sturdily and Spartan-like as to put to rout all that was not life, to cut a broad swath and shave close, to drive life into a corner, and reduce it to its lowest terms, and, if it proved to be mean, why then to get the whole and genuine meanness of it, and publish its meanness to the world; or if it were sublime, to know it by experience, and be able to give a true account of it in my next excursion. For most men, it appears to me, are in a strange uncertainty about it, whether it is of the devil or of God, and have somewhat hastily concluded that it is the chief end of man here to "glorify God and enjoy Him forever."

—From Thoreau's *Walden.*

I see a book kissed which I suppose to be the Bible, or at least the New Testament, which teaches me that all things whatsoever I would that men should do unto me, I should do even so to them. It teaches me further to remember them that are in bonds as bound with them. I endeavored to act up to that instruction. I say I am yet too young to understand that God is any respector of persons. I believe that to have interfered as I have done, as I have always freely admitted I have done in behalf of His despised poor, I did no wrong, but right. Now, if it is deemed necessary that I should forfeit my life for the furtherance of the ends of justice and mingle my blood further with the blood of my children and with the blood of millions in this slave country whose rights are disregarded by wicked, cruel, and unjust enactments, I say, let it be done.

—From John Brown's last speech.

With malice towards none, with charity for all, with firmness in the right as God gives us to see the right, let us finish the work we are in, to bind up the nation's wounds, to care for him who shall have borne the battle, and for his widow and his orphans, to do all which may achieve and cherish a just and a lasting peace among ourselves and with all nations.

—From Lincoln's Second Inaugural Address.

I expect that the Battle of Britain is about to begin. Upon this battle depends the survival of Christian civilization. Upon it depends all our British life, and the long continuity of our institutions and our Empire. The whole fury and might of the enemy must very soon be turned on us. Hitler knows that he will have to break us in this Island or lose the war. If we can stand up to him, all Europe may be free and the life of the world may move forward into broad, sunlit uplands. But if we fail, then the whole world, including the United States, including all that we have known and cared for, will sink into the abyss of a new Dark Age made more sinister, and perhaps more protracted, by the lights of perverted science. Let us therefore brace ourselves to our duties, and so bear ourselves that, if the British Empire and its Commonwealth last for a thousand years, men will still say, "This was their finest hour."

—Winston Churchill, a speech delivered to the House of Commons June 18, 1940. From *Blood, Sweat, and Tears.* Copyright 1941 by Winston S. Churchill. Courtesy of G. P. Putnam's Sons.

I feel that this award was not made to me as a man but to my work—a life's work in the agony and sweat of the human spirit, not for glory and least of all for profit, but to create out of the materials of the human spirit something which did not exist before. So this award is only mine in trust. It will not be difficult to find a dedication for the money part of it commensurate with the purpose and significance of its origin. But I would like to do the same with the acclaim too, by using this moment as a pinnacle from which I might be listened to by young men and women already dedicated to the same anguish and travail, among whom is already that one who will some day stand here where I am standing.

Our tragedy today is a general and universal physical fear so long sustained by now that we can even bear it. There are no longer problems of the spirit. There is only one question: when will I be blown up? Because of this, the young man or woman writing today has forgotten the problems of the human heart in conflict with itself which alone can make good writing because only that is worth writing about, worth the agony and the sweat.

He must learn them again. He must teach himself that the basest of all things is to be afraid; and, teaching himself that, forget it forever, leaving no room in his workshop for anything but the old verities and truths of the heart, the old universal truths lacking which any story is ephemeral and doomed—love and honor and pity and pride and compassion and sacrifice. Until he does so he labors under a curse. He writes not of love but of lust, of defeats in which nobody loses anything of value, of victories without hope and worst of all without pity or compassion. His griefs grieve no universal bones, leaving no scars. He writes not of the heart but of the glands.

Until he relearns these things he will write as though he stood among and watched the end of man. It is easy enough to say that man is immortal simply because he will endure; that when the last ding-dong of doom has clanged and faded from the last worthless rock hanging tideless in the last red and dying evening, that even then there will be one more sound: that of his puny inexhaustible voice, still talking. I refuse to accept this. I believe that man will not merely endure: he will prevail. He is immortal, not because he alone among creatures has an inexhaustible voice, but because he has a soul, a spirit capable of compassion and sacrifice and endurance. The poet's, the writer's, duty is to write about these things. It is his privilege to help man endure by lifting his heart, by reminding him of the courage and honor and pride and compassion and pity and sacrifice which have been the glory of his past. The poet's voice need not merely be the record of man, it can be one of the props, the pillars to help him endure and prevail.

—William Faulkner's Nobel Prize Award speech, Dec. 10, 1950. Reprinted by courtesy of Random House, Inc.

In the second place, standard English on the more formal levels is characterized by orderly structure. The expression and communication of ideas is a planned process, not a spontaneous outpouring. Ideas are grouped and arranged in some logical sequence. There is a serious attempt to show the interrelationship of ideas. As a consequence, paragraphs tend to be more fully developed than in informal writing; sentences acquire increased complexity as the thoughts they express become more mature.

Third, those who use the language in formal situations, in the serious discussion of serious ideas, tend, as a rule, to be relatively conservative in their attitude toward matters of grammar and usage. Among those who write for a living, among those who write occasionally, and among those to whom a "talk" to be given before the Rotary Club or the Chamber of Commerce is an event of magnitude, there is a tendency to appeal to an authority, to someone who knows what current usage is. The deference to "correct usage," in the sense of what other writers and speakers are doing, is strong among all users of the language. Grammarians may argue over the question of whether "It is me" is a solecism, a peccadillo, a sign of life in the language, or one of the seven deadly sins. The busy scientist with a radio talk to prepare turns to the author of a handbook, or grammar, or *Webster's New International Dictionary* with the attitude, "I know that you people don't make the language, but it is your business to find out what usage is. You are paid for that sort of thing."

And finally, standard English in the more formal situations generally tends toward an impersonal, objective attitude toward the subject matter expressed and communicated. One must not assume that the exclusion of the writer's or speaker's self is a requisite of the formal style. Indeed, some of the finest examples of formal writing are intensely personal in nature. In most cases they are personal because it is the personal element which is the vital substance of what is being said. Subjects in which the personal element is not vital, however, are usually treated objectively. More specifically, the sort of papers, reports, term essays, and discussions which you will write in college for your various courses are usually best treated impersonally and objectively.

Standard English: Informal Varieties. Before we begin to examine the characteristics of "informal" English, we must reaffirm the statement that the essential unity of standard English is much more important than the differences among its varieties. One does not stop writing formal English and begin writing informal English as if he were stepping through a door from one room to another.

In some writing traditionally labeled informal, as for instance in those informal essays that are written with skill and good taste, the total extent of informality consists of the attitude of the writer toward his material and toward his reader. You may find in them the same discriminating taste in choice of words, the same respect for present-day standards in grammatical correctness and in usage, the same mature structure as in the best formal writing. The only difference is that the writer frankly and freely interprets his subject through his own personality or through his own likes and prejudices.

From the writing that is informal only in attitude one may move down the scale through a large variety of levels and gradations of informality to writing that is as unceremonious and unconventional as slacks and sweater and a corncob pipe. Much of the writing that you will do in your college composition course will be informal in style and in attitude. In this classification can be included, among others, all of your autobiographical papers and sketches, sketches of persons and places, profiles, personal experiences, discussions of attitudes and likes and dislikes, your reactions to books that you have read, your personal letters, and talks before clubs and organizations.

In the following specimen of the informal style, notice how the words are chosen and arranged in order to dramatize a particularly easy sort of speaking voice, a voice that implies an easy, familiar relation with its listener.

I do not mean to suggest that the nature writer is or always should be on the mountain tops, either literally or figuratively. No one who actually looks at nature rather than at some fancy projected upon or read into her can ever fail to realize that she represents some ultimate things-as-they-are, not some ideal of things-as-he-thinks-they-ought-to-be. There is in her what we call cruelty and also, even more conspicuously, what we call grotesqueness and what we call comedy. If she warns the so-called realist how limited his conception of reality is, she is no less likely to bring the sentimentalist back, literally, to earth.

How much of the cruelty, of the grotesqueness, or of the sublimity any given man will see depends no doubt to some considerable extent upon his own temperament and I suppose it is some indication of mine when I confess that what I see most often and relish the most is, first, the intricate marvel and, second, the comedy. To be reminded that one is very much like other members of the animal kingdom is often funny though it is never, like being compared to a machine, merely humiliating. I do not too much mind being somewhat like a cat, a dog, or even an insect but I resent having it said that even an electronic calculator is like me.

Not very long ago I was pointing out to a friend the courtship of two spiders in a web just outside my door. Most people know that the male is often smaller than his mate and nearly everybody knows by now that the female of many species sometimes eats her husband. Both of these things were true of the common kind beside my door and the insignificant male was quite obviously torn between ardor and caution. He danced forward and then darted back. He approached now from one side and now from the other. He would and he wouldn't.

My friend, no nature student and not much given to observing such creatures, was gratifyingly interested. Presently he could contain himself no longer.

"You know," he said thoughtfully, "there is only one difference between that spider and a human male. The spider knows it's dangerous."

That, I maintain, both is and ought to be as much grist for a nature writer's mill as a sunset or a bird song.

—From Joseph Wood Krutch. "Some Unsentimental Confessions of a Nature Writer," New York *Herald Tribune Book Review,* June 15, 1952. Copyright 1952 by the New York *Herald Tribune.* Reprinted by permission of the publisher.

The following, too, is written in the informal style. The occasion is informal, the attitude of the writer is obviously personal, but his concern for quality is clear enough in what he says and in how he says it.

A publisher in Chicago has sent us a pocket calculating machine by which we may test our writing to see whether it is intelligible. The calculator was developed by General Motors, who, not satisfied with giving the world a Cadillac, now dream of bringing perfect understanding to men. The machine (it is simply a celluloid card with a dial) is called the Reading-Ease Calculator and shows four grades of "reading ease"—Very Easy, Easy, Hard, and Very Hard. You count your words and syllables, set the dial, and an indicator lets you know whether anybody is going to understand what you have written. An instruction book came with it, and after mastering the simple rules we lost no time in running a test on the instruction book itself, to see how *that* writer was doing. The poor fellow! His leading essay, the one on the front cover, tested Very Hard.

Our next step was to study the first phrase on the face of the calculator: "How to test Reading-Ease of written matter." There is, of course, no such thing as reading ease of written matter. There is the ease with which matter can be read, but that is a condition of the reader, not of the matter. Thus the inventors and distributors of this calculator get off to a poor start, with a Very Hard instruction book and a slovenly phrase. Already they have one foot caught in the brier patch of English usage.

Not only did the author of the instruction book score badly on the front cover, but inside the book he used the word "personalize" in an essay on how to improve one's writing. A man who likes the word "personalize" is entitled to his choice, but we wonder whether he should be in the business of giving advice to writers. "Whenever possible," he wrote, "personalize your writing by directing it to the reader." As for us, we would as lief Simonize our grandmother as personalize our writing.

In the same envelope with the calculator, we received another training aid for writers—a booklet called "How to Write Better," by Rudolph Flesch. This, too, we studied, and it quickly demonstrated the broncolike ability of the English language to throw whoever leaps cocksurely into the saddle. The language not only can toss a writer but knows a thousand tricks for tossing him, each more gay than the last. Dr. Flesch stayed in the saddle only a moment or two. Under the heading "Think Before You Write," he wrote, "The main thing to consider is your purpose in writing. Why are you sitting down to write?" And echo answered: Because, sir, it is more comfortable than standing up.

Communication by the written word is a subtler (and more beautiful) thing than Dr. Flesch and General Motors imagine. They contend that the "average reader" is capable of reading only what tests Easy, and that the writer should write at or below this level. This is a presumptuous and degrading idea. There is no average reader, and to reach down toward this mythical character is to deny that each of us is on the way up, is ascending. ("Ascending," by the way, is a word Dr. Flesch advises writers to stay away from. Too unusual.)

It is our belief that no writer can improve his work until he discards the dulcet notion that the reader is feeble-minded, for writing is an act of faith, not a trick of grammar. Ascent is at the heart of the matter. A country whose writers are following a calculating machine downstairs is not ascending—if you will pardon the expression—and a writer who questions the capacity of the person at the other end of the line is not a writer at all, merely a schemer. The movies long ago decided that a wider communication could be achieved by a deliberate descent to a lower level, and they walked proudly down until they reached the cellar. Now they are groping for the light switch, hoping to find the way out.

We have studied Dr. Flesch's instructions diligently, but we return for guidance in these matters to an earlier American, who wrote with more patience, more confidence. "I fear chiefly," he wrote, "lest my expression may not be *extra-vagant* enough, may not wander far enough beyond the narrow limits of my daily experience, so as to be adequate to the truth of which I have been convinced. . . . Why level downward to our dullest perception always, and praise that as common sense? The commonest sense is the sense of men asleep, which they express by snoring."

Run that through your calculator! It may come out Hard, it may come out Easy. But it will come out whole, and it will last forever.

—E. B. White, "Calculating Machine," from *The Second Tree from the Corner,* published by Harper & Brothers. Reprinted by permission of the author and publishers.

What are the characteristics of "informal" standard English? One notices immediately that informal English is *not* the language of the uneducated or the unintelligent, or of a lower social class—if there still *are* social classes. It is rather the English written and spoken by educated persons in situations where well-bred ease is more important than dignity or high seriousness. No part of the vocabulary of formal English is excluded from the vocabulary of informal English. There is, in addition, a certain freedom permissible in the use of occasional colloquial or slang expressions. Simple, everyday words are perhaps more common than literary, scientific, or technical terms. Contractions, like "they're," "can't," "didn't," are used more freely. It is evident, however, that there is in it the same conscientious regard for the conventions of correctness in grammar, in spelling, and in punctuation as in formal English. Sentences, too, are carefully built, and ideas are organized into paragraphs, although in some of the more journalistic types of informal writing both sentences and paragraphs may be shorter.

The Vernacular. There is a language below standard English —much more accurately, there is an endless variety of languages— in which the college student has only an academic interest. There have been times in the history of English, in the days before the radio, television, the airplane, the automobile, the daily newspaper and the weekly newsmagazine, a digest for every pocket, and an education for every child, when there still were social "classes," when rustics spoke dialects and educated persons spoke literary English. Now, the specialized vocabularies of small groups, like the language of jive, of the sub-debs, of racing, of airmen and marines, of various occupations, are made-to-order dialects of people who usually know standard English well enough and use it when the occasion demands it.

There have been many attempts to write entire books in the vernacular, notably Mark Twain's *Adventures of Huckleberry Finn*, James Stevens' *Brawnyman*, Vincent McHugh's *Caleb Catlum's America*, and, in a way, Sinclair Lewis's *Babbitt*, and the result has usually been an illusion—"slightly phony," as one critic remarked—rather than a transcript of actual speech. Although Mark Twain belongs to an older period, he was artist enough to make his interpretation of the vernacular of more than passing importance.

This place was a tolerable long, steep hill or ridge about forty foot high. We had a rough time getting to the top, the sides was so steep and the bushes so thick. We tramped and clumb around all over it, and by and by found a good big cavern in the rock, most up to the top on the side toward Illinois. The cavern was as big as two or three rooms bunched together, and Jim could stand up straight in there. . . .

We spread the blankets inside for a carpet, and eat our dinner there. We put all the other things handy at the back of the cavern. Pretty soon it darkened up, and began to thunder and lighten; so the birds was right about it. Directly it begun to rain, and it rained like all fury, too, and I never see the wind blow so. It was one of those regular summer storms. It would get so dark that it looked all blue-black outside, and lovely; and the rain would thrash along by so thick that the trees off a little ways looked dim and spiderwebby; and here would come a blast of wind that would bend the trees down and turn up the pale underside of the leaves; and then a perfect ripper of a gust would follow along and set the branches to tossing their arms as if they was just wild; and next, when it was just about the bluest and blackest—*fst!* it was as bright as glory, and you'd have a little glimpse of treetops a-plunging about away off yonder in the storm, hundreds of yards further than you could see before; dark as sin again in a second, and now you'd hear the thunder let go with an awful crash, and then go rumbling, grumbling, tumbling, down the sky towards the underside of the world, like rolling empty barrels downstairs—where it's long stairs and they bounce a good deal, you know.

—From Mark Twain, *The Adventure of Huckleberry Finn*, Chapter 9.

When a skilled writer sets out to color his writing by using slang, profanity, and what is known as "bad grammar," he does it to produce an effect, a mood perhaps, an impression of reality and genuineness. The following scene is from a book that does use the vernacular very well indeed, although the private first class who after three years in the army is now patiently trying to trim his GI vocabulary to civilian standards might smile a bit cynically at its restraint.

While the doctor and others worked on the bandages and the splint for the shattered arm, the medic with the pencil said:

"What got you, Jack?"

"God, I don't know. It was a tank. Where's the chaplain?"

"You don't need the chaplain, Jack," said the medic. "You're going to be okay. What got you? There weren't any tanks around a while ago."

"It was a grenade," said Jack, his hand still reaching for his face. "Where's the chaplain? God, why do you let me hurt like this?"

"How old are you, Jack?" asked the medic persistently. He had already marked "grenade," because the wounds showed that. It had been a German potato-masher grenade, because the holes in his body looked like bullet wounds, but didn't go clear through him, and they weren't as jagged as shell or mortar fragment wounds. Evidently the German had sneaked up while the boy was down in his hole.

Jack said he was twenty years old, he was a staff sergeant, and he was from Texas.

The questioning seemed heartless at this time, but there is a reason for it. If the patient is able to answer, it distracts him from his pain; and if the information isn't gained here, they have to get it back at the hospital.

Jack had guts. Of course he was scared. He knew he was hurt bad, and it's a shock to anybody to get hit. But when they told him he shouldn't reach for his face, he said okay a little sleepily, because the morphine was taking effect.

"Hold a flashlight," the doctor said to me. "The lantern isn't strong enough."

I grabbed a flashlight and held it on the boy while they worked on him. I thought, "Christ, twenty years old!" I felt like an old man at twenty-three. I looked at the holes which had riddled his right arm and practically severed his little finger, and I looked at the swollen bloody gashes on his leg. I looked at his horribly wounded face and head, and I thought of how twenty minutes ago he was sitting quietly in his hole wondering how soon he could get home.

I handed the flashlight to the medic who had finished filling out the slip, and I went over to the litter and sat on it with my head between my knees and tried to keep from being sick on the floor.

The medic took the flashlight without even a glance, and nobody looked at me. They went right on working. Pretty soon Jack's face was fixed and it didn't look so bad with a neat bandage and the blood washed off. His arm was fixed in a splint and it looked very neat indeed. He was wrapped up in blankets, and the ambulance came up and took him away. He was full of morphine and probably dreaming of home.

"I don't know what we'd do without morphine," the doc said.

I guess I looked a little foolish and white, and I started to open my mouth. I don't know what I was going to say, but the medic who had taken the flashlight turned to me and said:

"It's funny. I handle these guys every night, and some of them are really in awful shape. But last night one came in not hurt half as bad as Jack and I did the same thing you did."

Another medic said, "We keep some medicine to take care of those things."

They brought out a miracle—a half-filled bottle of Pennsylvania Rye. Now I know damned well one of those guys got that bottle in a Christmas package, and I know he could have sold it for a hundred dollars cash any-place between Florence and Bologna. Or he could have kept it to himself, and nobody would have blamed him. But we all had a slug of rye—the doc with his bloody hands and his eyes which were bantering once more, and the medics who were kidding each other again.

Whether the following scene illustrates the use of the vernacular or merely a type of fractured English is debatable, but there is nothing debatable about the fact that the book itself is wholly delightful and worth reading for the fun of it.

Naturally when I engaged myself for marriage with Helena Gerbertovna I went right away with heartful of happiness to carry the good news to my friends.

But seemed like they weren't so pleased. Vactangi showed long horse face. Challico sat dark blue in a corner. Even Illarion, practically American himself now, didn't give me any support. Only Dzea shaked my hand and that sadly. "You take a big chance, Bijo, to marry with an American girl." All he said.

"First place," Vactangi pointed out, "American young ladies don't like foreigner names. Now you have to change yours. One Russian, I knew him well, immediately he married American young lady she made him go in court take the name of Gerbert Goover. For honor. Next election Gerbert Goover don't wins. How he feels then, that Russian fellow? Be same with you."

"Main thing," Illarion said, "the American girls I met so far can only cook out of books."

"See. Something else you didn't know," Vactangi said. "Lose the book. Ph-i-i-t-t. No eat. You'll starve."

"I can buy another book," I said.

"And what's more," Challico had his turn, "American cooking every day just enough. Two peoples, two steaks. Three peoples, three steaks. Never cooking one extra piece for the pot's good luck. Company comes unexpected they gonna sit hungry. You'll die from shame before you're six months married."

"Yes," Vactangi said, "and after your funeral there won't be any table either. Maybe a cup of tea for who carries your burial box. I won't come."

"Never enjoy the pleasure at mealtime to call in strangers passing on the road to share your table." Challico shook his head. "Won't even be any use to get rich. You'll have a shiny five-hundred dollar, pull-a-button, push-a-button refrigerator and not one extra piece of baloney to keep inside."

"But you don't know the worst that's gonna happen in your house," Vactangi warned. "American young ladies all keep bodguts."

"Helena Gerbertovna has dog," I said. "Irishman setter named Veleike Kneeaz. Comes 'Duke' in English. But that's all."

"Bodguts means writing down moneys before you spending," Vactangi explained. "Suppose you not feeling good, we take for example. You want to stop in Russian Club drink glass of vodka, eat piece herring maybe, for your stomach. You have to write down in bodguts first:

I'm drinking whiskys . . . . . . 35¢
Eating piece herring, too . . . . . . 10¢

"Where you ever knew American young lady to find out such informations?" I asked him.

"That's enough, boys," Dzea said. "If they promised to each other can't help now. Damage is done." He shook my hand again. "Never mind, I stood your friend twenty years, Bijo Gogio, and I don't stop now."

—From George and Helen Papashvily, *Anything Can Happen*, Harper & Brothers, 1945. Reprinted by permission of the publisher.

The Student's Choice. A student of the English language should know something of its history, its forms and varieties, its resources and limitations, so that his attitude toward self-improvement will be realistic. The history of the language has been a history of innumerable changes. It is still a changing language. What *is* the realistic attitude in the face of changes in usage? The common-sense procedure is to ask, "What is being done at the present time by people of education, of taste, of social importance, people whose opinions I value?" It is not sensible, for instance, to use a double negative merely because you know that many great writers in the past have used double negatives. Neither is it sensible to anticipate future changes—to be so progressive that you want to be on the spot to welcome the future when it arrives. If you say, "Sir, I can't see nobody nowhere; I think it was only me and him putting away the goods," your employer will rudely set you right. The standards of the educated must be your standards for the simple reason that you as a college graduate will live among and communicate with those who have these standards.

What these standards are you can discover for yourself by wide reading and by long and careful observation of the practices of educated men and women. That is the way the authors of handbooks, grammars, and dictionaries have found out what current usage is. Some of these men have spent a lifetime doing little else but reading, checking, analyzing, and filing examples of usage.

Of course you do not have the time or the opportunity for this sort of individual research; you are satisfied to defer to the judgment of those "who are paid to do that sort of thing." That is a realistic attitude, too, but do not give up entirely your research and observation, for that may be fun. Observe current usage in the books that you read; listen to prominent men and women whom you may hear on television, and always, if you are in doubt or in a hurry, remember that a good dictionary, like *Webster's New Collegiate,* the *American College Dictionary, Webster's New World Dictionary,* or the Thorndike-Barnhart *Comprehensive Desk Dictionary,* will provide a pretty good reflection of general usage.

In most of the papers that you will write in college you will make a conscious choice of style, language, attitude, or point of view. Many times, it is true, your choices will be determined for you by the situation. If your instructor in history asks you to write a discussion of the causes of revolutions, you will naturally decide to give him, not a slangy, breezy sketch, but a serious, well-planned, and well-constructed essay in standard formal English. It is hard to see that any other decision is appropriate in such a situation. Similarly, a professional writer writing for the *New Yorker* uses the *New Yorker* style; a writer writing for *Harper's* uses a style appropriate for *Harper's.* Either he does this—or his manuscript is returned to him. To that extent he has no choice. But he does choose the language, the style, and the structure appropriate for each situation.

Frequently you will have to decide between a formal and an informal treatment of a subject. A subject like "Women Drivers" can be handled either with deep seriousness or with a light, perhaps with a humorous, touch. It depends on the particular phase of the subject that you decide to use, on the situation, and on the reader for whom you are writing. Your choice, whatever it is, should always consider writing as communication. You are not merely writing—you are writing for someone to read. In the final analysis, perhaps it is the reader, more than anything else, who determines the appropriateness of the choice of language, point of view, and treatment that you make.

The following books dealing with various aspects of the English language—its growth, its various levels of usage, the sources of its vocabulary, etc.—may be found in almost every college library:

Allen, Harold B. *Readings in Applied English Linguistics.* New York: Appleton-Century-Crofts, 1958.

Bloomfield, Leonard. *Language.* New York: Henry Holt & Co., 1933.

Bryant, Margaret M. *Modern English and Its Heritage.* New York: The Macmillan Co., 1949.

Curme, George O. *Syntax.* Boston: D. C. Heath & Co., 1931.

Evans, Bergen, and Cornelia Evans. *A Dictionary of Contemporary American Usage.* New York: Random House, 1957.

Fowler, H. W. *A Dictionary of Modern English Usage.* New York: Oxford, 1926.

Fries, C. C. *American English Grammar.* New York: D. Appleton-Century Co., 1940.

———. *The Structure of English.* New York: Harcourt, Brace & Co., 1952.

Gray, Louis H. *Foundations of Language.* New York: The Macmillan Co., 1939.

Greenough, James B., and George Lyman Kittredge. *Words and Their Ways in English Speech.* New York: The Macmillan Co., 1901, 1923.

Jespersen, Otto. *Growth and Structure of the English Language,* 9th ed. Oxford: Blackwell, 1948.

Kennedy, Arthur. *Current English.* Boston: Ginn & Co., 1935.

Krapp, George Philip. *The English Language in America.* New York: The Century Co., 1925.

McKnight, George H. *English Words and Their Background.* New York: D. Appleton & Co., 1923.

Nicholson, Margaret. *A Dictionary of American-English Usage.* New York: Oxford University Press, 1957. [Based on Fowler's *Modern English Usage.*]

Pei, Mario. *The Story of English.* Philadelphia: J. B. Lippincott Co., 1952.

Potter, Simeon. *Our Language.* Harmondsworth, England: Penguin Books, 1950.

Pyles, Thomas. *Words and Ways of American English.* New York: Random House, 1952.

Robertson, Stuart. *The Development of Modern English.* New York: Prentice-Hall, Inc., 1934.

Smith, Logan Pearsall. *Words and Idioms.* Boston: Houghton Mifflin Co., 1925.

Chapter 2

THE SENTENCE

A. GRAMMATICAL PATTERNS

What Is Grammar? Grammar, as we use the term here, is a description and analysis of the facts of language as it is used today.[1] We must remember, however, that the term "grammar" has meant more things to more people than any panel of linguists on a TV program could untangle in hours of discussion. One may speak of historical grammar, comparative grammar, or descriptive grammar. In its more inclusive aspects it may mean the study of word forms, pronunciation, syntax, parts of speech, the past history of the language, and so on. Our primary interest here is descriptive grammar, a label that explains not only itself but also the methods of the scientific grammarian. A scientist first observes and gathers the facts; then he tries to organize and analyze his facts, and finally to formulate certain generalizations that he calls laws. In grammar, similarly, the facts of usage always come first; the generalizations are based on usage.

Unfortunately, if we use the definition of the scientific grammarian or linguist, we are up against a real problem. If we study our definition carefully, it becomes obvious that there can be no such thing as good grammar or bad grammar. Everyone, from

[1] Compare, if you wish, the definitions used by: Robert C. Pooley, *Teaching English Grammar,* 1957, pp. 104–107; Margaret M. Bryant, *Modern English and Its Heritage,* 1949, p. 190; Charles F. Hockett, *A Course in Modern Linguistics,* 1958, p. 129.

the college professor to the illiterate, speaks grammatically, for the way each uses words for communication is *his* grammar. The complication arises from the fact that most educated people, including perhaps most of those very important ones who control the destinies of mankind, still do not believe this; to them grammar still means *good* grammar. And that, if we are realists, is a "fact of language" that we cannot brush away by a definition.

The scientific grammarian or linguist makes a distinction between grammar and usage; the ordinary person does not. When we point out that certain speech patterns are inappropriate or unacceptable on formal or dignified occasions among educated persons, that, to a grammarian, is a question of usage. It is a matter of choice, of preference, a matter of what is socially acceptable among the educated and what is not. In this book we shall try to observe the distinction between grammar and usage, knowing very well that occasional confusions are inevitable. We can define our terms, but we cannot by that act immediately change the mind-habits of everybody else.

Before we go on with a discussion of the grammar of the sentence, which is the concern of this chapter, let us clear up another problem. Most students, at some time or other, question the value of a knowledge of grammar as an aid to better writing. What part of grammar is useful? What part is useless? The answer must be different for every different person. Many people write well and speak well without knowing much about grammar, but for those who by reading this book admit their capacity for self-improvement, grammar is both a convenient chest of tools and a practical code of communication. It is like a chest of tools in that it enables them to build effective sentences and to repair faulty ones. It is a code or a technical vocabulary, understood by both teacher and learner, necessary in learning and teaching. Let us make this clearer by a few examples. How, for instance, can a student correct a sentence like this, "This is strictly between he and I," if he does not know something about pronouns, about prepositions, and about the uses of the objective case? How can a teacher explain the punctuation of phrases and clauses in a series if the student does not know what phrases and clauses are? When a person says, "I done pretty good in the test today," he expresses his thought with absolute clearness—but clearness itself is not always enough. How can this person learn what is acceptable among educated people, and how can a teacher help him learn it, if there is not some understanding of verb forms in current usage? The least we can say in defense of a knowledge of grammatical terms is that it is usually well for teacher and student to speak the same language.

The Parts of Speech. Words are classified according to their *function* or *use in the sentence* into what are called parts of speech. Notice that in this system of classification it is the *use in the sentence* which always determines the part of speech to which a word belongs. The parts of speech are nouns, verbs, pronouns, adjectives, adverbs, prepositions, conjunctions, and interjections. If you wish to group these parts of speech according to their functions, you may think of them as follows: nouns and pronouns are *naming* words; verbs are *asserting* words; adjectives and adverbs are *modifying* words; prepositions and conjunctions are *joining* words; interjections are *independents.*

1. A **noun** is a word that names something. It may name an object, a person, a place, or a quality. When a noun names a person, a place, or an object, it is called a concrete noun; when it names a quality or a mental concept, it is called an abstract noun. For the practical value of this information, see sections 22, 25, and 27. Nouns are also classified as proper and common. A proper noun is the official name of some individual person, place, or object; a common noun names any one of a class or kind. Proper nouns are capitalized; common nouns are not. See section 8.

Between me and my *friend* what unfathomable *distance!* All *mankind*, like *motes* and *insects,* are between us.—Thoreau.

Petrified *forests* consist of *trees* which *time* and *circumstance* have changed into *stone.*

On the *trip* to *Arizona, Gadsden* ran into *trouble* when his *car* stalled in the *desert.*

2. A **verb** is a word (or group of words) that asserts action, being, or state of being. See sections 3 and 6.

The sun *shines.* It *rained* yesterday. The children *did* not *go* to school. They *should have braved* the weather. My aunt *thinks* that they *are being spoiled.* They *will take* the bus today. We *shall be waiting* for them at the corner.

3. A **pronoun** is a word that takes the place of a noun. Pronouns are classified as personal, demonstrative, relative, interrogative, and indefinite. See section 4.

Personal:	I, you, he, she, it, they, we, them, thee, thou.
Demonstrative:	this, that, these, those.
Relative:	who, which, what, that, whoever, whatever, whichever.
Interrogative:	who, which, what.
Indefinite:	one, none, some, any, anyone, anybody, some one, somebody, no one, nobody, each, everyone, everybody, either, neither, both.

4. An **adjective** is a word that modifies (describes or limits) a noun or pronoun. It is probably most useful here to consider the articles *a, an, the,* and the possessive forms of nouns and pronouns, when used to modify nouns, as in the classification of adjectives. Pronouns have two forms of the possessive: the first form (*my, our, your, her, his, its, their*) when placed before a noun functions as an adjective; the second form (*mine, ours, yours, his, hers, its, theirs*) functions as a pronoun.

Adjective:

It was *an eloquent, sharp, ugly, earthly* countenance. *His* hands were *small* and *prehensile,* with fingers knotted like *a* cord; and they were continually flickering in front of him in *violent* and *expressive* pantomime.—R. L. Stevenson.

The place through which he made *his* way at leisure was one of *those* receptacles for *old* and *curious* things which seem to crouch in *odd* corners of *this* town, and to hide *their musty* treasures from *the public* eye in jealousy and distrust.—Dickens.

One of *our* boys found *your* kitten and noticed that *its* paw had been hurt.

Pronoun:

Yes, that kitten is *ours.* Please tell that boy of *yours* that any friends of *his* are welcome here.

5. An **adverb** is a word that modifies a verb, an adjective, or another adverb. Occasionally an adverb will modify a phrase, a clause, or a whole sentence. Adverbs express the following relations in a sentence: time, place, manner, degree, affirmation or negation, frequency. See also section 5.

Time:

He will come *tomorrow.* They will *soon* be here. May I leave *now?*

Place:

Put it *down.* Come *in.* Leave your dog *outside.* Your son was *here.*

Manner:

He answered *quickly.* I played *better* yesterday. She smiled *happily.*

Degree:

You are *very* kind. He is *too* good. They are *rather* dull.

Affirmation or negation:

Do *not* go there. *Certainly,* he will return. *Yes,* he is here. *No,* you must *not* see him.

Frequency:

She is *always* pleasant. She called *twice.* It rains *often.* It *never* snows.

6. A **preposition** is a word used to show the relation between a noun or pronoun, called its object, and some other word in the sentence. Many prepositions are single, short words: *at, by, in, for, from, off, on, up, above, after, around, before, behind, between, below, during, except, over, through, under, until, without.* There are also a number of so-called "group" prepositions: *by means of, in front of, on account of, in place of, with respect to.*

7. A **conjunction** is a word which connects words, phrases, or clauses. Conjunctions are co-ordinating and subordinating. Conjunctions used in pairs are called correlatives. Adverbs used as

connectives, either co-ordinating or subordinating, are called conjunctive adverbs.

The chief co-ordinating conjunctions are: *and, for, but, or, nor, yet, both . . . and, not only . . . but also, either . . . or, neither . . . nor.* At the present time, *so* is used as a co-ordinating conjunction in loose, informal writing and in colloquial speech, but its use should still be avoided in most writing except in direct quotation. Look up "so" in section 44.

The following are some of the subordinating conjunctions: *if, although, though, that, because, since, so that, in order that, as, unless, before, than, where, when.*

Correlative conjunctions are: *both . . . and, not only . . . but also, either . . . or, neither . . . nor.*

Some adverbs used as conjunctions are: *how, why, where, while, before, after.* Such connectives as *however, therefore, nevertheless, hence, accordingly,* are often classified as conjunctive adverbs. In modern prose they are commonly used as transitional expressions. There is no profit in quibbling over the question of whether they are transitions or conjunctive adverbs; the only important fact here is that in modern writing these expressions, with the exception of *hence,* are *not* placed at the beginnings of clauses in compound sentences. They are tucked away neatly within the clauses. See section 14 for a discussion of the punctuation which should be used with these transitional expressions.

8. An **interjection** is a word (or group of words) used as an exclamation expressing sudden or strong feeling. Note that an exclamation point is not the inevitable punctuation of an interjection. For mild interjections a comma or a period is sufficient.

The Verbals. The verbals—gerunds, participles, and infinitives—are hybrid forms. They come from verbs and have some of the forms and functions of verbs, but they serve primarily as other parts of speech. They may have tense forms, and they may be modified by adverbs. One important thing to remember about verbals is that they are not used to make independent statements.

1. A **gerund** is a verbal used as a noun.

He started *running* faster. [Note that *running* is the object of the verb *started*. It is modified by the adverb *faster*].

Writing a poem is not easy. [*Writing* is the subject of the verb *is*. It has *poem* as its object.]

I tried to get there without *breaking* the speed laws. [Object of the preposition *without*.]

His eligibility for office was established by his *having been* so successful as governor.

He was proud of *having won* the cup. [Note the tense form of the gerund in the last two sentences.]

2. A **participle** is a verbal used as an adjective. It is, of course, also used as a part of a verb phrase, as in: He *was reading* a book; but we are here concerned primarily with its adjective use. Note also such sentences as: The teacher *was asking* you a question, and Teasing him was *asking* for trouble, in which *asking* is a part of the verb phrase in the first combination and a gerund in the second.

The *excited* boy kicked at the *barking* dog. *Picking* up a stick, he threw it after the *frightened* animal. *Feeling* safer, he started to walk home. *Having told* us his story, he went to bed. [Note that *having told* modifies *he*. It takes an indirect object *us* and a direct object *story*. Observe the different tense forms illustrated.]

3. An **infinitive** is a verbal which may be used as a noun, an adjective, or an adverb. The infinitive may be recognized by its sign *to*, which precedes it. Occasionally the sign is omitted.

Mary wanted *to drive* a car. Used as a noun object of *wanted*. Note its object, *car*.]

She had no car *to drive*. [Used as an adjective to modify *car*.]

She was happy *to come* with us. [Modifies an adjective, *happy*.]

To watch her happiness was a pleasure.

We did not dare *let* her drive. [Note the omission of the sign *to*.]

Exercises

Exercise 1, Parts of Speech. In the following sentences name the part of speech to which each word belongs. The sentences are purposely made elementary. You should have no difficulty with this exercise. It is just a preliminary workout.

1. Tom and Sandra took their examinations in the morning.
2. Tom wrote his name in a heavy hand at the top of the paper.
3. Wearily he implored the ceiling for inspiration and knowledge.
4. Sandra, who had great fortitude, smiled sweetly at him.
5. She knew that spiritual courage was important.
6. Moreover, she had studied her lessons carefully.
7. Tom often depended on the impulse of the moment.
8. A golden opportunity was undoubtedly his.
9. Alas, he did not feel equal to the challenge.
10. With a sigh of resignation, he bent over his paper.

Exercise 2, Verbals. Identify the verbals in the following sentences. The verbals are gerunds, participles, and infinitives.

1. Going home is no fun; I hate to do it.
2. I saw the girls going home as I was coming in.
3. The contract, signed, sealed, and delivered, made me glad to take over the business.
4. The crowd having been scattered by the embattled police, the streets finally began to look as usual.
5. He appeared to remember what he was supposed to be doing, but doing it was another matter.
6. Many people like going to church, but others seem to be indifferent.
7. Mother took my protesting father to church to watch two strangers being married.
8. Wishing to avoid an argument, Father pretended to be enjoying himself.
9. Sitting in the next pew were two old and respected friends of his family.
10. Having bowed politely, he began to study the expressions on the faces of the assembled guests.

The Elements of the Simple Sentence. Defined in terms of form or pattern, a sentence is a basic unit of language, a communication in words, having as its core at least one independent verb with its subject. It gives the reader or hearer a feeling that it is a relatively complete unit, capable of standing independently or alone. Now this may sound a bit complicated, but it will gradually clear itself up as you study the explanations and examples below.

For a discussion of the various verbless, subjectless, or fragmentary units that are acceptable in writing and in speech, turn to section 1.

The **simple sentence** is one which contains a single independent clause. A simple sentence may have as subject more than one noun or pronoun and as predicate more than one verb.

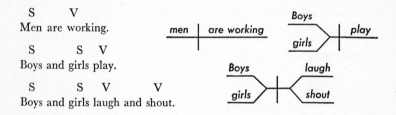

S V
Men are working.

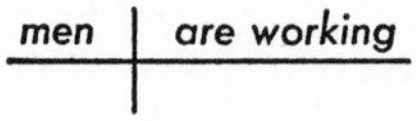

S S V
Boys and girls play.

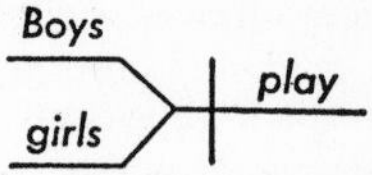

S S V V
Boys and girls laugh and shout.

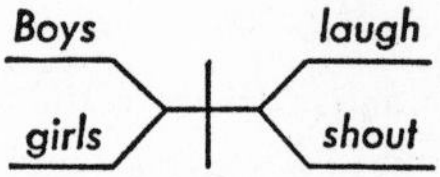

1. Complements. With certain types of verbs a third element—in addition to subject and verb—is essential to the formation of a complete expression. This element is called a complement. There are three main kinds of complements—direct objects, indirect objects, and subjective complements. Less common are the objective complement and the retained object.

a. The **direct object** of a verb denotes that which is immediately acted upon.

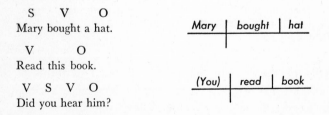

S V O
Mary bought a hat.

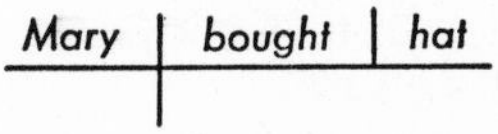

V O
Read this book.

V S V O
Did you hear him?

b. The **indirect object** names, without the use of the preposition, the one to whom or for whom the action is done.

Mother told *me* a story.

He taught *us* a lesson.

I gave the *dog* a bath.

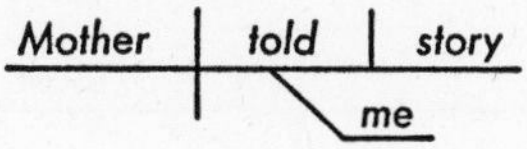

Note that when *to* or *for* are expressed, the substantive following becomes the object of the preposition, as in: Mother told a story to me; Dr. Jones taught mathematics to us; She gave a dollar to the man.

c. The **subjective complement** refers to the subject and describes or limits it. It is often called the *predicate substantive* if it is a noun or pronoun, and a *predicate adjective* if it is an adjective. See also section 5.

Tom is a *major* now.

The price seems *right*.

The milk tastes *sour*.

It looks *good* to me.

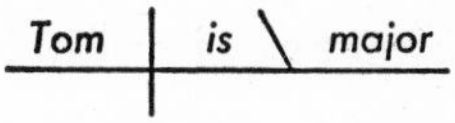

d. The **objective complement,** used with verbs such as *elect, choose*, *make*, *call*, *appoint*, or the like, refers to the direct object.

They made him their *chairman*.

They called him *foolish*.

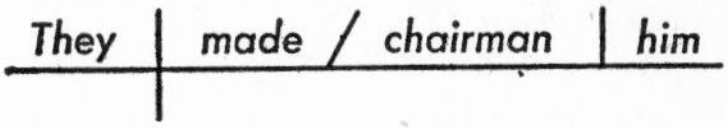

e. The **retained object** is used with a verb in the passive voice.

They were given some *food*.

He was taught a good *lesson*.

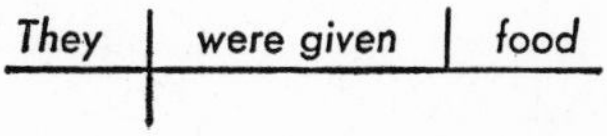

A simple sentence may have adjectives, adverbs, and phrases as modifiers.

The little boy gave his mother a red rose.

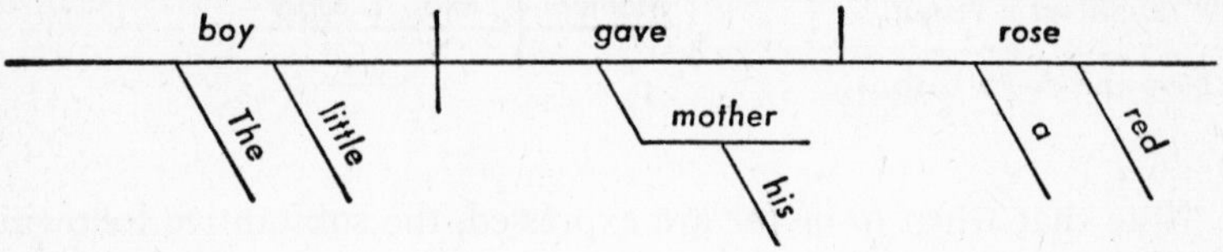

2. Phrases. In its general, loose sense, a phrase is any group of words. Thus we say that a man "phrases his thoughts" when he puts them into words, or that he expresses his ideas in "well-balanced phrases" when his sentences are well-built or rhythmical. The word "phrase" in its general sense has its place in the language. In the study of grammar, however, the word refers to one of three kinds: the verb phrase, the prepositional phrase, or the verbal phrase.

a. A **prepositional phrase** consists of a preposition, its object, and modifiers of the phrase or any of its parts.

A prepositional phrase may be used as an adjective.

The boy *with the books under his arm* is my brother. [The phrase modifies *boy*. Within the phrase is another phrase, *under his arm*, which modifies *books*.]

She married a man *of great wealth*. [The phrase modifies *man*.]

The father *of the child* [adjective] watched *from the window* [adverb].

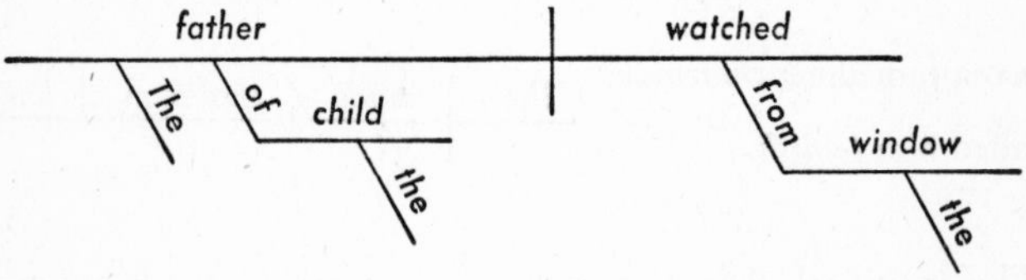

A prepositional phrase may be used as an adverb.

He plunged *into the pool*. [The phrase is an adverb of place or direction, modifying *plunged*.]

For an hour he played *in the water*. [Both phrases modify *played*. The first is an adverb of time, and the second is an adverb of place.]

Francis was true *to his word*. [The phrase is an adverb modifying *true*.]

Under the bridge two tramps had built a fire.

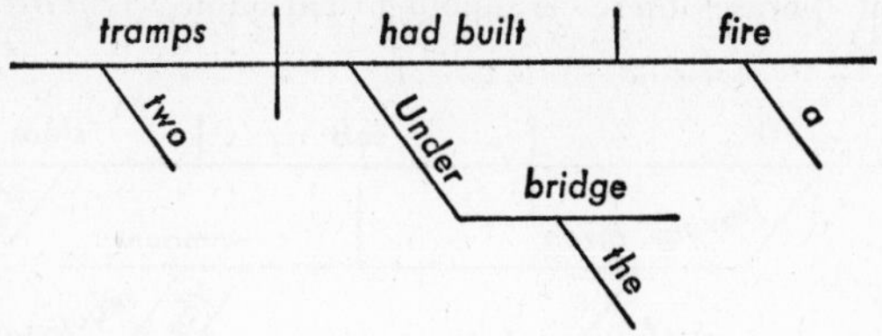

A prepositional phrase may be used as a noun.

The best time for study is *in the morning.* *On the mantel* would be a good place for it. [The first phrase is used as a noun subjective complement; the second is used as the subject of the verb *would be.*]

The best time *for study* is *in the morning.*

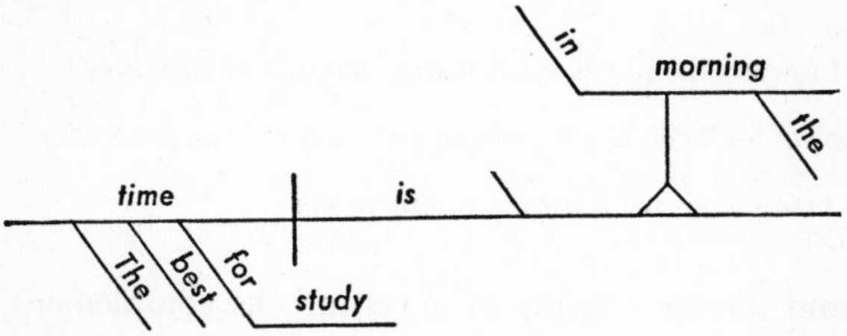

b. A **verbal phrase** consists of a participle, a gerund, or an infinitive and its complements and modifiers.

A **participial phrase** consists of a participle, its complement, if it has one, and any modifiers of the phrase or any of its parts. It is used as an adjective. A thorough understanding of the uses of participial phrases is of practical value to any writer because their misuse results in a stylistic fault known as the "dangling modifier." For a discussion of this see section 32.

The boy *now playing center* is a substitute. [The phrase modifies *boy.* The participle is modified by the adverb *now,* and it has for its object the noun *center.*]

Frightened by the sudden noise, the deer plunged into the brush. [The phrase modifies *deer.*]

His face, *freshly scrubbed,* shone in the morning light. [The phrase modifies *face.*]

Having given him the required amount, I left the store. [Notice that within the participial phrase there is another participle, *required,* modifying *amount.*]

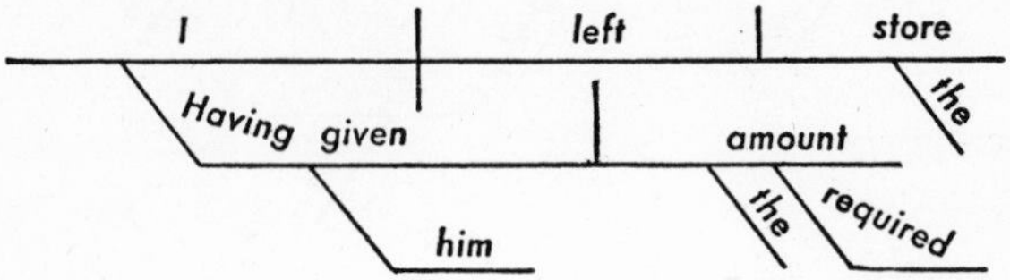

A special kind of participial phrase, called the **absolute phrase,** is made up of a substantive followed by a participle. It differs from the usual participial phrase in that it does not modify any single word in the sentence; grammatically it is an independent element. An absolute phrase cannot become a dangling modifier.

We hunted toward the north, *each taking one side of the ridge.*

Their navy having been destroyed, they were forced to surrender.

The game being over, we returned to our rooms.

A **gerund phrase** consists of a gerund, its complement, if it has one, and any modifiers of the phrase or any of its parts. A gerund phrase is always used as a noun.

Staying out late at night will not help your reputation. [The gerund phrase is used as the subject of the verb *will help.*]

Harry enjoyed *mowing the lawn.* [Object of the verb.]

You can get the address by *stopping at our house.* [Object of preposition.]

I should call that *violating the spirit of our agreement.* [The phrase is used as an objective complement referring to *that.*]

Hearing that song brings back sad memories to me.

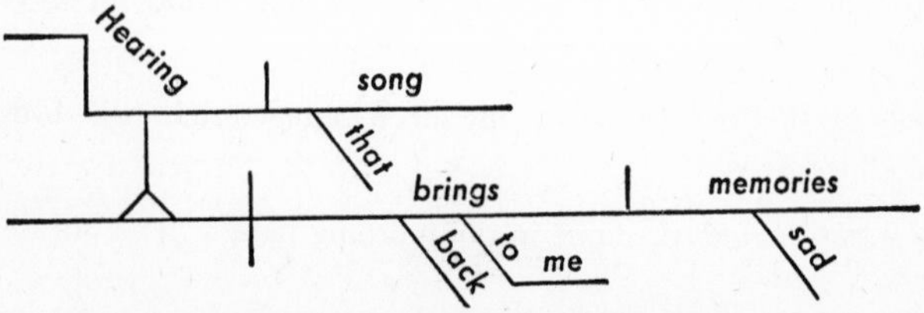

Mary objected to *my telling the story.*

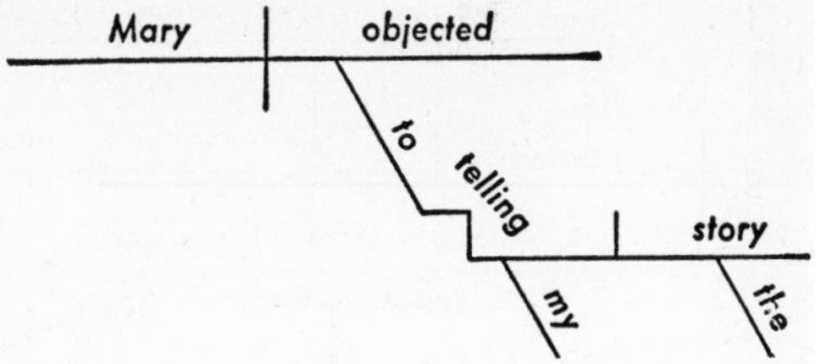

An **infinitive phrase,** like other verbal phrases, may have a complement and modifiers. In addition it may have what is called the assumed subject of the infinitive. The assumed subject of the infinitive is in the objective case. An infinitive phrase may be used as an adverb, an adjective, or a noun.

Tommy did not stop *to pick up his toys.* [An adverb, modifying the verb *did stop.*]

Their attempts *to cut the line* were futile. [An adjective, modifying the subject *attempts.*]

Whether to believe him or to call mother was a real problem for me. [A noun, used as the subject of the sentence.]

We knew *him to be the most hardened gambler of the regiment.* [Notice that the infinitive *to be* has *him* as its assumed subject.]

My orders were *to deliver the guns.*

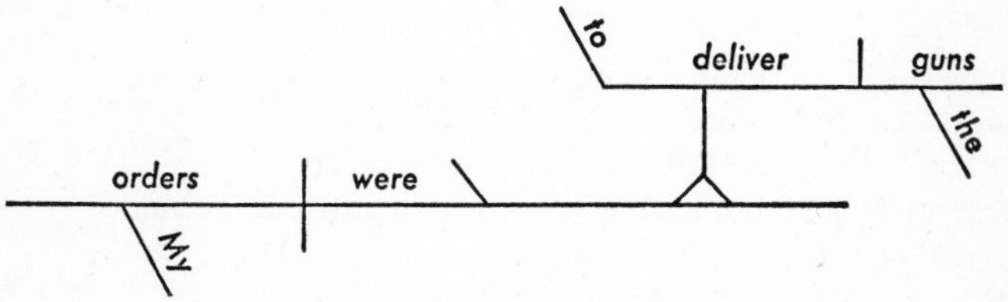

I am happy *to see you again.*

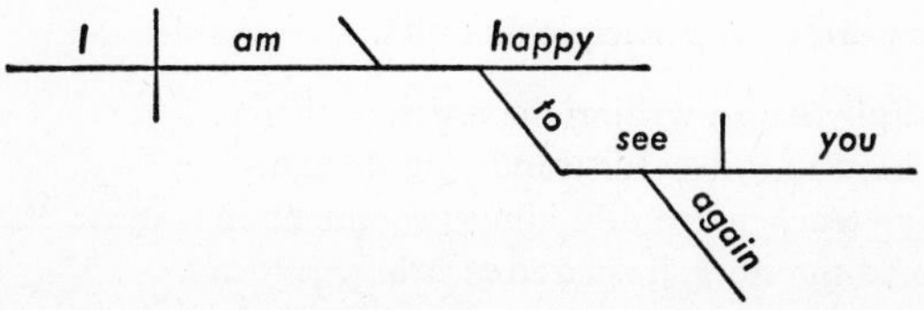

She wanted *me to drive the car.*

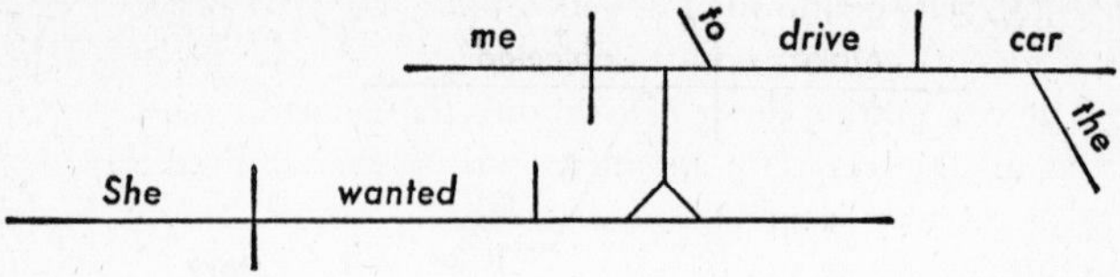

Exercises

Exercise 1, Subject, verb, complement. In each of the following sentences point out the subject, the verb, and the complement.

1. Two of the men handed tools off the truck.
2. The morning fog gave everything a ghostly appearance.
3. The break in the road had endangered traffic.
4. A man got some warning signs and set them up on the highway.
5. The foreman gave one of the workmen some directions.
6. The man nodded his head and called the driver of the bulldozer.
7. Soon the bulldozer had cleared the rubble from the highway.
8. The air was chilly and it smelled fresh.
9. In a while the men had given the pavement a coat of hot tar.
10. They had repaired the break before the traffic became heavy.

Exercise 2, Diagrams. Diagram the subject, verb, and complement (if any) in each of the following sentences.

1. We brought the men a light lunch.
2. A working man can always eat something.
3. Marge poured the hot coffee into the cups.
4. One tanned lad gave her a dazzling smile.
5. The color of his skin was a deep brown.
6. He was a sophomore at the state university.
7. He had found a job with a road construction crew.
8. Marge, who was also a student, seemed happy to meet him.
9. He told her his plans for the coming year.
10. The men thanked us and resumed their work.

Exercise 3, Participles. Pick out the participles in the following sentences and tell what word each participle modifies.

1. Tom dutifully began writing the assigned theme.
2. He tried hard to collect his wandering thoughts.
3. His smiling teacher had told him to comment on a story.
4. Having read the story, he glared at it in perplexity.

5. It dealt with a defeated and frustrated character.
6. The fellow belonged to the lost generation.
7. Tom glared at the story with rising anger.
8. Dared he risk putting down his scathing comments?
9. Lighting another cigarette, he started writing the required theme.
10. Being a recently demobilized Marine, he sought safety in imposing generalities.

Exercise 4, Participles and gerunds. Pick out each gerund and participle in the following sentences and tell how each is used.

1. Smiling with anticipation, the professor settled down to reading the stack of themes just handed in.
2. He found himself enjoying his students' writing more and more as the years went on.
3. Knowing that today's assignment had been challenging, he was especially eager to start.
4. But alas, the very first paper he opened was oozing with overwriting and fancy language.
5. Tearing his thinning hair, he began swearing softly.
6. This student's writing is even sillier than usual, he said to himself.
7. As he started grading the theme, his head began buzzing strangely with overused, meaningless language.
8. Irritated but not really surprised, he considered quitting for the day.
9. Did he really dislike grading themes after all?
10. Still, he thought to himself, grading themes is probably more fun than writing them, and with that, pulling himself together, he began inscribing a large red-inked "F" at the top of the paper.

Exercise 5, Phrases. In the following sentences pick out each phrase and tell whether it is prepositional, participial, gerund, or infinitive.

1. My brother urged me not to miss the concert.
2. I telephoned to Margie early in the afternoon.
3. Thanking me sweetly, Margie agreed to accompany me.
4. Getting two tickets was the problem of the moment.
5. As I knew the condition of my purse, I decided to get help from my friends.
6. A friend in need seems to be the only kind of friend that I have.
7. I found everyone in great need of financial help.
8. In despair I decided to test my brother's fraternal loyalty.
9. He had a long sermon to give me, but in the end he agreed to help me.
10. Looking very pretty, Margie added charm to an evening of pleasant music.

The Elements of the Compound Sentence. A compound sentence, as the name indicates, is made by compounding or joining two or more simple sentences. Such joining may involve the use of conjunctions and proper punctuation. See sections 13 and 14.

I warned her, but she was persistent.
She hit me, and I fell.

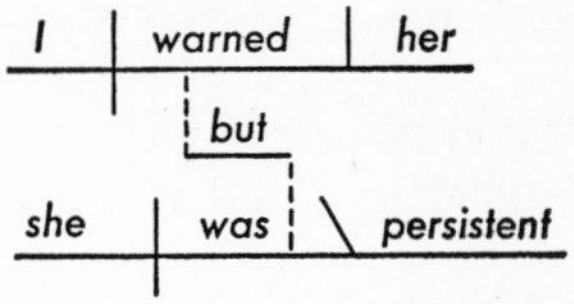

The Elements of the Complex Sentence. We have seen that simple sentences are units structurally and grammatically complete, and that compound sentences can be broken up into such complete and independent units. A thought expressed in a simple sentence is thereby given primary rank or importance. Ideas expressed in the co-ordinate units of a compound sentence are given equal billing, as it were. Now it is quite possible for communication to exist on that one level; the Anglo-Saxons came pretty close to writing and speaking in that manner. Modern English, however, developed a system whereby many differences in the relationship of one idea to another could be expressed by grammatical structure. It developed and perfected the dependent clause and the complex sentence.

But it should be added that this development and refinement has continued to the point where, for the sake of variety and emphasis, main ideas are occasionally expressed in dependent clauses, as in this very sentence you are now reading.

A complex sentence has at least one main clause, grammatically independent and able to stand alone, and one or more dependent clauses. A dependent clause is joined to the main clause by a relative pronoun, *who*, *which*, *that*, or by one of the numerous subordinating conjunctions, such as *after*, *although*, *as*, *because*, *before*, *if*, *since*, *unless*, *when*, *where*, *why*. Dependent clauses are used as nouns, as adjectives, or as adverbs. You can ordinarily recognize a dependent clause by the sign of its dependence or subordination, but occasionally the sign is missing, as in the following examples:

The one game *they did succeed in winning* was the only one played on the home floor.

The information *he brought* was invaluable.

I realized [*that*] *he had not understood the error* [*which*] *I had pointed out to him.*

The boy [*whom*] *he referred to* was the one who had begged, "Say [*that*] *it isn't so, Mister*!"

1. A dependent clause may be used as a noun.

As subject of a verb:	*What he did at the dance* shocked me greatly.
As object of a verb:	Harry thought *that he would not be recognized.*
As subjective complement:	This is *where I caught the largest salmon.*
As object of a verbal:	Be sure to accept *whatever she offers you.*
As object of a preposition:	It depends upon *how many will pay their dues.*
As an appositive:	His first argument, *that women are inferior to men*, was easily proved untrue. It has been suggested *that we adjourn.*

What he told the officers was never revealed. [Noun clause used as subject.]

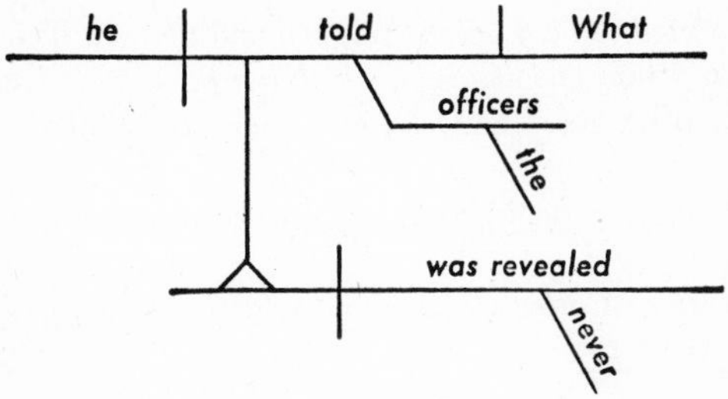

The teacher said *that the answer was correct.* [Noun clause used as object.]

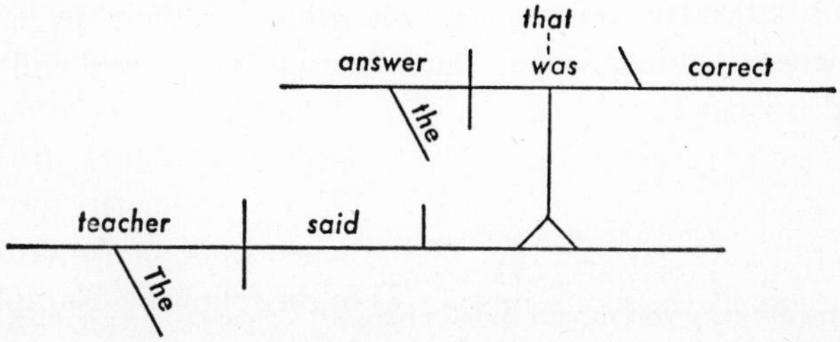

Give it to *whoever calls for it.* [Noun clause used as object of a preposition.]

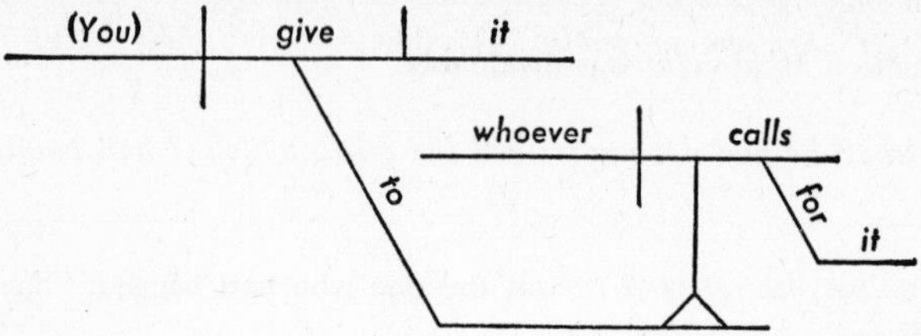

2. A dependent clause may be used as an adjective. Adjective clauses are either restrictive or nonrestrictive. An important thing to remember in this connection is that restrictive clauses are *not* set off by commas. See section 13 in the handbook.

Restrictive:

A teacher *who speaks poor English* is badly handicapped.
Algebra is the subject *with which I have the most trouble.*
I shall take you to the store *where I found the linens.*
That is the precise moment *when you must make your announcement.*
The reason *why I fainted* is that I was famished.
Do you know any trick *whereby you can make him confess?*

Nonrestrictive:

Our janitor, *who used to be a sailor,* strapped and tied our boxes.
I am reading *The Loom of Language, which is a fascinating book.*
It is too late to plant roses in December, *when the ground is usually cold or muddy.*
He usually gave his tests on Mondays, *when the class was too sleepy to care what happened.*
The book is *Webster's Collegiate Dictionary, with which you should be quite familiar by this time.*

Note here, if you are looking for structural signals as a means of identifying clauses, that the words, *where, when,* and *why* may introduce adjective clauses. If you think of them in terms of "place where," "time when," and "reason why," you will not be confused.

Adjective clauses:

We visited the *town where* my mother lived.
It was a *day when* everything went wrong.
I see no *reason why* you should remain here.

Adverbial clauses:

Put it back *where you found it.* [Modifies the verb *put.*]
We shall start *when you are ready.* [Modifies the verb *shall start.*]

Noun clause:

Tell me *why you are angry.* [Object of the verb *tell.*]

This is the boy *who brought the papers.* [Adjective clause modifying *boy.*]

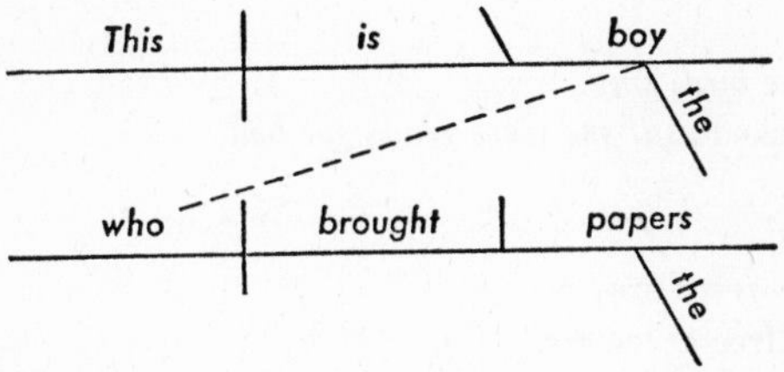

3. A dependent clause may be used as an adverb to show time, place, cause, purpose, result, condition, concession, manner, or comparison.

Time:

You may leave *when the whistle blows.*
Before you leave the room, close the windows and pull down the shades.
We played cards *until our father returned.*
After you finish your test, hand in your papers.
While Mother entertained her guests, we children played in the orchard.

Place:

These men will go *wherever they can find work.*

Cause:

I came late *because I was delayed by a wreck.*
As I could not understand the painting, I kept silent.
Since no one volunteered, James finished the work himself.

Purpose:

They came to America *in order that they might find religious freedom.*

Result:

Every door was locked, *so that it was impossible to leave the building.*
The night was so dark *that we could travel no farther.*

Condition:

If you want to go home, I shall call a cab.
Should you find yourself on the wrong trail, return to the starting point.
Children will not be admitted *unless they are accompanied by their parents.*

Concession:

Although I did not understand his question, I attempted a reply.
No matter what he says, I shall not be angry.

Manner:

Let us sing *as the birds sing.*
Marion Jean looked *as if she were ready for bed.*

Comparison:

They are as free *as we are.*
They are not so free *as we are.*
Ralph is older *than I am.*

Carol is prettier *than I am.* [An adverbial clause of comparison.]

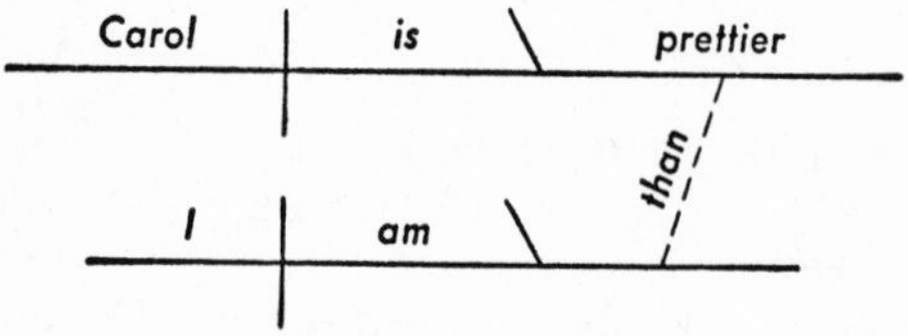

The whistle blew *before the ball was fumbled.* [An adverbial clause of time, modifying the verb *blew.*]

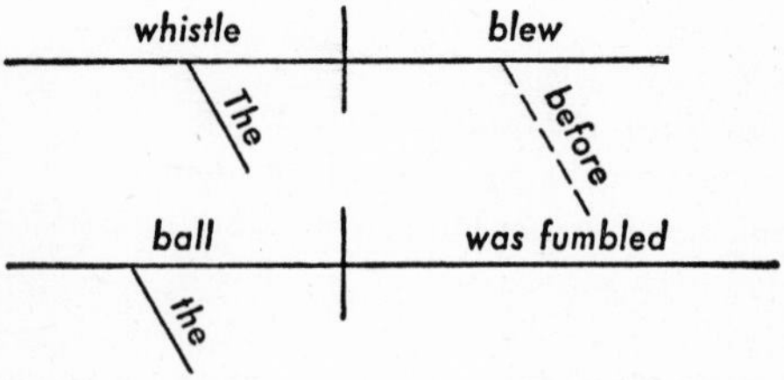

Elements of the Compound-complex Sentence. The compound-complex sentence is one which contains two or more independent clauses and at least one dependent clause.

A loud crash broke the silence, and everyone looked up to see what had fallen.

Someone rang the doorbell, but Mother, who was pouring the tea, chose to ignore the bell.

The door swung open, and a tall man, whose hat and overcoat were sprinkled with wet snow, stamped into the room.

Exercises

Exercise 1, Noun clauses. In the following sentences pick out each noun clause and tell whether it is used as the subject of a verb, as the complement of a verb or verbal, or as the object of a preposition.

1. The little boy refused to say what his name was.
2. A friendly policeman asked him where he lived.
3. No one seemed to know where his mother was.
4. One woman announced that she knew the little boy.
5. Why the boy was crying seemed to perplex the officer.
6. He tried to console the boy with whatever was at hand.
7. He decided to show the boy how the handcuffs worked.
8. Flashing a happy smile, the boy indicated that he wanted the officer's revolver.
9. "This is where he lives," said a woman, pointing at the apartment house.
10. Where he lived was quickly settled by the boy's mother, who came running out of the apartment house.

Exercise 2, Adjective clauses. Pick out the adjective clauses in the following sentences. Tell what word each clause modifies. Be able to tell which clause is restrictive and which is nonrestrictive.

1. The town where I was born is now a ghost town.
2. We decided to drive to Silver City, which was not far from the main highway.
3. We arrived there on a day when the temperature was in the nineties.
4. A red-bearded prospector, who seemed to be a public greeter, stopped our car.
5. Marion, who carried a 35 mm camera, took his picture.
6. We glanced down a street which hummed with activity.
7. Modern cars lined an avenue down which carriages had raced.
8. The ghosts we had expected to see must have retired to the hills.
9. I could see the reason why they preferred to remain invisible.
10. That day I buried some memories with which I had lived for some time.

Exercise 3, Adverbial clauses. Pick out the adverbial clauses in the following sentences.

1. The rain which had been threatening us all day came before we had finished our work.
2. We were working where the rocks had to be blasted out.
3. Because the traffic was heavy, we kept one lane of the road open.
4. Before each blast was set off, two men waved the traffic to a halt.
5. Ashley, who was more experienced than I, told me what to do.
6. Although we had never had an accident, we worked under constant tension.
7. When the highway was clear, I pressed the handle down, and a long strip of roadway shuddered as if it were writhing in agony.
8. While the traffic waited, the bulldozers quickly shoved loose rocks off the open lane so that the cars and trucks could proceed again.
9. I think that some of the drivers were as relieved as we were.
10. While we were clearing off the rocks, the downpour came; soon the cut was so muddy that we had to stop work for the day.

Exercise 4, Kinds of sentences. Pick out the dependent and independent clauses in the following sentences. These sentences have been purposely simplified, so that if your instructor thinks it worth your time, they may be used for practice in diagramming.

1. Some people have a perfect genius for saying nothing.
2. That which is called firmness in a parent is called obstinacy in a mule.
3. A bachelor is a souvenir of some woman who found a better one at the last minute.
4. Whoever comes will get a door prize.
5. Spring is almost here, and the crocuses are blooming.
6. I shall be ashamed if I cannot remember his name.
7. Westward the star of empire takes its way.
8. She wanted to know how she could renew her youth.
9. Harry is the boy who mowed your lawn yesterday.
10. If you love music, you will never be lonely.

B. RHETORICAL PATTERNS

The Problem of Effectiveness. "What is my trouble?" the puzzled student asks. "My verbs match their subjects, and my pronouns are backed up by the proper antecedents, and yet my writing is flat. It's dull as last season's campaign oratory. Why bother with grammar?"

That is a problem—why bother? There is a two-part answer to this question. In the first place, it is not enough to observe all the social sanctions in connection with what we call grammatical correctness. Something more is needed. Note that we say "something more," not "something in place of." One might say that "correct grammar" is like a pair of trousers: when a man has them on, no one notices him, but when he does not, he will be painfully conspicuous and embarrassed among people whose opinions he values. Let us repeat here—perhaps a trifle beyond the call of duty—that by "correct grammar" we refer to the language practices that are accepted by people of some education. These conventions are important to a college student because by his presence in college he has signified his intention to live and work among people of some education. Of course a person who is content to remain on the "has went—we was robbed" level has no problem; he needs only to open his mouth and do what comes naturally, and for his purposes his language will probably do well enough. He need not bother.

The second part of the answer to the question is that writing—and speaking, too—is an art, capable of cultivation and improvement. Let us be realistic about it and admit freely, before we go into this matter of improving something that is adequate, that for most routine occasions routine writing is good enough. We are here concerned with the student who is not satisfied with routine writing, the student who is disturbed by the fact that although he writes correctly and honestly, he is yet ineffective. His trouble may be that he has forgotten that writing is communication, that in communication there is not only a writer but also a reader, not only a speaker but also a listener. Communication by means of words is a game; someone is there pitching, not just throwing rocks into the air, but pitching for someone else to catch. The presence of the reader or the listener has a dominant effect on the way language is used. He must be reached somehow, his interest caught, his attention held; if he is not interested, the communication becomes a passport to the waste basket.

Some of the qualities of effective communication are stressed elsewhere in this book. It is well to review them here: the words you use must be exact, fresh, full of strength and vitality. Picture-making words are better than vague, general words. A fresh point of view will give flavor to your style; humor will lighten it. Even such devices as spacing on the page and using opaque paper are important. And as for speech, everyone knows how much depends on voice, tone, inflection, gestures, pauses, facial expression, and a pleasing personality.

In this chapter we are dealing primarily with the grouping or arrangement of words in sentences—not entirely, of course, inasmuch as no amount of skillful grouping of poorly chosen words can make effective sentences.

Long and Short Sentences. We can learn something by comparing the ways in which two men, both good writers, chose to report similar situations. The first man wrote his piece in very short sentences.

> Across the open mouth of the tent Nick fixed cheese cloth to keep out mosquitoes. He crawled inside under the mosquito bar with various things from the pack to put at the head of the bed under the slant of the canvas. Inside the tent the light came through the brown canvas. It smelled pleasantly of canvas. Already there was something mysterious and homelike. Nick was happy as he crawled inside the tent. He had not been unhappy all day. This was different though. Now things were done. There had been this to do. Now it was done. It had been a hard trip. He was very tired. That was done. He had made his camp. He was settled. Nothing could touch him. It was a good place to camp. He was there, in the good place. He was in his home where he had made it. Now he was hungry.
>
> He came out, crawling under the cheese cloth. It was quite dark outside. It was lighter in the tent.
>
> Nick went over to the pack and found, with his fingers, a long nail in a paper sack of nails, in the bottom of the pack. He drove it into the pine tree, holding it close and hitting it gently with the flat of the ax. He hung the pack up on the nail. All his supplies were in the pack. They were off the ground and sheltered now.
>
> Nick was hungry. He did not believe he had ever been hungrier. He opened and emptied a can of pork and beans and a can of spaghetti into the frying pan.
>
> "I've got a right to eat this kind of stuff, if I'm willing to carry it," Nick said. His voice sounded strange in the darkening woods. He did not speak again.

And now observe how differently another man says almost the same thing, "This is the place I have searched for, where for the moment I am happy and at peace."

There is a valley in South England remote from ambition and from fear, where the passage of strangers is rare and unperceived, and where the scent of the grass in summer is breathed only by those who are native to that unvisited land. The roads to the Channel do not traverse it; they choose upon either side easier passes over the range. One track alone leads up through it to the hills, and this is changeable: now green where men have little occasion to go, now a good road where it nears the homesteads and barns. The woods grow steep above the slopes; they reach sometimes the very summit of the heights, or, when they cannot attain them, fill in and clothe the combs. And, in between, along the floor of the valley, deep pastures and their silence are bordered by lawns of chalky grass and the small yew trees of the Downs.

The clouds that visit its sky reveal themselves beyond the one great rise, and sail, white and enormous, to the other, and sink beyond that other. But the plains above which they have travelled and the Weald to which they go, the people of the valley cannot see and hardly recall. The wind, when it reaches such fields, is no longer a gale from the salt, but fruitful and soft, an inland breeze, and those whose blood was nourished here feel in that wind the fruitfulness of our orchards and all the life that all things draw from the air.

In this place, when I was a boy, I pushed through a fringe of beeches that made a complete screen between me and the world, and I came to a glade called No Man's Land. I climbed beyond it, and I was surprised and glad, because from the ridge of that glade I saw the sea. To this place very lately I returned.

The many things that I recovered as I came up the countryside were not less charming than when a distant memory had enshrined them, but much more. Whatever veil is thrown by a longing recollection had not intensified nor even made more mysterious the beauty of that happy ground; not in my very dreams of morning had I, in exile, seen it more beloved or more rare. Much also that I had forgotten now returned to me as I approached—a group of elms, a little turn of the parson's wall, a small paddock beyond the graveyard close, cherished by one man, with a low wall of very old stone guarding it all around. And all those things fulfilled and amplified my delight, till even the good vision of the place, which I had kept so many years, left me and was replaced by its better reality. "Here," I said to myself, "is a symbol of what some say is reserved for the soul: pleasure of a kind which cannot be imagined save in the moment when at last it is attained."

—From Hilaire Belloc, *Hills and the Sea,* "The Mowing of a Field." Reprinted by permission of Charles Scribner's Sons and of Methuen & Co. Ltd., London.

We may notice that out of thirty-seven sentences in the Hemingway selection, twenty-seven are less than ten words long. Hemingway was obviously striving to give the effect of random thoughts and impressions going through the mind of his character, who at the end of a day of tramping was relaxed and happy and not disposed toward much thinking. In the Belloc selection, all except two sentences are over twenty words long. There is an air of reserve here; one feels that this is an occasion worthy of a bit of reverence. And yet both men wrote about the same thing and for the same kind of reader.

Uses of Subordination. A child normally expresses his thoughts and impressions in simple sentences. He will say, for instance, "My trike was lost. I found my trike. It was back of the garage. I lost it last night. It was wet. It was raining." The child's baby-sitter, several years older than he, probably would report the situation like this: "Bobby found his tricycle behind the garage. He left it there last night when it began to rain." An older person might have said: "Bobby found his tricycle behind the garage, where he had left it last night when it began to rain." As a child's mind matures and he begins to perceive that not all details and thoughts are of the same importance, he learns to give certain details of his communication a primary or a lesser position in a sentence. In other words, he learns to use subordination. He learns to place minor facts and ideas in dependent constructions in his sentences. The use of the complex sentence, it has often been said, is the sign of maturity in a person. The same thing can be said for the use of verbal phrases, prepositional phrases, appositives, and various types of single-word modifiers, which are also forms of subordination.

1. You should be familiar by this time with the various types of dependent clauses and with the structural signals that are used to

show their dependence on main clauses (see page 48). Let us see now what can be done with dependent or subordinate clauses to improve accuracy of expression, to give unity to sentences, and to relieve the monotony of too many clauses on the same level. As you observe each of the following revisions, ask yourself, "Does it improve the sentence? Does it produce a more accurate, compact, and pleasing expression?"

Immature:

I well remember a strange conversation I had with a man once. This man was a friend of mine. He and I had served together in the Marines.

Revised:

I well remember a strange conversation I once had with a friend of mine, with whom I had served in the Marines.

Immature:

The average recruit has just won his freedom from his parents. He objects violently to the whole idea of discipline.

Revised:

The average recruit, who has so recently won his freedom from parental authority, violently rejects the whole idea of discipline.

Awkward:

Do not be in too much of a hurry to join an organization. Study its membership before you join.

Revised:

Before you join an organization, investigate its membership.

Immature:

I have heard stories of the way freshmen were treated, but I have seen no bitter rivalry between classes thus far.

Revised:

Although I have heard stories of ill-treatment of freshmen, thus far I have observed no bitter rivalry between the classes.

Immature:

A newspaper has a duty to report the day's happenings. This report must be truthful. No one will deny this.

Revised:

No one will deny that it is the duty of a newspaper to report truthfully the day's happenings.

And now, before we leave this subject, let us examine a paragraph in two versions: first, as it would be written if every thought were given the importance of a separate statement, and second, as it would be written if lesser ideas were placed in subordinate constructions.

VERSION A:

A great deal of traditional cultural education was foolish. That must be admitted. Boys spent many years acquiring Latin or Greek. At the end they could not read a Greek or Latin author. Neither did they want to. Of course this was not true in a small percentage of cases. Modern languages and history are preferable to Latin and Greek. This is in every way true. They are more useful, and they give much more culture, and it takes less time. An Italian of the fifteenth century had to learn Latin and Greek. Everything worth reading was in those languages or in his own. These languages were indispensable keys to culture. Since that time great literatures have grown up in various modern languages. Development of civilization has been very rapid. A knowledge of antiquity has become less useful. A knowledge of modern nations and their comparatively recent history has become more useful in understanding our problems. The traditional schoolmaster's point of view was admirable at the time of the Revival of Learning. Now it is unduly narrow. It ignores what has been done since the fifteenth century. History and modern languages are not the only things contributing to culture. Science does that too. But science must be properly taught. Education should have other aims than direct utility. It is possible to maintain this. It is not necessary to defend the traditional curriculum. Utility and culture are not incompatible. They only seem to be. But they must be understood broadly.

VERSION B:

It must be admitted that a great deal of the traditional cultural education was foolish. Boys spent many years acquiring Latin and Greek grammar, without being, at the end, either capable or desirous (except in a small percentage of cases) of reading a Greek or Latin author. Modern languages and history are preferable, from every point of view, to Latin and Greek. They are not only more useful, but they give much more culture in much less time. For an Italian of the fifteenth century, since practically everything worth reading, if not in his own language, was in Greek or Latin, these languages were the indispensable keys to culture. But since that time great literatures have grown up in various modern languages, and the development of civilization has been so rapid that the knowledge of antiquity has become much less useful in understanding our problems than knowledge of modern nations and their comparatively recent history. The traditional schoolmaster's point of view, which was admirable at the time of the Revival of Learning, became gradually unduly narrow, since it ignored what the world has done since the fifteenth century. And not only history and modern languages, but science also, when properly taught, contributes to culture. It is therefore possible to maintain that education should have other aims than direct utility, without defending the traditional curriculum. Utility and culture, when both are conceived broadly, are found to be less incompatible than they appear to the fanatical advocates of either.

—From Bertrand Russell, *In Praise of Idleness and Other Essays.*

2. The substance of a co-ordinate clause may often be better expressed in a participial phrase. You must always, however, be on your guard against the danger of subordinating the wrong thought. Ask yourself, "Which is the important thought in my sentence? Which are the supporting details?"

Awkward:

My decision to enter college came suddenly, and I encountered several obstacles.

Improved:

Having made a sudden decision to enter college, I was unprepared for the difficulties which I encountered.

Immature:

The inexperienced camper usually sleeps on the ground for several nights, and so he decides that a bed of fir boughs is worth his effort.

Improved:

Having endured sleeping on the ground for several nights, the inexperienced camper usually decides that a bed of fir boughs is worth his effort.

Immature:

He looks at his teacher. His mind is in a whirl, his mouth is dry, so he makes some worthless answer.

Improved:

The confused student stares at his teacher—his brain in a whirl, his dry mouth stuttering some incoherent response.

3. A similar effect may be produced with gerund or infinitive phrases:

Awkward:

Their working hours were shortened. This resulted in more spare time for recreation and enjoyment.

Improved:

Shortening their hours of work resulted in more time available for recreation and enjoyment.

Immature:

The wife has children which she must clothe. She must take care of them and worry about them. The business woman does not have anybody except herself to whom she is obliged to pay any attention.

Improved:

The wife has children to clothe, to care for, to worry about; the business woman has no one to think of but herself.

Wordy:

The necessary preparation is simple. You get dressed and pull your old shotgun out of the corner. Then you are ready to start for the duck ponds.

Improved:

Having dressed and pulled the old shotgun out of the corner—all the preparation really necessary—the hunter is ready to start for the duck ponds.

4. A prepositional phrase may be used to express a detail more accurately and more concisely than a clause or a sentence.

Immature:

We wrote our papers at separate tables. There was a proctor in front of us. Another one stood behind us.

Revised:

We wrote our papers at separate tables, with one proctor in front of us and another behind us.

Immature:

The professor repeated his instructions. It was to help those who came late.

Revised:

For the benefit of the late-comers the professor repeated his instructions.

Immature:

When the examination was over, the students got together and compared their answers.

Revised:

After the examination the students flocked together to compare answers.

Immature:

I turned in my paper. I did not stop to go over my answers.

Revised:

I turned in my paper without a second glance at my answers.

5. A minor detail worth only a single word instead of a whole sentence or a clause is better expressed in a single word.

Wordy:

There were two new girls, and they both wore green rayon dresses that had short sleeves.

Revised:

The two new girls both wore short-sleeved dresses of green rayon.

Wordy:

The house was old. The lawn around it was enclosed by yew hedges. These hedges were neatly clipped.

Revised:

The lawn around the old house was shut in by neatly clipped yew hedges.

Wordy:

The window was closed. Through it came the sounds from the playground. Some boys were shouting angrily.

Revised:

Through the closed window there filtered into the room the angry shouts of boys on the playground.

6. An appositive may be used to express a detail that is not important enough to stand in a clause. Consider this piece of autobiographical writing:

I was born in Middleville, Ohio. It's a real small town. Most of the people in it are farmers. They raise cows for milk and a lot of apples. Still, it's the county seat of Whiteside County.

Now this is obviously a wordy passage, marred by many faults in addition to a lack of subordination. However, let us see what the use of appositives will do:

I was born in Middleville, Ohio, a small dairy and apple-farming community and the seat of Whiteside county.

The following group of revised sentences will further illustrate the use of the appositive:

Wordy:

I have an uncle who is a nuclear scientist. He works in an atomic laboratory and he urged me to come to college.

Revised:

An uncle of mine, a nuclear scientist in an atomic laboratory, urged me to come to college.

Immature:

I have a younger brother who is called Robie. He goes to high school and he is always in mischief. He wears his hair long and is always smiling. He, also, intends to be an engineer like my father.

Revised:

My younger brother Robie, a happy, mischievous, long-haired high-school lad, plans to become an engineer like his father.

Wordy:

Father is a congenial sort of person, and he hasn't made an enemy in his life.

Revised:

Father, a congenial sort of person, has not made an enemy in his life.

7. Occasionally the thought in a compound sentence is better expressed by a simple sentence with a compound verb.

Awkward:

The wise student budgets his time for study, and he prepares his lessons according to a schedule.

Revised:

The wise student budgets his time for study and prepares his lessons according to a schedule.

Variation in Order. In writing and speaking our primary concern must always be that our sentences fit the thoughts they are communicating. Most of them, without any conscious effort on our part, will fall into the established pattern of the English sentence, that of subject-verb-complement order. There is nothing *much* that we can or should wish to do about it, but occasionally a change of the normal order, either by inversion or by a shifting about of modifiers, will result in more accurate and more attractive expression of thought. In the following pairs of sentences, consider how the change in emphasis affects the meaning of the sentence.

In a home there is love. [What word is stressed here?]
There is love in a home. [What change of emphasis do you see here?]

They seldom come back for more.
Seldom do they come back for more.

The principal stormed into their midst.
Into their midst stormed the principal.

Aunt Sophronia came like a ship under full sail.
Like a ship under full sail came Aunt Sophronia.

They carry the mail through storms and floods.
Through storms and floods they carry the mail.

A candidate for a doctor's degree may write a novel or a play if he wishes.
If he so desires, a candidate for a doctor's degree may write a novel or a play.

Loose and Periodic Sentences. A periodic sentence is one in which the meaning of the main clause is not completed until the end of the sentence. A loose sentence is one in which various details are added after the meaning of the main clause is complete. Short sentences are often periodic; long sentences tend to be loose. Since the mind grasps the thought of a short sentence so quickly, it is only in long sentences that periodic structure has any noticeable psychological effect.

The periodic sentence builds suspense. It tends to hold up the meaning until the end, to force the reader to consider first the various details upon which the main thought is based. It makes him wait. Overuse of periodic structure is a little like an Ancient Mariner holding your lapel and breathing into your face while he tells his urgent story.

Notice in the following paragraph how a skillful writer can combine the two types. In the writing of beginners, which at times tends to flabbiness, the occasional conscious change from a loose to a periodic sentence is like tightening the bolts and screws on a car—it helps to stop the squeaks and rattles.

For the kind of courage which does not consist in repression, a number of factors must be combined. [periodic] To begin with the humblest: health and vitality are very helpful, though not indispensable. [loose] Practice and skill in dangerous situations are very desirable. [periodic] But when we come to consider, not courage in this and that respect, but universal courage, something more fundamental is wanted. [periodic] What is wanted is a combination of self-respect with an impersonal outlook on life. [periodic] To begin with self-respect, some men live from within, while others are mere mirrors of what is felt and said by their neighbors. [loose] The latter can never have true courage; they must have admiration and are haunted by the fear of losing it. [loose] The teaching of "humility" which used to be thought desirable was the means of producing a perverted form of this same vice. [periodic] "Humility" suppressed self-respect but not the desire for the respect of others; it merely made nominal self-abasement the means of acquiring credit. [loose] Thus it produced hypocrisy and falsification of instinct. [periodic] Children were taught unreasoning submission and proceeded to exact it when they grew up; it was said that only those who have learned how to obey know how to command. [loose] What I suggest is that no one should learn how to obey and no one should attempt to command. [loose] I do not mean, of course, that there should not be leaders in co-operative enterprises; but their authority should be like that of a captain of a football team, which is suffered voluntarily in order to achieve a common purpose. [loose] Our purposes should be our own, not the result of external authority; and our purposes should never be forcibly imposed upon others. [loose] This is what I mean when I say no one should command and no one should obey. [loose]

—From *Education and the Good Life* by Bertrand Russell. Published by Liveright Publishing Corp., N. Y. Copyright 1926 Boni & Liveright, Inc.

Parallel Structure and Balance. You must have noticed that as we go along in this chapter we are getting further and further away from the idea of everyday English for everyday occasions and deeper into the concept of language as an art. For most occasions workaday language will do. There are, however, other occasions. Ordinary English is like a truck: it will get you there, but many people like a more pleasant means of travel. Or you might say that simple language is like the food handed out from a chuck wagon: it is nutritive and most sustaining, but it lacks the graces of a table tastefully set and in pleasing surroundings, which many people enjoy and desire. Nor does language lose any of its solid virtues when it achieves a little grace and beauty; rather it gains in force, clarity, and directness.

One of the rhetorical devices that skillful writers resort to is known as the balanced or parallel construction. Let us examine this at two levels. First, we may see it as a pedestrian and thoroughly practical means of improving awkward sentences, by making a noun parallel with another noun, a gerund with another gerund, a phrase with another phrase, a clause with another clause. Notice how rephrasing the following sentences improves their effectiveness:

Awkward:

Choose a house that is spacious, with a good exposure to the sun and that people like to look at. [An adjective, a phrase, and a clause]

Parallel:

Choose a house that is spacious, sunny, and attractive to look at. [Three adjectives]

Awkward:

I have only one suggestion to make: cultivate friends who you think are loyal, have a cheerful disposition, and who are ambitious. [An adjective, a verb, and a clause]

Parallel:

I have only one suggestion to make: cultivate friends who you think are loyal, cheerful, and ambitious. [Three adjectives]

Awkward:

I was glad to be there for the lecture and to see how the models work. [A noun and a clause]

Parallel:

I was glad to be there for the lecture and the demonstration of models. [Two nouns]

Awkward:

The trouble with that book is its bad design and it costs too much. [A noun and a clause]

Parallel:

The trouble with that book is its bad design and high price. [Two nouns]

For a discussion of the "false parallel" see section 35.

When used beyond this workaday tightening up of flabby sentences, parallel structure becomes a conscious art. It could become a quaint mannerism, it is true, if it were carried too far. If it is used naturally, to fit the thought and the occasion, it will seldom be overused. You will not have frequent occasions to say, "To err is human, to forgive divine," or "You can take a boy out of the country, but you cannot take the country out of the boy."

Even Francis Bacon, writing in an age when rhetorical mannerisms were fashionable, did not often find it possible to balance phrases as he did in his essay about studies:

Reading maketh a full man;	
conference a ready man;	and
writing an exact man.	And therefore

if a man write little	—	he had need to have great memory;
if he confer little	—	he had need to have a present wit; and
if he read little	—	he had need to have much cunning,

to seem to know what he doth not.

You can find examples of skillful parallelism in the work of present-day writers, as in the following:

My remarks about society may have seemed too pessimistic, but I believe that society can only represent a fragment of the human spirit, and that another fragment can only get expression through art. And I wanted to take this opportunity, this vantage ground, to assert not only the existence of art, but its pertinacity. Looking back into the past, it seems to me that that is all there has ever been: vantage grounds for discussion and creation, little vantage grounds in the changing chaos, where bubbles have been blown and webs spun, and the desire to create order has found temporary gratification, and the sentinels have managed to utter their challenges, and the huntsmen, though lost individually, have heard each other's calls through the impenetrable wood, and the lighthouses have never ceased sweeping the thankless seas. In this pertinacity there seems to me, as I grow older, something more and more profound, something which does in fact concern people who do not care about art at all.

As one may suspect, the perfectly balanced sentence is like a four-leaf clover—it is still the three-leaf clovers that fill the haymow. Once in a long time we run across a man like Oscar W. Firkins, whose daily class lectures sounded like this:

Classicism seeks truth, but its care for form, its care for language, its care for dignity, its care for normality and for ethics, cut it off from many truths. The day comes when some truth-lover insists upon telling these untold truths. That day is the dawn of realism.

Classicism, then, is somewhat restricted on two sides, truth and beauty. Remove the restrictions on one side and you get romanticism; remove them on the other, and you get realism.

But most of us save parallelism for holiday and special occasions, such as seem to require a bit of show and eloquence.

In the following selection,[1] notice the pleasing rhythm throughout, the frequent use of balance, and here and there the effective use of climax, as: "You are the rulers and the ruled, the lawgivers and the law-abiding, the beginning and the end. . . . I say these things to you not only because I believe them to be true, but also because, as you love your country, I love my country, and I would see it endure and grow in light and become a living testament to all mankind of goodness and of mercy and of wisdom."

In theory, there is no duck so dead as a defeated candidate on the morning after election. To test this theory—and perhaps for other reasons, vaguely sentimental in nature—we picked up a book of Stevenson's speeches on the morning of November 5th, when we were punchy after the night's vigil with Univac and the pasty-faced characters on the television screen. Methodically we read a page or two, expecting to taste stale wine at the bottom of the glass. Greatly to our surprise, we found ourselves reading on and on, responding to familiar words that seemed not to have wasted or faded.

"You are the rulers and the ruled, the lawgivers and the law-abiding, the beginning and the end." (Surely we had had enough of speechmaking; surely there was a saturation point beyond which no further word could add its weight to the almost intolerable burden of the conscientious mind.) "I say these things to you not only because I believe them to be true, but also because, as you love your country, I love my country, and I would see it endure and grow in light and become a living testament to all mankind of goodness and of mercy and of wisdom."

The words still had the power to lift, to strengthen, and to reassure. They even furnished the text for the day: "Who leads us," we read, "is less im-

[1] From "Notes and Comments," the *New Yorker,* November 15, 1952. Reprinted by permission of the *New Yorker,* Copyright 1952 by The New Yorker Magazine, Inc.

portant than what leads us." And "A wise man does not try to hurry history."

The nourishment, the durability of this collection of campaign utterances struck us as something of a political miracle, in a time of wonders. And it seemed to us, too, that the new President-elect, if he should be in search of a small, inexpensive guidebook covering the main exhibits of the Fair, could hardly ask for a more compact and useful volume to steady him in hours of perplexity and trouble. With minor allowances for differences in party philosophy, there is not much in the published speeches of Adlai Stevenson that General Eisenhower couldn't, or doesn't, subscribe to with all his heart, and it is the country's good fortune that this is so.

We like America on the morning after election. It goes to work with a unique hangover—the sudden sobriety of unexultant victory and unregretful defeat, the firm acceptance of the goodness and wisdom and finality of the night's doings, without remorse, without headache. ("Your public servants serve you right.") There is little reason to believe, looking at the figures, that Governor Stevenson ever stood the remotest chance of getting elected in this year and under these circumstances. But because he was articulate beyond the usual powers of candidates, and because he chose to speak to the voters in exact, rather than in round, phrases, he performed a special service —not only for Americans but for people all over the earth. It is almost as though he served a three-month term of office that will be long remembered.

Governor Stevenson (who has been in politics only four years) had a way of pronouncing the word "political" that invested it with honor even in the middle of a slugging match, and that made politics seem the noblest of all works. He pronounced every syllable of the word "political," and he pronounced the first syllable "po," not "puh." He always seemed to utter the word with a mixture of affection, awe, and delight—as a mother bathes a brand-new infant. By so speaking, and so believing, he unconsciously elevated the theater of politics for millions of astonished and attentive listeners, and made the play exciting and at times great. For the millions who found the play, as he read it, exciting and rewarding, and who share his unflinching belief that politics is the noblest as well as the most dangerous of arts, we thank him for the infinite pains he took, for the courage he breathed, and for raising, for everyone, not only the standard of the Democratic Party but the standard of a democratic people.

Euphony and Rhythm. In your study of writing you soon reach a point beyond which grammar will not help you. You must depend upon your feeling for rhythm. Good prose should have a pleasant sound when it is read aloud. It should form patterns of sound—patterns which the reader somehow feels to be an appropriate and harmonious accompaniment of the thought expressed. The selections which are here used to illustrate rhythm are not models which anyone could expect you to imitate. They are merely samples of what can be done with prose. But please do read them aloud.

The first two are from well-known novels:

Only once in all that time he had again the glimpse of the earnestness in the anger of the sea. That truth is not so often made apparent as people might think. There are many shades in the danger of adventure and gales, and it is only now and then that there appears on the face of facts a sinister violence of intention—that indefinable something which forces it upon the mind and the heart of a man that this complication of accidents or these elemental furies are coming at him with a purpose of malice, with a strength beyond control, with an unbridled cruelty that means to tear out of him his hope and his fear, the pain of his fatigue and his longing for rest: which means to smash, to destroy, to annihilate all he had seen, known, loved, enjoyed or hated; all that is priceless and necessary,—the sunshine, the memories, the future—which means to sweep the whole precious world utterly away from his sight by the simple and appalling act of taking his life.

—From Joseph Conrad, *Lord Jim.* By permission of J. M. Dent & Sons, Ltd., London, copyright owners.

They [the English] had been the greatest poets in the world because the love and substance of great poetry were so rare among them. Their poems were so full of the essential quality of sunlight because their lives had known sunlight briefly, and so shot through with the massy substance of essential gold (a matchless triumph of light and color and material, in which they have beaten the whole world by every standard of comparison) because their lives had known so much fog and rain, so little gold. And they had spoken best of April because April was so brief with them.

Thus from the grim gray of their skies they had alchemied gold, and from their hunger, glorious food, and from the raw bleakness of their lives and weathers they had drawn magic. And what was good among them had been won sternly, sparely, bitterly, from all that was ugly, dull, and painful in their lives, and, when it came, was more rare and beautiful than anything on earth.

—Reprinted from *Of Time and the River* by Thomas Wolfe. Copyright 1935 by Charles Scribner's Sons. Used by permission of Charles Scribner's Sons.

The last selection was written many, many years ago, but it has lost none of its freshness and power:

A man may read a sermon, the best and most passionate that ever man preached, if he shall but enter into the sepulchres of kings. In the same Escorial where the Spanish princes live in greatness and power, and decree war or peace, they have wisely placed a cemetery, where their ashes and their glory shall sleep till time shall be no more; and where our kings have been crowned, their ancestors lie interred, and they must walk over their grandsire's head to take his crown. There is an acre sown with royal seed, the copy of the greatest change, from rich to naked, from ceiled roofs to arched coffins, from living like gods to die like men. There is enough to cool the flames of lust, to abate the heights of pride, to appease the itch of covetous desires, to sully and dash out the dissembling colors of a lustful, artificial, and imaginary beauty. There the warlike and the peaceful, the fortunate and the miserable, the beloved and the despised princes mingle their dust, and pay down their symbol of mortality, and tell all the world that when we die our ashes shall be equal to kings', and our accounts easier, and our pains and our crowns shall be less.—Jeremy Taylor (1613–1667).

Chapter 3

THE PARAGRAPH

What Is a Paragraph? The word "paragraph" comes from two Greek words, *para* beside and *graphein* to write. It was at one time a mark, usually ¶, written in the margin of a manuscript beside the place where a unit or subdivision of the text was to begin. The signal now used to indicate the beginning of a paragraph is indention, that is, beginning a line a little in from the margin. So you see that we can think of paragraphing as a form of punctuation.

When we inquire into the purpose of this type of punctuation of discourse, we find that the nature of the punctuated, or paragraphed, unit varies. In narration the paragraph unit is an incident or a speech of a character. In description it may be a scene or a picture, but description is more often woven into the story action than presented as separate units. In discussions of facts and ideas—usually spoken of as exposition—the common paragraph unit is a segment of thought, but there are also special purpose paragraphs such as those used for introductions and transitions. To speak of a paragraph of exposition as a related group of sentences with or without a summarizing sentence is perhaps as close as we can come to describing the actual practice of writers.

Before we continue our discussion of expository paragraphs, which is the main intent of this chapter, let us examine two selections, one narrative and the other largely descriptive.

The situation was still under control, although Bart was worried again, as any fire-boss would have to be with a twenty-mile dry wind and some snags still smoking. The crews that had rested through the night were back on the job, and so he now had thirty-eight men for patrol and mop-up. With the northeast wind the down-canyon side was again the dangerous one. He put the rested crews on that side, and scattered some of them back into the underbrush to watch for spot fires. The loggers and mill-men patrolled the rest of the line except for those who were getting the snags down. The snags were all that Bart was really concerned about, especially those that were already flaming, even though they stood well inside the fire-line. Something must be done about them, if possible.

He hurried down to where a falling-crew was at work.

"How about it?" he asked. "Do you want to try those hot ones?"

The men glanced at one another.

"We'll take a look," said one of them.

One snag was burning at the bottom, and was too hot for the saw, even if you had had a salamander-crew to work it.

They looked at another, appraised their chances with liberal profanity, and then got to work with the nonchalant air of men who were risking their lives and rather enjoying it. (After all, you didn't hire out as a faller at all, if you were interested in dying in bed.) Bart let them take the risk. If this fire ever jumped the line on a day like this, there would be a lot of trees burned and many lives in hazard.

While two men worked on the saw, another stood back and watched the burning top. Just as they finished the first undercut he yelled, and they ran. A thirty-foot slab of flaming three-inch bark came falling through the air. They dodged behind trees, and the slab hit where they had just been working, with a crash that would have brained any man alive.

They kicked the burning fragments out of the way, and got to work again.

—From George R. Stewart, *Fire.* Copyright 1948 by George R. Stewart. Reprinted by permission of Random House, Inc.

Looking up, I saw on a limb high above me the most gorgeous bird I had ever laid eyes on. Sunlight breaking through the leaves illuminated his perch, and, against the dark green of the foliage, his flame-colored flank plumes shone like live fire.

Slowly he hopped up the branch, dipping his head in a snakelike manner, grasping at little twigs and knobs and shaking them, his wings partly open and his plumes nervously twitching. Then, at the upper end of the limb, he turned sidewise and, like a child jumping with both feet at once downstairs from step to step, he made a series of little leaps down the pencil-size incline to the bottom.

Here, suddenly, he raised his wings, lowered his neck in a heronlike crook, and began to thump the wrists of his wings above his back—rapidly and strongly enough so that I could hear them distinctly 60 feet away. At the same time he cast his plumes upward and backward in a curving spray. The whole rear of his body shook like a feather duster.

Two other males flew to the limbs near by. One of them dared to land near the display perch itself, only to be charged and driven off by the indignant owner.

As for the females, six of them fluttered around within 5 to 50 feet of the dance limb. For the most part, they sat quietly aloof to the male's antics; but when he became greatly excited, lowered his head, and emitted a number of low, burring growls, they flew to perches directly above his gaudy plumes, and even down to a spot beside him.

Once, in Australia's Taronga Zoological Park, I had seen an Emperor of Germany Bird of Paradise reach such a peak of ecstasy that he swung head down from his perch like a shimmering pendulum, his plumes cascading from his flanks like fragile white fans. As I watched the Greater bird preening and prancing along his limb, with head low and plumes high, I wondered if he might not do the same.

And he did. A brilliant ball of plumage, he tumbled forward and swung beneath his perch, luminescent in the morning sun. A female flew to the limb and stood just above him. Reaching up, the male pecked and fenced with her in a kind of continuation of their ritual. Then, as if upon a signal, the dance ended, and all the birds soared off toward a large wooded canyon to feed.

—From E. Thomas Gilliard, "New Guinea's Rare Birds and Stone Age Men," *National Geographic Magazine*, April, 1953. Copyright 1953 by the National Geographic Society. Reprinted by special permission of the author and publisher.

What can we learn from these samples, one an uncomplicated narrative and the other a description strung on a thread of narrative? Both use the time order; that is, the details are told in the order in which they happen. As this same time order is used in an explanation of a process or in a presentation of some historical development, any facts that we learn from these two examples will apply also to some forms of exposition. The fact most useful to the student writer, and the only one that need concern us here, is that he can break up his narration into mouthfuls of reasonable size as he goes along, and if he wishes to stress some portion of it, he can put it into a separate paragraph. That is about all there is to it.

The fact-and-thought substance of most explanations and discussions, however, is not so easily divided up and arranged on the basis of something inherent in the substance. If you have ever stopped to analyze your own thought processes in the agonies of creating a theme, you know that thought material does not begin in any such orderly arrangement in your mind. More likely than not, it looks originally like a bit of primeval chaos, out of which you fish first this idea and then that one. An order is to be found in this chaos only after *you* have ordered it for presentation to your reader. Yours is the responsibility to arrange it, to group it into thought units, and to give it that forward movement.

When we analyze the nature of these thought units that writers present in paragraphs, we see at once that they come in a variety of forms and sizes. Traditionally we speak of elaborating or developing an idea into a paragraph. What is the size of this idea, and how much does a writer need to say about it? These are questions that have to be answered by each writer in terms of his subject, his purpose, his occasion for writing, and his readers. The same idea may be the subject of a sentence, a paragraph, a group of paragraphs, a chapter, or a book. It all depends on how much the writer wants to say about it. It is quite possible that an idea may be adequately *elaborated* for its specific purpose in a single sentence; on the other hand, it is also possible that another idea may take several paragraphs for an adequate *statement*. There are further possibilities. One idea may be developed by several paragraphs. One idea may be stated in a paragraph of a single sentence, and the various units composing it may be elaborated in a series of paragraphs following, each unit in a separate paragraph. An idea composed of several subordinate ideas may be stated in the first sentence of a paragraph, the first subtopic discussed in that same paragraph, and the other subtopics discussed in succeeding paragraphs.

But, of course, all this freedom does not mean that there are no standards; a poorly organized paragraph is still a bad paragraph.

Perhaps we should remind ourselves that paragraphing is strictly a utilitarian device in writing. Its purpose is to make communication by words more accurate and easier. It serves this purpose by breaking up the forbidding solidity of a page of type, by resting the eye, and by indicating the beginnings and endings of thought units. Chapters are like large paragraphs, and in intermediate sizes between the two are sections and subsections.

Length of Paragraphs. The length of a paragraph depends on several considerations: the thoroughness or completeness with which the writer wishes to develop the topic or idea he is trying to make clear, the class of readers for whom he is writing, and present-day conventions governing paragraph length. Essays written for serious or leisurely study may use more complete development of topics and therefore longer paragraphs. Essays written for hasty reading or for immature minds should use smaller units and therefore shorter paragraphs.

Better than arbitrary rules governing paragraph length is an actual word count of paragraphs as they are written by good writers. The following is a summary of such a count. Three samples were used: one a popular treatment of science, another a mixture of autobiography and essay, and the third an essay from *Harper's*.

	Exposition
Number of paragraphs below 100 words	15
Number between 100 and 200 words	31
Number between 200 and 300 words	18
Number between 300 and 400 words	5
Number above 400 words	1

An appreciation of the vast difference in paragraph length among various kinds of writing can be gained by a count of words in paragraphs composed by Eudora Welty in a short story:

	Fiction
Number of paragraphs below 25 words	8
Number between 25 and 50 words	11
Number above 50 words	1

The Topic Sentence. The typical paragraph of thought-and-fact writing, as we have said, is a group of closely related sentences with or without a summarizing sentence. This summarizing sentence is usually called a *topic sentence*.

Although a skilled writer can produce as clear, compact, and effective a paragraph without a visible topic sentence as with one, it is good practice for the beginner to use summarizing sentences in most of the expository paragraphs that he writes. The practice is an aid to straight thinking as well as a safeguard against spineless paragraphs. If a beginner writes a paragraph without a topic sentence, he should be sure that his paragraph does have a central idea and that his reader will have no difficulty in finding it.

Generally the topic sentence comes first in a paragraph, sometimes combined with a transitional phrase. Occasionally it comes last, when the writer wishes first to prepare his reader for the general idea. Sometimes the topic sentence comes both first and last; the entire idea may be repeated in the last sentence, or a part may be stated by the first sentence and a part by the last. And, finally, in some paragraphs the topic sentence appears within the paragraph whenever the writer is ready for it, usually after a preparation for it by means of examples or details. All of these methods will be made clearer by the sample paragraphs which follow.

How to Write a Paragraph. Perhaps the most practical approach to the subject of writing paragraphs is an attempt to reconstruct the mental processes that must have taken place in the writing of two or three sample paragraphs. The first one is taken from a book that describes "the big change" in American life. The author, Frederick Lewis Allen, must have observed that there have been changes in the daily sounds, sights, and sensations to which people are accustomed. In casting about for ways of grouping them he decided on those associated with horses and carriages as one, and after a very simple general statement as his lead-off, he proceeded to pack his paragraph with details.

Here is his paragraph—and a very good one it is:

The sights and sounds and sensations of horse-and-carriage life were part of the universal American experience: the clop-clop of horses' hoofs; the stiff jolting of an iron-tired carriage on a stony road; the grinding noise of the brake being applied to ease the horse on a downhill stretch; the necessity of holding one's breath when the horse sneezed; the sight of sand, carried up on the tires and wooden spokes of a carriage wheel, spilling off in little cascades as the wheel revolved; the look of a country road overgrown by grass, with three tracks in it instead of two, the middle one made by horses' hoofs; the special male ordeal of getting out of the carriage and walking up the steeper hills to lighten the load; and the more severe ordeal, for the unpracticed, of harnessing a horse which could recognize inexperience at one scornful glance. During a Northern winter the jingle of sleigh bells was everywhere. On summer evenings, along tree-lined streets of innumerable American towns, families sitting on their front porches would watch the fine carriages of the town as they drove past for a proud evening's jaunt, and the cognoscenti would wait eagerly for a glimpse of the banker's trotting pair or the sporting lawyer's 2:40 pacer. And one of the magnificent sights of urban life was that of a fire engine, pulled by three galloping horses, careening down a city street with its bell clanging.

—From Frederick Lewis Allen, *The Big Change*. Copyright 1952 by Frederick Lewis Allen. Reprinted by permission of Harper & Brothers.

The second example illustrates a different problem. Mr. Gilbert Highet, in a book called *The Art of Teaching*, has a section on the qualities of a good teacher. The good teacher, he says, must know his subject, know his pupils, and know much else. Now that is not a bad topic for a single-paragraph theme, or for a theme of three paragraphs. You might try it. But Mr. Highet writes a chapter of sixty-five pages on this subject. He says, in discussing the third topic, that a teacher must make a bridge between college and the world—by making his subject relevant, and then adds, "The best way to do it is for the teacher to make himself relevant." Not a bad idea, is it? You have probably thought it yourself many times. How would you make the general idea clear to your reader? Mr. Highet does it by the simple device of giving an example of what he means. Here is his paragraph:

The best way to do it is for the teacher to make himself relevant. Nine thousand times more pupils have learnt a difficult subject because they felt the teacher's vitality and energy proved its value than because they chose the subject for its own sake. If a youth, sizing up the professor of medieval history, decides that he is a tremendous expert in the history of the Middle

Ages and a deadly bore in everything else, he is apt to conclude that medieval history makes a man a deadly bore. If on the other hand he finds that the man is filled with lively interest in the contemporary world, that he actually knows more about it because, through his training, he understands it better, that the practice of the intellectual life, so far from making him vague and remote, has made him wise and competent, the youth will conclude without further evidence that medieval history is a valuable interest.

—From Gilbert Highet, *The Art of Teaching*, Alfred A. Knopf, 1951.

We can look at a paragraph as an elaboration or development of a unit idea to the extent that a writer deems necessary. What does elaboration or development mean? Essentially it means "make clear to the reader." It may at times also mean "make impressive" or "make convincing." The first quality of good writing, therefore, is clearness, the ability to communicate, to convey thought, information, emotions. If a reader cannot understand what is written, nothing else counts. In our preliminary examination of three rather long paragraphs written by professional writers we have noticed that clarity depends ultimately on the use of relatively specific and concrete details. This principle may serve as your key to good paragraphs—or, for that matter, to good essays and articles.

Were we to analyze a large number of expository paragraphs for their rhetorical structure, we should discover that there are several special devices which writers use to elaborate and present an idea to the reader. The most useful ones will be discussed and illustrated here.

1. Particulars and Details. The most common means of making an idea clear to the reader is to support it and build it up by particulars and details. It is used in nine out of ten of the expository paragraphs you read. How does the writer find his details? By observing, by thinking, by reading, by asking questions —just as he gets his details for any sort of communication. Which comes first, the details or the general idea? Well, it doesn't matter much. Probably the two have to be worked out together. In the finished paragraph as the reader sees it, however, the hammer and saw marks of building should not show much. Everything should be neatly ordered and properly displayed.

The following two paragraphs of particulars and details start out with a general statement, although we may be sure that the author's line of thinking was from observation of details to a general statement:

Sea otters, like humans, eat three meals a day. A few individuals take snacks between times but the main feeding of the herd corresponds to our breakfast, lunch and supper. They dive for their food, usually in comparatively shallow water but occasionally as deep as 150 feet. Slanting down obliquely, they descend with forelegs folded over their breasts and their webbed hind feet, twelve inches long and four inches wide, driving them forward with powerful thrusts. They can stay under water for as long as six minutes at a time. When they come to the surface, they bring shellfish, crustaceans, cuttlefish, sea urchins and similar creatures of the sea bottom. Turning over on their backs they eat at leisure, using the whole ventral surface of their bodies as a table. On a number of occasions one of these animals has been observed bringing a flat stone to the surface along with its shellfish. Carefully balancing the stone on its chest it uses it as an anvil on which it pounds the shell to break it open. . . .

At the end of the meal the sea otter licks its "fingers" to get the last of the taste and then washes vigorously. It rolls over and over. It scrubs the fur tablecloth on its chest and stomach. It rubs its forepaws together like a man using soap and water. It washes its face, even going behind its tiny ears. It splashes water over its head, chest and shoulders. Finally it smooths down its moustaches. This done it stretches out on its back for a long siesta. Before dozing off it usually wraps a strand of kelp about its body to keep it from drifting away from the herd. Similarly through the night the otters sleep on the waves anchored to the seaweed of the kelp beds.

—Reprinted by permission of Dodd, Mead & Company from *Autumn Across America* by Edwin Way Teale. Copyright © 1950, 1951, 1956 by Edwin Way Teale.

Here is another example of a paragraph in which the writer proceeds to clear up a general statement by means of particulars and details:

The rapid advances in aircraft design have added a new hazard for jet fighter pilots: shooting themselves down. Amazing as it may seem, aeronautical engineers have made it possible for a supersonic jet fighter plane to "catch up" with the fire from its own guns with sufficient speed to shoot itself down. If a plane, flying at 1,000 mph, fires a burst from its

20-millimeter guns, the shells leave the plane with an air speed (plane's speed plus muzzle velocity) of about 3,000 mph. They soon slow down, however, due to wind resistance, and the plane begins to overtake them. Normally, the shells drop sufficiently, because of gravity, to permit the plane to pass harmlessly over them. If a pilot fires his guns in level flight and then goes into a dive, however, its is possible for the plane to overtake and run into them with considerable force. If the shells happen to be explosive, great damage can be done to the plane. There is at least one instance known of a jet fighter pilot having shot himself down by this method.

—From *Science in Everyday Things* by William C. Vergara. Harper & Brothers, 1958. By permission of the author.

Particulars and details are used in paragraphs of characterization, as in the following brilliant example:

Physically he [James Otis] was a large man—"a great Leviathan." He had a short neck, bold, narrow eyes, and a big, eloquent mouth which looks, in his portrait, capable of taking in all the liquor credited to him and giving forth the fiery speeches. An obscure little lawyer of the moment, John Adams, said he "is extremely quick and elastic, his apprehensions as quick as his temper. He springs and twitches his muscles about in thinking." Friends said he was "rough, hasty, loved good cheer." But his enemies called him "rash, unguarded, foul-mouthed," or even "a rackoon" or "filthy scunk." And how he could talk! The wildness and magic (sometimes boredom) of his talk must have swept the Masonic lodges even as it swept through the diaries and letters of his contemporaries. It varied from dreams of a perfect British Empire uniting the whole peaceful world in bonds of love, with God over all, to dirty (and not very funny) stories, but it never stopped.

—Esther Forbes, *Paul Revere and the World He Lived In,* Houghton Mifflin Company, Boston, 1942. Reprinted by permission.

2. Examples or Typical Instances. The topic idea may be supported and presented by means of examples or typical instances. Let us assume, for instance, that you have just written: "An unpromising performance in college often leads to unusual success in later life." This statement is so contrary to all that people want to believe that its reception may consist of, "Hmmm. Doesn't sound probable. Just give me an example—two examples." That is exactly what you do. You write: "There is Dr. Blank, the great heart specialist. There are Generals White and Brown, brilliant leaders both of them, who stood near the bottom of their class at West Point. Then there is H. V. Jones, the head of Blank Steel Corporation." You have begun to make your point, and your reader is more receptive to your idea.

Notice in the following selection that the topic sentence is made to stand by itself, supported by another sentence that repeats the same idea, more or less. Then the author uses one paragraph for one example, carefully explained, and a second paragraph for a number of similar examples, with briefer comments.

This dropping into a sleep that seems so close to death is one of the strangest adventures of the animal world. The flame of life, for months on end, sinks so low it almost—but not quite—goes out.

During the summer a woodchuck breathes between twenty-five and thirty time a minute, reaching a hundred times when excited. Yet, during hibernation, it may breathe only once in five minutes. Normally its heart throbs about eighty times a minute. In emergencies it may jump to two hundred times a minute. During the long sleep of hibernation, however, its pulse may slow down to four or five beats a minute, just sufficient to keep its thickened and sluggish blood in motion. Its limbs grow rigid. Even though, like all hibernating animals, it rolls itself into a ball to conserve heat, its temperature drops as low as thirty-seven degrees F., only five degrees above freezing. Thus for months on end—for as much as five months and sometimes more—the hibernating woodchuck skirts the fine line that divides the living and the dead.

At the same time millions of other creatures—frogs buried in the mud of pond bottoms, bats hanging upsidedown in caverns, chipmunks rolled into striped balls of fur, bears hidden in dark and silent dens—would be lost in the depths of their winter sleep. Reptiles that would twine themselves into masses to reduce the evaporation of their moisture were already moving toward crevices in the various Rattlesnake Buttes of the Dakotas. To infusoria, to land snails, to bumblebees, to toads, to alligators, to grizzly bears the coming of fall brings the drowsiness and torpor of what the Indians called the Long Sleep. Even a bird, the desert poorwill, has been found hibernating in the southwest, its temperature down to sixty-four degrees F. For all these infinitely varied creatures their ability to hibernate turns the winter into one long night of slumber.

Often a topic sentence can be developed only by examples. It is hard to imagine any other method used in the following:

Another field that awaits scientific exploration is that of the joke-towns—*Podunk*, *Squedunk*, *Hohokus*, *Goose Hill*, *Hard-Scrabble*, and so on. Almost every large American city is provided with such a neighbor, and mention of it on the local stage arouses instant mirth. For many years *Hoboken* was the joke-town of New York, *Watt* was that of Los Angeles, and *Highlandtown* was that of Baltimore, but *Hoboken* won its way to metropolitan envy and respect during Prohibition, *Watt* has been absorbed in Los Angeles, and *Highlandtown* is now a glorious part of Baltimore. "The humorous connotation of certain Indian names," said the late George Philip Krapp, "has always been felt, and names like *Hohokus*, *Hoboken*, *Kalamazoo*, *Keokuk*, *Oshkosh*, *Skaneateles*, names of real places, have acquired more than local significance, as though they were grotesque creations of fancy. There is, however, no post office named *Podunk* in the United States Official Postal Guide. Just how this word came to be used as a designation for any small, out-of-the-way place is not known. It is an Indian word by origin, the name of a brook in Connecticut and a pond in Massachusetts, occurring as early as 1687. There is also a *Potunk* on Long Island." Here Dr. Krapp seems to have been in error, for an onomastic explorer, E. A. Plimpton, reported in the Boston *Herald* for February 8, 1933, that he had discovered a veritable *Podunk* in Massachusetts, not far from Worcester. Dr. Louise Pound says that *Skunk Center*, *Cottonwood Crossing*, and *Hayseed Center* are favorite imaginary towns in Nebraska, and that *Sagebrush Center* reigns in Wyoming, *Rabbit Ridge* in Kansas, and *Pumpkin Hollow* in the State of Washington. For Missouri Charles E. Hess reports *Gobbler's Knob*, *Possum Hollow*, *Hog Heaven*, *Slabtown*, *Hog-Eye*, *Skintown*, *Bugtown*, and *Puckey-Duddle*.

—From H. L. Mencken, *The American Language*, Alfred A. Knopf, 1936.

The following selection illustrates not only the use of examples and instances but also the manner in which topic sentences can be used to tie a group of paragraphs together:

As late as 1808, when the slave trade was abolished, numerous Southerners thought that slavery would prove but a temporary evil. [Summary of preceding paragraph]

But during the next generation the South was converted into a section which for the most part was grimly united behind slavery. [Topic sentence of the paragraph] How did this come about? Why did the abolitionist spirit in the South almost disappear? [Questions to be answered by what follows] For one reason, the spirit of philosophical liberalism which flamed high in Revolutionary days gradually became weaker. [One possible answer] For another reason, a general antagonism between puritanical New England and the slaveholding South became evident; they differed on the War of 1812, the tariff, and other great issues; and the South felt less and less liking for the so-called Northern idea of emancipation. [A second possible answer] But above all, certain new economic factors made slavery more profitable than it had been before 1790. [This third possible answer provides a topic sentence for the whole section to follow, comprising the following two paragraphs]

One element in the economic change is familiar—the rise of a great cotton-growing industry in the South. [First example of an "economic factor"; topic sentence of the first half of the paragraph] This was based in part on the introduction of improved types of cotton, with better fibers [one explanation of the rise of the cotton industry], but in much larger part on Eli Whitney's epochal invention in 1793 of the "gin" for cleaning cotton [second explanation]. Cotton culture rapidly moved westward from the Carolinas and Georgia, spreading over much of the lower South to the Mississippi River and, eventually, on into Texas. *Another factor which placed slavery on a new basis was sugar growing.* [This second "economic factor" provides a topic sentence for the second half of the paragraph.] The rich, hot delta lands of southeastern Louisiana are ideal for sugar cane; and in 1794–1795 an enterprising New Orleans Creole, Étienne Boré, proved that the crop could be highly profitable. He set up machinery and vats, and the crowds which had come from New Orleans to watch the boiling-off broke into cheers when the first sugar crystals showed in the cooling liquid. The cry, "It granulates!" opened a new era in Louisiana. A great boom resulted, so that by 1830 the state was supplying the nation with about half its whole sugar supply. This required slaves, who were brought in, in thousands, from the Eastern seaboard.

Finally, tobacco culture also spread westward and took slavery with it. [Third "economic factor" and topic sentence of this paragraph] Constant cropping had worn out the soil of lowland Virginia, once the greatest tobacco region of the world, and the growers were glad to move into Kentucky and Tennessee, taking their Negroes with them. Thereafter the fast-multiplying slaves of the upper South were largely drained off to the lower South and West. This diffusion of slavery relieved many observers, because it lessened the risk of such a slave insurrection as Nat Turner's Rebellion, a revolt of sixty or seventy Virginia slaves in 1831—which, incidentally, did much to increase Southern fear of emancipationist doctrines.

—From *The Pocket History of the United States* by Allan Nevins and Henry Steele Commager, published by Pocket Books, Inc. Copyright, 1942, 1951, ©, 1956, by Allan Nevins and Henry Steele Commager.

3. Definition. A definition is usually an answer to an implied question: What do you mean by this? In what sense are you using this or that word? In the illustration that follows, James B. Conant is concerned with defining the word "empirical" in a special sense for his own purpose. He has to do this because he *needs* this word, or one like it, to make a distinction. Here is his situation. He has just made plain, in preceding paragraphs, that what is usually called "the scientific method" is in fact true of almost any activity in which some one tries to figure something out. He gives the example of an electrical failure in one's house, and he shows that the steps usually associated with "scientific method," such as hypothesis and experiment, are perfectly relevant to the problem of replacing a light bulb or a fuse. But Mr. Conant wants to distinguish this sort of practical activity from true science, the discovery and expression of principles and theories. Therefore he employs, with great care as you will see, the word "empirical" to characterize the kind of information that we use every day to solve practical problems. In these two paragraphs he defines his term by contrast (with science), and by example.

All this information is conveniently called "empirical," which means essentially cookbook information. John Tyndall, in a famous address of a popular nature on fermentation, wrote, "Hitherto the art and practice of a brewer have resembled those of the physician, both being founded on empirical observation." (And I am giving this quotation to define my use of the word "empirical.") "By this is meant the observation of facts apart from the principles which explain them, and which give the mind an intelligent mastery over them. The brewer learned from long experience the conditions, not the reasons, of success. But he had to contend, and still has to contend, against unexplained perplexities."

At the time Tyndall was writing one could say that the art of wine making and beer manufacture was empirical. The work of Pasteur and subsequent microbiologists and chemists has greatly lowered the degree of empiricism. Still, even today, there are many procedures in these industries which are simply based on experience and cannot be related to the concepts and theories of chemistry or biology. It is convenient to characterize a given practical art or a branch of science by assigning to it a degree of empiricism. If one wants to find an activity where the degree of empiricism is very low, I suggest turning to the work of the surveyor. Long ago the science of optics was developed so that it is possible to calculate by mathematical formulas the shapes of mirrors and lenses and to construct the optical part of a surveyor's instruments. Furthermore, Euclidian geometry provides a mathematical framework for the observation of the surveyor. Therefore, one can say that the surveyor's work represents an applied science in which the degree of empiricism is essentially zero. At the other end of the scale I would put the labors of any excellent cook, for in spite of all our knowledge of the chemistry of proteins, fats, and carbohydrates, the recipe for a good sauce or a good dessert is still entirely empirical.

—From *Modern Science and Modern Man* by James B. Conant. Columbia University Press, 1953. Reprinted by permission.

4. Comparison or Contrast. Comparison is telling what a thing is like. Usually the more familiar thing or idea is used to explain the less familiar one. If you were to explain the game of badminton, for instance, you could show how it was similar to tennis, the more familiar game. In what ways is piloting a plane like driving a car? How are Canadians like their friends in the United States? Contrast, on the other hand, is telling what a thing is not like. How does college life as you see it now differ from college life as you thought it would be? How does the American way of living differ from the Oriental way? How does democracy differ from communism? How does propaganda differ from news? These are typical subjects which invite treatment by contrast, not in paragraphs alone but also in entire essays or articles.

A white-collar employee of an American corporation visiting a Soviet institution of comparable rank will be in for some surprises. [Topic sentence] For one thing the offices of the establishment will be secondary to the plant, instead of vice versa which is usually the case in the United States. Also the visitor will note that a considerable number of executive officers in a Russian industrial organization, even engineers, are women. On a superficial level other points can be mentioned. First, there is little of the personal byplay and banter that accompany much American business endeavor and office routine; no coffee break, for example. Bosses are aloof. Second, lunch takes place in a cafeteria on the premises, maintained by the establishment; no corner drugstore, bar, or hotdog stand. Third, nobody has to catch the 5:25; commuting, if any, is by bus. Another point is that jobs are different in function. No Soviet plant has a public relations department or advertising department, office for employer-employee relationships, or even a sales manager and staff. Salesmanship, the first of all occupations in America, does not exist in our sense at all.

—From *Inside Russia Today* by John Gunther. Harper & Brothers, 1958. Reprinted by permission.

The following, with its sparks of grim humor that so few people associate with the author, may inspire you to compare and contrast your chosen occupation with others:

The great liability of the engineer compared to men of other professions is that his works are out in the open where all can see them. [Topic sentence] His acts, step by step, are in hard substance. He cannot bury his mistakes in a grave like the doctors. He cannot argue them into thin air or blame the judge like the lawyers. He cannot, like the architects, cover his failures with trees and vines. He cannot, like the politicians, screen his shortcomings by blaming his opponents and hope that the people will forget. The engineer simply cannot deny that he did it. If his works do not work, he is damned. That is the phantasmagoria that haunts his nights and dogs his days. He comes from the job at the end of the day resolved to calculate it again. He wakes in the night in a cold sweat and puts something on paper that looks silly in the morning. All day he shivers at the thought of the bugs which will inevitably appear to jolt its smooth consummation.

On the other hand, unlike the doctor his is not a life among the weak. Unlike the soldier, destruction is not his purpose. Unlike the lawyer, quarrels are not his daily bread. To the engineer falls the job of clothing the bare bones of science with life, comfort, and hope. No doubt as years go by people forget which engineer did it, even if they ever knew. Or some politician puts his name on it. Or they credit it to some promoter who used other people's money with which to finance it. But the engineer himself looks back at the unending stream of goodness which flows from his successes with satisfactions that few professions may know. And the verdict of his fellow professionals is all the accolade he wants.

—From Herbert Hoover, *The Memoirs of Herbert Hoover: Years of Adventure.* Copyright 1951 by Herbert Hoover. Reprinted by permission of The Macmillan Company.

Here is an interesting comparison of the reading of poetry with the playing of music:

Second, poetry must never be read as an exercise in "reading-speed," that deplorable mental-mangle for increasing the rate of destruction of textbook English. The fastest reader is not the best reader any more than the best conductor of Beethoven is the man who gets the orchestra through the *Eroica* in the shortest elapsed time. Why not take a stop watch to the Symphony, if this is your measure? Obviously because music declares its own pace. But so does good poetry. By rhyme, by the word-values of the poem, by the sequence of syllables, and by all these taken together, good poetry contains its own notation. [He explains how by specific details.] "We broke the brittle bright stubble like chaff" can no more be read at the same rate as "Bury the great duke with an Empire's lamentation" than *allegro vivace* can intelligently be played *adagio*. [He uses specific examples for further clarification.]

—From "What Does It Take to Enjoy a Poem," *Mid-Century American Poets,* by John Ciardi. Twayne Publishers, 1950. By permission of the author.

5. Analogy. Analogy is a form of comparison. It is used when the writer wishes to make something clear by comparing it with something from a different, and to the reader a more familiar, field of experience. A brief analogy is called a metaphor, as for instance Washington Irving's "A sharp tongue is the only edged tool that grows keener with constant use." A metaphor or an analogy has the power to illuminate a piece of writing, if it is well done, and the apprentice writer should try his hand at it more often, even at the risk of failure. Observe in the following paragraph how brilliantly Hawthorne uses analogy to describe the psychoanalyst's probing of his patient's subconscious:

Then after long search into the minister's dim interior, and turning over many precious materials, in the shape of high aspirations for the welfare of his race, warm love of souls, pure sentiments, natural piety, strengthened by thought and study, and illuminated by revelation,—all of which invaluable gold was perhaps no better than rubbish to the seeker,—he would turn back discouraged, and begin his quest towards another point. He groped along as stealthily, with as cautious a tread, and as wary an outlook, as a thief entering a chamber where a man lies only half asleep,—or, it may be, broad awake,—with purpose to steal the very treasure which this man guards as the apple of his eye. In spite of his premeditated carefulness, the floor would now and then creak; his garments would rustle; the shadow of his presence, in a forbidden proximity, would be thrown across his victim. In other words, Mr. Dimmesdale, whose sensibility of nerve often produced the effect of spiritual intuition, would become vaguely aware that something inimical to his peace had thrust itself into relation with him. But old Roger Chillingworth, too, had perceptions that were almost intuitive; and when the minister threw his startled eyes towards him, there the physician sat; his kind, watchful, sympathizing, but never intrusive friend.

—Nathaniel Hawthorne, *The Scarlet Letter,* Chapter 10.

6. Methods in Combination. In analyzing paragraphs to learn the methods used by professional writers, you must not be confused by a possible complexity of paragraph structure. A writer may use these methods singly or in various combinations, and the combinations may be intricate. It is not always possible to pick out a sentence and say, "This is example; this is definition." Frequently you will find several methods used in the same sentence. At times you may even find that example, analogy, or definition is used to make clear, not the topic idea, but a subordinate idea. Remember also that some of the words or even sentences in a paragraph must do other things than develop the topic idea. They may be used to relate the topic idea to ideas that came before it or that may come after it, or to establish connections between the subordinate ideas in the paragraph.

Almost every resource of the skilled writer is used in the following paragraphs, which, although part of a novel, are essentially expository. Note the analogies—"the unchained prowling beasts," "the long opulent Victorian afternoon and golden evening." Notice how at the end he repeats this phrase to tie everything together. Notice the wealth of examples and concrete details.

I often think of that dinner party in Richard's rooms as the midmost point of my life. I have spent my years almost equally between two centuries, and that was the last year of the first of them. People are apt to see this twentieth century in which humanity now weeps and mourns as a time of cataclysm. We are living in a loft over the stable; the floor is desperately thin; and we can hear the beasts stirring beneath us. And we know that they are not good chained comfortable beasts that come at our call and work in our service. Sometimes our hair stands on end as we listen, in a night's dark loneliness, to their unchained prowling, the scuffle of great pads, the rasp of breath coming out of hot red throats, and we picture their eyes lifted to their ceiling, which is our frail floor: the light green or golden pitiless eyes shining over the jaws that drip hungrily. Sometimes in dream the floor dissolves, and we are the beasts and the beasts are we, and all is chaos. And those who have known only this latter half of what has been my life think with envy of that first half, seeing it as green pastures and tranquil waters and talking of the long opulent Victorian afternoon and golden evening.

It wasn't so. The beasts were there then. The beasts are always there. Always our loft is perched between them and the stars, that seem to look implacably down on them and us, as if serenely and indifferently expecting the moment when the fools in the loft will become so heavily embroiled that they will smash the floor beneath their feet.

They were always embroiled, but they go on adding to the weight of their embroilment; and the only question is whether they will stop or whether the weight will become too much.

They were always embroiled. I have lived long enough to have no illusions about that. I am nearing my ninetieth year as I write this. I was born in a time when my living eyes could look at the Dook who had been at Waterloo. And then I watched the great glass bubble go up and heard the talk of peace on earth. And then I saw the Crimean men, legless and armless and eyeless and hopeless, sitting under the railings of Hyde Park, holding out their tin mugs for coppers, as we rode inside the Park and Mama bowed or did not bow, and Papa became a knight because he had helped to win the war. And I loved Lord Burnage who had ridden in the desperate moment of that war, and I had stroked the flank of the lovely beast that helped Tennyson to make the poem that moved us all to pride and wonder. And there had been the savage horror of mutiny in India; and I had watched my half brother Justin drive away, through the soft airs of a Cornish morning, because they were still embroiled, and he had never come back, and already that was so long ago that the moment when the path was empty and we turned back into the renovated house seemed, as the century ended, a moment lost in the mists of dream.

There had been embroilment in China, and Gordon had died at Khartoum, and the Boers had swept us off the hill at Majuba; and I had seen wooden ships with sails become ironclads with boilers, and rifles become machine guns, and cannon balls become explosive shells; and finally, at the turn of the century, the little soldier on the gray horse whom Nika had excitedly watched leading the grand parade to St. Paul's on Diamond Jubilee day had led a grand parade to Oom Paul, and many who went with him did not come back, and among them were Richard and Trimmer and poor Tom Chadderton.

And this was the long Victorian afternoon and golden evening.

—Howard Spring, *The Houses in Between,* Harper & Brothers, 1951.

In the next two selections we can study two versions of a common device in paragraphing. First, a general idea is stated in a topic sentence. Then this idea is broken up into several parts, and each part is given a separate paragraph.

The Soviet Union's cosmic rocket added a new member, if a miniscule one, to the system of planets revolving around the sun since eons past. Its success is a dramatic step toward sending rockets to seek out secrets of the solar system—and perhaps to explore some of the measureless space beyond. And it has stimulated men further to look up at the "stars that sweep, and turn, and fly," and ponder the nature of the universe. [This introduces the next idea, which is the heart of the piece.]

Space, from earthman's point of view, has three main divisions. [Main topic sentence] *The first and smallest is the solar system.* [Topic sentence of first subdivision] The sun, with a diameter of 864,000 miles and its mighty force of gravitation, holds the nine known planets in their elliptical orbits. In addition, the solar system includes thirty-one satellites of the planets (not counting the earth's artificial satellites); thousands of asteroids, which are rather like tiny planets; comets and meteors. As astronomical distances go, the size of the solar system is not astronomical: it is only about 7,350,000,000 miles across. [Particulars and details to clarify the topic sentence]

The next division of space is "our" galaxy: an aggregation of about 100 billion stars. [Second topic sentence] Our sun is an average star in this "Milky Way." The nearest star to us after our sun is so distant that it takes light four and one-half years to travel to us. The galaxy itself is so vast that it takes light 100,000 years to travel from one edge of it to the other. Yet ours is a medium-sized galaxy. [Particulars and details]

Beyond our "Milky Way" is the third division of space—all the rest of the universe. [Third topic sentence] In the unimaginable reaches of this really outer space are countless numbers of aggregations of suns. All these galaxies rotate and move in space. The most powerful telescopes can find no end to them. [Again, particulars and details]

—From "To the Planets and Beyond," the *New York Times Magazine*, Jan. 11, 1959. Reprinted by permission.

There are two reasons for using this method of grouping ideas, shown in the preceding and in the following selections: the writer may wish to set off, to emphasize, to point to each topic separately; he may wish to break up a forbiddingly large block of solid print.

Now, in writing plays, there are, in this matter of the moral, three courses open to the serious dramatist. [Topic sentence] The first is: To definitely set before the public that which it wishes to have set before it, the views and codes of life by which the public lives and in which it believes. This way is the most common, successful, and popular. It makes the dramatist's position sure, and not too obviously authoritative.

The second course is: To definitely set before the public those views and codes of life by which the dramatist himself lives, those theories in which he himself believes, the more effectively if they are the opposite of what the public wishes to have placed before it, presenting them so that the audience may swallow them like powder in a spoonful of jam.

There is a third course: To set before the public no cut-and-dried codes, but the phenomena of life and character, selected and combined, but not distorted by the dramatist's outlook, set down without fear, favour, or prejudice, leaving the public to draw such poor moral as nature may afford. This third method requires a certain detachment; it requires a sympathy with, a love of, and a curiosity as to, things for their own sake; it requires a far view, together with patient industry, for no immediately practical result.

—John Galsworthy, *Candelabra,* "Some Platitudes Concerning Drama," Charles Scribner's Sons, 1933, pp. 3–4. Reprinted by permission.

Note the use of analogy, comparison, contrast, definition, and details in these paragraphs:

Every culture is a precipitate of history. [Analogy] In more than one sense history is a sieve. [Analogy] Every culture embraces those aspects of the past which, usually in altered form and with altered meanings, live on in the present. [Explanation of analogy] Discoveries and inventions, both material and ideological, are constantly being made available to a group through its historical contacts with other peoples or being created by its own members. However, only those that fit the total immediate situation in meeting the group's needs for survival or in promoting the psychological adjustment of individuals will become part of the culture. [Two sentences given to the "sieve" aspect of history] The process of culture building may be regarded as an addition to man's innate biological capacities, an addition providing instruments which enlarge, or may even substitute for, biological functions, and to a degree compensating for biological limitations—as in ensuring that death does not always result in the loss to humanity of what the deceased has learned. [Example follows a general statement]

Culture is like a map. [Comparison] Just as a map isn't the territory but an abstract representation of a particular area, so also a culture is an abstract description of trends toward uniformity in the words, deeds, and artifacts of a group. [Further comparison] If a map is accurate and you can read it, you won't get lost; if you know a culture, you will know your way around in the life of a society. [Comparison]

Many educated people have the notion that culture applies only to exotic ways of life or to societies where relative simplicity and relative homogeneity prevail. Some sophisticated missionaries, for example, will use the anthropological conception in discussing the special modes of living of South Sea Islanders, but seem amazed at the idea that it could be applied equally to inhabitants of New York City. And social workers in Boston will talk about the culture of a colorful and well-knit immigrant group but boggle at applying it to the behavior of staff members in the social-service agency itself. [Two examples]

—From Dr. Clyde Kluckhohn, *Mirror for Man.* Copyright 1949 by McGraw-Hill Book Company, Inc. Reprinted by permission of the publisher.

The two paragraphs that follow reveal an interesting plan. The first sentence is both a transition and a statement of the topic. The paragraph itself is largely a preliminary statement of the topic of the next paragraph—"the introduction of the closed car." Notice how supporting details are introduced into the general topic statement of the second paragraph. And observe again how concrete and specific details give body and authority to a paragraph.

Ford's energetic driving down of prices helped to make the automobile more popular, [transition] but equally responsible were a series of vital improvements: [statement of new topic] the invention of an effective self-starter, first designed by Charles F. Kettering and installed in the Cadillac in 1912; the coming, within the next two or three years, of the demountable rim and the cord tire; but above all, the introduction of the closed car. [New topic taken up in next paragraph] As late as 1916 only 2 per cent of the cars manufactured in the United States were closed; by 1926, 72 per cent of them were.

What had happened was that manufacturers had learned to build closed cars that were not hideously expensive, that did not rattle themselves to pieces, and that would be painted with a fast-drying but durable paint; and that meanwhile the car-buying public had discovered with delight that a closed car was something quite different from the old "horseless carriage." It was a power-driven room on wheels—storm-proof, lockable, parkable all day and all night in all weathers. In it you could succumb to speed fever without being battered by the wind. You could close its windows against dust or rain. You could use it to fetch home the groceries, to drive to the golf club or the railroad station, to cool off on hot evenings, to reach a job many miles distant and otherwise inaccessible, to take the family out for a day's drive or a week-end excursion, to pay an impromptu visit to friends forty or fifty miles away, or, as innumerable young couples were not slow to learn, to engage in private intimacies. One of the cornerstones of American morality had been the difficulty of finding suitable locale for misconduct; now this cornerstone was crumbling. And if the car was also a frequent source of family friction ("No, Junior, you are *not* taking it tonight"), as well as a destroyer of pedestrianism, a weakener of the churchgoing habit, a promoter of envy, a lethal weapon when driven by heedless, drunken, irresponsible people, and a formidable convenience for criminals seeking a safe getaway, it was nonetheless indispensable.

—From Frederick Lewis Allen, *The Big Change.* Copyright 1952 by Frederick Lewis Allen. Reprinted by Permission of Harper & Brothers.

Unity in Paragraphs. Everything that has been said so far about the paragraph bears directly on the problem of unity in paragraph structure. A paragraph of exposition is a unit of structure, and it follows that the inclusion of material not related to the central idea violates paragraph unity and makes the paragraph confusing and ineffective. Careful observation of many paragraphs will give you a feeling for the size and extent of the thought unit that can be presented in a paragraph. Observation will also lead you back to the principle so often stressed here—that a topic sentence, whether written or implied, is still your best safeguard of unity.

Arrangement or Order in Paragraphs. Frequently the topic sentence can also be made the best safeguard of a logical, effective arrangement of parts in a paragraph. If the writer, for example, says, "In its foreign policy our nation must take one of three courses," you expect him to continue by specifying each of these courses in turn. If he begins, "Light can be thrown on this subject by tracing the development of the meaning of the word *propaganda,*" you expect him to use the historical order. In other words, a topic sentence is not only a statement of the central idea but also, at times, an indication and a forecast of arrangement.

The writer of a paragraph should use the order which best fits his material and his purpose. If he is explaining a process, he should use the order of happening, usually called the chronological order. If he begins with a general statement, he should proceed from the general to particulars. If he wants to build up to a conclusion, he should go from particular details to his general statement. In some paragraphs, especially in short ones, it does not matter what order is used. The writer's common sense will usually warn him against gross confusion.

The ideal paragraph has often been defined as one in which each sentence grows so naturally out of the one before it that the reader *feels* the natural, logical growth of the paragraph idea. It is pointless to quibble over the question whether such a paragraph is any closer to the ideal than the one which is liberally sprinkled with connective words. Good paragraphs may be written either with or without connecting links or transitions. When two ideas are set side by side, the mind naturally assumes that the ideas are related. Not many paragraphs, however, are so simple that the ideas in them may be stacked like bricks in a pile. If a writer is building a wall, instead of piling bricks, he may need to work out a complex pattern, and—to extend the analogy—he may find it necessary to use mortar.

Transitions in Paragraphs. The mortar that holds the bricks of thought together in a paragraph may be of several kinds. Assuming that the thoughts have been properly arranged, they may be further tied to each other by the following means:

1. **Conjunctions and other connectives,** such as *and, but, yet, however, therefore, consequently, moreover.*
2. **Transitional or directive expressions,** such as *accordingly, and then, again, at the same time, as a result, in the meantime, for example, for instance, on the other hand, first, second, finally, in conclusion, similarly, conversely, in other words.*
3. **Pronouns,** such as *this, that, these, those, his, her, its,* which carry the reader's mind back to the antecedent.
4. **Repetition of key words,** which are sometimes called "echo" words.
5. **Parallel structure,** through which the reader is led back to ideas phrased in similar forms.

Whatever has been said about connectives within a paragraph applies to connectives between paragraphs, except that here the connecting links may occasionally be longer. As within paragraphs, the links may be words or phrases; frequently these are the opening parts of the topic sentences. More rarely the topic sentence is preceded by an entire sentence of transition, and still less frequently the transition is a paragraph by itself.

But, again, your best method of learning how to use connectives is to analyze some paragraphs written by experienced writers.

The first sentences of this book were written nearly two years ago. Outside my window on that spring morning, as on this, a bird sang. Outside a million windows, a million birds had sung as morning swept around the globe. Few men and few women were so glad that a new day had dawned as these birds seem to be.

Because my window looks out on a southern landscape, my bird is a cardinal, with feathers as bright as his half-whistled song. Farther north in the United States he would be a robin, more likely than not—less colorful and somewhat less melodious but seemingly no less pleased with the world and his place in it. Like us, robins have their problems but they seem better able to take them in their stride. We are likely to awake with an "Oh, dear!" on our lips; they with "What fun!" in their beaks. Mr. Sandburg's peddler was remarkable because he seemed so terribly glad to be selling fish. Most robins seem terribly glad to be eating worms.

For some time I have been thinking that I wanted to write a book about the characteristics and activities of living things. During the week or two just before, I had been wondering with what activity or characteristic I should begin. Reproduction, growing up, and getting a living are all, so I said to myself, fundamental activities. Combativeness in the face of rivals, solicitude for the young, courage when danger must be met, patience when hardships must be endured, are all typical characteristics. But my cardinal proposed a different solution. Is any characteristic more striking than the joy of life instead?

Repeats "outside window." Pronouns "that" and "this." "Bird" repeated by "birds." Repeats "morning." "Sung" echoes "sang." Pronoun "these." Repeats "birds." Again repeats "Window." Repeats "bird." Contrasts "north" with "southern" above. Repeats "robin." "Their" contrasts with "us." Pronouns. "We" ties in with "us." "They" ties in with pronouns above. Note repetition of phrase "terribly glad." Repeats two key words —"activities" and "characteristics." Pronoun refers to "I." Again repeats key word. Note use of parallel structure. Repeats key word. "My cardinal" refers to "cardinal" in first sentence of second paragraph.

—From *The Great Chain of Life* by Joseph Wood Krutch. Houghton Mifflin Co., 1956. By permission of the author and the publisher.

Exercises

Exercise 1. In one of your textbooks (history, sociology, economics, psychology) find examples of paragraphs developed entirely by examples, by analogy, by comparison and contrast, by particulars and details. Bring these to class and be prepared to analyze them for the class. Point out the topic sentence, if there is one, in each of the paragraphs. Point out the transitional phrases or sentences in each of the paragraphs. Find one paragraph which is entirely transitional.

Exercise 2. Bring to class examples of the following:

1. A paragraph with a topic sentence at the end
2. A paragraph beginning with a transitional sentence
3. A paragraph used as a transition between two topics of an essay
4. A paragraph summarizing a section of an essay or chapter

Exercise 3. In one of your textbooks find several paragraphs of definition. What other methods are used to develop these paragraphs?

Exercise 4. Try to determine which method of paragraph development is called for by each of the following topic sentences:

1. Competitive sports teach many virtues useful in later life.
2. It is important to distinguish the artist from the artisan.
3. The study of science in college is fundamentally different from that in a high-school science course.
4. Just what is a police state?
5. Life in Colonial Boston was quiet and dignified.
6. The sack dress was a catastrophe in the history of American fashion.
7. There are three possible approaches to the problem.
8. Most homeowners have very little conception of the gadgets in their houses.
9. Sometimes I get too much excited.
10. The one-family farm is on its way out.

Exercise 5. Write a paragraph with a topic sentence which forecasts the structure of the paragraph. Here are some suggestions:

1. There are two possible alternatives in the future of the American Communist Party.
2. It is possible to isolate only three qualities of the good student: native intelligence, early education, and motivation.

3. All the factors in the outbreak of the Civil War can be summarized under two headings.

Exercise 6. In the following passage, revise and combine the sentences, inserting transitions where necessary, in order to produce a logical and readable paragraph:

Students of the English language have divided its historical growth into three main periods; the Old English Period, from 450 to 1100, was the first one. The Middle English Period lasted from 1100 until 1500. The Modern English Period began in 1500 and lasted up to the present time. The people of England did not stop speaking one kind of language and begin speaking another in any one year. The change was gradual. There were definite historical events occurring at the times mentioned which caused a more rapid change in the language of the people of England. The Angles, Saxons, and Jutes invaded England in 449. The Norman Conquest occurred in 1066. The English Renaissance began about 1500.

(After you have finished this exercise, you might turn to page 4 in this book to see one way of solving these problems.)

Exercise 7. Here is a short list of fairly abstract and complicated subjects. In a single paragraph, try to give an informal definition of one of them: courtesy, the scientific method, good writing, non-representational art, morale.

In your paragraph use definitive statements, particulars and details, examples and analogy. In the margin at the left of your paper label each device as you have used it.

Exercise 8. Write a paragraph which depends largely on contrast. Here are a few suggested subjects:

1. Liberal and vocational education
2. Democratic and Republican
3. The "movie" West and the real West
4. Popular music and jazz
5. Living at home and living at a college

Chapter 4

THE PROCESS OF PLANNING AND WRITING

Selecting an Appropriate Subject. Many of the papers which you will write in college will be on subjects chosen or prescribed by the occasion or by some person, such as your instructor in a course in history, or political science, or sociology. Some of your papers will be summaries or reports based on assigned reading. Some will be more or less brief discussions in answer to examination questions. Such situations as these will place their own limitations upon what you will say, how you will organize your material, and what attitude you will adopt toward your material.

Frequently, however, especially in a course in English composition, you will be given a broad or general subject, which you must narrow down to a usable topic, or a type of writing to experiment with, such as a personal essay, a profile, a narrative sketch, or a pattern of structure to imitate. The choice of specific subject will be left to you. The suggestions which follow are designed to help you explore the various resources at your command. If you do not need this help, no harm has been done. The suggestions are here; you may turn to them if you feel the need of help, or you may use better ideas of your own.

The primary source of material for writing, after all, is experience—experience understood in the broad sense. Everything that you know has come to you, in one way or another, through personal experience. You have learned by living, by doing things, by going to school, by reading, by observing, and by listening. As a convenient grouping of subjects about which you know something, through the fact that you have lived, read, observed, and listened, let us try the following:

1. Home and family
2. School and college
3. Work
4. Sports and games
5. Hobbies and amusements
6. Your home town
7. Friends and social life
8. Religion
9. Reading
10. Developing attitudes and values

Now let us try narrowing these general subjects to something more specific and usable.

The Autobiographical Sketch. Instead of writing a narrative account of your life, listing in chronological order such items as when and where you were born, who your parents were, where you went to school, where you lived, etc., tell about the development of your interest in music, about your religious life, about your attitude toward democracy or toward a life work. The following plan may suggest an idea that you could use:

[Title] DEVELOPMENT OF A FAITH

I. Earliest ideas about God and heaven
   A. Influence of home training
   B. Influence of Sunday School
II. Influence of church membership
   A. Social activities
   B. Music and ceremony in church ritual
   C. Growing familiarity with Bible and religious concepts
III. Disturbing influences on faith
   A. Scientific study
   B. Distracting social influences in the environment
   C. Reading
IV. A tentative statement of faith

Another interesting way of treating autobiographical material is to concentrate on the development of a dominant trait in your character or personality. First, analyze yourself and your nature.

Are you an introvert or an extrovert? Are you normally happy, gloomy, irritable, friendly, lonely, timid? What has made you the way you are? Write a paper in which you explain yourself. The following are a few suggestions for thesis sentences that you might use:

1. For eighteen years I have almost never had an unhappy moment.
2. My life has been dominated by the fact that I am an only child.
3. For eighteen years I have lived with fear.
4. It is a tragic thing that a girl's personality can be molded by the fact that she wears thick glasses and has a bad complexion.
5. I am the child of divorced parents.
6. All my life I have not been allowed to forget that my parents were born in Europe.

You might bring out your dominant trait by means of a typical incident, as in the following:

I was a shy infant and, alas, was frightened by my father, who was the most gentle and tender of men. Something about his black mustache alarmed me. Far from running to meet him on his return, I avoided him and turned away my head when my mother brought me to him. This grieved him deeply, and after seventy years I am still enraged with myself whenever I think of it.

Otherwise I seem to have been a well-behaved child, generally quiet and obedient, giving little trouble. So the only anecdote which came down to me from these years of my early childhood is quite surprising. (My friends say it throws definite light on my subsequent character.) One morning at breakfast, when I started to get down from my high chair, my mother turned to me and said, "Baby, you must say, 'Please excuse me.'" And I replied, "I won't." So my mother of course said, "Then you may not get down until you say 'Please excuse me.'" But I resolutely refused.

There was great agitation in the household. Everyone tried to persuade me. My brother Harry, who loved me dearly, especially begged me to be good. My nurse wept. My high chair was moved from the breakfast table over to a corner, and there I remained sitting. My father said, "That child should be punished," put on his hat, and went out of the house. It was a Sunday morning but no one went to church. After some hours the family gave in. I was removed from the high chair and allowed to go about my daily routine.

The following morning when I had finished my breakfast, no one said anything to me at all. My mother made no suggestions, but I turned to her gravely and said, "*Now* I will say 'Please excuse me.' " It was, I suppose, my mother's use of the word "must" that Sunday morning that touched some chord in my infant disposition. Apparently I was quite willing to do anything that seemed reasonable and proper, but, however reasonable it might be, not to do it under any kind of pressure. All my life this latent quality has continued to exist. Any kind of pressure or threat stirs up some mulish trait in my disposition.

—Virginia C. Gildersleeve, *Many a Good Crusade,* 1954. By permission of The Macmillan Company, publishers.

Or you may concentrate on the growing-up period of your life, on something that made you grow up in a hurry:

[Title] MY FIRST TASTE OF MATURITY

I received my first taste of maturity about five or six years ago, but yet I can remember every detail. How old was I? About twelve. I used to go to Hines Veterans Hospital to play the piano, entertain the boys, and give them cigarettes. Twelve years is a very young age, and I was young; I was innocent of the things life entailed.

One night in December, I entered the Hines Hospital with the purpose of entertaining the patients. I hopped up onto the movable piano ensemble, and the head nurse wheeled me along the corridor to Ward A.

Each ward contained forty boys, and as we entered the first ward, I saw forty heads duck under the covers. The room was silent. Suddenly one of the patients peeked out from beneath the covers and yelled, "Hey fellas, it's only a kid." In almost perfect unison, each man lifted his head from underneath his blanket. They greeted me with enthusiasm. I played a few ballads on the piano, and then with a sudden bang, I burst into a red-hot boogie woogie piece. The sounds of loud, appreciative applause and shouts clamoring for more came like the first sight of a "welcome" mat. I played two additional boogie woogie pieces, and I stopped.

I reached for a large box filled with cigarettes and proceeded to distribute them to the veterans. One of the veterans had paralyzed hands, and he asked me to light his cigarette. Clumsily, I pushed the cigarette between his lips and lit it for him. I lingered a few moments to exchange polite conversation with him. During the conversation he said to me, "You know, honey, you're the prettiest girl I've seen in a long time." I was flattered, but because of the self-consciousness of a twelve-year-old girl, I blushed and walked away. Later, my young mind started to function when a nurse mentioned to me that he was blind.

I went to four other wards; I played for four more hours, almost continuously. My thumb started to throb with pain as I beat out the boogie basses. I did not stop because I knew that I had only one more number to complete, and then I would be finished for the evening; then I could go home. My throbbing thumb kept in rhythm with my music. It seemed to beat out, "You are pretty; he is blind. You are pretty; he is blind. . . . "

When I finished the piece, the head nurse asked me to play for a patient down the hall. He was in a private room, and only the hopeless patients had private rooms. I told her that I would be glad to do anything that I could for him. The piano was pushed just outside the room. He could see me, but I could not see him. He requested boogie woogie, and with my throbbing thumb, I played boogie as though my blood kept in rhythm with each beat of music. How my thumb ached! The beat, beat, beat of the pain again called out, "You are pretty; he is blind. You are pretty; he is blind. . . . " My thoughts were confused, and I wanted desperately to stop playing. I could not endure the pain in my thumbs any longer. I had to stop, but yet I had to continue. That boy in the room wanted to hear it. Just at that moment, the head nurse whispered to me, "You may stop now. He can't hear you any more."

That night I left the hospital with my first taste of maturity. I did not like it; it was bitter.

—From a student paper. Reprinted by permission.

The Autobiographical Incident. If you choose to write about some interesting experience of yours, you should discard the obvious possibilities, such as the automobile accident, the trip to the mountains, the boating accident, the big fire downtown. Much more effective is some apparently minor incident, so written that it acquires importance in the telling.

There were the annual excitements, too, of Chautauqua and the Champaign County Fair. My clearest memory of the fair I have preserved in the story "Dollar Bill," where a boy who accurately corresponds to me teases his mother for money with which to go to the grounds on a day when the rest of the family have not planned to go. She gives him a dollar, the smallest amount she can find in her purse, and presses upon him the importance of his bringing half of it back; admission for him as a child will be a quarter, and with the other quarter he can buy good things to eat and drink. He goes at last, a little ashamed of having teased her into consenting, but comforted by the prospect of the lemonade and hamburgers he can buy with the second quarter. But a scoundrel at the window, pretending not to notice he is under age, gives him an adult ticket with only half a dollar in change, so that he enters the grounds not merely in shame but in despair. He tries to get interested in the free exhibits; smells hamburgers cooking; decides that one such indulgence will be forgiven by his mother; goes up to the counter; is given a sandwich; and before he can eat it hears the man telling him his half-dollar is counterfeit. I do not tell in the story how my father, when we all went the next day, passed the bad coin in the same window and heard nothing further from it. I looked at the implements and animals again, and in the grandstand saw pacing and trotting races. There was no horse like Dan Patch, the world's champion pacer whom we had read about and admired; but the sulkies, the drivers with their silk caps, the starters and the judges, not to speak of the horses themselves, so gaily harnessed and at the finish line so dark with sweat, were a spectacle of which I could never get enough.

—From *The Autobiography of Mark Van Doren,* © 1958 by Mark Van Doren. Reprinted by permission of Harcourt, Brace and Company, Inc.

Have you ever passed through a "phase"? That is excellent material for a paper—if you have a little ability to laugh at yourself.

I was still at the infantile stage, moreover, when misery seemed to me picturesque, even the groans of poor devils regretting their existence, and I was full of my own histrionics, dramatizing everything I did, sometimes in the manner of Sentimental Tommy. I delighted in holes in my trousers and the bottoms of my shoes, wearing at the same time a flower in my buttonhole or dressing as far as I could in the opposite extreme. I felt I acquired a secret strength by reacting in this way against the popular pattern of the young business man, a type that seemed to me as insipid and banal as the rows of young maple trees on suburban streets. I supposed that by so doing I somehow connected myself with the venerable race of unworldly or vagabond writers who had shared this cult of shabbiness, poverty and failure. Occasionally, wishing to appear old-fashioned, I wore my grandfather's round sleeve-buttons, and, longing for an excuse to wear tortoise-shell glasses, I had my eyes examined, finding that they were all too tiresomely normal. I passed through the mimetic phases that young writers usually undergo, imitating this man's gestures and that man's walk, while, at the same time, I was inept on the actual stage, with neither the talent nor the presence of mind of an actor.

—From *Scenes and Portraits,* by Van Wyck Brooks, published by E. P. Dutton and Company, Inc., 1954. Reprinted by permission of the author and publisher.

First Impressions of College. Was there ever a college freshman who was not asked to record his first impressions of his brave new college world? The following, done by a great artist, will make you stretch yourself hard if you try to do something like it.

In order to place this question fairly before you, I will describe, for memory has kept the picture bright, one of those rare but, as Queen Victoria would have put it, never-to-be-sufficiently-lamented occasions when in deference to friendship, or in a desperate attempt to acquire information about, perhaps, the French Revolution, it seemed necessary to attend a lecture. The room to begin with had a hybrid look—it was not for sitting in, nor yet for eating in. Perhaps there was a map on the wall; certainly there was a table on a platform, and several rows of rather small, rather hard, comfortless little chairs. These were occupied intermittently, as if they shunned each other's company, by people of both sexes, and some had notebooks and were tapping their fountain pens, and some had none and gazed with the vacancy and placidity of bull frogs at the ceiling. A large clock displayed its cheerless face, and when the hour struck in strode a harried-looking man, a man from whose face nervousness, vanity, or perhaps the depressing and impossible nature of his task had removed all traces of ordinary humanity. There was a momentary stir. He had written a book, and for the moment it was interesting to see people who have written books. Everybody gazed at him. He was bald and not hairy; he had a mouth and a chin; in short he was a man like another, although he had written a book. He cleared his throat and the lecture began. Now the human voice is an instrument of varied power; it can enchant and it can soothe; it can rage and it can despair; but when it lectures it almost always bores. What he said was sensible enough; there was learning in it and argument and reason; but as the voice went on attention wandered. The face of the clock seemed abnormally pale; the hands too suffered from some infirmity. Had they the gout? Were they swollen? They moved so slowly. They reminded one of the painful progress of a three-legged fly that has survived the winter. How many flies on an average survive the English winter, and what would be the thoughts of such an insect on waking to find itself being lectured on the French Revolution? The enquiry was fatal. A link had been lost—a paragraph dropped. It was useless to ask the lecturer to repeat his words; on he plodded with dogged pertinacity. The origin of the French Revolution was being sought for—also the thoughts of flies. Now there came one of those flat stretches of discourse when minute objects can be seen coming for two or three miles ahead. "Skip!" we entreated him—vainly. He did not skip. There was a joke. Then the voice went on again; then it seemed that the windows wanted washing; then a woman sneezed; then the voice quickened; then there was a peroration; and then—thank Heaven!—the lecture was over.

The Narrative Incident. Have you ever been called on the carpet by an outraged parent? Then the following incident will appeal to you. Study this for the author's brilliant use of concrete details. Then write a paper like it.

But there, alas, was the rub—as Morison himself would ruefully admit. He was himself such a mad, scape-grace sort of fellow that his acts sometimes passed all the bounds of decorum and propriety, and for that reason "the governor" was always "having him in upon the carpet."

There, in fact, was the whole setting. The governor existed for the sole purpose of "having him in upon the carpet"—one never saw them in any other way, but when Morison spoke about it one saw them in *this* way with blazing vividness. And this picture—the picture of Morison going in "upon the carpet"—was a very splendid one.

First, one saw Morison pacing nervously up and down in a noble and ancient hall, puffing distractedly on a cigarette and pausing from time to time in an apprehensive manner before the grim, closed barrier of an enormous seventeenth-century door which was tall and wide enough for a knight in armor to ride through without difficulty, and before whose gloomy and overwhelming front Morison looked very small and full of guilt. Then, one saw him take a last puff at his cigarette, brace his shoulders in a determined manner, knock on the panels of the mighty door, and in answer to a low growl within, open the door and advance desperately into the shadowed depths of a room so immense and magnificent that Morison looked like a single little sinner walking forlornly down the nave of a cathedral.

At the end of this terrific room, across an enormous space of carpet, sat "the governor." He was sitting behind a magnificent flat desk of ancient carved mahogany; in the vast shadowed depths behind him storied rows of old bound volumes climbed dizzily up into the upper darkness and were lost. And men in armor were standing grimly all around, and the portraits of the ancestors shone faintly in the gloom, and the old worn mellow colors of the tempered light came softly through the colored glass of narrow Gothic windows which were set far away in recessed depths of the impregnable mortared walls.

Meanwhile, "the governor" was waiting in grim silence as Morison advanced across the carpet. The governor was a man with beetling bushy eyebrows, silver hair, the lean, bitten and incisive face, the cropped mustache of a man who had seen service in old wars, and commanded garrisons in India, and after clearing his throat with a low menacing growl, he would peer fiercely out at Morison beneath his bushy brows, and say: "Well, young man?"—to which Morison would be able to make no answer, but would just stand there in a state of guilty dejection.

And the talk that then passed between the outraged father and the prodigal son was, from Morison's own account, astonishing. It was a talk that was no talk, a talk that was almost incoherent but that each understood perfectly, another language, not merely an economy of words so spare that one word was made to do the work of a hundred, but a series of grunts, blurts, oaths and ejaculations, in which almost nothing was said that was recognizable as ordered thought, but in which the meaning of everything was perfectly conveyed.

The last outrageous episode that had brought Morison into his present position of guilt "upon the carpet" was rarely named by name or given a description. Rather, as if affronted decency and aristocratic delicacy could not endure discussion of an unmentionable offense, his fault was indicated briefly as "that sort of thing" (or simply "sort of thing," spoken fast and slurringly)—and all the other passions and emotions of anger, contrition, stern condemnation and reproof, and, at length, of exhausted relief and escape, were conveyed in a series of broken and jerky exclamations, such as: "After *all!*" "It's not as if it were the first time you had played the bloody fool!" "What I mean to say is!" "Damn it all, it's not that I mind the wine-woman-song sort of thing—young myself once—no plaster saint—never pretended that I was—man's own business if he keeps it to himself—never interfered—only when you do a thing like this and make a bloody show of yourself—you idiot!—sort of thing men can understand but women!—it's your mother I'm thinking of!" and so on.

Morison's own speech, in fact, was largely composed of phrases such as these: he blurted them out so rapidly, scarcely moving his lips and slurring his words over in such a broken and explosive way, that when one first met him it was hard to understand what he was saying:—his speech seemed to be largely a series of blurted-out phrases, such as "sort of thing," "after *all,*" "what I mean to say is!" and so on. And yet this incoherent and exclamatory style was curiously effective, for it seemed to take the listener into its confidence in rather an engaging manner which said: "of course there's no need to go into detail about all this, because I can see you are a man of the world and the same kind of fellow as I am. I know we understand each other perfectly, and the truth of what I am saying must be so self-evident that there's no point in discussing it."

Descriptions. Most of the description that you read consists of brief pictures so interwoven with narrative that it is impossible to say what is description and what is incident. The Ernie Pyle piece below is a good example. Occasionally, however, a writer presents a larger picture, in which we may point out and study a few basic principles. If a writer sets out to do a large picture, he must establish his point of view, that is, he must tell the reader where he is when he views his scene. If he changes his position, he must inform the reader of the change. Technically that is known as the "moving point of view." He may also unify his picture by means of a summarizing statement, or by giving his scene a dominant tone.

Do you have a favorite brook or river? Make a list of the changes in its moods, and then a list of the characteristic things that happen along its banks, morning, daytime, evening and night. There is your material for a descriptive sketch like this one of the Carmel River:

> The Carmel is a lovely little river. It isn't very long but in its course it has everything a river should have. It rises in the mountains, and tumbles down a while, runs through shallows, is dammed to make a lake, spills over the dam, crackles among round boulders, wanders lazily under sycamores, spills into pools where trout live, drops in against banks where crayfish live. In the winter it becomes a torrent, a mean little fierce river, and in the summer it is a place for children to wade in and for fishermen to wander in. Frogs blink from its banks and the deep ferns grow beside it. Deer and foxes come to drink from it, secretly in the morning and evening, and now and then a mountain lion crouched flat laps its water. The farms of the rich little valley back up to the river and take its water for the orchards and the vegetables. The quail call beside it and the wild doves come whistling in at dusk. Raccoons pace its edges looking for frogs. It's everything a river should be.

—From *Cannery Row.* Copyright 1945 by John Steinbeck. Reprinted by permission of The Viking Press, Inc.

Read the next piece for the effect produced by a tremendous massing of concrete details. Of course you are not an experienced journalist like Ernie Pyle—and we hope there will never again be an invasion beach—but you can produce a readable description by imitating his method. String it on a walk somewhere, and point out things and comment on them as you walk.

I walked for a mile and a half along the water's edge of our many-miled invasion beach. I walked slowly, for the detail on the beach was infinite.

The wreckage was vast and startling. The awful waste and destruction of war, even aside from the loss of human life, has always been one of its outstanding features to those who are in it. Anything and everything is expendable. And we did expend on our beachhead in Normandy during those first few hours.

For a mile out from the beach there were scores of tanks and trucks and boats that were not visible, for they were at the bottom of the water—swamped by overloading, or hit by shells, or sunk by mines. Most of their crews were lost.

There were trucks tipped half over and swamped, partly sunken barges, and angled-up corners of jeeps, and small landing craft half submerged. And at low tide you could still see those vicious six-pronged snares that helped snag and wreck them.

On the beach itself, high and dry, were all kinds of wrecked vehicles. There were tanks that had only just made the beach before being knocked out. There were jeeps that had burned to a dull gray. There were big derricks on caterpillar treads that didn't quite make it. There were half-tracks carrying office equipment that had been made into a shambles by a single shell hit, their interiors still holding the useless equipage of smashed typewriters, telephones, office files.

There were LCTs turned completely upside down, and lying on their backs, and how they got that way I don't know. There were boats stacked on top of each other, their sides caved in, their suspension doors knocked off.

In this shore-line museum of carnage there were abandoned rolls of barbed wire and smashed bulldozers and big stacks of thrown-away life belts and piles of shells still waiting to be moved. In the water floated empty life rafts and soldiers' packs and ration boxes, and mysterious oranges. On the beach lay snarled rolls of telephone wire and big rolls of steel matting and stacks of broken, rusting rifles.

On the beach lay, expended, sufficient men and mechanism for a small war. They were gone forever now. And yet we could afford it.

We could afford it because we were on, we had our toe hold, and behind us there were such enormous replacements for this wreckage on the beach that you could hardly conceive of the sum total. Men and equipment were flowing from England in such a gigantic stream that it made the waste on the beachhead seem like nothing at all, really nothing at all.

But there was another and more human litter. It extended in a thin little line, just like a high-water mark, for miles along the beach. This was the strewn personal gear, gear that would never be needed again by those who fought and died to give us our entrance into Europe.

There in a jumbled row for mile on mile were soldier's packs. There were socks and shoe polish, sewing kits, diaries, Bibles, hand grenades. There were the latest letters from home, with the address on each one neatly razored out—one of the security precautions enforced before the boys embarked.

There were toothbrushes and razors, and snapshots of families back home staring up at you from the sand. There were pocketbooks, metal mirrors, extra trousers, and bloody, abandoned shoes. There were broken-handled shovels, and portable radios smashed almost beyond recognition, and mine detectors twisted and ruined.

There were torn pistol belts and canvas water buckets, first-aid kits, and jumbled heaps of life belts. I picked up a pocket Bible with a soldier's name in it, and put it in my jacket. I carried it half a mile or so and then put it back down on the beach. I don't know why I picked it up, or why I put it down again.

Soldiers carry strange things ashore with them. In every invasion there is at least one soldier hitting the beach at H-hour with a banjo slung over his shoulder. The most ironic piece of equipment marking our beach—this beach first of despair, then of victory—was a tennis racket that some soldier had brought along. It lay lonesomely on the sand, clamped in its press, not a string broken.

Two of the most dominant items in the beach refuse were cigarettes and writing paper. Each soldier was issued a carton of cigarettes just before we started. That day those cartons by the thousand, water-soaked and spilled out, marked the line of our first savage blow.

Writing paper and air-mail envelopes came second. The boys had intended to do a lot of writing in France. The letters—now forever incapable of being written—that might have filled those blank abandoned pages!

Always there are dogs in every invasion. There was a dog still on the beach, still pitifully looking for his masters.

He stayed at the water's edge, near a boat that lay twisted and half sunk at the waterline. He barked appealingly to every soldier who approached, trotted eagerly along with him for a few feet, and then, sensing himself unwanted in all the haste, he would run back to wait in vain for his own people at his own empty boat.

—From Ernie Pyle, *Brave Men,* Henry Holt & Co., 1944. Reprinted by permission.

Interpretations of Home and Friends. You can always find material for descriptive and expository papers in your home life—anything from short profiles of your father or your mother to longer discussions interpreting your family life in terms of its relation to American democracy. Or you can take a single brief incident out of your home life and make it interesting and significant. Interesting always is a return to your home after an absence, to lay old ghosts or to relive the past. Here is how one college student did it:

I braked the car carefully to the curb, turned off the ignition, and slid into the adjoining seat so that I might have a better view of the block. At first glance I could see that everything, yet nothing, had changed in the interim. How long was it? A hasty check on my fingers showed at least ten years, possibly eleven.

Eleven years. Somehow, I felt a wave of relief come over me when I saw that the old apartment house was still as it had been. I looked at the same dirty tan bricks, the same recessed courtyard with its claustrophobic tulip bed and overly ornate fountain, the same row of windows now hung with Venetian blinds, the same women sitting complacently by the curb and rocking their eternal baby carriages. Once again I could hear the mutter of dismay as I ran full tilt past their slumbering offspring, all guns blazing a salute to youth.

Across the street stood the neighborhood candy store. Gone was the grimy, bepostered window of the depression era. Now all was chrome and sparkling glass—modern, efficient, and characterless. To walk into such a store and ask for two cents' worth of candy or a three-cent ice cream stick would be, the fancy overhead sign proclaimed, an incongruity.

My apartment house (again I was recalling and reliving the jealous possessiveness with which the city child strives to make himself or his little clique an entity in the mass) stood at one end of the block. At the other end stood another apartment of very similar design. In between there had been a lot, the scene of many a fight, game, or bonfire. Now an ugly edifice of screaming red brick went clamoring upwards for eight eye-offending stories.

They could take away the lot but not the children. The game could have been the one I stepped away from eleven years ago, except that this one was being played in the gutter instead of in the lot. The street was fairly wide, with go-slow-children-at-play signs posted on the telephone poles. Though the angle between the foul lines had been made drastically acuter, I gathered that the game had not otherwise suffered in its transition from sandlot to asphalt. The cries of the younger children at play filled the valley of the street and brought remonstrating glances from the line of carriage-rockers on the sidewalk.

The push carts and the rag pickers were conspicuously absent; the only vendor to be seen was a lone fish peddler standing stolidly beside his truck. They, too, had gone with the depression. I suddenly felt very sorry for this generation of youngsters who had never known the succulence of a fresh street-baked sweet potato resplendent in its orange wrapper covering or the thrill of a traveling-truck merry-go-round whirling in its wild romance of sound and color.

I looked longingly around for a familiar face, or one of the "old gang." Surely some of the friends of ten years ago must still live here. Then as my gaze was roaming fruitlessly to and fro, I chanced to look squarely into the eyes of a boy of my own age who was walking by. He was stopped short, as if by a physical force, and we stared at each other for a split second. As he continued down the block, I let out the brake and drove quickly off.

—From a student paper. Reprinted by permission.

Occupations. The profession you expect to enter after you leave college, the work you have done during your vacations, or the job that you have while you are attending college—all have material for many interesting discussions. Here are two or three suggestions.

If you have ever worked at a serious job anywhere, plan a descriptive paper which will give the reader a vivid, detailed picture of your first day on the job. Use a narrative framework on which to hang your details. Use word pictures constantly; give your impressions of the appearance of the place, pictures of people as types and as individuals, sense impressions of sounds and smells.

If you have decided on your life occupation, you may write a serious analytical discussion of your chosen profession. The following scheme may give you a few hints as to how to treat your subject.

[Title] ENGINEERING IS MY LIFE

I. Opportunities in the profession of engineering
   A. Industrial
      1. Reconstruction of war-torn countries
      2. Development of backward countries
      3. Transportation
         a. Railroads

b. Ocean transportation
c. Air transportation
d. Highways
4. Chemistry
a. Plastics
b. Textiles
B. Public service
1. Reclamation projects
2. Governmental projects
II. Desirable personal qualities
A. Interest in scientific processes
B. Love of outdoor life
C. Creative imagination
D. Capacity to grow
III. Necessary preparation for the profession
A. Adequate professional training
B. Vital need of wide cultural training
1. Thorough training in writing and speech
2. Command of some foreign language
3. The social sciences
4. Psychology
5. Wide reading
IV. The personal satisfactions in the profession
A. Assurance of a lifelong job
B. Association with interesting people
C. Constant variety of work
D. Satisfaction of doing something for mankind

But this outline is for a fairly long paper.

You are not limited to the main line, you know. Some writers, right now, are stewing over the place of wives in the social hierarchies associated with big business. Do you feel like stewing a bit over the problem? Or you can write about the hobbies, or the private interests, of professional men. Like the following:

I have only one more thing to say: to be an employee it is not enough that the job be right and that you be right for the job. It is also necessary that you have a meaningful life outside the job.

I am talking about a genuine interest in something in which you, on your own, can be, if not master, at least an amateur expert. This something may be botany, or the history of your county, or chamber music, cabinetmaking,

Christmas-tree growing, or a thousand other things. But it is important in this "employee society" of ours to have a genuine interest outside of the job and to be serious about it.

I am not, as you might suspect, thinking of something that will keep you alive and interested during your retirement. I am speaking of keeping yourself alive, interested, and happy during your working life, and of a permanent source of self-respect and standing in the community outside and beyond your job. You will need such an interest when you hit the forties, that period in which most of us come to realize that we will never reach the goals we have set ourselves when younger—whether these are goals of achievement or of worldly success. You will need it because you should have one area in which you yourself impose standards of performance on your own work. Finally, you need it because you will find recognition and acceptance by other people working in the field, whether professional or amateur, as individuals rather than as members of an organization and as employees.

This is heretical philosophy these days when so many companies believe that the best employee is the man who lives, drinks, eats, and sleeps job and company. In actual experience those people who have no job outside their jobs are not really successful people, not even from the viewpoint of the company. I have seen far too many of them shoot up like a rocket, because they had no interests except the job; but they also came down like the rocket's burned-out stick. The man who will make the greatest contribution to his company is the mature person—and you cannot have maturity if you have no life or interest outside the job. Our large companies are beginning to understand this. That so many of them encourage people to have "outside interests" or to develop "hobbies" as a preparation for retirement is the first sign of a change toward a more intelligent attitude. But quite apart from the self-interest of the employer, your own interest as an employee demands that you develop a major outside interest. It will make you happier, it will make you more effective, it will give you resistance against the setbacks and the blows that are the lot of everyone; and it will make you a more effective, a more successful, and a more mature employee.

—From "How To Be an Employee," by Peter F. Drucker, *Fortune*, May, 1952. Copyright by Time Inc. 1952.

The Profile. A profile is a short biographical sketch which depends for its effect on a few well-chosen, vivid facts and details. The subject of a successful profile need not be famous—or notorious; as a matter of fact, the writer of a profile often takes some totally obscure person and tries to make the reader feel that that person is worth knowing. On the other hand, many profiles, like some of those in the *New Yorker,* are of celebrities. You may take your choice.

If your instructor approves the idea, write a profile of one of your former teachers, one whom you have known fairly well. Select one whom you have liked and admired. Go to the library and consult some local "who's who" in education or science for background facts. Then organize your profile on the basis of a number of the following divisions.

I. An interview, in which you introduce your subject and give us a quick picture of his appearance
II. A glimpse of him at work, in class or in his office
III. A cutback to the facts about his career, education, etc.
IV. His dominant traits
V. A typical classroom performance (your big scene)
VI. What others say about him

You need not use all of these divisions, but if you want to compress, remember that I, III, and V are pretty essential. The others are expendable.

If you want to do a more ambitious biographical piece, one that will take you to some of the reference books in the library, try writing a biographical sketch of (1) the author of a book you are reading; (2) a pioneer of your locality; (3) the man who represents you in Congress; (4) a well-known scientist who is connected with your college or university. Be careful to give all your borrowed information in your own words!

The following sympathetic interpretation was written by a college freshman.

She is grey haired, yes. She speaks explicitly and yet subtly, with a skill which apparently only age and experience can supply. From years of teaching them she knows the best ways to reach and impress high school seniors. Still, I refuse to call her old in any sense. Her face has worry lines, and sometimes an ill look, but her voice and her dry, sometimes sarcastic humor are ageless and timeless. When you are listening to her it is easy to forget that hundreds of students have preceded you and that hundreds more will probably follow you.

The early morning classes blur into one another, and looking back upon them I cannot remember exactly how she looked to me the first morning. I must have seen her in school before I had her for class, for ours was a small high school, but I have no recollection of it. There were so many other teachers who resembled her—women with crimped grey hair, out-of-date clothes, clumping "sensible" shoes, old-fashioned jewelry. She was taller than most, though, a gaunt, big-boned, large-featured woman whose teeth were much too prominent when she smiled, but who had nonetheless a certain homely dignity.

After her appearance had become a familiar sight to me, I began to learn the more interesting things about her. There is one mannerism which has become a part of her—a rubbing of hand against forehead. I do not recall exactly when I came to know that that was her silent reaction to anything that saddened or hurt or annoyed her. Sometimes she spoke of what was bothering her. (And it might have been anything from the government's waste of surplus food to the fact that Howard had not yet handed in his book report.) Sometimes she merely passed a hand over her forehead as if to clear her mind of matters which would not interest her nine o'clock English class, turned a page in her plan book and spoke of other things. Only once did I ever see her express annoyance in any other way but that.

She had a standard answer to my explanations for unfinished work. It was invariably polite, invariably gave the flattering impression of one adult speaking to another: "Well, that's understandable. You'll get it in to me as soon as possible, won't you." The latter was never a question, despite its phrasing, and so effective was the psychology that in this case, at least, it worked even when its victim knew that it was psychology.

Her entire teaching method was built on the psychological basis that if the student was made to understand that she thought him capable of good work and energetic enough to do it, he would do his best to live up to her expectations. She was patient, and she never scolded, but the student who overstrained that patience inevitably got his reward at report-card time. She had long since become accustomed to the fact that not all students could see the beauty of English literature, and that composition was torture to a great many, but she simply could not understand the student who would not *try* to know and enjoy both.

She favored brains, and she was an intellectual snob in that she could not conceal her preference for the student who excelled in intellectual skills. To her a machine was an incomprehensible collection of wires and screws, and an automobile the most unpredictable and unreasonable of machines; she never admitted that the student who knew the inside of a car might be as skilled in his way as the one who liked what is inside a book. Her preferences in pupils showed sometimes, in comparisons which were truthful and sharply drawn, but cruel for the student in question. I pitied those she criticized, but it did not affect my lasting admiration of her mind and teaching.

She had a liking for precise and correct speech, a little on the conservative side always. She had a phrase for muddled or ambiguous work—"I fail to see the significance of it" (spoken earnestly and sorrowfully), which perhaps illustrates as well as anything her fussiness about words.

Many students found her somewhat ludicrous, and a few hated her, of course, but I found in her a charm and a beauty few other teachers approached. I remember weeping just a little when she read aloud Countee Cullen's bitter sonnet, "Yet Do I Marvel," and I have often wished every Shakespeare student could have the benefit of her reading, vocal acting and speech-by-speech explanation.

I remember many such isolated instances and incidents, but one such remains with me as a perfect closing touch to high school—not the whipped cream on the sundae, exactly, but perhaps the cherry atop the final product. Despite memories that have blurred and melted together since I graduated, the remembrance of one May morning is still sharp and clear. It was the type of morning usually found only in a Faith Baldwin novel; it had rained at dawn, and every lilac bush in town was in bloom. The sun was warm, but not yet hot, and in the shade and long shadows the dampness of the rain lingered. Every molecule of air contained an atom of the fresh smell of rain, and at least one atom of essence of lilac. Our classroom was on the shady side of the building, and as the class slowly and reluctantly filed in, a small breeze methodically pushed the odor of lilac in one open window and out another. We had a vocabulary test scheduled for that morning, and we resignedly sat down and began spreading out paper and pen.

"I think it's much too pleasant a morning to do ordinary work, people," said Celia Hutchinson, and she began to read. She read every line of poetry about lilacs she had been able to find. I think I shall remember for a long time sitting near the open windows in the cool spring morning while the voice I knew so well read:

> Go down to Kew in lilac-time, in lilac-time, in lilac-time;
> Go down to Kew in lilac-time (it isn't far from London!) . . .

—From a student paper. Reprinted by permission.

The Brief, Informal Book Review. If your instructor wishes you to produce a formal analysis or critical interpretation of a piece of literature, he will probably give you explicit directions to follow. But there is another sort of informal report based on readings that is enjoying increasing popularity in our time. More and more in recent years, the tempo of book publication has increased to the point where no one can expect to read all the new books, even those restricted to a particular field of interest. Readers therefore must depend on the reports of others in order to select the particular books they may want to buy and read. To meet this demand for quick and ready information, there has developed in newspapers and magazines a special kind of review: a very short, informal description of a book, with some brief information about the author, and at least an implied evaluation of his work. You will find such brief reports in *Time,* in the *New Yorker,* and in several other magazines and newspapers that are likely to reach serious readers of books.

Sometimes such an informal review can be accomplished—or at least attempted—in a single paragraph. In the example below you will note the almost breezy tone adopted by the anonymous reviewer. Thus he speaks of armies being "licked" instead of defeated, and he humorously speaks of Russia as an "amoeba" that "doesn't mind amputations." But beneath the informality there is much serious purpose, and much important information is presented in quick and palatable form.

Seven Roads to Moscow, by Lieutenant-Colonel W. G. F. Jackson (Philosophical Library). This is an interesting study of all the invasions of Russia, written by a British Army officer who has taught at the Royal Staff College and at Sandhurst. During the Middle Ages, Russia was successfully invaded a few times, but in the eighteenth, nineteenth, and twentieth centuries, Charles XII of Sweden, Napoleon, and Hitler all tried it and were licked. The story of their campaigns, which Colonel Jackson tells in considerable detail, is an awe-inspiring record of military ineptitude. The invaders lopped off huge stretches of territory and only then discovered that Russia, like an amoeba, doesn't mind amputations. The Russian armies retreated, wondering why they had not been able to stop the enemy at the border; these confused retreats later looked like wisdom, because by the time the Russians were ready to counterattack, the invaders were exhausted from chasing them. Since the French imagined they could avoid the mistakes that the Swedes had made, and the Germans were certain they would avoid the mistakes that the French had made, and none of them did anything except make mistakes, Colonel Jackson's moral—don't invade Russia—seems unimpeachable.

—From the *New Yorker,* January 24, 1959. Reprinted by permission; © 1959 The New Yorker Magazine, Inc.

In attempting such a brief review yourself, you should keep in mind at least three purposes. First, you should indicate something of the author's reputation or qualifications. Second, you should carefully but in large strokes sketch the contents of the book. Third, you should indicate by some evaluative remark your notion of the author's success. In the review above, for example, it is perfectly clear from some of the adjectives used ("an interesting study," "seems unimpeachable") that this is a favorable judgment.

Directions, Processes, Organizations. The "how to do it" and "how it was done" literature of America is impressive in extent, and some of it, at least, is impressive in literary quality. The ability to give accurate directions is extremely important and should be cultivated just as strictly as the more "creative" kinds of writing. Here are a few suggestions that you may find useful:

1. Take two points rather far apart in your city, such as your home in the suburbs and a downtown theater. Write a short paper of directions in which you tell a total stranger to the city how to reach your home by starting from the point downtown. Do *not* once use any of the directions of the compass—north, east, south, west—in your explanation. Depend entirely on an accurate record of landmarks and distances.

2. Explain to an unmechanical friend how to start and drive a farm tractor. Do not use a single technical term without explaining it in clear, untechnical language.

3. Tell one of your younger friends what he is to do to register in college. Take him from one building to another, and explain every step of the procedure in words that he cannot fail to understand.

An explanation of a process is not necessarily a set of directions to be followed by someone. Thousands of them are written merely because there are people who like to know how things work. If you try one of the following subjects, you might try making it simply an interesting explanation, not a set of directions to be followed:

1. Photographing children
2. Making a blueprint
3. Making an enlargement
4. Life-saving blood
5. Making a bird-feeding station
6. How to sail a boat
7. How to use a fly rod
8. The outdoor fireplace
9. An informal dinner party
10. Transplanting wild flowers
11. Taming a wild animal
12. Delivering newspapers
13. One issue of the school paper
14. Making Christmas cards
15. The efficient baby sitter
16. Training a dog to obey
17. A day at the soda fountain
18. How to model clothes
19. Operating an elevator
20. The "hello" girl's day

An explanation of an organization calls for somewhat more extensive treatment than an explanation of a process. It is a particularly effective device for practicing outlining techniques, as you must be careful that your divisions are co-ordinate and that they are mutually exclusive and not overlapping. Here are a few topics that you may use:

1. A military unit
2. Your fraternity or sorority
3. The college you are attending
4. The induction center
5. The Boy Scouts of America
6. The 4-H clubs
7. Camp Fire Girls or Girl Scouts
8. A consumers' co-operative
9. The county fair
10. A business organization

One world of activity in which "how to do it" writing has an important role is sports. Here the problem of expressing in precise language just what one does with one's own body is crucial. Here is a set of directions for doing the "flutter kick" in swimming:

In the flutter, the water is squeezed, thrust, and kicked away, imparting a forward drive. It is most effective when the power comes from the hips and thighs, the rest of the legs controlled but relaxed, the knees slightly bent, the ankles loose. The ankles may be turned slightly inward in pigeon-toed fashion and should be completely relaxed so that they flop loosely, the toes pointed to eliminate resistance.

The kick is, of course, a series of beats, the legs moving alternately up and down. As it is lifted toward the surface, the leg is relaxed at the knee and bends slightly, the bend increasing until the leg is near the surface. The downward thrust is a whiplash motion in which the whole leg is straightened, imparting a snap to the lower leg and the ankle. The effect is to drive the water down along the thighs and snap it away; or, to look at it in another way, the legs both in the upward and in the downward beat catch hold of the water and drive the body forward.

The first rule for practicing the flutter kick is to make the thighs do the lifting and thrusting. If those big muscles in the thighs and lower back do the work, the kick will not be as tiring as it would be if it were primarily a knee kick, incorrectly used by many swimmers. By applying force from his thighs, the swimmer will give an undulating movement to his legs somewhat like that of a piece of rope when one end of it is snapped. At first there should be little, if any, bending of the knees. The swimmer can let his legs twist inward slightly, rolling the knees closer together and pointing the toes inward and downward.

—From Harold S. Ulen and Guy Larcom, Jr., *The Complete Swimmer,* 1949. Reprinted by permission of The Macmillan Company, publishers.

A good test of a "how to do it" article is this: can you, from reading it, put the process into operation yourself? Can you, in a word, *do* it? This test is particularly appropriate when you are reading an account of a process that is utterly unfamiliar to you.

Here is Vilhjalmur Stefansson's explanation of the method used by Eskimos in catching fish under ice:

In getting ready to fish through ice you fasten your floats to one edge of the net and your sinkers to the other, so that one edge of the net shall be held at the surface of the water and the other down vertically. Then you cut two holes in the ice about forty feet apart (for that is a common length for Eskimo nets) and each a foot or eighteen inches in diameter. Between these two holes you cut a series of smaller holes just big enough to stick your arm into the water, and perhaps six to eight feet apart. Next you take a stick of dry, buoyant wood that is eight or ten feet long. You shove it down through one of the end holes until it is all in the water, when it floats up and rises against the ice. You have a string tied to the stick and this stick you fasten to one end of the net. Then you lay the string so that, while one end is still visible at your hole, the other end is visible below the next hole six or eight feet away. You now go to the second hole, put your hand into the water and slide the stick along under the ice until you can see it through the third hole. The stick, of course, pulls the string in after it and by the time you have worked the stick along to the furthest hole your net is set. You now take a rope that is about ten feet longer than the net and tie each end of the rope to one end of the net so as to make an "endless chain," the net being under the water and the rope on top of the ice.

During the night the holes all freeze over. You allow the small holes to remain frozen permanently but each time you go out to tend the net you open the two end holes and pull the net out of one of them. As you pull the net out the rope part of your endless chain is pulled into the water. When you have picked all the fish out of the net, you pull on your rope and thus drag the net back into the water.

—From *Hunters of the Great North,* copyright, 1922, 1950, by Vilhjalmur Stefansson. Reprinted by permission of Harcourt, Brace and Company, Inc.

"Local Color" Articles. America's literary renaissance after the Civil War began when writers realized that their own communities were worth writing about. Since that time the literature of "local color" has piled up until now its bulk exceeds that of any other type. Every section of America, every state, every city has its stories, poems, novels, and essays of praise or interpretation. The supply of good material is apparently inexhaustible.

You may treat the available "local color" material in various ways. For instance, you may choose to write an article based on reading in the library and, perhaps, on a few interviews. A project of this sort will be fairly ambitious, an article, let us say, of two thousand words or so. The article should be accompanied by an outline.

1. You may investigate the history of your community and write a paper on some interesting phase of it, such as (a) the pioneer days, (b) the coming of the railroad, (c) the rivalry for the county seat, (d) Civil War days, (e) the founding of the college, etc.

2. You may investigate local science—geology, botany, etc.—and write an article on (a) the geologic structure of the region, (b) the birds of the region, (c) the characteristic vegetation, etc.

3. You may look up the lives and achievements of some of the local celebrities and tell about their work.

There are undoubtedly unusual and interesting customs in your home community that can be explained in readable articles or essays.

Then there is always one's home community, a subject of infinite possibilities. One good way of treating this subject, a way which has been tried successfully by many students, is to begin with a personification of your home town, which you will use as the dominant theme of your whole analysis. Then organize your essay on the basis of some of the following topics, but remember that this plan calls for a long paper:

1. Cultural resources
2. The teen-agers
3. What the people live on
4. Contact with the past
5. Politics and government
6. The school system
7. Tribute to beauty: parks, etc.
8. Recreation
9. Industrial domination
10. Commuters
11. Its environment
12. Relation to democracy

But for the ordinary short paper a personification alone may do very well.

[Title] BAGHDAD-BY-THE-BAY

What is San Francisco?

To anyone trying to put a typewriter finger on its complexities and perplexities, that's a question with a hundred answers—no one of them completely satisfying.

The truth lies somewhere between the old and the new, the progressive and the backward, the fog and the sunshine. Even those who have searched longest for it are confused afresh each day, for in any part of the city, a totally unexpected and unexplored San Francisco can be discovered—just around the next corner in the very next moment.

Basically, it is a city of tremendous scenery, of a view from every hilltop and a vista from every window—and yet, it is a city of spectacular ugliness, too. Of dank alleys where children abandon their search for playground space, of Victorian gingerbread that has gone moldy and sour, of tiny box-like houses with false stucco fronts that fail to hide the sham of such short-sighted "planning."

It is a city whose fine residential sections are breathtakingly lush, with row after row of marching mansions set in fields of landscaped beauty—and yet there is a hollowness behind this impressive façade, too. Many of these great homes have been divided internally into small apartments that make them nothing more than super boarding houses. And in many another mansion—this is a crowning anomaly in these days of housing shortages—only one person and a servant live in the emptiness of twenty-two rooms, surrounded by the ghosts of a tradition that died almost as it was born.

For in San Francisco, tradition is a great thing, and this, too, is strange to a city less than one hundred years old. There is a firm, entrenched aristocracy founded, in many cases, on antecedents no more noble than bartenders who knew a good thing when they saw it in the Gold Rush days, or on bonanza speculators who weren't above an outrageous double-cross that left their partners impoverished and themselves multimillionaires.

And yet, it is a tradition already slipping, in its third generation, on its quicksilver foundations. Great fortunes have filtered through the soft fingers of a dozen inheritors in only a few decades, and the residue no longer will finance the high-flown scale of living necessary for a landed gentry to remain landed.

Nevertheless, it is this tradition of wealth and pomp that, even in its November throes, is most strongly imprinted on San Francisco. There is still an atmosphere of good living and sparkling champagne about the city, still a reverential attitude toward culture and all that goes with it, still an unmocking respect for dignity and age and history.

This short yet powerful background of great and sudden wealth leaves the San Franciscan of today almost neurotic in his confusion between what changes must be made and what institutions must be clung to, come what may. Every plan for civic improvement has to be considered not only in the light of what good it will do, but also from the misty standpoint of how great a change it will make on the face of a city whose contours have become frozen because most San Franciscans love it the way it is, not the way it should be.

The San Franciscan's unique civic pride, renowned the world over, is made up of many things—some of the strongest of them rooted deep in the past. When he looks out over the Bay, he sees not only the great bridges, but also the long-gone fleets of white and orange ferryboats that used to dot its surface. He goes to a tiny, out-of-the-way North Beach restaurant because it revives memories of the nights when it was a speak-easy. When he walks through Golden Gate Park, he talks of the days when his father used to stroll along the same paths. He has an instinctive distaste for chromium and glitter and anything that seems typical of Hollywood, and he usually has to struggle slightly to overcome a slight coolness toward outsiders who fail to respond immediately to the nostalgic "pull" of San Francisco.

In short, this descendant of the brawlers and adventurers of the Gold Rush days has become a conservative, looking to his yesterdays for his pattern of tomorrow.

However, the analytical observer may conclude that it is just this attitude, reflected in a thousand musty, dusty corners of San Francisco, that gives the city a charm that is peculiarly Old World—a charm that can be found in few other American cities, and certainly in no other in the West.

Young in years but ancient in sentiment, San Francisco today is at once gay and wise, erratic and yet settled in its ways. It is a city that has lived centuries in a hundred years, only to be born again each day in its own salty magic of wispy fog that floats across the hilltop like grayish memories that refuse to die.

Eternally, San Francisco is Baghdad-by-the-Bay.

—From Max Yavno and Herb Caen, *The San Francisco Book*, Houghton Mifflin Company, 1948. Copyright 1948 by Max Yavno and Herb Caen. Reprinted by permission of the publisher.

One way of producing something new and interesting is to look at a familiar place at some odd or unusual hour of the day, at sunrise perhaps, or in the quiet of early Sunday morning. The student who wrote the following saw Washington Square in New York City on an early morning in winter, and she chose to unify her picture of the place by imposing upon it a mood. That is an idea that you might try.

[Title] WASHINGTON SQUARE

Early morning is a morbid time in a city, and a park such as Washington Square can easily heighten the impression of chilly gloom.

There on one particularly dismal January morning I saw two children playing in the jail-like area that is supposed to represent a playground. One child was lying on the dark cement. In his bulgy snowsuit he looked like drawings I've seen of an amoeba, a squirming blob of muddy brown that, except for its movement, could scarcely be distinguished from the playground surface. The other child held a rubber sword to the snowsuit's bloated skin and waved his free arm about wildly, a gesture that made his dangling red mitten dance on its cord like a partially severed hand.

"You're dead! You're dead!" Oddly, it was the blob that shouted.

The words were directed at his companion, I suppose, but they seemed a concise description of the whole park. Branchy skeletons of trees stood motionless. Dead leaves lay in heaps about them. The wind that might have stirred those leaves or rattled the rope tendons of the bone white flagpole was also dead. The only movement in Washington Square was that of a black baby carriage and the shuffling woman who pushed it, a woman with gray hair, gray skin, and a matching coat. The carriage squeaked loudly as she forced it over cracked walks outlined in uneven rows of weatherworn benches; but the child in it, if there was one, stayed silent. Over this graveyard park stood Washington Arch, a huge unlettered tombstone, a gray monument to some forgotten time, perhaps, when the Square had been filled with color and life.

Suddenly one of the children laughed, and I looked up to see the cause of his amusement—a man had slipped and nearly fallen on one of the muddy walks. I noticed that several other persons were now crossing the park and that automobiles were going by. For a moment the park was full of the many sounds of people and traffic; for a moment I thought that the park was not dead after all. I imagined Washington Square, like the rest of the city, had merely been sleeping and would now awake.

But the cars had passed, the people were gone, the park was again silent; and I wasn't sure.

—From a student theme. Reprinted by permission.

Personal Essays. Although the personal essay has been ridiculed or gently sniffed at by writers who are eager to be on their way from where they are to where they are not, it is still a favorite with many writers and readers. In a way the personal essay does not fit into our restless civilization. It requires calmness of spirit, repose, and the ability to enjoy the flavor of life. Essentially, the personal essay is a discussion not of a subject but of a writer's attitude toward a subject. Its tone should be pleasant, easy, well-bred, never violent or argumentative.

[Title] LADIES ON THE HIGHWAY

That men are wonderful is a proposition I will defend to the death. Honest, brave, talented, strong and handsome, they are my favorite gender. Consider the things men can do better than women—mend the plumbing, cook, invent atom bombs, design the Empire waistline and run the four-minute mile. They can throw a ball overhand. They can grow a beard. In fact, I can think of only two accomplishments at which women excel. Having babies is one.

The other is driving an automobile.

Don't misunderstand me. Some of my best friends are male drivers. And they seldom go to sleep at the wheel or drive 90 on a 45-an-hour road or commit any other of the sins of which statistics accuse them. But insurance companies have been busy as bees proving that I don't get around among the right people.

New York State—where I live—has even made it expensive to have sons.

Car insurance costs much more if there are men in the family under 25 driving than if there are only women. Obviously the female of the species make the best chauffeurs.

They ought to. They get the most practice. Aside from truck- and taxi-drivers, it is women who really handle the cars of the nation. For five days of the week they are in command—slipping cleverly through traffic on their thousand errands, parking neatly in front of the chain stores, ferrying their husbands to and from commuting trains, driving the young to schools and dentists and dancing classes and Scout meetings. It is only on Saturdays and Sundays that men get their innings, not to speak of their outings, and it is over week ends when most of the catastrophes occur.

Not that men are responsible for *all* the accidents. Some are caused by women—by the little blonde on the sidewalk at whom the driver feels impelled to whistle. Or by the pretty girl sitting in the front seat for whom he wants to show off his skill, his eagle eye, and the way he can pull ahead of the fellow in the red sports car.

But it isn't caution and practice alone which make the difference between the sexes. It's chiefly an attitude of mind. Women—in my opinion—are the practical people. To them a car is a means of transportation, a gadget more useful, perhaps, than a dishwasher or a can opener, but no more romantic. It is something in which we carry the sheets to the laundry, pick up Johnnie at kindergarten and lug home those rose bushes.

Men, the dear, sentimental creatures, feel otherwise. Automobiles are more than property. They are their shining chariots, the objects of their affections. A man loves his car the way the Lone Ranger loves his horse, and he feels for its honor on the road. No one must out-weave or out-race him. No one must get off to a better jack-rabbit start. And no one, but no one, must tell him anything while he's driving. My own husband, ordinarily the most good-tempered of men, becomes a tyrant behind the wheel.

"Shouldn't we bear south here?" I inquire meekly on our Saturday trips to the country. Or, "Honey, there's a gray convertible trying to pass."

"Who's driving!" he snarls like Simon Legree, veering stubbornly north or avoiding, by a hair, being run into.

Women drivers, on the other hand, *take* advice. They are used to taking it, having had it pressed on them all their lives by their mothers, teachers, beaus, husbands, and eventually their children. And when they don't know their routes exactly, they inquire at service stations, from passers-by, from traffic officers. But men hate to ask and, when they are forced to do so, seldom listen.

Have you ever overheard a woman taking down directions on the phone? "Yes," she says affably. "I understand. I drive up that pretty road to the Danbury turn-off. Then I bear left at the little antique shoppe that used to be a barn—yellow with blue shutters. Then right at a meadow with two beech trees in it, and a couple of black cows. Up a little lane, just a tiny way beyond a cornfield, and that's your place. Yes. With a Tiffany-glass carriage lamp in front. Fine. I won't have any trouble." Nor does she.

A man has too much pride to take such precautions. "O.K." he says impatiently. "Two point seven miles off the Post Road. A left, a rotary, another left. Six point three to—oh, never mind. I'll look it up on the map."

When they don't insist on traveling by ear, men travel by chart. I've nothing against road maps, really, except the way they clutter up the glove compartment where I like to keep tissues and sun glasses. But men have a furtive passion for them.

When my husband and I are planning a trip, he doesn't rush out like me to buy luggage and a new wardrobe. He shops for maps. For days ahead of time he studies them dotingly; then *I* am forced to study them en route. Many a bitter journey have I taken past the finest scenery in America with my eyes glued to a collection of black and red squiggles on a road map, instead of on the forest and canyons we had come all the way across the country to behold.

"Look!" I cry to him as we rush up some burning autumn lane. "Aren't the trees glorious!"

"What does the map say?" he mutters. "I've marked a covered bridge about a quarter of a mile along here. That's where we turn."

If we should ever approach the Pearly Gates together, I know exactly how the conversation will run. "See all the pretty stars," I'll be murmuring happily. "And, oh, do look over there! Isn't that the City of Gold?"

"Never mind your golden cities," he'll warn me sternly, as he nearly collides with a meteor. "Just keep your eye on the map."

—Phyllis McGinley, published originally as "Women Are Better Drivers." Reprinted from *The American Weekly* © 1959 by Hearst Publishing Co., Inc.; by special permission of the author and publishers.

The next is a charming little essay written by a college freshman:

[Title] PENCIL TRACKS

A returned paper without the instructor's written criticism, no matter how good the grade may be, is like a drink of cold lemonade without any sugar in it. Nothing in the world is so disappointing; nothing leaves the student with such a flat feeling as does the search through the essay, the history report, or whatever the paper may be, for the note of praise or criticism which is not there. It is like cracking a nice large hazel nut and finding the shell empty.

They are such personal things—confidential words from the instructor to the student, which no one else may see or hear, unless the student chooses to show them to a pal. They mean a great deal more to him than the grade-mark up in the right-hand corner of the paper. Personally, I should rather receive a grade of C on a paper if it was accompanied by a note from the professor who graded it, than a nice big, red A without the note.

It doesn't make much difference where these notes are written, just so they are there. I have found them scattered here and there, at the top of the page, along the margins, and between the lines, all over my papers from one end of the page to the other. It is real sport hunting them, one that arouses a good deal of enthusiasm, especially when the hunter can be quite sure the end of the search is going to bring him the prize he is hoping for, a note which tells him what was good and what was bad in his paper.

It doesn't make much difference, either, to what racial class these notes belong. Whether they are red, green, blue, or just plain lead-gray, they accomplish their purpose just as efficiently as if they were written in gold.

Sometimes they are exceedingly difficult to decipher, owing to the fact that they tumbled into their places so fast they were slightly jammed and crowded into their corners; but they are there, and they tell the student everything he wants to know, frankly, quickly, and decisively just when he wants to know it the most.

There is no doubt about it. He likes to see them smile; but if they frown, he knows something he has written is all wrong and he'll have to get busy and make it right. How much easier it is to do that when those little notes keep repeating their message to him over and over again until he has satisfied their demands.

Some of them make the student's ears burn with their twinging, biting sarcasm. They arouse his anger, and he swears he'll "make the prof eat those words yet." He reads them again and again until their meaning has been seared into his soul. It hurts; but he'll never again forget to cross his *t's* or dot his *i's*.

Then, of course, there are the prim, neatly written, fine exhibitions of penmanship that the student finds at the end of his paper, exactly three lines below the last line of his own writing. They are carefully indented, standoffish paragraphs of exposition. Very worthy, they are, as they would have the reader know. For my part, however, I prefer the scrawly ones perched intimately over the left ear of one of my phrases, or stepping on the toes of a flowery adjective.

No matter how they look, where they are, nor what they say, those confidential notes, in search of which the student eagerly scans his paper, are welcome. Without them, a grade of A-plus could not be perfect.

—From a student paper. Reprinted by permission.

Planning the Paper. The planning of your paper begins when your instructor tells you that you are to write, let us say, an eight-hundred-word theme on some local custom, on some new development of science, on the author of the book you happen to be reading—whatever the particular subject may be. You begin by thinking in terms of the space which you have to fill, just as the professional writer begins to plan when his editor asks him to write a five-hundred-word filler on a new grass for shady lawns, a two-thousand-word article on a new hybrid corn, or a six-thousand-word article on the commercial uses of radar. You begin to think in terms of space to fill and readers to interest. What do you have to say that is new, that has not been said over and over again, and, most important at the moment, that can be effectively said in eight hundred words? This process of thinking in terms of a limited space to fill is what in academic language is called "limiting the subject."

Limiting the Subject. The natural tendency of the apprentice writer is to think of subjects in the large. Subjects like "Home and Friends," "Amusements," "Politics," "Reading," or "Vacations" are not subjects for short papers; they are warehouses of subjects. Each contains the materials for innumerable essays, articles, anecdotes, descriptions, whatever you wish to write. The larger the subject, the more hopeless it seems and is. It must be narrowed, cut down, limited to usable size.

Let us illustrate the general principle of limiting a subject by using an example. Let us say that you are interested in antiques, a general subject about which many books have been written. You know something about antiques because your mother and your older sister have several cupboards filled with early American glass. You too have a few choice pieces as the beginning of a collection. Your subject is already beginning to limit itself. What can you tell your reader—in eight hundred words—that is not old and general? Your answer may be the natural result of your own experiences: you decide to give point and direction to your article by concentrating on a single objective, on the idea that an amateur collector of glass develops through three stages. State this objective in the form of a "thesis" or summarizing sentence: "An amateur collector of early American glass develops through three stages: first, he buys everything in sight; second, as his knowledge and taste grow, he discards all except a few of his choicest pieces; third, he begins to see that the pleasure of owning a few perfect things is worth more than a large collection." There you have a target to shoot at, a rough plan of operations, and some idea of the ammunition you are going to use. Up to this time most of your planning has been done in your head. Now jot down your main ideas on a sheet of paper, write down under each main head a few of the details as they occur to you, and you have a working plan.

You will probably change your plan as you proceed, but that is what every writer must do. Change will improve your finished product as long as you keep to your main objective and your first general plan. Your paper will have direction, purpose, organization, and clearness.

Perhaps you will get a better idea of limiting a subject by examining the following groups of limited subjects derived from larger units:

General subject: Home and family life

1. Life in an apartment house
2. Taking care of the baby
3. I am an only child
4. Father comes home at night
5. Getting acquainted with Father
6. The well-planned kitchen
7. A freshman son to his father
8. Sister falls in love
9. Life in Suburbia
10. My parents have separated

General subject: Hobbies

1. Hunting birds with a camera
2. Old guns fascinate me
3. The sports car club
4. Indian relics in my state
5. Mother collects antique glass
6. My arrowhead collection
7. Wood carving
8. Remaking old cars
9. The bow-and-arrow hunter
10. The rock hunter

General subject: Travel

1. Bicycle trips in Maine
2. Exploring in a canoe
2. Places I have slept in
4. Touring with a trailer
5. Glacier Park trails
6. We explore Bryce Canyon
7. I like to meet people
8. Traveling by bus
9. A walking trip in England
10. The trouble with sleeping bags

Nature of the Plan or Outline. Every paper written needs a plan, although some plans spend their life cycles in the heads of the writers without ever emerging on paper in the form of outlines. Some plans take the form of a series of notes on the back of an old envelope. The experienced writer may plan almost subconsciously; some writers say that they do all their outlining in their heads, whereas many others say that they write out elaborate outlines on paper. But the inexperienced writer has everything to gain by using paper and pencil to record and clarify the planning that goes on in his head. Even when a paper is written offhand, as the outpouring of an inspired idea, an outline of the finished paper is an excellent check for organization and logic. If there are flaws in the product of the writer's inspiration, an outline will reveal them.

The Informal Outline. A short paper should have a short outline. In fact, a few notes on the back of an old envelope might do well enough. Let us illustrate: You plan to write a thoughtful little essay on childhood memories. You decide to begin by commenting on the difficulty of remembering things that at the time must have been very vivid to you. Then you go as far back as you can into your childhood and tell a few of the things you remember. You close with a paragraph of comment on the possible reasons why those things and not a million others have remained in your memory. A very poignant and appealing little essay may be written in this way—and yet what slaughter of wistful details could result if this material were forced into the procrustean bed of a formal outline!

The Process of Synthesis. An outline is often spoken of as a process of dividing a subject. It is assumed that the thought mass exists in its entirety in the writer's mind, and in preparing it for the market he methodically slices it up into gobs called topics and subtopics. That may be true for some. For most of us outlining is a process of synthesis, not division. We usually begin with a problem and the necessity of doing something about it. Our first suggestion is probably a very ill-favored, disreputable little idea, something trying to crawl into the woodwork or hiding in the underbrush. We pull it out and look it over. It seems promising

—after it has had its face washed and its clothes changed. Then we look about again—by thinking, by reading, by observing—and pull out other ideas to add to it. We jot down these ideas on paper. Pretty soon, if we are fortunate, we have enough, or perhaps more than enough for our purpose. Then and only then can we begin to select and arrange and divide.

Let us remind ourselves here that in this process of writing a paper or a speech many things go on at the same time. We do not select a subject first, limit the subject second, plan next, outline next, and so on. We may think of a good illustration—and write it down quickly before it fades away; we are conscious of the persons who will read what we say; we have a sudden inspiration of a clever opening paragraph; we think of another important idea that just has to have a place somewhere; we add another thought brick to the structure. And so our essay grows. But the process cannot be explained in that way.

Order of Presentation. The order in which you present your material to your reader will depend partly on what you have to say and partly on the sort of reader you are addressing.

1. The Chronological Order. If you are telling how something is made, how a game is played, how a system grew or developed in the course of time, you will naturally use the order of happening, called the chronological order. In discussions like the following the chronological order is inherent in the material: how to clean a rifle, how to organize and manage a formal dance, how to prepare for a final examination, how to operate a bulldozer, the history of tennis, the development of consumers' co-operatives, learning how to tap-dance. When a subject does not naturally call for this order, you can often achieve a clearer presentation by changing your approach so that you can use the order of time.

2. The Inductive Order (Order of easy acceptance). Occasionally you may gently lead your reader toward an unpalatable idea—like a salesman at your door—by starting with a presentation of a number of facts, instances, or observations that support your main idea. It may be used where it is necessary to prepare a reader's mind for a new idea, but inasmuch as most articles are read quickly the device of surprise has limited uses. It can be tried, however. For instance, if you are advocating the adoption of an honor system in your school, you may get a more favorable reaction from your readers if you convince them first that a system of strict, paternalistic supervision has resulted in widespread dishonesty. If you are urging the establishment of teen-age night clubs, you can begin by picturing first the existing undesirable conditions.

3. Order of Enumeration. If you can divide your subject into several parts of equal importance, you may indicate the division in your opening paragraph and then discuss the parts one by one in the selected order. For convenience, we shall label this order the order of enumeration. "Communism differs from socialism in four important aspects," you begin. "Before the Diesel engine can be used in light motor cars, automotive engineers must solve the following three problems." "The comments of those veterans who are not interested in more free education fall into three general groups." You can see from these examples how a considerable number of subjects will adapt themselves to this sort of treatment. You must remember, however, that a formal enumeration of parts implies a serious and formal treatment of the subject. The lighter, more informal subjects should be handled more informally.

Almost any textbook will give you examples of the order of enumeration. The following piece, from a book about professions, should be studied for its skillful use of analogy and details as well as for order:

> The first requirement for an accountant is analytical power. Perhaps the best illustration of what we mean by analysis is found in the attempt to distinguish two things absolutely familiar to everyone—running and walking. Everyone can tell whether another person is walking or running; yet few people can quickly analyze the two gaits. The difference is not in speed, for the same person can walk faster than he may sometimes run; nor is it in the length of step, for he can take longer steps in walking than he may sometimes take in running; nor is it in the pitch of the body, nor in the bend of the knee, nor in the height of the step, nor in the violence of exertion, nor in various other apparent but unimportant things. It lies in a single factor or element in one gait that is not in the other. Analysis of the two gaits discovers it.
>
> A person who does not find delight in studying things in such fashion,

picking them to pieces, finding the relations of their parts, and then comparing them with other things, is not cut out for an accountant. An accountant must have what we call the philosophic mind, a mind which finds pleasure in discovering what things really are as contrasted with what they appear to be.

The second requirement for an accountant is a knowledge of business practice and experience, for otherwise he will not know what facts about business need study and record, and will not know what light such study and record can throw on the future conduct of the business. If, for example, he does not know that in certain trades it is customary to allow large discounts for early payment of bills, he will not be trustworthy in calculating how much a firm in that business is likely to collect on sums owed it. If he does not know that certain chemicals collect moisture from the atmosphere, he will not be trustworthy in interpreting in terms of value reports of quantities of chemicals on hand in terms of weight. If he does not understand manufacturing processes, he will not direct the bookkeepers so that their records can be used to show whether this or that process is more or less economical than another.

The third requirement is imagination,—the last thing people usually think of as a requirement, or even a virtue, in an accountant. One of the purposes of accounting is to serve as a guide for the future. The records of the past must be so clear, and must be so clearly interpreted (as a historian interprets the facts of history so that they may help us in solving problems of the present and the future), that the policy of the business may be intelligently directed largely on the basis of the information that the accounting gives.

—William Morse Cole, "The Profession of Accounting," from Clayton H. Ernst's *What Shall I Be?* Reprinted by permission of the publishers Appleton-Century-Crofts, Inc.

4. Order of Easy Comprehension. If your subject is an organization, or a complicated piece of machinery, or an idea hard to grasp, you may start with the simple elements of your subject and gradually work toward those more difficult to understand. You may call this order "from easy to hard," if you wish, or "from known to unknown."

5. Order of Division. And finally, there is the method of division—the method used in perhaps ninety-eight per cent of all expository essays, papers, articles, and books. It is a simple method and a good one. In his process of planning the writer says to himself, "Now, I have a certain number of main facts or ideas to give to my reader in the time and space I have for all this. There doesn't seem to be any reason why one should come first and another last." If there is a topic which seems more important than the others, it should be placed last and given more space. Traditionally the end position is the position of advantage and importance, although it does no harm for the writer, when he comes to his "and finally," to tell the reader directly that this final idea is the most important one.

Conventions of the Formal Outline. There are a number of conventions governing the formal outline which the student should observe:

1. The parts of the outline, heads and subheads, should be labeled by alternating figures and letters as follows: I, II, III, etc., A, B, C, etc., 1, 2, 3, etc., a, b, c, etc. Periods, not dashes, should be placed after these numbering figures and letters.

2. No punctuation is needed after the topics in a topic outline. In a sentence outline, each sentence should be punctuated in the conventional manner.

3. The heads in any series should be of equal importance. That is, the heads numbered I, II, III, IV, etc., should actually be divisions of the whole paper; heads numbered with capital letters should be co-ordinate divisions of heads numbered with Roman numerals; and so on.

4. Whenever possible, co-ordinate heads should be expressed in parallel form, that is, in a given series, nouns should be made parallel with nouns, adjectives with adjectives, and so on. But although parallel structure is desirable and logical, clearness and directness should never be sacrificed on the altar of strict parallelism. There are times when nouns and gerunds can live side by side in a formal outline.

5. In a topic outline, all heads and subheads must be topics. In a sentence outline, all heads and subheads must be sentences. Sentences should not run over from one head to another.

6. Each head and subhead should be as specific as it is possible to make it in an outline. Vague topics and sentences are bad because they tend to hide flaws in the logic or organization of the outline.

7. Using such headings as "I. Introduction, II. Body, III. Conclusion" is unnecessary and undesirable. Such divisions do not indicate correctly the structure of most essays or articles. Many papers written by students are too short for a formal introduction or conclusion. In most long papers the conclusion is simply the main topic which the writer wants the reader to hear about last—for reasons explained elsewhere. Separate introductions are used more often than separate conclusions in essays of six thousand words or more, but in the outline it is better to use a topic which tells what is said in the introduction than to use the vague "Introduction" itself.

8. Since an outline represents a grouping of parallel parts, it is illogical to have a single subhead under any head. A single subhead can usually be combined with its head with benefit to the logic and organization of the outline.

The conventions of outlining are illustrated by the following examples. These were done by a college freshman for a fairly short paper. For other examples, see "Engineering Is My Life," page 114, and the outline of the library paper.

[Title] AS THE TWIG IS BENT

TOPIC OUTLINE

Thesis: My life has been dominated by the fact that I am a college professor's daughter.

I. The restrictions placed upon my life and actions
    A. Checks upon my natural impulses
    B. My goldfish-bowl existence
    C. The necessity of graduating with honors from local college
II. The advantages of being a professor's daughter
    A. Frequent opportunity for travel
    B. Possession of a permanent home town
    C. Less difficulty in getting an education
III. The necessity of leading a quiet life

A sentence outline is similar in organization to a topic outline. It differs from a topic outline in that every topic and every subtopic is translated into a complete sentence. This sentence states the central idea of each head or subhead. The sentence outline has two advantages over the topic outline: (1) it forces the writer to study his material carefully so that he has something specific to say for each head and subhead, and (2) much more than the topic outline it is able to convey information to the reader. The topic outline merely states the topics about which the writer intends to say something; the sentence outline actually summarizes what he has to say.

[Title] AS THE TWIG IS BENT

SENTENCE OUTLINE

Thesis: My life has been dominated by the fact that I am a college professor's daughter.

I. Many things are taken for granted because I am a college professor's daughter.
   A. A restraining hand is placed upon my impulses.
   B. I am destined to live in a town where all my actions are known and where I have to live up to my father's standards of respectability.
   C. It is taken for granted that I will graduate with honors from the college in my home town.

II. There are several advantages resulting from being a professor's daughter.
   A. I have had frequent opportunity for travel.
   B. I have had a permanent home town.
   C. I have had a few of the sharp stones removed from the long road to an education.

III. Only a girl who loves a quiet life should choose to be born into a professor's family.

Beginning the Paper. Every writer faced with the task of setting his ideas down on paper is conscious of the overwhelming importance of an effective beginning. It is like first meetings—the first interview with your employer, the first introduction to your mother-in-law. There is something terrifying about it simply because it must be got over with first. In writing, students spend entirely too much time getting started.

"The best way to begin is to begin. Do not write introductions. Just plunge in." All this is sound advice but not very helpful to the beginner. One might as well tell him to learn how to dance by plunging in—some persons do dance that way—or to play bridge, or to swim. After all, one must know what he is to do after he plunges in. Another bit of advice, a trifle more helpful, is, "Just write down anything about your subject. Keep going until you get well into your first main topic. Then in revision cross out the first two paragraphs."

There are, however, a number of specific devices which a writer may use to introduce his subject appropriately and interestingly. After he has experimented with a few of them, he will no doubt invent variations of his own.

1. Begin by specifying the phase or aspect of the subject to which you intend to limit your discussion. In formal papers, such as the research article, this sort of beginning is often a help to both writer and reader. The announcement of the subject need not be stiff and artificial. Notice how easily the introducing is performed in the following specimen:

> On one of my bookshelves is a long row of smallish volumes, bound in red cloth with gold lettering and marbled edges, all carrying on their practically uniform title pages the legend, "Handbook for Travelers. By Karl Baedeker."
>
> For well over forty years the author of those volumes has been for me very literally a guide; likewise he has been a friend, if friendship lies in constant readiness to aid, to safeguard, and to counsel. So much he has been to many others, throughout the world. But what comparatively few realize is that Karl Baedeker is also a philosopher—a man with a personality, a consistent set of principles for action, and a *Weltanschauung* of his own—to borrow an untranslatable word from his native language. It is with this personality, with Karl Baedeker the man, that I am now concerned.
>
> —From W. G. Constable, "Three Stars for Baedeker," *Harper's Magazine*, April, 1953. Copyright 1953 by Harper & Brothers. Reprinted from *Harper's Magazine* by special permission.

2. Begin with an incident, real or imagined, out of which the discussion arises, or which illustrates the point of the discussion.

> A puff of wind comes down the street. An old newspaper stirs in the gutter, jumps up on the sidewalk, spirals up to second-story height and

flaps about there for a moment; then, with a new burst of energy, it sweeps upward again, and when you last see it, it is soaring high above the roof tops, turning over and over, blinking in the sunlight.

The wind has picked up a piece of paper and blown it away. What of it? A generation ago, in philosophical discourse, one might have chosen this as an example of an event completely void of significance, completely chance. But not in the air age. The tiny occurrence demonstrates an important fact concerning the air ocean—one that is only now becoming the practical knowledge of practical airfaring men: there are winds which blow neither east nor west, neither north nor south, but in the third dimension: straight up.

—Wolfgang Langewiesche, "Winds That Blow Straight Up," *Harper's Magazine*, August, 1945. Reprinted by permission of the author.

Some years ago when I was the dinner guest of a famous club in Boston, the chairman of the evening introduced me in the following words: "Our guest tonight is an economist. I need hardly remind you, gentlemen, of the large part played in our life today by our economists. Indeed, it has been calculated that if all the economists were laid out in a line, end to end, starting at the Mexican border, they would reach—" The orator paused impressively and added: "nowhere."

That, I may say, was a few years ago. What was a genial joke then is a plain fact now. In my opinion that is exactly where economics stands. At a time when the world is in danger of collapse from the dilemma of wealth and want, the economists can shed no light, or rather only a multitude of cross lights that will not focus to a single beam—in place of a lighthouse, wrecker's signals, or at least, fireworks, elaborate and meaningless.

How has this come about? What has happened to our economic science?

—Stephen Leacock, "Lost in the Jungle of Economics," *New York Times Magazine,* August 20, 1939. Reprinted by permission.

3. Begin with a pertinent story or anecdote.

One of the oldest Texas stories, dating back probably a hundred years, is of the early-day booster who wrote to an influential friend back East dilating upon the manifold beauties and wonders of the region, and closing with the observation: "All Texas needs is more water and a little better class of people." To which the friend replied, "Why, man, that's all hell needs."

Well, where are we now?

—From Stanley Walker, "Everything's True about Texas," *Harper's Magazine*, March, 1950. Copyright 1950 by Harper & Brothers. Reprinted from *Harper's Magazine* by special permission.

4. Begin with some fact or series of facts related to your subject which shows the importance or the timeliness of your subject.

How high can taxes rise without economic trouble? The question is timely. People have always grumbled about taxes, but during the past three or four decades—as a result of two hot wars and the high defense costs of the cold war, to say nothing of the gradually rising expense of government services of many sorts—most of us have watched our taxes climb to such unprecedented heights that we must have sincerely wondered what the effective limit was. . . .

—From Colin Clark, "The Danger Point in Taxes," *Harper's Magazine*, December, 1950. Copyright 1950 by Harper & Brothers. Reprinted from *Harper's Magazine* by special permission.

5. Begin with a question or a series of questions, the answers to which will constitute your article or essay.

The main purpose of this article is to tell you what the astrophysicists have discovered recently about the inner workings of the sun. And this will bring up their answers to a number of age-old cosmological questions. What is the sun made of? How hot is it? Is it simply hot on the surface, or is the whole body hot, inside and outside? These are some of the things which puzzle people. Much more important is this one. What is the source of the sun's energy? Is it growing hotter, or colder? How long will it continue to radiate light and heat at just the rate required by living creatures on the Earth?

—From Fred Hoyle, "The Sun and the Stars," *Harper's Magazine*, January, 1951. Copyright 1951 by Harper & Brothers. Reprinted from *Harper's Magazine* by special permission.

What would happen if all the children in the world learned another language along with their own? Not just *another* language, but *the same* language?

—From Mario Pei, *One Language for the World*, Devon-Adair, 1958, p. xiii.

6. Begin by commenting on the need of a new discussion of an old subject.

There was a time not long ago when a snob was a snob and as easy to recognize as a cock pheasant. . . . But now the social snob, while not extinct, has gone underground (except for professionals such as head waiters and metropolitan-hotel room clerks), and snobbery has emerged in a whole new set of guises, for it is as indigenous to man's nature as ambition and a great deal easier to exercise.

—From Russell Lynes, "The New Snobbism," *Harper's Magazine*, November, 1950. Copyright 1950 by Harper & Brothers. Reprinted from *Harper's Magazine* by special permission.

7. Begin by stating your intention to refute something said or published.

"The average Yaleman, Class of '24," *Time* magazine reported last year after reading something in the New York *Sun*, a newspaper published in those days, "makes $25,111 a year."

Well, good for him!

But, come to think of it, what does this improbably precise and salubrious figure mean? Is it, as it appears to be, evidence that if you send your boy to Yale you won't have to work in your old age and neither will he? Is this average a mean or a median? What kind of sample is it based on? You could lump one Texan oilman with two hundred hungry free-lance writers and report *their* average as $25,000-odd a year. The arithmetic is impeccable, the figure is convincingly precise, and the amount of meaning there is in it you could put in your eye.

—From Darrell Huff, "How to Lie with Statistics," *Harper's Magazine*, August, 1950. Copyright 1950 by Harper & Brothers. Reprinted from *Harper's Magazine* by special permission.

8. Begin by pointing out the fascinating nature of your subject.

To many Americans one of the most fascinating scientific developments of the postwar world has had to do with the weather. Man has always been supinely and sublimely submissive to the weather, but now (he has read in his paper, heard on his radio) at long last he has learned how to *do something* about it.

—From C. Lester Walker, "The Man Who Makes Weather," *Harper's Magazine*, January, 1950. Copyright 1950 by Harper & Brothers. Reprinted from *Harper's Magazine* by special permission.

Writing the Paper. After you have thought your subject through, worked it over in your mind, laid out your general plan and supplied as many details as you could, you will probably want to write rapidly without pausing too often to ponder over the perfect sentence or the exact word. Write rapidly if that is the way you write naturally. Write slowly and carefully if slow and careful writing is your best method. Among professional writers no two work alike. Some write fast and revise slowly, changing words and phrases, crossing out and rewriting, copying the revised manuscript and then rewriting again, sometimes as many as fifteen times. Some chisel out every word in creative agony in their first draft—and never revise.

Although no two writers use an outline alike, the apprentice writer can profit, here as elsewhere, by observing the practice of the skilled writer. A short outline for a short paper is probably so well fixed in the writer's mind by the time he has finished it that he can give it a quick survey, lay it aside, and proceed to write his paper from memory. In the composition of a long paper with a complex outline, especially when the writing is done from notes, it is well to study the notes and the outline dealing with a small unit, lay both aside for the time, and write from memory. The writer does go back—and should, too—for a recheck of his material before his revision of his first draft. There is such a thing as an outline-ridden paper. A writer gives himself freedom to add illustrations, examples, and typical cases that do not show in the outline. He should also have the freedom to cut if that seems best in the writing.

Proportion. The amount of space that you give to each of the topics in your paper will depend on what you have to say and on your purpose in writing.

In general, certain things are unimportant. Long, rambling beginnings, formal conclusions, and digressions from the central idea should be severely pruned or grubbed out entirely.

As for the rest, the principle is simple. Keeping in mind the old rule of "an interesting beginning and a strong ending," you will give relatively more space to the important topic which you have saved for the end of your paper. That is the fact or idea that you want to stress, both by placing it at the end and by saying more about it. You may, of course, introduce your last topic by some such phrase as, "And, finally, the most important—," but telling your reader that an idea is most important is not the same as making him think and feel that it is. For this you need concrete details. You need evidence. And you also need to allow a certain amount of time for the idea to sink into his mind.

Substance: Use of Details. To reach the mind of your reader, to make him understand and to persuade him to accept, you must usually be specific and concrete. Generalities seldom convince. A vague essay on the need for international understanding and co-operation may get a reader's passive mental agreement, but a concrete picture of it in a novel or a play will reach his heart too. A lecture on man's inhumanity to man is one thing; a newsreel showing the inside of a concentration camp is something very different. Your outline and much of your note-taking are often a series of generalities. They are the skeleton of your paper, with all the emotional appeal, the personality, and the warmth of a skeleton. You must cover the skeleton with living flesh. Explanations, specific details, instances, illustrations, concrete examples—out of these you build your finished essay.

One way of placing yourself in a better position to put substance into your writing is to keep substance in mind from the beginning, during your preliminary note-taking and outlining. Be specific from the start. Actually few ideas come into your mind as abstractions, unless you are merely pushing other people's words around like billiard balls. Abstractions usually start with an actual occurrence of some sort. An abstraction like "the need for international understanding" is likely to mean, if it means anything at all to you, something that *happened* in your experience. Perhaps it was a conversation with a South American; perhaps it was something you read in a foreign book; perhaps you saw a French movie. Whatever it was, your notion of the need for international understanding was a logical connection you made between all the pious and abstract talk you have heard on this subject and something definite that was part of your own life. When you begin your note-taking and outlining, do not forget this connection. We all know the sort of note or outline heading that means almost nothing, and that gives the writer almost no help for proceeding. "Need for international understanding vital:" what can you do about that except repeat it in other and even duller words? But suppose your notes read something like this: "Conversation with Juan, acquaintance from Havana. Passionate defense of Castro's executions. 'You don't understand Cuba,' he says. Does he understand America?" This is only a beginning, but it is promising. Obviously, abstract terms and headings are always necessary to hold an argument together and to give it direction. But when your abstractions become disembodied from the drama and experience of daily events that gave them birth, you are on your way to writing mush.

The Ending. In the writing process, stopping is much simpler than starting. In a short paper, after the writer has discussed the last phase of his topic adequately, no literary device surpasses the finality of lifting the pen from the paper or pulling the paper out of the typewriter. The short essay, sketch, article, or discussion has no room for summaries or formal conclusions.

In an article of several thousand words, a quick restatement of the thesis idea is effective. If a summing up of the central idea is inconvenient, the reader's mind should be directed to some important thought related to the main subject, not to a subordinate detail.

An anecdote, an epigram, a clever quip may be used to end as well as to begin a paper. This device is especially effective if it turns the reader's mind to the beginning of the paper and serves to tie the whole thing up in a neat package.

1. Darrell Huff, in "How to Lie with Statistics," ends his paper with an anecdote. Turn to page 144 to see how he began it.

> Is this little list altogether too much like a manual for swindlers? Perhaps I can justify it in the manner of the retired burglar whose published reminiscences amounted to a graduate course in how to pick a lock and muffle a footfall: The crooks already know these tricks. Honest men must learn them in self-defense.[1]

2. Wolfgang Langewiesche, in "Winds That Blow Straight Up," takes the reader back to his opening incident. (See page 141.)

[1] All selections from *Harper's Magazine* reprinted by permission of the authors and of *Harper's Magazine*.

That's the dynamite packed in the puff of wind which picks up a piece of paper.[1]

3. H. Tracy Hall, in "Ultrahigh Pressures," begins his article: "There is a nice symbolism in the fact that man was able to hit the moon before he could sink a three-mile shaft through the earth's crust. . . . But man has barely begun to approach in his laboratories the outstanding characteristic of the nether world—its enormous static pressure." In his concluding words he restates and summarizes his main thesis:

A new era in high-pressure work, both in the laboratory and on the production line, is clearly on the way. The race to skim the cream is beginning. It should be a fascinating and rewarding sweepstakes.[2]

4. Fred Hoyle, in "The Sun and the Stars," summarizes his main point in a single straightforward sentence.

So we may conclude that although mankind may engage in foolish personal destruction, the Earth itself is safe.[1]

5. Russell Lynes, in "The New Snobbism," uses a sprightly comment on his main idea as a means of listing the main points of his essay.

It will not have escaped the reader (and so I might as well admit it) that this cursory attempt to classify and define snobs is an example not only of Intellectual Snobbism, but of Moral, Sensual, Occupational, Political, Emotional, and above all Reverse or Anti-snob Snobbism. I am sure there is no greater snob than the snob who thinks he can define a snob.[1]

6. C. Lester Walker, in "The Man Who Makes Weather," uses a reference to a humorous commentary on the success of his weatherman.

[1] All selections from *Harper's Magazine* reprinted by permission of the authors and of *Harper's Magazine*.

[2] This selection from the November, 1959, issue of *Scientific American* reprinted by permission of the author and of *Scientific American*.

They have been hailing the success of the Schaefer technics by running cartoons of the airplane pilot nonchalantly lassoing the thunderstorm clouds.[1]

7. Stanley Walker, in "Everything's True about Texas," begins and ends his account with anecdotes.

There is a very old story of the Easterner who was being driven by a rancher over a blistering and almost barren stretch of West Texas when a gaudy bird, new to him, scurried in front of them. The Easterner asked what it was.

"That is the bird of paradise," said the rancher.

The stranger rode in silence for a time and then said: "Pretty long way from home, isn't he?"

It's a long way still, but we're edging closer.[1]

An so the search for the perfect ending, like the search for the Holy Grail, goes on; the perfect ending, *La commedia è finita,* appears once in an age. And let us not forget that Shakespeare, after Hamlet's perfect last line, "The rest is silence," continues with fifty more lines of trivia.

Exercises

Exercise 1. Select a number of subjects that can be developed by using the chronological order. Construct a preliminary outline for your subject. Here are a few suggestions. See also page 122.

1. Registration day
2. A day at the shop
3. A day on the job
4. Cleaning a rifle
5. Prepare for inspection
6. How to bind a book
7. Planting a rose bush
8. How to explore the city

Exercise 2. Plan a sketch of some place, such as a town, a summer resort, a college, etc., which you can write in imitation of John Steinbeck's characterization of the Carmel River, page 110.

1. My home town isn't very large, but it has everything that a little town should have.
2. Our city block is like thousands of other blocks, but it has everything that a block should have.

[1] All selections from *Harper's Magazine* reprinted by permission of the authors and of *Harper's Magazine.*

3. Few people have ever heard of the little village which I call my home, but it has everything that a village should have.

Exercise 3. Use some of the following general subjects for practice in cutting down a large subject to a phase of it suitable for a paper of eight hundred words.

1. Commuting
2. Life on a farm
3. College traditions
4. Careers for women
5. Bird watching
6. Reading for recreation
7. Basketball
8. Drag races
9. Teen-age gangs
10. Modern music

Exercise 4. Select a subject that you want to use for your essay. Write four beginnings for it. With the help of your instructor pick out the most successful one and use it in writing your paper.

1. Begin by using an imagined incident which illustrates the point of your paper or out of which a discussion of your subject may seem to arise.
2. Begin with evidence of the importance or the timeliness of your subject.
3. Begin by stating your purpose in writing.
4. Begin with a question or a series of questions.

Chapter 5

WRITING THE LIBRARY PAPER

Importance of the Library Paper. Almost every class that you attend in college demonstrates the importance of knowing how to prepare a paper based on printed materials which may be found in a library. The lecture on the Magna Charta in your history class, for instance, the explanation of the "single-tax" theory in your economics class, the talk on protozoans in your biology class—these and hundreds of thousands of other class lectures are all "papers based on research in a library." The same is true of countless numbers of papers written to be read before clubs, civic groups, study organizations, and so on.

You may, of course, have occasion later in your life to prepare a paper based on original experiments, or perhaps on the study of original documents in the British Museum. If that time comes, you will learn the first rule of scholarship: "Before you begin your project, first learn what has already been done in your field." In other words, go to the libraries.

There are other values and skills to be got from writing a library paper:

1. You will get practice in preparing the term papers that will be required in many of your courses.

2. You will get a great deal of interesting and perhaps useful information about a special subject.

3. You will learn how to sift material as well as to find it, to judge its worth, to organize it, and to present it in pleasing form. And that is a skill that will be useful some day, whether you compose a talk for your club meeting or write an article for your company journal or for *PMLA*.

The Use of the Library. A study of the resources of the library may be taken up under three main headings: (1) the card catalogue, (2) the general reference library, (3) the indexes to periodicals, bulletins, and newspapers.

The Card Catalogue: Basic Guide to the Library. The starting point for your exploration of the library is, logically, the card catalogue, for this is a collection of cards listing every book (including reference books), bulletin, pamphlet, and periodical which the library owns.

The cards are arranged alphabetically according to authors, titles, and subjects. In other words, every book in the library should be listed on at least three separate cards. You can therefore find a book if you know the author's name, or the title, or the subject with which it deals. Magazines and bulletins are usually listed by title; that is, the card catalogue will tell you whether or not the library owns a certain magazine or series of bulletins. The card will tell you which volumes are bound and shelved, and which are stacked unbound in a storeroom. In most libraries there will be a duplicate list of periodicals for use in the reference library room. For detailed information about the contents of these periodicals and bulletins and newspapers you will have to consult the periodical indexes. (See page 160.)

Let us examine a typical library card, shown on page 153.

1. DU740.M96 is the call number, according to the Library of Congress system. (See page 156.)
2. "Mytinger, Caroline" tells you the author's name, last name given first. Ordinarily the date of the author's birth is added after the name.

3. "New Guinea . . . 1946" tells you the title of the book; the author's name, written in the natural order; the place of publication; the name of the publisher; and the date of publication.
4. The fourth line tells you that the book has eight pages numbered in Roman numerals, one leaf blank, 441 pages numbered in Arabic numerals. The book has illustrations, plates (one double plate), and the shelf height of the book is 22 centimeters.

```
DU740 Mytinger, Caroline.
M96
        New Guinea headhunt, by Caroline Mytinger. New York,
      The Macmillan Company, 1946.

        viii p., 1 l., 441 p. illus., plates (1 double) 22cm.

        Map on lining-paper.
        "First printing."

        1. New Guinea—Descr. & trav.  2. Ethnology—New
      Guinea
      I. Title.

        DU740.M96          919.5          42–226

        Library of Congress      [20]
```

5. The next two lines are "notes," only seldom of interest to a student looking for a book.
6. The next two lines give you the subject references under which the book may be found listed in the card catalogue. You will find the book listed under: New Guinea—Description and travel, Ethnology—New Guinea, and under the title of the book.
7. "DU740.M96" is the Library of Congress cataloguing symbol or call number.
8. "919.5" is the class number under the Dewey Decimal system.
9. "42–226" is the order number used by librarians in ordering cards.
10. "[20]" is the key to the printing of the card.

The card just examined is an author card. A title card is just like an author card, except that the title is typewritten at the top.

K The spirit of liberty.
H14

Hand, Learned, 1872–

The spirit of liberty; papers and addresses, collected, and with an introd. and notes, by Irving Dilliard, 2d ed. enl. New York, Knopf, 1953.

xxx, 285 p. port. 22^{cm}.

1. Law—U. S.—Addresses, essays, lectures. 2. U. S.—Civilization—Addresses, essays, lectures. I. Title.

K - H14 304 53–7605

Card showing that the library has a certain periodical:

H1 **Political** science quarterly, a review devoted to the historical,
P8 statistical and comparative study of politics, economics and public law . . . v.1-73.

Mar. 1886–1959

Boston, New York, Ginn and Company, [etc., etc.] 1886–59 v. tables, charts, maps. 24 cm

Vols. 1–23 (1886–1908) edited by the Faculty of political science of Columbia university; v.24–date (1909–date) edited for the Academy of political science in the city of New York by the Faculty of political science of Columbia university.

Managing editors: 1886–93, Munroe Smith.—1894–1903, W. A. Dunning.—1904–13, Munroe Smith.—1914—T. R. Powell.

H1.P8

(continued on next card)

A subject card is an author card with the subject typed, usually in red, above the author's name at the top.

```
HC103    U. S.--Economic conditions
 B57
         Bogart, Ernest Ludlow, 1870–

           . . . Economic history of the American people, by Ernest
         Ludlow Bogart . . . New York, London [etc.] Long-
         mans, Green and co., 1930.

           xii p., 1 l., 797 p. illus. (maps) diagrs. 22½cm. (Longmans'
         economics series)

           "First edition."
           "Bibliographical note" at end of each chapter.

           1. U. S.—Econon. condit.  2. U. S.—Indus.—Hist.
                                                    30—28303

           Library of Congress            HC103.B57

         —— ——— Copy 2.
         Copyright  A29217          [33z3]          330.973
```

Call Numbers. A "call number" is a symbol or group of symbols used by libraries to designate any particular book. The call number for any book is placed in the upper left-hand corner of the card-catalogue card, on the spine or bound end of the book, and usually on the inside of the back cover as well. Books are arranged on shelves according to their call numbers. Call numbers usually consist of two parts: the upper part is the classification number, and the lower part the author and book number.

For the ordinary undergraduate, a knowledge of the systems used in devising call numbers is relatively unimportant. To satisfy a natural curiosity on the part of many students and to make library work a little more interesting, the following brief explanation is given.

Two systems of classification are used by libraries in this country: the Library of Congress system and the Dewey Decimal system.

The Library of Congress system, found more frequently in college than in public libraries, uses the letters of the alphabet, followed by Arabic numerals or additional letters, as the basis of its classification.

A	General works	M	Music
B	Philosophy—Religion	N	Fine arts
C	History—Auxiliary sciences	P	Language and literature
D	History and topography	Q	Science
E and F	American history	R	Medicine
G	Geography—Anthropology	S	Agriculture
H	Social sciences	T	Technology
J	Political science	U	Military science
K	Law	V	Naval science
L	Education	Z	Bibliography and library science

The Dewey Decimal system, devised by Melvil Dewey, uses a decimal classification for all books. The entire field of knowledge is divided into nine groups, with an additional group for general reference books. Each main class and subclass is shown by a number composed of three digits.

000	General works	500	Natural science
100	Philosophy	600	Useful arts
200	Religion	700	Fine arts
300	Sociology	800	Literature
400	Philology	900	History

The following table shows the first subdivision under the literature class and the beginning of the intricate system of further subdividing under the 820 group.

810 American
820 English
  821 English poetry
  822 English drama
    822.3 Elizabethan drama
      822.33 Shakespeare

830 German
840 French
850 Italian
860 Spanish
870 Latin
880 Greek
890 Minor literatures

The Reference Library. The reference library consists of all the general works, such as encyclopedias and dictionaries, and collections of pamphlets, bibliographies, guides, maps, pictures, and the like, which are to be consulted for some specific information rather than to be read in their entirety. Reference books ordinarily cannot be taken from the library. The following list of reference books should be a starting point for your explorations of the reference room of your library. Get acquainted with these books. Find out where they are shelved. Examine them, and examine others like them that you find on the shelves.

In the following list, the date given is usually the date of the latest revision. In this changing world, the date of publication may be very important in a reference book.

1. The General Encyclopedias

Encyclopaedia Britannica. 24 vols. Chicago: Encyclopaedia Britannica Company. Since 1940 the *Britannica* has been kept up to date by continuous revision. Hence a date is necessary with a reference to any printing or revision of the work since 1940. For editions before 1940, give the number of the edition.

Encyclopedia Americana. 30 vols. New York: Americana Corporation. Like the *Britannica,* the *Americana* is now kept up to date by continuous revision. Hence the date is necessary with any reference to it.

Chambers's Encyclopaedia. London: George Newnes, Ltd., 1950.

New International Encyclopedia. 23 vols. plus 4 supp. vols. New York: Dodd, Mead and Company, 1902–1930. It has not been revised since 1930.

A student using the *Britannica,* the *Americana,* and the *New International* should consult the annual supplements, the *Britannica Book of the Year,* the *Americana Annual,* and the *New International Year Book,* for additional information.

2. The Special Encyclopedias

The Catholic Encyclopedia. 16 vols. New York: The Gilmary Society. Supp. I, 1922. Supp. II, 1950–1954. Although this work deals primarily with the accomplishments of Roman Catholics, its scope is very general. It is useful for subjects relating to medieval literature, history, art, and philosophy.

The Jewish Encyclopedia. 12 vols. New York: Funk and Wagnalls Company, 1925.

Encyclopaedia of the Social Sciences. 8 vols. Ed. by Edwin R. A. Seligman and Alvin Johnson. New York: The Macmillan Company, 1937.

3. The Year Books

Britannica Book of the Year. Chicago: Encyclopaedia Britannica Company, 1938 to date.

Americana Annual. New York: Americana Corporation, 1923 to date.

New International Year Book. New York: Funk and Wagnalls Company, 1907 to date.

World Almanac and Book of Facts. New York: The New York *World-Telegram,* 1868 to date.

Information Please Almanac. New York: The Macmillan Company, 1947 to date.

Economic Almanac. New York: National Industrial Conference Board, 1940 to date.

Statesman's Year-Book. London: Macmillan & Co., Ltd.; New York: St. Martin's Press, 1864 to date.

4. Guides to Reference Books

Murphey, Robert W. *How and Where To Look It Up.* New York: McGraw-Hill Book Company, 1958.

Shores, Louis. *Basic Reference Sources.* Chicago: American Library Association, 1954.

Cumulative Book Index (called *United States Catalog* up to 1928). New York: H. W. Wilson Company, 1928 to date. This is a catalogue of books in print in any given year. It is invaluable for checking exact titles, author's names, dates of publication and revisions, and so on.

5. Biographical Information

Current Biography: Who's News and Why. New York: H. W. Wilson Company, 1940 to date. Published monthly, with six-month and annual cumulations.

Webster's Biographical Dictionary. Springfield, Mass.: G. & C. Merriam Company, 1943. A one-volume pronouncing biographical dictionary of over 40,000 names. It includes living persons.

Dictionary of American Biography. 21 vols. New York: Charles Scribner's Sons, 1928–1943.

Dictionary of National Biography. 22 vols. London: Oxford University Press, 1885–1949. The word "national" is sometimes confusing to students; it refers to the "nationals" of the British Empire, more recently the British Commonwealth of Nations.

Who's Who. London: A. & C. Black, Ltd.; New York: The Macmillan Company, 1949 to date.

Who's Who in America. Chicago: A. N. Marquis Company, 1899 and biannually to date.

Biography Index. New York: H. W. Wilson Company. 1947 to date. This is a guide to biographical information in books and magazines.

Biographical information can also be secured in books and magazines, through the aid of various periodical indexes, and in very compressed form in your own desk dictionary.

6. Dictionaries and Books of Synonyms

Webster's New International Dictionary, 2nd. ed. Springfield: G. & C. Merriam Company, 1934 to date. This is the famous "Webster's unabridged," the dictionary almost universally appealed to as the final authority in spelling, meaning, pronunciation, derivation, and usage.

New Standard Dictionary. New York: Funk and Wagnalls Company, 1935 to date.

New Century Dictionary. 3 vols. New York: The Century Company, 1927–1933. Based on the original *Century Dictionary,* 12 vols., 1911.

Oxford English Dictionary. New York: Oxford University Press, 1933. A corrected reissue of *A New English Dictionary on Historical Principles,* 1888–1933. The purpose of this work is to give the history of every word in the English language for the last 800 years. It contains many quotations illustrating meanings of words in various periods and full discussions of derivations and changes in meanings and spellings.

Dictionary of American English on Historical Principles. 4 vols. Chicago: University of Chicago Press, 1936–1944. This is especially useful to the student who wishes to learn the historical changes in the use and meaning of words in American English.

Webster's Dictionary of Synonyms. Springfield: G. & C. Merriam Company, 1942. A dictionary of discriminated synonyms with antonyms and analogues and contrasted words.

For other books dealing with the English language see the bibliography at the end of Chapter 1.

7. Gazetteers and Atlases

The Columbia Lippincott Gazetteer of the World. A revision of *Lippincott's Gazetteer* of 1905. New York: Columbia University Press, 1952.

In a world of quickly changing national boundaries, atlases are out of date almost as soon as they are printed. Most of the following, however, are kept up to date by frequent revisions. Look for the date on the book that you are using.

Rand McNally Commercial Atlas and Marketing Guide. Chicago: Rand McNally and Company.

Encyclopaedia Britannica World Atlas. Chicago: Encyclopaedia Britannica Company. Revised annually.

Webster's Geographical Dictionary. Springfield: G. & C. Merriam Company, 1949.

8. Books on Literature

Cambridge History of English Literature. 15 vols. Cambridge University Press, 1907–1927.

Cambridge History of American Literature. New York: The Macmillan Company, 1933.

Literary History of the United States. 3 vols. Ed. R. E. Spiller, *et al.* New York: The Macmillan Company, 1948.

9. Books of Quotations

Bartlett, John. *Familiar Quotations.* Boston: Little, Brown and Company, 1955.

Mencken, H. L. *A New Dictionary of Quotations on Historical Principles from Ancient and Modern Sources.* New York: Alfred A. Knopf, 1942.

Stevenson, Burton. *The Home Book of Quotations.* New York: Dodd, Mead and Company, 1956.

10. Books on Mythology, Classical Literature

The Oxford Classical Dictionary. Oxford: Clarendon Press, 1949.

Hamilton, Edith. *Mythology.* Boston: Little, Brown and Company, 1942.

Indexes to Periodicals (Magazines, Bulletins, Newspapers). Indexes to periodicals are usually shelved in the reference room of the library.

When you wish to find something published in a periodical, you need to know two things: (a) Does the library subscribe to that periodical? (b) In what issue was the article published? The answer to the first question is on a card, found in either the general catalogue or an additional special card file kept in the reference room. For an answer to the second question you must look into a periodical index.

Bulletins are listed in most indexes. In compiling your bibliography you must remember that a bulletin is treated as a periodical if it is published at regular intervals, and as a book if it is a separate, single publication.

There is a special index for material published in newspapers.

Poole's Index to Periodical Literature, 1802–1881, and supplements from 1882 to 1906. To be able to use this index intelligently, you must known that: it is a subject index only; it has no author entries; all articles having a distinct subject are entered under that subject; articles having no subject, like poems and stories, are entered under the first word of the title; no date is given, only volume and page, but not inclusive paging; the periodicals indexed are principally of a general nature.

Readers' Guide to Periodical Literature, 1900 to date. The special features of this index are: the entries are under author, title, and subject; it gives volume, inclusive paging, date; it indicates illustrations, portraits, maps, etc.; it indexes book reviews up to 1904; it has a list of 597 books in the second and third cumulated volumes. Since for the average student this is the most important of the indexes, a sample of its entries is given below:[1]

> INSECT control. See **Insects, Injurious and beneficial—Control**
>
> INSECTICIDES
>
> **Insecticides tempt insects. Sci N L 62:204 S 27 '52**
>
> **Insects v. insecticides. R. L. Metcalf. il tab Sci Am 187:21-5 O '52**
>
> **It's news: plant bites bug. T. E. Stimson, jr. il Pop Mech 98:65-9+ S '52**
>
> **Separation and detection of the pyrethrin-type insecticides and their derivatives by reversed phase paper chromatography. F. P. W. Winteringham. bibliog Science 116:452 O 24 '52**
>
> **Systemics fight bollworm. Sci N L 62:130 Ag 30 '52**
>
> Injurious effects
>
> **Death in the Florida marshes. H. R. Mills il Audubon Mag 54:285-91 S '52**
>
> **Wildlife in a chemical world. J. P. Linduska il Audubon Mag 54:144-9+, 248-52 My-Jl '52**

International Index to Periodicals, 1907 to date. This is the best index to the scholarly journals. It also indexes some foreign language journals, especially German and French.

[1] Reproduced by courtesy of The H. W. Wilson Company.

Agricultural Index, 1916 to date. A subject index to periodicals, bulletins, books, and documents.

Art Index, 1929 to date. Author and subject index.

Dramatic Index, 1909 to 1950. An annual subject index to articles on drama, the theater, actors and actresses, playwrights, and plays.

Education Index, 1929 to date. Author and subject index.

Engineering Index, 1892–1906. *Engineering Index Annual,* 1906 to date. A classified subject index from 1906 to 1918, and an alphabetical index from 1919 to date.

Experiment Station Record, 1899 to date. A record and digest of current agricultural literature.

Index to Legal Periodicals, 1908 to date.

Industrial Arts Index, 1913 to date.

New York Times Index, 1913 to date. Although this is an index to *The New York Times,* it can be used as an index to any daily newspaper in the United States, since the same major news stories will probably be found in all daily papers on the same day they appear in the *Times.*

Public Affairs Information Service, 1915 to date. Indexes periodicals, books, documents, and pamphlets relating to political science, sociology, and economics; the best source of last-minute information on problems in these fields.

Quarterly Cumulative Index Medicus, 1927 to date. *Index Medicus,* 1879–1926. An author and subject index to 1,200 periodicals in the field of medicine, and to books and pamphlets.

The Library Paper. The library paper, variously known as the investigative theme, the term paper, or the research article, is an exposition which aims to present the results of careful and thorough investigation of some chosen or assigned subject. You will no doubt have occasion to write term papers based on laboratory experiments, or on questionnaires, or on your own critical reactions to something that you have read; papers of that sort are organized and written like any other expository paper. The information given here applies primarily to papers based on published material.

Let us summarize here the values or purposes of the library paper:

1. It will teach you how to use the library efficiently.
2. It will acquaint you with the methods of scholarly documentation, that is, the use of bibliography and footnotes.
3. It will increase your ability to take usable notes.

4. It will teach you how to organize and combine material from a number of different sources.

5. It will give you practice in presenting material in a way to interest your readers.

Choosing the Subject. As soon as the library paper is assigned, many students will ask themselves: "Now what subject do I know something about?" A major in English may want to investigate some author or literary movement. A student of forestry may want to write on conservation. A student of home economics may want to write on nutrition or antique furniture. In some ways this attitude is commendable; in other ways it is a mistake. A student should indeed be interested in the subject of his investigation, but his interest may as well bring the thrill of exploring a field entirely new to him.

His choice of field, however, must be limited by certain practical considerations. The following kinds of subjects are *not* satisfactory; they lead only to frustration and unhappiness:

1. Those that are too broad. Broad or general subjects are starting points. They must be limited or narrowed to usable dimensions.
2. Those from the writer's own experience or those based on interviews or experiments. Material of this sort, however, may be used to supplement information got from reading.
3. Those on which little has been published anywhere.
4. Those on which the local library has little material.
5. Those that are so technical that the writer cannot understand his material, much less present it intelligibly to others.
6. Events so recent that only newspaper comments are available.
7. Those that are too narrow or too trivial for a paper of the suggested length.

Deciding on the General Field. It is impossible to list all the general interests that will appeal to students everywhere. The lists given here are merely suggestive:

1. Something related to the course you are taking or expect to take in college, such as literature, history, medicine, and so on.

2. Something coming out of your experience, such as war service, life in a foreign country, the occupation of your parents. But remember that this is but the starting point for your library work.

3. Something related to your hobbies, your special talents, or your reading interests, such as photography, archaeology, exploration, sports, flying.

The advice of your instructor may be the last word on your choice of subject. If you have freedom of choice, however, or if you are urged to present several choices for his approval, the following list of general fields may help:

1. Archaeology
2. Art
3. Aviation
4. Biography
5. Dancing
6. Exploration
7. History
8. Language and literature
9. Medicine
10. Music
11. Nature
12. Photography
13. Psychology
14. Sciences
15. Sports
16. Warfare

Limiting the Subject. After you have indicated your general field of interest, you will, with the help of your instructor, select some part or aspect of it that can be effectively presented in the given space and time. If you are interested in literature, you may decide to write about Carl Sandburg. In a paper of about three thousand words you cannot tell everything about Sandburg. You may, however, choose to tell about his stories for children, or his glorification of industry, or his championship of the common man. Or if you are interested in the subject of industrial diseases, you might select some one disease, such as silicosis. In choosing your subject, always remember that you cannot narrow or limit a subject by excluding from it essential details. A research article should be interesting. Interest comes from the concrete details, the examples, or the imaginative touches that you can give your writing.

Now let us take two or three of these general fields and suggest in each one of them several topics narrowed down to what you could present adequately in the time and space at your disposal:

General subject: Archaeology

1. The Rosetta stone
2. Stonehenge
3. Site of ancient Troy
4. Easter Island statues
5. Cave paintings
6. A Mayan site in Mexico

General subject: Photography

1. Close-ups of insects
2. Close-ups of flowers
3. Use of special lenses
4. Microphotography
5. Hunting with a camera
6. Underwater photography

General subject: Sciences

1. Rockets to the moon
2. Artificial diamonds
3. Making weather maps
4. Animal luminescence
5. Sargasso Sea
6. Hibernating animals
7. The sense of smell
8. Splitting the atom
9. Radioactive isotopes
10. Operation of heat pumps
11. Migrating butterflies
12. The Dead Sea Scrolls

Before you make your final decision, it might be well for you to spend an hour or two browsing in the library. First look in the card catalogue. Check through some of the periodical indexes to find out the extent of the published material in your field. Notice in what types of periodicals your information is found, and make a preliminary check, either through the general card catalogue or through a special list of periodicals, to see which of the sources are available in your library. Look in the *Britannica* to see what that has on your topic. After you have done that, you are ready to begin collecting your bibliography.

It might be well to review here the steps ahead of you, so that you will proceed without too much loss of time in a project that can be full of frustrations:

1. Deciding on a general subject or field of investigation
2. Preliminary check of library and some general reading
3. Limiting the subject

4. Preparing a working bibliography
5. Reading and note-taking
6. Preparing an outline
7. Writing first draft of paper
8. Writing final draft with footnotes
9. Preparing final bibliography

Preparing a Working Bibliography. A bibliography is a list of books, articles, bulletins, or documents relating to a given subject or author.

When a student begins work on a library paper, it is wise for him to arm himself with a supply of 3 x 5 cards. On these cards he makes a list of references—one and *only one* to each card—that he hopes will be useful to him. He gets his references from the card catalogue, the general reference books, and the periodical indexes. Since there is always a great deal of wastage and frustration in this sort of project, he should take out insurance by getting many more references than he expects to use. As he proceeds with his reading, he will constantly upgrade his bibliography by adding new references and by discarding those that he finds useless.

Bibliographic Forms. It is unfortunate that bibliographic forms have not been standardized as completely as have the parts of an automobile. Recently, however, the Modern Language Association has moved in the direction of standardization in the general field of literature, language, and the social sciences. The result of the move has been the publication of the *MLA Style Sheet.*[1] Although this pamphlet concerns itself primarily with the preparation of "*learned articles* in humanistic fields," it has been "increasingly recommended to undergraduate and graduate students as helpful in the preparation of term papers and theses."[2] The forms of bibliographies and footnotes used here are based on the *MLA Style Sheet,* insofar as the recommendations of the MLA are applicable to undergraduate work.

There are other forms used for bibliographies and footnotes, how-

[1] Copies of the Style Sheet may be obtained from the Treasurer of the MLA, 6 Washington Square North, New York 3, New York. The price is fifty cents.

[2] *MLA Style Sheet,* supplement, p. 24.

ever, and your instructor may well recommend modifications of the MLA style. Use the form that your instructor recommends.

Every bibliographic reference consists of the three parts necessary for a complete identification of the printed work used, and these parts are generally arranged in this order:

1. *The author's name.* (Always write the last name first. If the article or pamphlet is unsigned, begin with the title.)
2. *The title.* (If it is a book, underline the title. If it is an article, essay, or any subdivision of a larger work, enclose in quotation marks.)
3. *The facts of publication:*
   a. For a book, give the place of publication, the name of the publisher, and the date.
   b. For a magazine article, give the magazine, the volume number, the date, and the pages.
   c. For a newspaper article, give the name of the newspaper, the date, the section, the page, and the column.

The sample bibliography cards illustrate the arrangement of items and the punctuation in various types of references as shown on page 168.

Bulletins are treated like books if they are occasional, and like magazine articles if they are issued periodically (at regular intervals).

Occasional bulletin: Parker, William Riley. *The MLA Style Sheet.* New York: MLA, 1951.

Periodical bulletin: "Amazing Gibberelic Acid." *Agricultural Research,* USDA, V (Sept. 1956), 12–13.

Gathering Material and Making Notes on Reading. It is assumed that before you begin to take notes you have collected a few fairly promising bibliography cards. Take your cards with you to the library. Look up a few of the most promising of your references. You might start with the encyclopedia articles. Your purpose is to make a preliminary exploration of your field. Read for

Article in an encyclopedia.
Initials of author identified in vol. I. Date of copyright from back of volume. Title of article in quotes. Underline title of reference book.

> Atkinson, Richard J. C.
> "Stonehenge." Encyclopaedia Britannica,
> 1958, XXI, 440-441.

Book by a single author.
Copy call number. Underline title of book.

> 818 W5818s
> White, E. B.
> The Second Tree from the Corner.
> New York: Harper & Brothers, 1954.

Book by two or more authors.
All names after the first are in normal order.

> QC173 B4
> Bethe, Hans Albrecht, and Philip Morrison.
> Elementary Nuclear Theory.
> New York: John Wiley & Sons, 1956.

Book by a number of authors or by a number of editors. Et allii (and others) abbreviated *et al.*

> PS92 L5
> Spiller, Robert E., et al., eds. 3 vols.
> Literary History of the United States.
> New York: The Macmillan Company, 1949.

Book edited.

> 811 M611x
> Millay, Edna St. Vincent.
> Collected Poems. Ed. by Norma Millay.
> New York: Harper & Brothers, 1956.

Signed magazine article.
STONEHENGE, England
New, exciting discoveries at mysterious Stonehenge. J. Stern. il House & Gard 112: 52 S '57

> Stern, J.
> "New, exciting discoveries at mysterious Stonehenge."
> House and Garden, CXII (Sept. 1957), 52+.

Unsigned article.
STONEHENGE, England
Mystery in stone. il NY Times Mag p84 S 7 '58

> "Mystery in Stone."
> New York Times Magazine, Sept. 7, 1958, p. 84.

Newspaper article.
(From *New York Times Index* for 1958.) Neuberger, (Sen) Richard L.: Article in Defense of the Politician; illus, N2, VI, p 13

> Neuberger, Senator Richard L.
> "Article in Defense of the Politician."
> New York Times, Nov. 2, 1958, sec. VI, p. 13.

general information. While you are exploring, make a note of the most important topics that seem to be related to your particular project. These topics, properly arranged, will become your first rough outline. They will be the headings you will use on your note cards when you begin to take notes.

Use of Note Cards. When you go to the library you should have with you a generous supply of note cards. These may be either the 3 x 5 cards that you use for your bibliography or some slightly larger size, such as the 4 x 6. If you cannot obtain cards, you may cut notebook paper into slips approximately 4 x 5 in size. It is not good practice to copy your notes into your notebook.

The Preliminary Outline. After your preliminary exploration of your field you will be ready to construct a topical outline of your paper. This topical outline will be based partly on what you have learned about your subject and partly on what any intelligent and mature person would want to be told if he were reading an article about your subject. Do not underestimate this second source of your preliminary outline. A writer must always keep his reader in mind. It is a mistake to assume that anything that is there—like a mountain to climb—must become a part of your paper.

As you read more extensively and take notes, you will wish to modify your outline, to drop unsatisfactory topics and to add new ones. The "preliminary outline" is just that—preliminary or experimental. But it will give you a necessary guide for your note-taking.

Methods of Identifying Notes. One system of identifying notes —an indispensable precaution if you are to avoid utter confusion later on—is to write at the top of the card the heading or topic which tells where the note fits into the outline and at the bottom of the card an abbreviated reference to identify the source of the note. This may consist of the author's last name, an abbreviated title, and the exact page reference. See the sample note cards on pages 171–172.

The second method—a very simple one—is to number all of your bibliography cards, and, instead of the reference at the bottom of the note card, to write the number of the bibliography card with the exact page reference.

But be sure to use the method that is recommended by your instructor.

The Form of Notes: Sample note cards are given on pages 171–172, but before you study them, you should review the following well-defined principles of note-taking:

1. Most of your notes will be in the form of a condensed summary. Get what is essential and get it accurately, but do not waste words. In order to avoid any chance of unconscious plagiarism, try to paraphrase what you read; that is, try to *use your own words,* not the words of your source.
2. If you wish to quote the exact words of the author, copy your material in the form of a direct quotation and put quotation marks around it.
3. Let your first unbreakable rule be "One topic to a card." Do not include in your notes on the same card material relating to two or more topics. You may have as many cards as you wish relating to the same topic, but you must label each card and give the exact source of your notes on each card.
4. Let your notes be so accurate and so complete that they will make sense to you when they become cold.
5. Use headings or topics which represent actual divisions of your outline, as closely as it is possible for you to anticipate the outline you will use. Avoid the unnecessary and confusing multiplication of topics and subtopics.
6. And, finally, remember that every note card must have three pieces of information:
   a. The exact source of your material.
   b. The heading or topic which shows where your information belongs.
   c. The information itself.

Reading and Skimming. Your first attempts to take notes on your reading may result in a few scattered entries and much wasted time. But you will soon discover that your English composition course has taught you more than merely how to write a few themes. You will begin to realize that at least half its value lies in what it has taught you about reading. You have been taught to organize themes so that their contents may be comprehended by your reader easily, quickly, without confusion, without wasted effort. Those who write books, chapters, essays, or articles employ the same principles of writing that you have learned—so that *you* may get the information you want, easily, quickly, without confusion, without wasted effort. In a book you examine first the table of contents, the index, the chapter headings, and the topics of the minor divisions. In an essay or article you look for a formal statement of plan or purpose at the beginning of the selection. Then you glance through the essay, reading a topic sentence here, another one there, until you come to what you want. This process is called "skimming."

Evaluating Your Sources. You will also learn to use signs indicating the value of your source. Look at the date of publication to see if it contains information recent enough for your purpose. In some fields, such as chemistry and medicine, information even a few months old may be highly misleading or absolutely worthless. Investigate the author, too. Is he an authority in his field? What is his reputation for scholarship or for honesty? If you are examining an article in a magazine, let the reputation of the magazine help you to determine the reliability of your author. Above all, beware of the mistake so often made by too many people—the mistake of assuming that anything in print is necessarily true.

Sample Note Cards. If you follow the instructions on pages 169–170, you will have no trouble in taking usable notes. These are summaries. No sample card is necessary to illustrate a direct quotation.

> <u>Origins of Name</u>
> The terminology of railroading was used extensively. The name of "president" was given to two of the early leaders, Levi Coffin and Robert Purvis. The routes of escape were "lines." The fleeing slaves were known as "freight" or "packages," and the places where they stopped to hide or to get help were "stations."
> <u>Britannica</u>, 1958, <u>XXII</u>, 681-682

> Attitudes in South
> Example: An incident which happened in South
> a year before Fugitive Slave Law was passed.
> Richard Dillingham, a Quaker, was arrested
> in Nashville, Tenn. with three stolen slaves.
> In court he pleaded humanitarian reasons.
> His attitude praised by *Nashville Daily*
> *Gazette*, Apr. 13, 1849. His penalty could have
> been death. Court gave him minimum -
> three years in prison. Dillingham avowed
> his gratitude for court's leniency.
> Macy, *Antislavery Crusade*, p. 122

The Final Steps: Writing the Paper. If your mental processes are like ours—that includes college professors as well as college students—you worked up your outline gradually as you collected notes. The whole process has been one of synthesis, of gradual putting together, which of course includes throwing away unusable material as well as filling in unexpected gaps. By the time you are ready to write, you have a pretty good idea of the limits or the extent of your paper. You have worked out your approach to your subject and perhaps to your reader. It may be that you have even thought of an interesting beginning. So you take your note cards and your outline, and on the table in front of you you spread out the note cards for your first section. You read them over to freshen in your mind the sequence or flow of thought—and then you are on your own.

As you write, whenever you use borrowed material, put the reference in parentheses in the right place in the text. You will copy your footnotes at the bottom of each page as you prepare the final draft of your paper. If you can prepare a finished paper without a first draft, without changes and revisions, without false starts or brilliant ideas that blinked out and had to be replaced, you are just too good for this course.

The Final Outline. For most of us, the final outline is the one we hand in and not the one we write the paper from. In other words, the outline is usually in a state of flux until the paper itself is finished. It is subject to change until the last moment. If something that looked good to you at first now seems to be out of place, throw it out and improve the outline. The outline is your blueprint, a simplified diagram of your paper, a help to you and to your reader, but it is no help to anyone if it forces you to construct something that at the last moment you feel is wrong. Change it if it needs changing.

For the approved form of the outline, go back to the section on planning and writing a paper, Chapter 4.

Footnotes: Where Needed. Whether in a college term paper or in a scholarly research article, footnotes are required for two purposes:

1. To acknowledge and identify every direct quotation. Quoted material should always be quoted exactly word for word and enclosed in quotation marks. The only exception to this rule is that no footnotes are used with familiar sayings or proverbs which everyone knows to be quoted.
2. To acknowledge and identify all material, all information that has been used in the paper or thesis in paraphrased, reworded, or summarized form. Of course, facts of general knowledge need not be credited to any one source.

It is only honest and decent to give proper credit for borrowed material. Failure to do so is plagiarism, which is not looked upon with favor in schools and colleges, or among writers.

In professional work a footnote may also be used to define a term used in the text, to give additional information that does not fit into the text, and to explain in detail what has merely been referred to in the text.

Numbering and Spacing Footnotes. To indicate to the reader that a footnote is being used, place an Arabic numeral immediately *after* and a little above the line of the material referred to. Do not put a period after the number, either in the text or with the footnote at the bottom of the page. Place the same number *before* and a little above the line of the note at the bottom of the page.[1]

[1] *The MLA Style Sheet*, p. 12.

Footnotes should be numbered consecutively, starting from 1, in a paper intended for publication; in a typed or handwritten paper, however, it is often required that they be numbered beginning with 1 on each page. You should use the style that your instructor recommends.

The Form of Footnotes. The first time that you use a footnote to refer to any source, you should give the same information given in the bibliographic entry, plus the exact page from which your material is taken: the author's name (but in the natural order, *not* with the last name first), the title of the work, the facts of publication, and the exact page reference. Later references to the same source are abbreviated. If only one work by the same author is used, the author's name with the page reference is enough. If more than one work by the same author is used in the footnotes, the author's name and a shortened form of the title (with exact page reference, of course) will suffice. In footnoting, clearness and brevity are more important than any set forms.

The forms illustrated here are those recommended by the *MLA Style Sheet*. If you use another form, you must use that form for both bibliography and footnotes. Use the one that your instructor specifies.

Bibliographic entry:

Van Doren, Carl. *The Great Rehearsal.* New York: Viking Press, 1948.

Footnote, first use:

[1] Carl Van Doren, *The Great Rehearsal* (New York: Viking Press, 1948), p. 162.

Footnote, later uses:

[2] Van Doren, p. 177.

The *MLA Style Sheet*, with commendable good sense, discourages the use of such abbreviations as *ibid*, *op. cit.*, and *loc. cit.* In the "old days" these and many other Latin abbreviations were considered the marks of very learned scholarship. It was considered proper to have footnotes pullulate on every page. One common jest—not too funny at that—of the graduate schools was that an article was not scholarly unless the footnotes took up more space on the page than the text.

Footnote, for a book with two or more authors:

[3] Hans Albrecht Bethe and Philip Morrison, *Elementary Nuclear Theory* (New York: Wiley, 1956), p. 32.

For an edited book:

[4] Emily Dickinson, *Bolts of Melody*, ed. Mabel Loomis Todd and Millicent Todd Bingham (New York: Harper, 1945), p. 207.

For a translated work of two or more volumes:

[5] H. A. Taine, *History of English Literature*, trans. H. Van Laun (New York, 1889), IV, 296.

For an article in a collection of articles:

[6] W. A. Shaw, "The Literature of Dissent," *Cambridge History of English Literature* (New York: Macmillan, 1917), X, 422.

For an article in an encyclopedia:

[7] Richard J. C. Atkinson, "Stonehenge," *Encyclopaedia Britannica* (1958), XXI, 440.

For a signed magazine article:

[8] J. Stern, "New, Exciting Discoveries at Mysterious Stonehenge," *House and Garden,* CXII (Sept. 1957), 52.

For an unsigned magazine article:

[9] "Better a Free World," *Newsweek,* XXXVII (March 19, 1951), 60.

For a signed newspaper article:

[10] Sen. Richard L. Neuberger, "Article in Defense of the Politician," *New York Times,* Nov. 2, 1958, sec. VI, p. 13.

For an unsigned newspaper article, simply begin with the title. A bulletin published as a separate or occasional publication is treated like a book; one issued periodically or as part of a regular series is treated like a magazine article.

Abbreviations in Footnotes. Although the number of abbreviations used in research papers at the graduate-school level is large—and often confusing to the lay reader—only a few are of immediate concern here:

anon.	anonymous
c., ca.	*circa* "about"
cf.	*confer* "compare"
ch., chap.	chapter
chs., chaps.	chapters
col., cols.	column, columns
ed.	edited, edition
e.g.	*exempli gratia* [eg-zem'plī grā'shi-a] "for example"
et al.	*et alii* [et ā'li-ī] "and others"
f., ff.	and the following
ibid.	*ibidem* [i-bī'dem] "in the same place" (It refers to the note immediately preceding. The *MLA Style Sheet* recommends either the author's name or an abbreviated title as being unambiguous and almost as brief.)
i.e.	*id est* "that is"
l., ll.	line, lines
loc. cit.	*loco citato* [loco si-tā'to] "in the place cited" (It refers to the same passage cited in a recent note. It is used with the author's name but is not followed by a page number.)
op. cit.	*opere citato* [ŏp'ĕ-rē sī-tā'tō] "in the work cited" (The *MLA Style Sheet* calls this "the most abused of scholarly abbreviations," and recommends instead the use of the author's name alone or with an abbreviated title.)

Roman Numerals. Because Roman numerals have a restricted use, students are sometimes unfamiliar with them. The following brief explanation may be helpful:

The key symbols are few in number: 1 = I, 5 = V, 10 = X, 50 = L, 100= C, 500 = D, 1,000 = M.

Other numbers are formed by adding or subtracting. The three main principles involved are: (a) A letter following one of equal or greater value is added value; (b) A letter preceding one of greater is subtracted value; (c) When a letter stands between two of greater value, it is subtracted from the last in the group and the remainder is added to the first. Try this explanation with the following examples:

Rule a					
2	II	20	XX	200	CC
3	III	30	XXX	300	CCC
6	VI	60	LX	600	DC
7	VII	70	LXX	700	DCC
Rule b					
4	IV	40	XL	400	CD
9	IX	90	XC	900	CM
Rule c					
19	XIX	59	LIX	1900	MCM

Sample Outline and Library Paper. The following sample outlines and library paper are reproduced here, not as perfect models to imitate, but as examples of conscientious and competent work at the college freshman level:

[Title] THE UNDERGROUND RAILROAD

TOPIC OUTLINE

<u>Thesis sentence:</u> During the early years of our American nation, slaves in our southern states attempting to escape to Canada were assisted by an organized system known as the Underground Railroad.

I. Early history: the Quakers
    A. "Incorporation" in 1804 and growth
    B. Origin of name, 1832
    C. Mixed northern attitudes toward slavery
        1. Black laws in some northern states
        2. Antislavery Quaker groups in Ohio and Pennsylvania
II. Fugitive Slave Law of 1850
    A. Reaction in North
        1. Resistance in Chicago
        2. Sympathy with hardships suffered by fugitives
        3. Hostility to cruel slave-hunters

B. Reaction in South
1. Economic value of slaves to owners
2. Harsh treatment of slave smugglers
3. Some help for fugitives, especially among Negroes

III. Negro attitudes toward slavery
A. Early resignation
B. Contact with antislavery northerners
C. Religious influence

IV. The Railroad at its height
A. The Ohio record
B. Methods of travel
1. Night travel by land
2. By ship
3. By railroad
C. Some famous operators
1. Levi Coffin
2. Thomas Garrett
3. Invaders of the South
4. Negro operators: Harriet Tubman

[Title] THE UNDERGROUND RAILROAD

SENTENCE OUTLINE

I. The Quakers of Pennsylvania were the first white group to help escaped slaves.
A. Although there were people who would help escaping slaves at a far earlier time, it was not until 1804 that the Underground Railroad was "incorporated" at Columbia, Pennsylvania.
B. It did not receive its name until 1832.
C. During these early years there was much proslavery sentiment, even in the North.
1. A number of northern states passed "black laws."
2. The strong Quaker groups in Ohio and Pennsylvania who helped slaves were in a minority.

II. The crisis in the fugitive slave trade came in 1850, when the Fugitive Slave Law was passed by the United States Congress.
A. Many people in the North prided themselves more upon its breach than its observance.
1. The Chicago City Council condemned the law and refused to let the Chicago policemen enforce it.
2. The escaping slaves aroused much north-

ern sympathy, even though their poor physical condition was not typical.
3. The barbarous and vulgar slave-hunters further aroused northern hostility toward the law.

B. In the South, most people were proslavery and supported the law.
1. The slaves involved a very sizable financial investment for their owners.
2. There was consequently much harshness against anyone who aided fugitive slaves.
3. Nevertheless there was some sympathy with the antislavery crusade even in the South, especially of course among the Negroes themselves.

III. The feelings of the slaves themselves toward freedom were very important in the growth and success of the Underground Railroad.
A. At first, slavery seemed to the Negro the natural condition of the majority of men.
B. After contact with antislavery Northerners, however, the Negroes became determinedly antislavery.
C. Their deep religious convictions supported this belief in freedom.

IV. The Underground Railroad enjoyed its greatest development during the 1840's in Ohio and Pennsylvania, though other routes to Canada were also used.
A. Judging from the records of one Ohio station, the total number of fugitives can be set at between 40,000 and 80,000.
B. In different parts of the country the fugitives traveled by different methods.
1. They usually traveled overland by night and were concealed at the homes of operators during the day.
2. Along the Atlantic coast, they were hidden in ships.
3. Sometimes railroads were used.

C. Most of the people who helped the slaves during this period did not encourage them to escape from their masters, but helped them when the slaves came to their doors for assistance.
1. Levi Coffin was one of the most famous of these people.

2. Thomas Garrett, another Quaker, lost his fortune helping the fugitives.
3. A very few men were foolhardy enough to invade the South in an effort to free the slaves.
4. The real heroes on the Underground Railroad were the Negroes, such as Harriet Tubman.

THE UNDERGROUND RAILROAD*

By George R. Powers

Ever since slavery was introduced into the ancient world, there have always been slaves who, in search of freedom, have attempted to escape from their masters. During the early years of our American nation, many slaves in our southern states attempted to escape. With no place in particular to go, most of these slaves merely wandered aimlessly about or were captured before they were out of sight of their homes. Before long, however, they learned that in the wilds of Florida they could live like free men.[1] But, although they enjoyed almost complete freedom in Florida, they realized that their masters could take them back if they were found. This unstable existence caused them to look for a land where they could enjoy complete freedom and safety. Before too many years passed, they learned that they could have complete security in Canada. In order to reach Canada, however, they needed help. Before long, they learned that the Quakers and other northern abolitionists were willing to aid them in their flight from their masters. Although the slaves were helped on an entirely individual basis in the early years, this help was later organized into the system called the Underground Railroad.

Although the early history of the Underground Railroad is rather vague, most authorities agree that the Quakers of Pennsylvania were the first white group to help escaped slaves. It is uncertain when the Quakers first started aiding the

[1] Jesse Macy, The Anti Slavery Crusade (New Haven: Yale University Press, 1919), p. 112.

* From The Green Caldron: A Magazine of Freshman Writing, published at the University of Illinois. Reprinted by permission.

fugitives, but it is known that they were actively rendering aid during George Washington's lifetime. According to Washington's correspondence, it is clear that he was not sympathetic with the beliefs of the Quakers. Once when speaking of some escaped slaves, he said, "a society of Quakers formed for such purposes have attempted to liberate them." At another time, when speaking of one of his own escaped slaves, he said:

> The Gentleman in whose care I sent him has promised every endeavor to apprehend him; but it is not easy to do this, when there are numbers who would rather facilitate the escape of slaves than apprehend them when run away.[2]

Although there were people who would help escaping slaves at a far earlier time, it was not until 1804 that the Underground Railroad was "incorporated" at Columbia, Pennsylvania.[3] Several incidents in which fugitive slaves were mistreated by their masters so greatly aroused the anger of these Pennsylvanians that they began to help the fugitives on a large-scale basis. After this beginning at Columbia, the Underground Railroad spread rapidly throughout the northern states. As early as 1816, the Underground Railroad was firmly entrenched in Pennsylvania and Ohio.[4] Shortly after it had been established in Ohio, "lines" were laid in Michigan and Indiana and were soon carrying a large share of the fugitive-slave traffic. Because of the beliefs of Illinois' early settlers, the Underground Railroad did not become active in Illinois until 1838 or 1839. By that time, routes for the escaping fugitives were already in operation in Iowa and the New England states.[5]

Even though the Underground Railroad was very active by 1830, it did not receive its name until it was named by a disappointed slaveholder in

[2] Henrietta Buckmaster, Let My People Go (New York: Harper and Brothers, 1941), p. 19.

[3] Ibid., pp. 23-24.

[4] Wilbur Henry Siebert, "The Underground Railroad for the Liberation of Fugitive Slaves," American Historical Association Annual Report, 1895 (1896), p. 396.

[5] Ibid., p. 397.

1832. This owner was right behind his escaping slave when they reached the bank of the Ohio River. The master watched the slave swim the river and then crossed by boat. However, when he reached the other side, the slave, who had been helped by a group of Ohio Quakers, had mysteriously disappeared. Later, when asked what had happened, the bewildered owner answered, "He must have gone on an underground road." This name spread rapidly among the operators of the system, and before long they were calling themselves names such as "conductors," "stationmasters," "brakemen," and "firemen." Their houses became known as "depots" and "stations."[6] Two of their early leaders, Levi Coffin and Robert Purvis, were called "President." Those who escaped were called "packages" or "freight" and traveled on routes that were known as "lines."[7]

The personal feelings and beliefs of the people involved determined whether the Underground Railroad would be a success in any given region. By merely looking at the Mason and Dixon line, one might think that everyone north of the line would be antislavery while everyone south of the line would be proslavery. This was true for the most part, but there were some exceptions. The group that was most notable in this respect was the transplanted southerners who lived in southern Illinois and Indiana. These men would do everything in their power to assist in the capture of an escaped slave. On the other hand, it was quite often possible to find people in the South who were willing to help the fugitives.

There were some areas in the northern states, such as southern Illinois, where the people were very hostile toward the fugitives. Surprising as it may seem, these people were a majority in several northern states. As a result of this dislike for the Negroes, a number of states passed "black laws."[8] In fact, these "black laws" were

[6] Buckmaster, p. 59.

[7] "Underground Railroad," Encyclopaedia Britannica (1949), XXII, 681.

[8] James Harris Fairchild, "The Underground Railroad," Western Reserve Historical Society Tracts, Tract No. 87 (Cleveland: Leader Printing Co., 1895) p. 98.

so strict that one Massachusetts abolitionist wanted to know if the Illinois Black Code had been drawn up by men from Alabama.[9] This question really was not as nonsensical as it sounds, for many of the early Illinois settlers did come from southern states and were definitely in favor of slavery.[10]

Although they were in a minority, there were groups of people in the northern states who helped the fugitives. This minority was at its strongest in Ohio and Pennsylvania. In fact, it was through Ohio that the largest number of the fugitives passed on their way to Canada.[11] In northern Ohio the time came when the Underground Railroad was no longer an underground movement, but an affair in which the people openly violated the fugitive slave laws. Because of the feeling of the people, it was in northern Ohio that the slave-hunter met the most trouble. There he had to move as carefully and cautiously as the slave he was trailing in order that the local townsmen would not discover his motive. If he was lucky to capture the slave whom the people so carefully protected, he was forced to go to the courthouse and show his papers. In cases where the people could find any flaw in his papers, the slave was released.[12]

As far as the northerners were concerned, the crisis in the fugitive slave trade came in 1850, when the Fugitive Slave Law was passed by the United States Congress. The general provisions of the law and the reactions it created in the minds of the people of the northern states were most succinctly stated by A. J. Baughman when he said:

> The fugitive slave law not only required people to assist in returning slaves to their masters, but made it a penal offense to refuse to do so, which made the law so

[9] O. L. Schmidt, "Illinois Underground Railway," Illinois State Historical Society Journal, 18 (1925), 705.

[10] Ibid.

[11] Booker T. Washington, The Story of the Negro (New York: Doubleday, Page and Company, 1909), I, 226.

[12] Fairchild, p. 106.

> unpopular in the North that many people prided themselves more upon its breach than its observance.[13]

The way the northerners met the challenge of the Fugitive Slave Law is best shown by the reactions of the Puritans in northern Illinois. These people, unlike those of southern Illinois, were willing to aid the escaping fugitives.[14] When the Fugitive Slave Law was passed, the Chicago City Council condemned the law and refused to let the Chicago policemen enforce it.[15] To back up their condemnation of the law, the people of Chicago became more defiant than ever towards the slave-hunters, and were known to tar and feather any slave-hunters they caught in the territory.[16]

To be truthful, it must be admitted that the view of slavery which the people of the North received was not an entirely true one. This misconception about the nature of slavery was caused, for the most part, by the personal appearance of the slaves when they reached the northern states. These slaves, after having traveled long distances, were in very poor physical condition when they came to the operators of the Underground Railroad. These escaping slaves also brought many tales of hardship with them, which, although possibly true, were not typical of a slave's life.

In many ways, the slave-hunters were even more miserable beings than the slaves they were pursuing. These men, whose job it was to track down the fugitives, were of the lowest southern class.[17] They were "men whose natural utensils were the bull-whip, the pistol, and the Bowie knife; and their language and bearing corresponded with these weapons."[18] Because of the actions of the slave-hunters, it has been said:

> The frustration of the purposes of those in pursuit of fugitives and the threats

[13] A. J. Baughman, "The Underground Railroad," _Ohio Archaeological and Historical Quarterly_, 15, (1906), 189.

[14] Schmidt, p. 706.

[15] _Ibid._, p. 710.

[16] _Ibid._, p. 713.

[17] Fairchild, p. 94.

[18] _Ibid._, p. 95.

> and demonstrations made by them while seeking their lost property, created distrust and hatred on both sides.[19]

Considering all these facts, it is not surprising that the northerners felt that they were justified in helping the fugitives escape.

The views of the southerners on the question of slavery were also important. Although there were notable exceptions, most southerners were pro-slavery simply because of what the slaves were worth to them. The slaves of the period were to the masters as horses were to the farmers of fifty years ago. A slave was worth five hundred to one thousand dollars. Considering this sizable investment, it is no wonder that the owner would follow the fugitive for months or even years.[20]

With this monetary value as their main reason, the southerners were, as a class, very harsh with anyone who aided fugitive slaves. This strictness is best shown by what happened when one young man attempted to smuggle some slaves out of Missouri. One day this man, who lived in Illinois, was approached by a Negro who asked him to cross the Mississippi River that evening and help some fugitive slaves escape. Upon crossing the river that evening, he realized too late that he had fallen into a trap. He was met on the shore by an angry group of Missourians and was carried off to jail in a hurry. Although there was no real evidence against him, he was tried and convicted on three counts "for stealing slaves, for attempting to steal them, and for intending to attempt to steal them." That man spent five years in the Missouri penitentiary for a crime that he never committed.[21]

But not all southerners were as harsh with those who helped the slaves as the Missourians. As in the other case, this can be best shown by citing a law case. When Richard Dillingham was captured in Nashville, Tennessee, with a fugitive slave, he, like everyone else, expected to receive the death penalty. The southern jury showed pity and agreement with his purpose and only sent him to the state penitentiary for three years.[22]

[19] Siebert, p. 402.
[20] Fairchild, p. 91.
[21] Ibid., p. 103.
[22] Macy, p. 122.

Besides those sympathetic with the antislavery crusade, such as the members of the jury, there were others in the South who were actively engaged in helping the fugitives escape. Some of these people had come from northern states and had brought northern ideas with them. Most surprising of all, however, is the fact that even members of slaveholding families were known to help the fugitives.[23] Although these southern whites helped a great deal on the Underground Railroad, the main operators in the South were the colored people. They could often smuggle members of their own race to the north and to freedom more easily than could the white agents, for a white man seen traveling with a Negro would arouse suspicion.

A knowledge of the beliefs and ideas of the slaves helps one to understand the growth and success of the Underground Railroad. The feelings of the slaves were very important, for if the slaves had not wanted freedom, the Underground Railroad would never have come into existence. These beliefs of the Negro were best stated by Booker T. Washington, who wrote:

> Slavery . . . appeared to the native African . . . to be the natural condition of the majority of men. It was only after the African slaves learned the language of their masters and possessed themselves to some extent of their masters' ideas that they began to conceive that the natural condition of man was not slavery but freedom.
>
> When the fugitive slaves came in contact with the antislavery people of the North they made the acquaintance for the first time of a people who hated slavery in a way and with an intensity which few of them had ever felt or known. They learned . . . to believe in freedom for its own sake. They became, as a result, the most determined of antislavery people, and many of them devoted their lives most unselfishly to securing the freedom of other members of their race.[24]

Most of the people of this period were very religious and considered the Bible to be the final

[23] Ibid., p. 123.

[24] Washington, I, 231 232.

authority in any argument. Instead of going to the Constitution to decide the slavery question, most of the people turned to the Bible. In the northern states, many law cases involving slaves were won because of the Mosaic law which said, "Thou shalt not deliver unto his master the servant which is escaped unto thee."[25] Of course, the southerners could also support their claim that the slaves should be returned by appealing to the Bible and quoting the passage where Paul sent the slave, Onesimus, back to his master.[26]

Since the personal feelings of the people in any region determined whether the Underground Railroad would be a success, it was most active in those parts of the country which were strongly antislavery. As it might be guessed, the Underground Railroad had its greatest development in Ohio and Pennsylvania. The records of the Alum Creek settlement of Quakers in Delaware County, Ohio, during 1844 show that large numbers of fugitives passed through Ohio.[27] Over a period of five months, forty-seven Negro fugitives stopped at that one station on their way to Canada. If this number at one station is considered representative, it appears evident that an estimate setting the total number of fugitives at between 40,000 and 80,000 is very likely true.[28] On the other hand, few routes crossed southern Illinois and other areas hostile to the Negroes.

Because of the illegal nature of the Underground Railroad, the fugitives usually had to travel at night. They were hidden at the homes of the operators during the day and were smuggled on to the next station under cover of darkness. During the day the fugitives were hidden in secret rooms, hollow haystacks, and dense thickets.[29] Occasionally, in order to throw the slave-hunters off the track, the fugitives were moved by wagon during the day.[30]

In different parts of the country the fugitives traveled by different methods. Along the Atlantic

[25] Fairchild, p. 97.
[26] Schmidt, p. 704.
[27] Siebert, p. 400.
[28] Ibid., p. 399.
[29] Schmidt, p. 708.
[30] Fairchild, p. 104.

coast, the slaves were concealed in ships and in this way were smuggled into the free northern states. Once they arrived in the free states, they traveled on to Canada by foot, steamboat, or even railroad.[31] Although Canada was still the goal, travel through the Midwest was somewhat different from that in the East. Almost all of the travel in the Midwest was done at night and on foot. Sometimes, however, railroads were used for transporting the slaves. The Illinois Central carried some of the fugitives who passed through this area on their way to Canada.[32]

No account of the Underground Railroad would be entirely complete without some information about the personalities of the operators. Most of the men who helped the slaves would not encourage them to escape from their masters. They would help only when the slaves came to their doors to plead for help.[33] Levi Coffin, the president of the Underground Railroad, was one of the most famous of these people. For thirty-three years, from his home in Cincinnati, Ohio, he helped about one hundred fugitives a year to escape. Because of his shrewdness, he was able to save himself from prosecution and fines.[34] However, another Quaker, Thomas Garrett, was not quite so lucky as Coffin. After many lawsuits had swept away his ample fortune, Garrett still believed in his convictions strongly enough to say, "Friend, I have not a dollar of property in the world, but if thee knows a fugitive that needs a breakfast this morning, send him to me."[35]

There were even some men, although very few, foolhardy enough to invade the South in an effort to free the slaves. While some succeeded for awhile in these attempts, they were usually caught sooner or later. In an effort to free the wife of Peter Still, a Negro abolitionist, Seth Concklin, a Shaker abolitionist, was killed.[36] After Concklin had brought a group of slaves up the Tennessee, Mississippi, and Wabash Rivers, he

[31] Macy, p. 123.
[32] Siebert, p. 298.
[33] Fairchild, p. 99.
[34] Ibid., pp. 104 105.
[35] Ibid., p. 105.
[36] Washington, I, 221.

was captured at Vincennes. A little later he was killed while trying to escape. Another abolitionist, Calvin Fairbanks, made a practice of going into the South and smuggling out slaves.[37] Although he could claim that no fugitive in his care was ever captured, he was taken in 1844 and was forced to spend many years in jail. What happened to these men is representative of the fate of many who invaded the South.

Although most of the operators of the Underground Railroad were white, the real leaders and heroes were the Negroes. Perhaps the most famous of the colored operators was Harriet Tubman. She helped so many slaves escape that her people began to call her "Moses." After she herself had escaped from slavery in 1849, she returned many times to the South and helped bring out others. It has been said that she helped over three hundred slaves escape.[38] She, like Calvin Fairbanks, was able to say that no fugitive under her care was ever recaptured. Then, during the Civil War, she worked for the Union Army's secret service.[39] It was Negroes like her who really made the Underground Railroad a success. For they, in doing this work, set themselves up as examples for others of their race and proved that they really wanted freedom.

[37] Buckmaster, p. 123.
[38] Washington, I, 222.
[39] Ibid., p. 223.

BIBLIOGRAPHY

Baughman, A. J. "The Underground Railway." Ohio Archaeological and Historical Quarterly, XV (1906), 189-191.

Buckmaster, Henrietta. Let My People Go. New York: Harper and Brothers, 1941.

Coffin, Levi. Reminiscenses of Levi Coffin, the Reputed President of the Underground Railroad. Cincinnati: Western Tract Society, 1876.

Fairchild, James Harris. "The Underground Railroad." Western Reserve Historical Society Tracts, Tract No. 87. Cleveland: Leader Printing Company, 1895.

Macy, Jesse. The Anti-Slavery Crusade. New Haven: Yale University Press, 1919.

Schmidt, O. L. "Illinois Underground Railroad." Illinois State Historical Society Journal, 18 (1925), 703-717.

Siebert, Wilbur Henry. The Underground Railroad from Slavery to Freedom. New York: The Macmillan Company, 1898.

____________. "A Quaker Section of the Underground Railroad in Northern Ohio." Ohio Archaeological and Historical Quarterly, XXXIX (1930), 479-502.

____________. "The Underground Railroad for the Liberation of Fugitive Slaves." American Historical Association Annual Report, 1895 (1896), 393-402.

Smedley, Robert C. History of the Underground Railroad in Chester and Neighboring Counties of Pennsylvania. Lancaster, Pa., 1883.

Still, William. The Underground Railroad. Philadelphia: People's Publishing Company, 1879.

"Underground Railroad." Encyclopaedia Britannica (1958), XXII, 681-682.

Washington, Booker T. The Story of the Negro. New York: Doubleday, Page and Company, 1909.

Chapter 6

LETTER WRITING

A letter is, in a sense, a theme, governed by the same laws of writing that govern every other kind of composition. It must be clear, well organized, coherent. It must be correct in spelling, grammar, and punctuation. And it should be interesting. Interest in a letter, as in other forms of composition, can be created by concreteness, by originality, by vitality. But a letter is also governed by certain other laws, or conventions, of usage, which the letter writer cannot ignore without serious penalty. Since everyone has occasion to write letters—personal letters, business letters, informal or formal social notes—the college student should know the correct usage in the different types of letters.

These are the parts of a letter:

1. The heading
2. The inside address
3. The salutation or greeting
4. The body of the letter
5. The complimentary close
6. The signature

For each of these parts usage has prescribed certain set forms. These forms must not be ignored or altered, especially in business letters. Conformity, not originality, is a virtue here.

The Heading. The parts of a heading, written in the following order, are the street address, the name of city or town, the name of the state, the date. A letterhead takes the place of a typed address. On paper with letterheads, the writer types the date, either directly under the letterhead or flush with the right-hand margin of the letter.

[*Letterhead*]

March 20, 1960 (or) March 20, 1960

On paper that does not have a letterhead, the writer types the heading at the right according to one of the following forms:

Block form with open punctuation; that is, the end punctuation is omitted.

327 East Walnut Street
Springdale, Minnesota
March 20, 1960

Indented form, with closed punctuation. End punctuation is usually omitted.

76 Belmont Street,
Canton, Iowa,
March 20, 1960

Whichever form he uses, the writer should be consistent throughout the letter—in the heading, the inside address, and in the address on the envelope.

The Inside Address. In a business letter the inside address is the address of the person written to. In a personal letter the inside address is usually omitted. It may, however, be written at the bottom of a personal letter, in the lower left-hand corner. The first line of the inside address should be flush with the left-hand margin of the letter. Either the block form or the indented form may be used.

Mr. H. G. Warren
Warren & Swazey, Builders
132 First Avenue
Ogden, Maine

Dear Mr. Warren:

(or)

Parr Oil Company
205 Monroe Street
Helena, Illinois

Gentlemen:

In a business letter it is always correct to use a personal title with the name of the person addressed. The use of a personal title is correct even when a business title follows the name. A business title should not precede the name. Correct personal titles are:

Mr., Mrs., Miss, Dr., Professor, Messrs. The business title may follow the name of the person addressed if the title is short, or it may be placed on the line below it if the title is long:

Mr. T. C. Howard, Secretary
Pueblo Rose Society

Dr. James Pendleton
Superintendent of Schools

Mr. William R. Jones
Personnel Manager

Mrs. Theodore Jackson
Secretary, Salem Women's Club

The Salutation or Greeting. The following forms are correct for business and professional letters:

Gentlemen:
Dear Sir:
My dear Sir:
Dear Mr. Jackson:

Ladies:
Dear Madam:
My dear Madam:
Dear Miss Blank:

In personal letters the range of greetings possible is unlimited, but somewhere between the inappropriately formal *Sirs, Madam, Gentlemen*, at one extreme, and the mushy *My own Lovey-Dovey* at the other, one might mention the following as usually appropriate:

Dear Jack,
My dear Chambers,

Dear Mr. Howard,
Dear Miss Brown,

For correct usage in addressing government officials and other dignitaries, see *Webster's New World Dictionary*, pp. 1717–1719, or the *American College Dictionary*, p. xxxiii.

A colon is used after the salutation in business letters; either a colon or a comma may be used in personal letters. A comma is considered less formal.

The Body of the Letter. The composition of business letters is a subject much too complex to be discussed here. A good letter obeys the principles of good writing. It should be clear, direct, coherent, dignified, and courteous. A student who can write a good class paper should be able to write a good business letter.

The following are useful guides to the various types of business letters:

Saunders, Alta Gwinn. *Effective Business English,* 3rd ed. New York: The Macmillan Company, 1949.

Smart, Walter K., and L. W. McKelvy. *Business Letters,* 3rd ed. New York: Harper and Brothers, 1950.

Taintor, Sarah Augusta, and Kate M. Monro. *The Secretary's Handbook,* 8th ed. New York: The Macmillan Company, 1958.

The Complimentary Close. Correct forms for business letters are:

Yours truly,
Yours very truly,
Very truly yours,
Respectfully yours,
Faithfully yours,
Sincerely yours,
Yours sincerely,
Cordially yours,

It is now considered bad taste to use a participial phrase in closing a letter, such as *Hoping for an early answer.* A comma is the usual punctuation after the complimentary close. Only the first letter of a complimentary close is capitalized. In ordinary formal business letters, *Yours truly* or *Yours very truly,* is the accepted form; in business letters between men who know each other well, *Yours sincerely* and *Cordially yours* are used.

The Signature. For the ordinary person it is correct to sign a business letter as he would sign a check. If possible, he should write his name legibly. Since a legible signature is impossible for many persons, it is desirable to type the name under the signature.

Some of the conventions which govern the form of a signature are:

1. Neither professional titles, such as *Professor, Dr., Rev.,* nor academic degrees, such as *Ph.D., LL.D., M.A.,* should be used with a signature.
2. An unmarried woman should not sign herself as Miss Laura Blank, but she may place *Miss* in parentheses before her name if she feels that it is necessary for proper identification.
3. A married woman or a widow signs her own name, not her married name. For example, *Diana Holoday Brown* is her own name; *Mrs.*

George Brown is her married name. She may place *Mrs.* in parentheses before her signature, or her married name in parentheses under it.

4. When a secretary signs her chief's name to a letter, she may add her own initials below the signature.

The following is an example of a typical business letter:

37 North Cove Road
Los Gatos, California
June 18, 1959

Acme Camera Shop
876 Fifth Street
Palo Alto, California

Gentlemen:

I am returning to you a lens which you sent me, on my order, on June 16. The lens is a 35-mm F 2.5 (wide angle) P. Angenieux Retrofocus, with a bayonet mount to fit the Exacta camera. The number of the lens is 463513.

You will notice by holding the lens against a bright light that there is a distinct scratch on the front element. As the lens is guaranteed to be free from imperfections, I am returning it to you for a replacement.

Will you kindly send me a new lens as soon as you can? I must have it by June 25, as I am leaving then on a camera trip to Utah.

You have my check for $120, dated June 12, in payment.

Yours very truly,

Martin H. Hanson

Martin H. Hanson

Letters of Application. One of the most difficult and probably most important letters that you will have to write is the letter of application. Of course it is impossible to say what will appeal to every employer, but certain general guides can be set up. It is true that usually you have to fill out a printed form. Well, so will five hundred others applying for the same job. It is the letter you write that will help you to stand out in this crowd.

A letter should be direct, sincere, and informative. It must not be vague and general; it must not grovel in undue modesty or boastfully promise what you cannot deliver.

A typical letter of application has the following components:

1. An introductory statement in which the writer states that he has heard of a possible vacancy
2. Personal data
3. Record of education
4. Record of experience
5. References
6. Request for an interview

Probably the most important section—to the writer—is the one in which he shows how his education or experience has a vital bearing on the job for which he is applying. This analysis is hard to write, but you must try it. Your job depends on it.

37 Twenty-third Street
Corvallis, Oregon
April 15, 1959

Mr. F. C. McVey
Personnel Officer
Baird & Summers, Contractors
35 Division Street
Salem, Oregon

Dear Mr. McVey:

Mr. James Ryan, one of the engineers on your staff, has informed me that you will need several truck drivers for your road construction jobs early in June. I wish to apply for a job as gravel truck driver.

I am 20 years old, six feet tall, and I weigh 182 pounds. I am unmarried.

Two years ago, when I was eighteen, I graduated from Central High School, where I took the college preparatory course with emphasis on mathematics and physics. I also played football in my junior and senior years.

When I was in high school I spent my weekends and vacations working for Bert's Texaco Station and Garage, where I learned a great deal about the operation, service, and maintenance of various types of trucks. Mr. Bert Jenkins will write you about my work there.

Since then I have worked at various jobs to earn money for my college education. I am now finishing my first year in the school of engineering at Oregon State College. After I graduated from high school I spent a year working for the Ochoco Ranch, near Knappa, Oregon, where I drove tractors, trucks, cultivators, and harvesters. Last winter I drove a bulldozer for Bruce & Stewart, clearing the old Camp Adair site near Corvallis. Then last summer I had a job with Pelican Builders of Klamath Falls, for whom I drove gravel trucks and cement mixers. I believe that my experience should qualify me for the job for which I am applying.

The following employers for whom I have worked have given me permission to use their names as references:

Mr. H. D. Winslow
Ochoco Ranch
Knappa, Oregon

Mr. Edwin Stewart
Bruce & Stewart
Corvallis, Oregon

Mr. Karl Swensen
Pelican Builders
Klamath Falls, Oregon

I should appreciate an opportunity to call at your office for an interview at any time that you designate. My telephone is Plaza 3-5948.

Yours very truly,

Henry Williamson

Henry Williamson

Invitations, Acceptances, Regrets. An informal invitation should be written in an easy, natural, and cordial manner. It should not be typed.

1520 East 34th Street
May the fifth

My dear Mrs. Fowler,
Will you and Mr. Fowler dine with us on Saturday, May the fourteenth, at seven o'clock? We shall probably drive out to the Oasis to dance afterwards. We shall be very glad if you are able to come.

Sincerely yours,
Beatrice W. Scott

Dear Mrs. Fowler,
Mr. Scott and I shall be greatly pleased if you and Mr. Fowler can come to an informal dinner at our apartment on Saturday, May the fourteenth, at seven o'clock. If you feel like dancing afterwards, we shall drive out to the Oasis for an hour or two.

Sincerely yours,
Beatrice W. Scott

1520 East 34th Street
May fifth

My dear Mrs. Scott,
Mr. Fowler and I are delighted to accept your very kind invitation to dine and dance with you on Saturday, May the fourteenth, at seven o'clock. We are looking forward to seeing you again.

Sincerely yours,
Marion Fowler

46 West Clinton Avenue
May sixth

My dear Mrs. Scott,
Mr. Fowler and I regret exceedingly that we are unable to accept your invitation for dinner on Saturday, May the fourteenth, as unfortunately we have another engagement for that evening.

Sincerely yours,
Marion Fowler

46 West Clinton Avenue
May sixth

Formal social notes are written in the third person. No abbreviations are used. Dates and hours are written in full. The following examples will serve for ordinary invitations, acceptances, and regrets. For correct forms in engraved invitations and announcements it is usually better to depend upon the stationer.

Mrs. Prentiss requests the pleasure of Miss Roxbury's company at dinner on Friday evening, May the thirteenth, at seven o'clock.
620 Monroe Street,
May the fifth.

Miss Roxbury accepts with pleasure the kind invitation of Mrs. Prentiss to dinner on Friday evening, May the thirteenth, at seven o'clock.
1224 Franklin Road,
May the sixth.

Miss Roxbury regrets that she is unable to accept the kind invitation of Mrs. Prentiss to dinner on Friday evening, May the thirteenth, at seven o'clock.
1224 Franklin Road,
May the sixth.

Faults to Avoid

1. Do not omit pronouns, prepositions, and articles where they are grammatically necessary. If your letter should begin with *I* or *we*, begin with *I* or *we*.

   Bad: Received your letter yesterday.
   Am writing to you in reply . . .
   Have not heard from you . . .

   Right: I received your letter yesterday.
   I am writing to you . . .
   I have not heard from you . . .

2. Do not close a letter with a sentence or a phrase introduced by a participle.

   Bad: Hoping to hear from you soon . . .
   Hoping for an early answer . . .
   Thanking you again for your past favors . . .
   Trusting to hear from you by return mail . . .

3. Do not write *yours*, *your favor*, or *your esteemed favor* for *letter*.

   Bad: In reply to yours of the 20th . . .
   Your esteemed favor at hand, and in reply . . .

4. Avoid certain trite and stilted expressions frequently used in business letters.

Bad: In reply would say . . .
Yours of the 10th inst. received . . .
And contents thereof noted . . .
Your valued favor . . .
And oblige, Yours truly . . .
Enclosed please find . . .

Exercises

Exercise 1. Write a letter to a friend who lives in your home community explaining to him the value of the course you are now taking in your college.

Exercise 2. Write a letter to your college newspaper in which you correct a wrong impression produced by a news story which has appeared in the paper. Make your letter courteous, dignified, and logical.

Exercise 3. Write a letter to your dean in which you request permission to take your final examinations several days before the scheduled period. Give your reason clearly and convincingly.

Exercise 4. As secretary of a student organization, write a letter to the members urging them to pay their dues.

Exercise 5. You plan to work at one of the national parks during the summer. Write a letter of application. Apply for some position that you could fill. Give adequate information about yourself and your qualifications.

Exercise 6. Write to a friend asking him to accompany you on a fishing and camping trip.

Exercise 7. Write to your hostess thanking her for the pleasant time you have had at her home. She is your roommate's mother.

Exercise 8. A man for whom you worked last summer owes you thirty dollars. Write him a letter that will induce him to pay what he owes you.

Part 2

A HANDBOOK OF WRITING AND REVISION

GRAMMAR AND USAGE

THE SENTENCE FRAGMENT

1. Fragmentary sentences are generally avoided in expository writing, in both formal and informal varieties of standard English.

A grammatically complete sentence is a pattern of communication in words that is based on a verb with its subject. That is the essential core of a complete sentence—at least one verb with its subject or subjects. Structurally it must be an independent unit, capable of standing alone. See "The Elements of the Simple Sentence," pages 39–40.

Now this means simply that dependent units, such as phrases, clauses, appositives, and other such groups of words, are not sentences and should not be written as sentences. When any one of these dependent units is written and punctuated as a sentence, it is called a *sentence fragment.*

Of course there are also nonconforming patterns in writing and speech—especially in informal speech—which we may call legitimate fragments, or non-sentences, or unconventional sentences, as we fancy. The exact naming is less important than your understanding of these patterns. They are discussed later in this section.

The ineffective sentence fragment, a result of ignorance or carelessness, is the affliction of only the first few papers written in a college composition course, because sentence sense is something that is easily and quickly mastered. It must be mastered quickly, moreover, if you are to progress to more vital matters related to good writing. If you still do not know what a sentence is, turn back to pages 39–52 and study the definitions, the examples, and the diagrams that you find there.

An ineffective sentence fragment may be revised by: (1) attaching the fragment to the sentence from which it was split off, (2) completing its form by adding the necessary words, (3) rewriting the passage. The following examples show some of the revisions that are possible:

Fragment:

After the war I returned to college. *Thinking, of course, that I would meet all my old friends there.*

Complete:

After the war I returned to college, thinking, of course, that I would meet all my old friends there. [Revise by joining the fragment to the rest of the sentence.]

Complete:

After the war I returned to college. I thought, of course, that I would meet all my old friends there. [Revise by changing the phrase into a sentence, supplying both subject and verb.]

Fragment:

The room was comfortable and clean but sparsely furnished. *No rugs. No curtains.*

Complete:

The room was comfortable and clean but sparsely furnished. There were no rugs or curtains. [Revise by incorporating the two fragments into a separate sentence.]

Fragment:

Wrecks do occur on this four-lane highway which runs for seventy miles without a curve. *Mainly because drivers fall asleep. Hypnotized by the monotony, probably.*

Complete:

Wrecks do occur on this four-lane highway which runs for seventy miles without a curve, probably because the drivers, hypnotized by monotony, fall asleep at the wheel. [Revise by rewriting and joining to the main part of the sentence.]

Fragments of various kinds, verbless and subjectless sentences, with or without understood additions that would make them complete grammatically, are commonly used in speech. In narrative writing they are necessary to reproduce dialogue naturally. They are also used for special stylistic effects by some writers. In some of the fragments either the subject or the predicate is understood; in others, no amount of ingenious interpretation will supply a missing subject or verb. We must accept them for what they are—language patterns correctly punctuated as sentences.

1. *The command.* (The typical pattern of the imperative sentence omits the subject.)

Open the door, Marjie. Come into the kitchen. Take off your wet coat and hang it near the radiator. Now sit down and tell me all about it.

2. *The question.*

Broke it, did he? How badly? Can't be repaired? Isn't yours? Whose, then? On approval from Tiffany's? How terrible.

3. *The exclamation.*

Well played, George. Not bad, not too bad. Oh, missed it this time. How awfully amusing.

4. *Bits of dialogue.*

"How old are you?" he asked.
"Sixteen. Why?"
"Look young for your age, don't you?" he said. "Any identification with you?"

5. *Special effects—the "pointing at" method of description.*

Ye Art Shoppe, Prop. Mrs. Mary Ellen Wilks, Christian Science Library open daily free. A touching fumble at beauty. A one-room shanty of boards recently covered with rough stucco. A show-window delicately rich in error: vases starting out to imitate tree-trunks but running off into blobs of gilt—an aluminum ash-tray labeled "Greetings from Gopher Prairie"—a Christian Science Magazine—a stamped sofa-cushion portraying a large ribbon tied to a small poppy, the correct skeins of embroidery-silk lying on the pillow.

—From *Main Street* by Sinclair Lewis. Copyright Harcourt, Brace & Co., 1920.

It will help you to write complete sentences if you know what the trouble spots are and what you should do about them. There are four main types of ineffective sentence fragments:

1a. A dependent clause should not be written as a complete sentence.

If you remember that a dependent clause usually begins with a subordinating conjunction, such as *because*, *although*, *when*, *as*, *if*, *as if*, you can guard against some types of fragments. Another thing to remember is that in this type of error the clause usually *follows* the main clause.

Fragment:

Then he faced me and repeated his request. *Although I had understood him well enough the first time.*

Complete:

Then he faced me and repeated his request, although I had understood him well enough the first time. [Join the fragment to the main clause that precedes it.]

Fragment:

Frowning mournfully, Belinda studied the explanations. *Which, by the way, were more confusing than the problem they tried to explain.*

Complete:

Frowning mournfully, Belinda studied the explanations, which, by the way, were more confusing than the problem they tried to explain. [Join the subordinate clause to the main clause.]

1b. A verbal or a prepositional phrase should not be written as a complete sentence.

Fragment:

The railroad made Virginia City a lumber center. *Its population leaping from three hundred to five thousand in three years.* [This is a participial phrase, of the special type called the absolute phrase. See page 44.]

Complete:

The railroad made Virginia City a lumber center. Its population leaped from three hundred to five thousand in three years. [Change the participle to a verb to make a complete sentence. You may also join the phrase to the main clause.]

Fragment:

I had left home to seek adventure. *To get away from the dullness of the small town.* [This is an infinitive phrase.]

Complete:

I had left home to seek adventure, to get away from the dullness of the small town. [You may also change the fragment to a sentence by supplying a subject and a predicate, "I wanted to get away . . . ."]

1c. *An appositive phrase should not be written as a complete sentence.*

Guard against this fault especially when the phrase is introduced by such words as *namely, for example, such as,* and the like.

Fragment:

New problems face the girl entering college. *Such as budgeting her money and her time for studying.* ["Budgeting" is in apposition with "problems."]

Complete:

New problems, such as budgeting her money and her time, face the girl entering college.

Fragment:

It was a vast, desolate, forbidding region. The home of the lava bear and the hungry coyote. ["Home" and "region" are appositives. Correct by joining the phrase to the main clause.]

Complete:

It was a vast, desolate, forbidding region, the home of the lava bear and the hungry coyote.

1d. *Any verbless chip or fragment of a sentence, whether you can classify it or not, should not be allowed to stand as a sentence.*

Some fragments are written because the writer was in too much of a hurry to think; others are written because the writer has carried over into writing the exclamatory nature of very informal speech. The following examples will make the points clear.

Fragment:

Unexpectedly I dropped in on her daughter. *Just a friendly call, no party.* [The writer of this was making note jottings, not sentences. Rewritten, this might read, "I intended this to be just a friendly, informal call."]

Fragment:

Just a long, long sleep. That's the way the old Indian spoke of death.

Complete:

Just a long, long sleep—that's the way the old Indian spoke of death. [The dash indicates a sharp break in the construction. In a more ordinary form, this could read, "The old Indian spoke of death as being a long, long sleep."]

Exercises

Exercise 1. Copy the following sentences. Some of them are complete. Some are fragments. If a sentence is complete, underline its subject once and its verb twice. If the group of words is a clause, encircle the subordinating conjunction. If it is a verbal phrase, encircle the verbal.

1. Belinda can never resist bargain-day surprises at Nolan's.
2. Although she rarely purchases anything of importance.
3. The other day she talked Clarence into going with her.
4. Clarence explaining patiently his inability to cut another class.
5. After a long debate he agreed to go with her.
6. Which was not what he had in mind at first.
7. Fortunately being able to get excused from his class.
8. Both of them were elbowed and jostled by the crowd.
9. Belinda, frustrated again, came home empty-handed.
10. Clarence proudly showing her his new spring hat.

Exercise 2. In some of the following word groups you will find sentence fragments. Eliminate each fragment either by joining it to the main clause or by rewriting it as a complete sentence. Be able to tell whether rule 1a, 1b, or 1c applies.

1. Working in a book store has taught me many things. About people rather than about books.
2. Belinda dropped in the other day. Bringing with her Chauncey and Clarence, her inseparable companions.
3. College students often come in to browse among our books. Especially as the book store is next to the coffee shop.

4. An English professor paused at my counter. "Oh, that mine adversary had written a book," he quoted.
5. He swatted the counter with a copy of *College English.* In which, as he explained, his book had suffered a review.
6. Belinda, passing by, nodded vaguely at us. Her thoughts, I am sure, were somewhere else.
7. Belinda was a girl of strange enthusiasms. Her two immediate ones being photography and poetry.
8. Would she exclaim over a volume by Dylan Thomas or a new Westenar F 2.0 lens? A hard question to answer.
9. Chauncey came up, took her by the arm, and steered her to the coffee shop. Clarence following.
10. Glancing through the glass partition, I could see them drinking coffee and talking excitedly. Probably about something dreadfully intellectual.

RUN-TOGETHER SENTENCES

2. *Two or more complete sentences should not be run together without any punctuation or with only a comma between them.*

A sentence made up of two or more independent, co-ordinate clauses, properly joined and punctuated, is called a *compound sentence.* (See pages 48, 52.) The usual means of joining these independent clauses are (1) a semicolon, (2) a conjunction, (3) a comma and a conjunction, (4) a semicolon and a conjunction. (See also sections 13 and 14.)

2a. *The comma splice may be corrected in several ways.*

The use of a comma to join independent, co-ordinate clauses (except in certain infrequent situations which will be discussed later) is called a "comma splice" or a "comma fault." It should be avoided in college writing, especially in serious discussions of serious subjects. It may be corrected in one of the following ways. The student should choose the method of revision that produces the most effective sentence.

1. By subordinating one of the two independent sentences. (Since the student put both statements in the same sentence, he must have felt that one was closely related to the other.)

Splice:

The boys were sent to a good preparatory school, they would be safe there and properly looked after.

Better:

The boys were sent to a good preparatory school, where they would be safe and properly looked after.

Splice:

They wouldn't study very much, no one expected them to.

Better:

Because no one expected them to, they would not do much studying.

2. By inserting a co-ordinating conjunction after the comma. (These conjunctions are *and, but, for, or, nor, yet.*)

Splice:

Anxiously I searched the clouds below for a break, we were running out of gas.

Better:

Anxiously I searched the clouds below for a break, for we were running out of gas.

3. By using a semicolon instead of a comma if the sentences are close enough in thought to be combined into a compound sentence.

Splice:

A quarterback spins the football as he throws, that is to prevent the ball tumbling over and over in its flight.

Better:

A quarterback spins the football as he throws; that is to prevent the ball tumbling over and over in its flight.

If you wish to subordinate, however, you would write the sentence like this:

Right:

To keep a football from tumbling over in its flight, the quarterback gives it a spin as he throws it.

4. By using a period to separate the two co-ordinate clauses.

Splice:

We wondered what first led him to choose army life, it could have been his fear of loneliness or a wish for security.

Better:

We wondered what first led him to choose army life. It could have been his fear of loneliness or a wish for security.

The use of a comma to join co-ordinate clauses is more common in novels, stories, and some types of journalistic writing than it is in serious expository prose. Although it is hard to make general statements here, it is safe to say that this practice is the exception, not the rule.

In serious discussions—with which we are primarily concerned here—the comma is used by most writers to join co-ordinate clauses in the following situations:

1. When the clauses are arranged in the "a, b, and c" order.

Example:

I couldn't properly understand the text, many a word was new to me, and I had to pass on, reading as I did at odd moments, or in the horse cars.—George Santayana, *Persons and Places.*

2. When the series of statements takes the form of a climax.

Example:

I came, I saw, I conquered.
The leaves are turning to gold, squirrels are fattening, hunting time is near.

3. When the statements form an antithesis, or are arranged in the "it was not merely this, it was also that" formula.[1]

Examples:

It was more than an annoyance, it was a pang.—Winston S. Churchill.
To allow the Mahdi to enter Khartoum would not merely mean the return of the whole of the Sudan to barbarism, it would be a menace to the safety of Egypt herself.—Lytton Strachey.

[1] See article by David S. Berkeley, Oklahoma State University, in *College English,* February, 1953, p. 289.

Warning: You should guard against the comma splice in the two special forms: with dialogue tabs, like "he said," and with conjunctive adverbs, like "however," "moreover," and so on. The examples will make the point clear.

Dialogue:

"That's right," said Paul. "I'd almost forgotten her name." [A period is the usual punctuation, although a semicolon is occasionally used.] "No one remembers the good things I have done," she complained; "no one ever does." [Semicolon used here.]
"Yes, I know, sir," said Jones. "I warned him to be careful." [Period used here.]

Adverbs:

The prisoner told a long story of atrocities; however, his companion did not agree with his version of what had happened to them. [Use a semicolon before the conjunctive adverb. Better still, use a semicolon and hide the adverb within the second clause.]
When I registered for engineering, I had two high-school subjects to make up; moreover, I had forgotten most of the algebra I ever knew. [Use a semicolon before the conjunctive adverb.]

2b. *Two sentences run together without any mark of punctuation between them may be corrected just as a comma splice is.*

The fragmentary sentence, the comma splice, and the run-together or "fused" sentence are probably all symptoms of the same infirmity—carelessness rather than ignorance of what constitutes a sentence. If a student knows what a sentence is, he should not let slovenly carelessness mar his writing. After all, his writing is judged not by the knowledge he has but by the knowledge he uses. If he does *not* know what a sentence is, he should go back to pages 39–52 and study the explanations and the examples that he finds there.

Fused:

At first I wondered if I should speak to her she seemed to be so wrapped up in her thoughts.
I almost decided to walk by and pretend I did not see her she might think I was intruding.
I was lonesome I decided to speak and I said hello in a weak voice.

Unified:

She seemed so wrapped up in her thoughts that at first I wondered if I should speak to her. [Subordination]
Fearing that she might think I was intruding, I almost decided to walk by and pretend not to see her. [Subordination]
As I was lonesome, I decided to speak to her, and I said hello in a weak voice. [Subordination]

As a rule, subordination is the best cure for the run-together sentence, as it is for the comma splice.

Supplementary Exercises

Sections 1 and 2 of the handbook deal with what is usually called "sentence sense," that is, the ability to recognize and to write complete and unified sentences. If you do not have this sentence sense, you must go back to the elementary drill of sentence analysis or diagraming.

Exercise 1. In the following exercises each sentence begins with some element before the subject. Copy these sentences. Below each sentence, diagram and label the subject and the verb of the *main clause* of that sentence.

1. One day five years ago while exploring the Arches Monument, I picked up a pretty pebble from the dried-up bed of a stream.

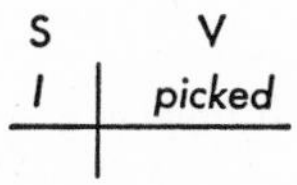

2. For some reason that I cannot recall now, that bright pebble marked the beginning of my interest in geology.
3. Half in earnest and half in fun, I asked the guide if he could identify that pebble.
4. With the air of a patient teacher, he examined the piece of rock.
5. Tossing the pebble back to me, the guide explained that the pebble was undoubtedly a piece of chalcedony.
6. Since park rangers and naturalists are trained to be patient, his answer encouraged me to continue my questions.
7. As we were standing under Landscape Arch, my next question urged him to explain why the arch was not made of the same kind of stone.

8. Smiling the happy smile of a true teacher, he proceeded to give us a short lecture.
9. In prehistoric days, some Indians must have used the shelter of the arch as a winter campground.
10. Having no TV or comic books to take up their time, they busied themselves during the winter making arrowheads out of chalcedony, which they had brought in from other places.

Exercise 2. Correct each of the following sentences by subordinating one of the run-together co-ordinate clauses.

1. Rock-hunting is my favorite hobby it is both interesting and educational.
2. Last summer we explored the Kootenai River, it is a well-known source of beautiful agates.
3. Agates are easy to find in river beds, they are polished by the action of the water.
4. The river water is ice-cold in spring it is not too comfortable for barefoot exploring.
5. We picked up a great many specimens however we threw most of them away.
6. Not every shiny pebble is an agate, we found that out before our trip was over.
7. We spent one vacation in central Oregon, we hoped to find thunderbird eggs there.
8. A thunderbird egg looks like dull grey rock, however, it may contain a beautiful agate inside.
9. Once we found a moss agate on the Oregon coast, many agate beds can be found there.
10. We decided to invest in an agate-tumbling machine, they are inexpensive to operate.

Exercise 3. Revise each of the following sentences by using subordination of a rank below that of a subordinate clause (a phrase or an appositive).

1. A rock hunter must have two virtues they are curiosity and patience.
2. Petrified wood is not hard to find, it is a form of agate.
3. We heard about the obsidian mountain near John Day, we decided to take a close look at it.
4. We got there during the deer-hunting season, it was a poor time for two amateur rock hunters.
5. A stooping rock hunter may not have horns, still to an eager hunter he looks like a deer.

Exercise 4. Correct each of the following by any method that you think is good. Be able to explain the method that you use.

1. Mother and Father were discussing my future, they were determined to make a career woman out of me. A good one, too.
2. Mother wanted me to have a college education, however, she had never attended college herself.
3. Father was sure that practical experience was good. Especially in business.
4. I wasn't so sure myself, I had other ideas. Having fallen in love with the lifeguard at Seaside Beach.
5. I was persuaded to try college for a year, it couldn't do me any harm. Nor much good either I explained to my parents.

SUBJECT AND VERB

3. *A verb agrees with its subject.*

Actually there is nothing very difficult about the general principle that you should match singular subjects with singular verbs and plural subjects with plural verbs. In most cases, you can "play it by ear," for you will usually recognize when a particular use is not in conformity with good habits of language. For example, almost no one would match a singular subject with a plural verb in such a sentence as "The man were on the front porch." You know that is wrong. And if someone should say, matching a plural subject with a singular verb, "The men was on the front porch," you would probably recognize that without much trouble as a familiar but distinctly substandard use of English.

The difficulties arise when the sentences are not so simple as those examples. Problems in agreement can be listed under two main categories:

1. When several other words intervene between your subject and verb, or when your word order is unusual, you may forget just what your subject was and so make an error.

2. When the subject seems to be singular and plural at the same time—"everybody," "gymnastics," "the whole family," "either of us," "a group of people"—you can become confused as to just what rule ought to apply. This is especially true because there is some shifting taking place in current practice, and people are asking not so much whether a subject is singular or plural in gram-

matical form, but whether it is singular or plural in *meaning* in a particular sentence. It is no wonder you are sometimes confused. But a study of the examples given below, plus some clear-headed common sense, should remove much of your difficulty over this tricky business of agreement.

It is often helpful for a student, especially the visual-minded one, to make a quick mental diagram of the grammatical subject and verb of a sentence.

3a. Plural words that intervene between a singular subject and its verb do not change the number of the subject.

Examples:

The *racket* of all those engines *was* deafening. [*Racket was*, not *engines were*. "Of all those engines" is a phrase modifying *racket*, and this of course does not change the number of *racket*.]

One of the many techniques he explained to us *was* that of flycasting. [*One* of them was *fly-casting*, not all of them.]

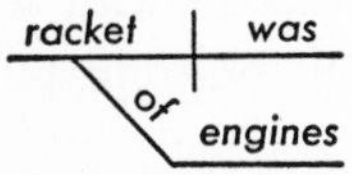

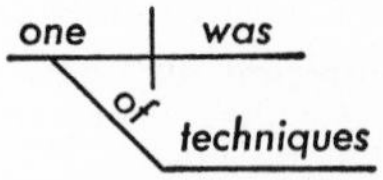

3b. When words are added to a singular subject by with, together with, as well as, in addition to, except, *and* no less than, the number of the subject remains singular.

Examples:

The *teacher*, as well as his principal, *was* exonerated.
The *boy*, together with his mother, *was* left standing there.

Often, particularly in informal English, *with* and *together with* are considered as effectively making the subject plural, and a plural verb is used. Watch for the omission of commas as a hint that the subjects are to be treated as more than one, like a compound subject.

Informal:

The *boy* together with his *mother were* left standing there.

3c. *In sentence patterns that depart from the typical subject-verb-complement order, watch especially for the following situations:*

1. The subject following the verb.

Examples:

Imbedded in the concrete walks *was* the *print* of a man's hands. [*print was*]
Stacked against the wall of the shelter *were* eleven *cases* of hand grenades. [*cases were*]

2. Introductory *it.*

Introductory *it,* as in "It is the people who matter," is always followed by the singular verb, no matter whether the noun that follows is singular or plural. *It* in such cases has been called a *dummy subject,* preparing the way for the real subject to come. Nevertheless it controls the verb, and no one would say, "It are the people."

Examples:

It is the fundamental *issue* that we should keep in mind.
It is the *colleges* that must take up the burden.

3. Introductory *there.*

In present-day English, usage seems to be divided in regard to the number of the verb when the "dummy" *there* introduces a sentence.

In sentences in which the noun that follows the verb is plural in form, most writers and speakers will use a plural verb.

Examples:

There *were* eleven *men* in our group.
There *are* two *explanations* of his conduct.
There *seem* to be three *deer* hidden in that brush.
[No literate person would be likely to say: *eleven men was, there is two, there seems to be three.*]

When the subject following the verb consists of a number of nouns the first of which is singular, there is a definite tendency, in both speech and writing, to make the verb singular. Those who are strongly conscious of the requirements of grammatical agreement, and who have time to plan their sentences, will doubtless use the plural verb in such cases.

Examples:

From Long Island to San Francisco, from Florida Bay to Vancouver's Island, there *is* one dominant race and civilisation, one language, one type of law, one sense of nationality.—Frederic Harrison, *Memories and Thoughts.*[1]
At Valenciennes, where there *was* a review and a great dinner . . . .—Lytton Strachey, *Queen Victoria.*
There *is* much manganese and chrome, and enough uranium in the slag heaps of the Johannesburg gold mines to make its extraction worth while.—*Harper's Magazine*, July, 1952.

3d. *The verb agrees with its subject, not with its subjective complement.*

If the difference in number between subject and subjective complement produces an awkward sentence, it is better to rewrite the sentence.

Right:

The main *reason* he looked so sick *was* the late hours he kept.

Better:

He looked so sick because he kept so many late hours.

3e. *A compound subject joined by and takes a plural verb.*

Again, do not be distracted by unusual word order or by intervening phrases.

Examples:

Bed and *table were* both solid maple.
Bed and *table*, purchased the week before at the local department store and placed in his garage, *were* both solid maple.
Solid maple too *were* the *bed* and *table.*
Were both *bed* and *table* solid maple?

[1] Examples here used are quoted from David S. Berkeley's "An Agreement of Subject and Verb in Anticipatory *There* Clauses," *American Speech*, May, 1953. By kind permission.

Tests showed that the *quality* and *amount* of solid maple used in the construction *were* above specifications.

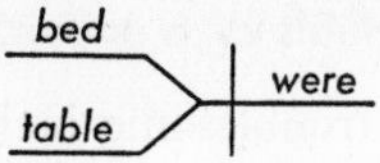

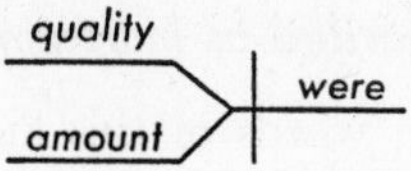

When several singular subjects, however, represent the same person or thing, or when they form one collective idea, a singular verb is used.

Examples:

Our *ally* and *neighbor* to the South, the Republic of Mexico, *maintains* a quiet border.
The *sum* and *substance* of the book *is* that all men are created unequal.
Many an *athlete* and *hero has* grown fat and disillusioned.

3f. When subjects are joined by neither–nor, either–or, not only–but also, *the verb agrees with the nearer subject.*

Example:

Neither the *students* nor their *teacher is* quite prepared.

Often, however, in order to avoid awkward-sounding situations, it is better to recast the sentence altogether.

Awkward:

Neither *you* nor *I am* going now.

Better:

You are not going now and neither am I.

3g. *After* each, every, each one, everyone, everybody, anybody, nobody, either, *and* neither *the singular verb is used in formal English.*

Example:

Each of us *is* quite able to see the point.

But in informal situations, especially in conversation, *neither* is often felt to be plural, especially when followed by some phrase like *of them.* The same usage applies to *none.*

3h. *With a collective noun a singular verb is used when the group it names is regarded as a unit, and a plural verb when the noun is regarded as indicating the individuals of a group.*

Common words of this kind that are troublesome include *number, family, group, data,* and *public.*

Examples:

The *number* of failing papers *was* surprising. [*The number* is usually considered as a single unit.]
A *number* of things *are* going wrong. [*A number* refers to individual items and is therefore plural.]
The whole *family is* here. [Family considered as a single unit.] The *family are* all attending different churches. [In this less common use, the members of the family are referred to individually.]

Since there is considerable range for individual choice in the use of collective nouns, you must let consistency be your guide. Once you have spoken of a group as a single unit, you cannot, without some explanation, refer to it in the plural.

Consistent:

The *platoon are* removing their knapsacks. They *are* getting ready for a mock charge.
The class *was* assembled promptly, and proceeded with *its* assignment.

3i. *When the subject is a title, the name of a book, a clause, a quotation, or other group of words expressing a single idea, the verb is singular.*

Examples:

Tales of the Vienna Woods is a delightful composition.
All men are created equal is a statement of dubious truth.
Voices is a well-known magazine of verse.

This rule also applies to subjects involving *numbers.* Expressions of quantity, distance, time, amount, etc., are matched with singular verbs when the subject is felt to be a unit.

Examples:

Fifteen years is a harsh jail sentence.
Five hundred words is plenty for most themes.
Ten dollars is a ridiculous price for a theatre ticket.

But:

Ten dollars were marked in red ink. [Here the dollars are considered as individual bills.]

3j. Several words ending in s are governed by special rules of usage.

A number of nouns ending in *ics* (physics, mathematics) are considered singular when they refer to single branches of study, but are often plural when they refer to physical activities (acrobatics, tactics).

Other words likely to cause trouble are listed below:

Usually singular: news, measles, mumps, gallows.
Usually plural: scissors, tidings, riches, trousers, means.
Either singular or plural: headquarters, politics, alms.

Examples:

Ethics deals with problems of morality.
Economics is not a difficult study.
The *acoustics* at the Metropolitan *are* superb.

3k. A singular verb is used with a relative pronoun referring to a singular antecedent, and a plural verb is used with a pronoun referring to a plural antecedent.

Examples:

I like people *who are* lively.
I like a man *who shows* energy.

In this connection, the "one of those who" construction requires special treatment. In a sentence like *She is one of those girls who always get into trouble,* the verb in the subordinate clause is logically plural because *who* refers to *girls.* But in actual practice the singular verb is very common: *She is one of those girls who always gets into trouble.*

Exercises

Exercise 1. Some of the difficulty with agreement, as we have seen, is simply a matter of making sure just what the subjects and verbs in complicated sentences are. In the following sentences underline each subject once and each verb twice.

1. Whoever was there was making a great deal of noise.
2. The sound of the bells was heard all over three counties.
3. The president, as well as his entire cabinet, was there.
4. Since all the new office buildings have been built, there is an increasing need for improvement in transportation facilities.
5. It was considered that a statement to the newspapers was appropriate.
6. The secretary and member *ex officio* was present.
7. The secretary and the member *ex officio* were present.
8. Neither had any interest in the other.
9. There were always a number of cars and trucks parked along the sidewalks.
10. A large assortment of candied fruits was handed to him.

Exercise 2. Correct the errors in each of the following sentences. Tell what rule applies.

1. The subways in the wintertime often gets very cold.
2. The whole point of these courses are to teach you to think.
3. When the pair of scissors was not to be seen, she called out, "The scissors is not here."
4. The trouble with all those radiators were the rusty pipes.
5. There is usually, somewhere underneath the surface, at least two reasons for everything.
6. I find the garlic, together with the onion and paprika, are too sharp for the salad.
7. *The Grapes of Wrath* make very good reading.
8. Fifty dollars were just too much for me to pay.
9. Measles are an irritating disease, and so is mumps.
10. One of the several methods indicated in the manuals for professionals were preferred by most experts.

Exercise 3. Some of the following sentences contain errors; some are correct. Point out each mistake that you find, correct the sentence, and tell what rule applies.

1. The whole series of books are dedicated to the president.
2. Our friend and fellow-student, Jonathan Jones, is always welcome here.
3. He and Edith makes a very handsome pair.
4. A handsome pair like Andrew and Betty makes one believe in love after all.
5. Economics are probably his hardest subject.
6. Do you find that athletics are your pleasantest activity?
7. Then *The Bells of St. Mary* was played, and on the church steps Mr. and Mrs. Goldsmith, that fine-looking pair, was to be found.
8. I found that her glance and her inquisitive eyebrow was most attractive.
9. The student council has reached its decision, and Roberts, as well as Robinson, are to be punished.
10. His use of phrases and clauses was deplorable.

PRONOUNS

4. Be careful to use the right form of the pronoun.

Nouns in modern English change their form for the plural and for the possessive. Plurals are discussed in section 21. The possessive forms are discussed in section 15. There are very few problems connected with the form changes of nouns.

Pronouns, however, change their forms for person, number, and case, and thereby cause the student of the English language numerous difficulties. In English there are three cases: the nominative or subjective, the possessive, the objective. There are also three persons: the *first* person indicates the speaker; the *second* person indicates the one spoken to; the *third* indicates the one spoken about.

The forms of the personal pronoun are shown in the table below:

	First Person	Second Person	Third Person		
	Masculine or feminine		*Masc.*	*Fem.*	*Neuter*
SINGULAR NUMBER:					
Nominative:	I	you	he	she	it
Possessive:	my, mine	your, yours	his	her, hers	its
Objective:	me	you	him	her	it

PLURAL NUMBER:

Nominative:	we	you	they
Possessive:	our, ours	your, yours	their, theirs
Objective:	us	you	them

The relative and interrogative pronoun *who* has only three forms:

Nominative:	who
Possessive:	whose
Objective:	whom

There are also a number of *indefinite* pronouns, such as *another, anybody, anyone, anything, both, each, either, everybody, everyone, everything, few, many, neither, nobody, none, one, somebody, someone.* Those that can be so used form the possessive by adding an apostrophe and *s.*

Examples:

Everybody's business is nobody's business. It is still anyone's game.

The intensive pronouns (used for emphasis) and the reflexive pronouns (used to point the action back toward the subject) are *myself, himself, herself, itself, yourself, yourselves, ourselves, themselves.*

Intensive:

The governor *himself* presented the award.

Reflexive:

The boy hurt *himself.* They washed *themselves* quickly.

Although in the past the pronouns compounded with *-self* were often used in place of the simple personal pronouns, at present such use is generally regarded as appropriate only in informal, conversational English.

Standard (formal and informal):

The committee was made up of Dr. Brogan and *me.*
We thought that Mrs. Wollin and *you* should talk to her.
The Dean let Jim and *me* go home for the week end.

Informal:

The committee was made up of Dr. Brogan and *myself*.
The Dean let Jim and *myself* go home for the week end.

NOMINATIVE CASE

4a. The nominative case is used when the pronoun is the subject of a verb.

The student must watch out for three trouble spots in connection with the use of the nominative case:

1. A parenthetical expression, such as *they think, they say, we believe,* etc., between *who* (*whoever*) and the verb may confuse the writer.

Examples:

Jones is one senior who we think could teach this class. [Not *whom we think,* but *who could teach*]
A young man who we believe was the driver of the car is being held. Who did you say brought us these cherries? [Not *whom did you say*]
We agreed to accept whoever they thought was the best foreman. [Not *whomever*]

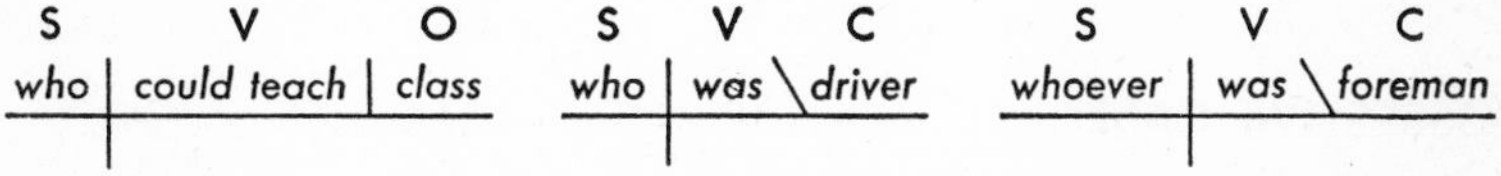

2. The fact that a *who* or *whoever* clause follows a preposition may confuse the writer into using the wrong case.

Examples:

Give the keys to *whoever* calls for them. [Not *to whomever. Whoever* seems to be attracted into the objective case by its position after the preposition. But it is the subject of the verb *calls.* The whole clause is the object of the preposition.]
At these dances every girl has to dance with *whoever* asks her. [Not *with whomever*, but *whoever asks*]

3. In clauses of comparison, with *than* and *as,* the nominative is used with the implied verb.

Examples:

Do you know anyone who can talk faster than *she* [talks]?
No one knows it better than *I* [know it].
I feel that we are as good as *they* [are].

4b. *In standard literary English, the nominative case form is used when the pronoun is a subjective complement after the verb be.*

In conversation, *it's me* is generally accepted. Some educated persons might say, *it's us,* or *it's them,* but since others, whose opinion the student may value highly, would regard such forms as signs of slovenly language habits, it might be well to avoid extreme informality. But it is a question of manners—usage or conventions—not a question of morality.

Standard (formal and informal):

It was *we* who discovered the fire, Mr. Hines. It was *they* who called the fire department. And I think it was *he* who ran in and woke up the sleeping boys.

The occasion to use *it's me, it's us, it's him* does not arise often in college writing. When used in reporting dialogue, however, these forms and others like them must be reported accurately.

POSSESSIVE CASE

4c. *The apostrophe is not used with personal pronouns to form the possessive case; the apostrophe is used, however, with those indefinite pronouns that can be used in the possessive.*

Personal pronouns, possessive forms: my, mine, your, yours, his, her, hers, its, our, ours, their, theirs.
Indefinite: anybody's, anyone's, everybody's, nobody's, no one's, one's, somebody's.

Wrong:

The furniture is *their's,* but the house is *our's.*
The bush is dying; *it's* leaves are covered with mildew.

Right:

The furniture is *theirs*, but the house is *ours*.
The bush is dying; *its* leaves are covered with mildew.

Note carefully the distinction between *it's,* which means *it is,* and *its,* which is the possessive form of *it.* Note also that when *else* follows the indefinite pronoun, such as *anybody, somebody, someone,* the apostrophe and *s* are added to *else,* not to the pronoun.

Right:

It's [contraction of *it is*] *anybody's* guess *whose* [possessive form of *who*] horse will win this race.
Would you like to ride in somebody *else's* car?
I wouldn't trust someone *else's* judgment.

4d. *In standard English of the more formal varieties, the general practice is to use the possessive form of the pronoun when it precedes a gerund.*

Please note that here we do not use *general* in the sense of *universal.* We mean, "Most do; some don't." It is easy enough to find exceptions in the writing of reputable authors.

Examples:

No historian can justify *his ordering* an assault an hour before the armistice.
We were told about *his running* away from home.
His taking your car without asking is unusual for him.

In these sentences the verbals *ordering, running, taking* are gerunds. They are used as object, as object of a preposition, and as subject, in that order. When the verbal is a participle, however, the objective case is correct.

Examples:

We watched *them playing* a game of tennis. [Them in the act of playing]
The men saw *him entering* the apartment. [Him in the act of entering]

With nouns introducing or modifying gerunds, usage varies. There are situations in which the possessive is desirable; there are others in which it is difficult or clumsy, and therefore it gives way to the objectve.

Examples:

Mother did not approve of *John's running* off to South America.
I do not like the idea of *girls marrying* before they are out of school.
The very thought of so many *officers being murdered* horrifies everyone.

4e. *Instead of the apostrophe s form, the of phrase may be used to show possession when the situation calls for it.*

1. Ordinarily for inanimate objects: the top of the pile, the bottom of the barrel, the pages of the book, the legs of the table (but not *the pen of my aunt*). But notice such forms as: in an hour's time, it cost a month's pay, a week's wages, a year's absence. In some cases either form may be used; in other cases only one form is possible.

2. To shift the position of a word so that it will stand closer to its modifier.

Example:

The popularity of the teacher who never gives hard tests is assured. [Not "The teacher's popularity who never gives, etc."]

The double possessive is a construction long established in standard English.

Right:

friends of Howard's, an acquaintance of my mother's, that old sweetheart of mine, a cousin of his, an old schoolmate of Jack's

OBJECTIVE CASE

4f. *The objective case of the pronoun is used when the pronoun is the direct or indirect object of a verb or verbal.*

Direct object:

We liked *him*. Mother called *her*. Father tried to pay *him*. Punishing *him* did little good.

Indirect object:

Mother served *them* their dinners. I agreed to read *him* a story.

No one is likely to make a mistake in the objective case of a pronoun when the pronoun immediately follows the verb or verbal of which it is the object. For instance, no one would say, "I saw *she* at the game," or "Father took *I* and Bob to the game." Difficulties arise, however, in two types of constructions:

1. With *who* and *whom,* when these appear out of their normal S-V-O pattern. Here we have to distinguish between the more or less formal, literary pattern and the conversational, informal pattern. In questions, when *who* begins the sentence, *who* is used in informal speech for both the subject and the object forms.

Formal usage:

Whom can this government send to the summit meeting? [Government can send *whom.*]
General Dean was the officer *whom* the Koreans captured early in the war. [Koreans captured *whom.*]

Conversational:

Who did you call, Mother?
Who did you see?
I wonder *who* she is going to ask this time.

2. When the pronoun is the second of two objects connected by *and.*

Examples:

Mrs. Hill invited *her* and *me* to stay with her over the week end. [not *her and I*]
Dr. Hall told Harry and *me* that we had passed the course. [not *Harry and I*]

4g. *The objective case form is normally used after* than *and* as *in clauses of comparison to show that it is the object of an implied verb.*

Examples:

My father always liked Tom more than [he liked] *me.*
Did you give Tom as much as [you gave] *me?*

4h. *The objective case form is normally used when the pronoun is the object of a preposition.*

Here again trouble arises not when the pronoun immediately follows a preposition, as in, "I spoke to *her*" [not *to she*], but when the pronoun comes before its preposition or when it is the second of two objects.

Informal, conversational usage accepts "who" as the objective form, especially in questions, in which the pronoun may begin a sentence or a clause, such as, "*Who* did you call for?" or "*Who* are you going with?"

Standard formal usage:

No one was quite sure *whom* the warning was intended for. [for *whom*]
Whom can we turn to in this dreadful crisis? [to *whom*]
The officer stared thoughtfully after the man *whom* he had just talked with. [with *whom*]
The sergeant pointed to Jonas and *me* and motioned us to report to the captain. [not *Jonas and I*]
Just between you and *me*, the boy is a hopeless dancer. [not *you and I*]

A common error in speech and writing occurs in connection with a pronoun that is linked with a noun in the objective case, as with "of we men," or "for we students."

Examples:

We girls decided to leave.
Some of *us* girls decided to leave.
The dean sent a warning to several of *us* men.

4i. *The objective case is proper when the pronoun is the assumed subject or the complement of the infinitive to be.*

Examples:

She thought Oswald to be *me*.
We wanted *him* to be our chairman.
A girl whom I believed to be *her* waved to me from a passing car.

AGREEMENT WITH ANTECEDENT

4j. A pronoun should agree with its antecedent in number, gender, and person.

An antecedent is the word or words to which a pronoun refers. If the antecedent is singular, the pronoun should be singular; if it is plural, the pronoun should be plural.

Examples:

One girl brought *her* lunch.
Three girls brought *their* lunches.
A boy brought *his* lunch.
The man and *his* dog were leaving *their* house.
It is assumed that *I, who am* the oldest son, will inherit the title.
We prefer to speak to *you, who are* their leader.

Here as elsewhere, when questions of usage arise, we must distinguish between what is customary in formal usage and what is accepted, at least by a great many educated persons, in conversational, informal situations. There are differences of opinion and attitude, you know: it is these differences that complicate our attempts to get at the truth.

The problem of agreement will be analyzed in terms of certain typical situations, which are also typical trouble spots.

1. In situations that call for more or less formal English, it is customary to use a singular pronoun to refer to any of the following: *anybody, anyone, everyone, everybody, nobody, no one, somebody, someone, person.*

In informal English, especially in conversation, these words, although they take singular verbs, are quite generally felt to be collectives (plural in sense), and the pronouns referring to them are often plural. In addition, all sorts of special situations arise. For instance, *each, every, everybody, everyone* have a general meaning of "all, or a group, but taken individually." Apparently it is the "group" sense that is dominant in influencing the number of the pronoun referring to one of these words. In some cases, when the group consists of both males and females, the speaker uses the plural form because he feels that neither *his* nor *her* is quite accurate. Finally, in some situations, such as in this sentence, "Everybody started to laugh, but in a moment *they* realized that the speaker was not joking," the singular form just would not make sense. In the words of the military communiqué, the situation is confused.

Formal agreement:

England expects every man to do *his* duty. [No question of gender here.]
Everyone must do *his* part in this war.
Nobody has a right to think that *his* happiness is more important than the happiness of others.

Generally acceptable in conversation:

Everyone did *their* best.
Each child must bring *their* lunch to school.
Somebody left *their* hat here.

Every student should realize, however, that many persons feel a twinge of pain when they hear expressions of this sort. He should therefore choose his words with due regard to the situation, lest he offend those whose opinions are important to him.

2. Either a singular or a plural pronoun may be used to refer to a collective noun, depending upon whether the noun designates the group as a whole or the members of the group.

Consistency is the governing principle. The construction should be either singular or plural but not both.

Inconsistent:

The band *is* playing *their* best selection now. [The verb is singular but the pronoun is plural.]

The team *is* now on the floor, taking *their* practice shots at the basket. [Verb and pronoun indicate a shift in number.]

Consistent:

The band *is* playing *its* best selection now.

The team *are* on the floor now, taking *their* practice shots at the basket. [*The team* is thought of as being more than one person.]

3. Ordinarily the masculine pronouns, *he, his, him,* are used to refer to one of these "group taken individually" words, not *he or she, his or her, him or her.*

Right:

Every person in the audience was requested to sign *his* [not *his or her*] name to the petition.

4. In modern usage, the relative pronoun *who* is used to refer to persons and occasionally to animals, but *whose* may refer to persons, animals, or things, especially when *of which* produces an awkward construction. The relative pronoun *that* may refer to both persons and things. The relative *which* may refer to animals, things, and ideas.

Examples:

A critic is one *who* tells of the adventures of the soul among masterpieces. My brother, *who* is a New York critic, delights in modern art. It is a taste *that* I cannot understand. He once gave me a painting *which* I hung upside down in my room. It is a masterpiece *whose* meaning is obscure. My dog, *whose* critical taste is instinctive, barks at it.

5. Except in the most formal writing, American usage prefers *he* and *his* when *one* is the antecedent.

Formal:

One must not lose one's temper when one is being criticized. [Most people would regard this as slightly affected.]

Right:

A person must not lose his temper when he is being criticized.
If one were to read between the lines, he would quickly detect the irony in Swift's calm proposal.

6. Pronouns used in apposition are in the same case as their antecedents.

Examples:

The prize was divided among *us* three, George, Alice, and *me.* [not I]
Mother had told *us—him* and *me*—to meet her at Clark and Broadway.

Exercises

Exercise 1, Case of pronouns. In the following sentences tell whether each of the italicized pronouns is used as the subject of a verb, the complement of a verb or verbal, or the object of a preposition.

1. "Would *you* care to drive out to our lake cottage with Nancy and *me* today?" asked Gail.
2. Gail's cottage was a subject that several of *us* talked about in whispers.
3. Gail had asked Nancy and *me* once before, but *we* had to tell *her we* could not go.
4. *It* was understood that *everyone* was to take her swimming suit.
5. *We* girls wondered *who* could have borrowed mine.
6. Nancy, *who* was a little more orderly than *I*, said, "Try to remember *whom you* lent it to."
7. As *I* usually give things to *whoever* asks for *them*, *neither* of *us* had hopes of finding my suit.
8. Gail, *whom* no one excels in generosity, solved the problem.
9. *It* was *she* who lent *me* one of her swim suits.
10. And *who* do *you* think was there to meet *us?*

Exercise 2, Case and number. In the following sentences correct every error in the case and number of pronouns. Explain why you make these changes.

1. Harry Links was the one who we really wanted for our president.
2. Some of we men decided to support whomever was nominated by the committee.
3. Harry is one man whom I am sure will restore discipline to the house.
4. No one in their right mind will say that noise is conducive to study.
5. Harry once told Marty, Tom, and I that everybody should forget their "kiddish" ways when he enters college.
6. At the time we men wondered to who he was referring.
7. Since then I realized that no one could profit from his advice more than me.
8. When the meeting was called to order, everyone took their seats.
9. A fairly large group, including Tom, my roommate, and I, had prepared a slate of candidates whom we thought would be acceptable.
10. No one was more surprised than us when Harry Links, the man who we all wanted, was elected by unanimous vote.

Exercise 3. Correct every error in each of the following sentences. Assume that these sentences appeared in college themes, not in informal conversation. If you think that any of these are acceptable in conversation, explain your reasons.

1. If a person does not try to improve their English, you will never feel secure among people of education.
2. When we went to register late, Professor Hall told my roommate and I that he had already assigned the first theme.
3. He remarked that for the first week everybody was required to bring their dictionary to class.
4. I realized that here was an opportunity for every student to improve themselves.
5. Professor Hall is a teacher whom I feel sure will be a great inspiration to my roommate and I.
6. When we entered the classroom for the first time, we saw that everybody was busy with their work.
7. Across the room I saw a boy who I had not seen for three years.
8. It is pleasant to meet a friend and exchange news and gossip with them.
9. This boy spoke to my roommate and I and suggested that some of we graduates of Central High should get together.
10. When Mr. Hall called the roll, he asked each student to stand up and introduce themselves to the class.

Exercise 4. Decide which of the following sentences conform to standard formal usage in the forms of the pronouns used. Decide which are acceptable in informal conversation. Then make the changes that would be necessary according to formal usage.

1. The college president's son, who everybody thought was a pretty steady boy, decided to quit school.
2. If I were him, I would try to finish my education before I married.
3. His leaving school might not have been any concern of our's except that he was a member of our fraternity.
4. He had once told Harry and I that he needed some mature responsibilities.
5. We know Madge, who he intends to marry, and just between you and I, his wish will be granted.
6. Some of we men remarked that, after all, every man has a right to choose their own ways of being unhappy.
7. A hasty marriage has it's own problems, and a person may be wise if they do not add the problems of education to them.
8. It was strange that him leaving college caused little comment, but I suppose that everybody thought that it concerned he, and he alone.
9. He came to see us and told Harry and I who he wanted for his best man.

10. Whom do you suppose will take his place now as the steadying influence at our house?

ADJECTIVES AND ADVERBS

5. *Distinguish between adjectives and adverbs, and use the correct forms of each.*

An adjective, as everybody knows, is used to modify a noun, and an adverb is commonly used to modify a verb, an adjective, or another adverb. One superficial sign of distinction between the two is that most adverbs end in *-ly*.

Adjective:

He is a *violent* man. She is a *lazy* girl.

Adverb:

He smashed the fence *violently*. She swam *lazily* toward the shore.

Some difficulty can arise because a few adjectives, like *lively, kindly,* also have the *-ly* ending, and because a few common adverbs, like *there, here, very, too, then,* do not. Usually these are not hard to recognize.

Adjective:

He is a *manly* fellow. She is a *lively* hostess. *The early* bird gets the worm.

Adverb:

Put it down *here*. I went along *too*. *Then* they went home.

Actually the difference between adjectives and adverbs depends not on a distinctive form or ending but on the way the words function in sentences. Thus a number of familiar words are used as either adjectives or adverbs, depending on function. In the list below, note that when the word is used as an adjective, it modifies a noun, and when it is used as an adverb, it modifies a verb, an adjective, or another adverb.

Examples:	Adjective	Adverb
deep	He dug a deep hole.	He dug down deep.
early	I am an early riser.	I went home early.
fast	He is a very fast driver.	He drove much too fast.
little	It is a little book.	The book is little understood.
right	I wish I had the right answer.	I wish I could do it right.
well	He is not well yet.	He is very well equipped.

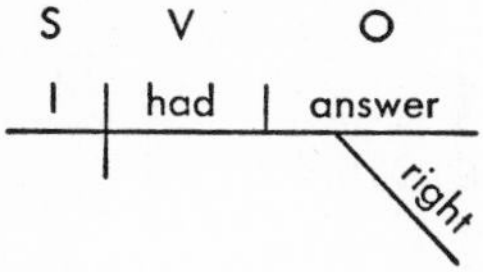

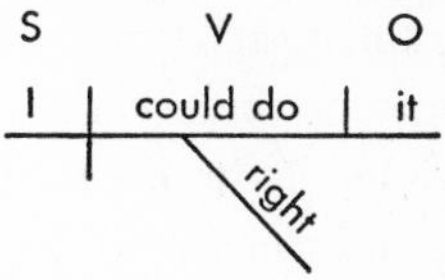

5a. The clumsy or awkward use of a noun form as an adjective should be avoided.

In our flexible language, as we have seen, words commonly used as nouns can also function as adjective modifiers, as in: a *bird* dog, a *house* cat, an *ivory* tower, an *iron* rod, a *silk* dress, a *flower* pot, the *city* streets, the *Chicago* fire. These are absolutely natural and legitimate uses. The objection is to the awkward use of a group modifier before a noun, as in the following examples:

Poor:

The Nevada Board of Health and Welfare decision to sue was applauded.
The principal speaker was the University of Minnesota law school dean.

Better:

The decision to sue on the part of the Nevada Board of Health and Welfare was applauded.
The principal speaker was the dean of the law school at the University of Minnesota.

5b. The adjective form is used as a complement after certain verbs, like be, become, appear, seem, prove, remain, look, *and the verbs of the senses, like* smell, taste, feel.

Examples:

The girl was *quiet*. [The *quiet* girl]
The little boy appears *happy*. [The *happy* little boy]

Hyacinths smell *sweet.* [*Sweet* hyacinths]
This water tastes *bad.* [*Bad* water]
The report proved *true.* [*True* report]

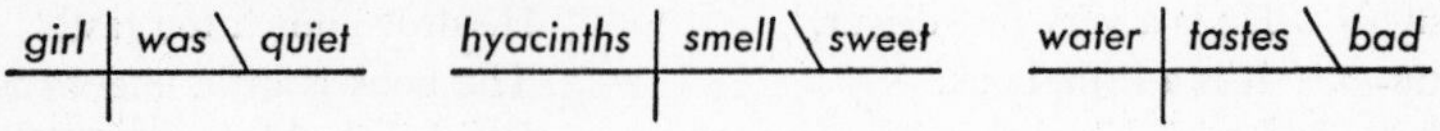

In informal conversation, "I feel badly" is as generally used by people of education as "I feel bad."

With some of these verbs, when the word in the predicate refers to the manner of the action and not to the subject, it is, of course, an adverb, and the adverb form must be used.

Adverb:

The boy appeared *unexpectedly.* The man felt *carefully* for the door. She looked *quickly* at me.

5c. *When a word modifies a verb, an adjective, or another adverb, the adverb form is used.*

1. Adverb modifying a verb.

Wrong:

Last summer I managed to improve my golf game *considerable.*
He talks *clever,* but his arguments are shallow.

Right:

Last summer I managed to improve my golf game *considerably.*
He talks *cleverly,* but his arguments are shallow.

2. Adverb modifying an adjective.

Wrong:

The sergeant seemed *real* glad to see us again.
It was *awful* good of you to come and help me.

Right:

The sergeant seemed *really* glad to see us again.
It was *awfully* (or *very*) good of you to come and help me.

3. Adverb modifying another adverb.

Wrong:

The stock market dropped *considerable* faster than it went up.

Right:

The stock market dropped *considerably* faster than it went up.

Most of the difficulties here center about a few words, of which the following are typical: *bad—badly, good—well, sure—surely, real—really, most—almost, awful—awfully, considerable—considerably.*

The words *most* and *almost* are a special problem. In formal usage, *almost* is the accepted modifier in such expressions as: Almost all were saved; summer is almost here; we almost never see him; almost everyone respects him. But in informal conversation *most* is widely used in those situations, and occasionally it appears in writing of a serious character.

5d. Certain nonstandard uses of adjective and adverb should be avoided: type, like, -wise.

These coinages, originating partly on Madison Avenue in New York and partly among users of substandard English, are to be avoided in most written work.

1. *Type* as an adjective.

Undesirable:

This *type* screw won't go into that *type* wood.

2. *Like* as a vague and loose adverb.

Poor:

I slid down the hill *like* and then I saw this sort of glow *like* in the sky.

3. *-wise* as an adverbial suffix in awkward coinages.

Undesirable:

Moneywise I was in favor of it, but fraternitywise I had to vote against it.

5e. *When an adverb has two forms (the short and the -ly forms), any differences in their use or meaning should be carefully observed.*

The following adverbs—and a few others—have two forms:

bright—brightly	high—highly	near—nearly
cheap—cheaply	late—lately	right—rightly
close—closely	loose—loosely	tight—tightly
deep—deeply	loud—loudly	wrong—wrongly

The adverbs in these pairs are not always interchangeable. Nor is there any quick and easy way of learning how to distinguish them in meaning and function. Using them in sentences, as in the following, will help.

Idiomatic:

Go slow. Drive slow.
Go slowly. Drive slowly.
The boy slowly opened the door.
Lately the son has been staying out late.
The dog crept close to me.
Nobody was near.
He was highly respected.

Not good idiom:

The boy slow opened the door.
Late the son has been staying out lately.
The dog crept closely to me.
Nobody was nearly.
He was high respected.

5f. *Use the correct form of the comparative and the superlative.*

The positive form of an adjective or adverb assigns a quality to the word it modifies, as in *a big bed, he walked quickly.* The comparative degree is formed by adding *-er* to the positive, or by using *more* or *less* with the positive, as in *a bigger bed, he walked more quickly.*

The superlative degree is formed by adding *-est* to the positive form or by using *most* or *least* with the positive. The superlative degree ranks the modified word highest in a class. It implies that there are at least three things in the class: *the biggest bed in the house.* (See also section 36.)

The comparative degree, then, is used when referring to two

persons or things; the superlative is used when three or more persons or things are involved.

Comparative:

He was *taller* than his brother.
Of the two boys, Penwick was *more intelligent* and *more co-operative.*

Superlative:

He was the *tallest* boy on the basketball team. [More than two]
Penwick was the *most intelligent* and the *most co-operative* boy in school. [Highest in a group consisting of more than two]

Some words are compared irregularly:

much	more	most	many	more	most
good	better	best	bad	worse	worst
well	better	best	little	less, lesser, littler	least, littlest

Adjectives of more than one syllable rarely take *-er* and *-est* to form comparatives and superlatives. Forms like *famouser* or *magnificentest* are not modern English. In formal writing, there is some objection to comparative or superlative forms of adjectives that name qualities thought of as absolute, such as *most perfect, most unique;* but these forms, and others like *straightest, blacker, most complete,* are found in both formal and informal English.[1]

In modern English one does not combine two superlatives to form a kind of super-superlative.

Wrong:

That is the *most unkindest* thing you could have said.

Right:

That is the *most unkind* thing you could have said.

The same principle applies to forming comparatives.

Wrong:

He finally reached the *more remoter* regions of the country.

[1] Bergen Evans and Cornelia Evans, *A Dictionary of Contemporary American Usage*, pp. 105–107.

Right:

He finally reached the *more remote* regions of the country.

Exercises

Exercise 1, Recognition. Copy the following sentences. Underline each adjective once and each adverb twice.

1. It was a long, lonely road, but he walked it bravely.
2. He was much too proud to try so humble a task.
3. Shakespeare speaks of the branches of trees in late autumn as "bare ruined choirs, where late the sweet birds sang."
4. After I had played it wrong a few times, I learned the right way.
5. That man is a lighthouse keeper.
6. She advertised in the Help Wanted column for a light housekeeper.
7. He seems very well today, after sleeping well last night.
8. Things look bad everywhere today.
9. He is a princely host, and the whole Glen Rock community enjoyed his hospitality.
10. He arrived very early, even for such an early riser as he is.

Exercise 2, Correct forms. Correct the error in the form or use of the adjective or adverb in each of the following sentences.

1. The texture of the rug feels roughly underfoot.
2. Which is the best, this one or that one?
3. The University of North Carolina Committee on Admissions chairman addressed the group.
4. She is almost ready; the work is near done.
5. We drove steady for near ten hours; then we felt utterly tired out.
6. I never saw a sumptuouser banquet.
7. I sure do feel bad from time to time.
8. The patient looks sickly and unhealthily to me.
9. What she said made me feel cheaply.
10. Mr. Nelson's examination in Philosophy 4 was real hard.

Exercise 3, Correct forms. In each of the following sentences select the correct form of the adjective or adverb.

1. The salesman's talk sounded so (convincingly, convincing) that I bought a set of his plastic dishes.
2. After the first defeat things looked rather (bad, badly) for the American army.
3. After a while the frantic prisoner was persuaded to come (quiet, quietly) with us.

4. The game has started, and may the (better, best) team win.
5. The jackets were heavy but they did not feel (warmly, warm).
6. Why don't you do it (different, differently)?
7. I got up much too (late, lately) this morning.
8. I have a great deal of trouble getting up on time (late, lately).
9. Who would have thought the peaches would look so (good, well)?
10. I observed his face (good, well).

VERB FORMS

6. *The appropriate form of the verb should be used.*

A student who is uncertain about the right form of a verb turns to his dictionary for help. Let us see what he finds:

Webster's New Collegiate	*American College Dictionary*
lead (lēd), *v.t.;* LED (lĕd); LEAD'ING.	**lead** (lēd), *v.,* **led, leading,** *n.*
lay, *v.t.;* LAID (lād); LAY'ING.	**lay** (lā), *v.,* **laid, laying,** *n.*
rise (rīz), *v.i.;* ROSE (rōz); RIS'EN (rĭz''n); RIS'ING (rīz'ing).	**rise** (riz), *v.,* **rose, risen, rising,** *n.*
jump (jŭmp), *v.i.*	**jump** (jŭmp), *v.i.*

These examples illustrate the fact that a dictionary gives what are known as the "principal parts" of a verb, or as many of them as are necessary. Verbs are regular or irregular. The **regular** verbs form their past tense and their past participle by adding *-d*, *-t*, or *-ed* to the present: *I jumped, I have jumped, I was jumping.* The **irregular** verbs change the present stem form to make the past tense and the past participle: *I rise, I rose, I have risen.* From the principal parts we get the key to all the forms of the verb—or its conjugation. You can see from the examples given that one part is enough to give us the key to a regular verb. Two parts in addition to the present—the past tense and the past participle—are needed in an irregular verb. When the dictionary does not list the past participle, it is assumed that it is the same as the past tense, as in *I lead, I led, I have led; I lay it down, I laid it down, I have laid it down.*

An abridged conjugation of the verb *take* is given below. For other forms and their uses, see section 6a. The principal parts of the verb *take* are *take, took, taken.*

INDICATIVE MOOD

ACTIVE VOICE		PASSIVE VOICE	
Present Tense			
Singular	*Plural*	*Singular*	*Plural*
I take	we take	I am taken	we are taken
you take	you take	you are taken	you are taken
he takes	they take	he is taken	they are taken
Past Tense			
I took	we took	I was taken	we were taken
you took	you took	you were taken	you were taken
he took	they took	he was taken	they were taken
Future Tense			
I shall (will) take	we shall (will) take	I shall (will) be taken	we shall (will) be taken
you will take	you will take	you will be taken	you will be taken
he will take	they will take	he will be taken	they will be taken
Present Perfect Tense			
I have taken	we have taken	I have been taken	we have been taken
you have taken	you have taken	you have been taken	you have been taken
he has taken	they have taken	he has been taken	they have been taken
Past Perfect Tense			
I had taken	we had taken	I had been taken	we had been taken
you had taken	you had taken	you had been taken	you had been taken
he had taken	they had taken	he had been taken	they had been taken

Future Perfect Tense

I shall (will) have taken	we shall (will) have taken	I shall (will) have been taken	we shall (will) have been taken
you will have taken	you will have taken	you will have been taken	you will have been taken
he will have taken	they will have taken	he will have been taken	they will have been taken

IMPERATIVE FORMS: take, be taken
INFINITIVE FORMS: to take, to have taken, to be taken, to have been taken
GERUNDS: taking, having taken, being taken, having been taken
PARTICIPLES: taking, taken, having taken, being taken, having been taken

TENSES

6a. The correct tense forms of the verb should be used.

1. **The present time.** Present time may be expressed by three main verb forms. The simple present tense form usually expresses general or habitual action: *I work, he teaches, she lives in Albany, they drive a Lincoln.* To express action as going on at the present time we use the **progressive** form of the present: *I am working, he is teaching, she is living in Albany, they are driving a Lincoln.* There is also a "do" form, which is used for emphasis (*I do work*), for negations (*she does not teach*), and for questions (*does she live in Albany?*).

2. **The past time.** Past time is usually expressed by the past tense, as in *I studied, she played the piano, he taught, I worked.* Past time may also be indicated by the present tense form (called the **historical present**), as *The captain looks at me, and I stare back at him, and he says to me . . . .* It is a device that can easily be abused in student writing.

3. **The perfect tenses.** The **present perfect** tense shows that an act has been completed prior to the present.

Examples:

Yes, I *have taken* a course in English grammar.
The boys *have been taken* to the gymnasium.

The **past perfect** tense shows that an act was completed before some specified or understood time in the past.

Examples:

I *had registered* for the course before I spoke to him.
He *had* already *paid* his fees.

The **future perfect** tense indicates a future act as past in relation to a specified or understood future time. This tense is not used as often as the others.

Examples:

I *shall have finished* my work by the time you arrive.
By ten o'clock all the dresses *will have been sold.*

4. **The future time.** Future time may be indicated in several ways. It may be indicated by the *present tense with an adverb or an adverbial phrase of time.*

Examples:

We *attack soon.*
We *take* the train *tomorrow morning.*
My last examination *comes on Saturday.*

The future may be indicated by using *"going to"* and *"about to"* with the verb.

Examples:

He *is going to give* us an easy examination.
They *are going to take* an early train.
He *is about to make* a special announcement.

Shall—will, should—would. The future may be indicated by using *shall* or *will* with the verb. In his study of English, the college student should be aware of the fact that the use of *shall* and *will* is the center of much controversy. He should know that strong differences of opinion exist. In modern informal speech, most people use *will* and *would* (or the contractions *I'll, he'll, he'd, you'd*) for all persons. Some people use *shall* and *should* for the first person, and *will* and *would* for the second and third persons, in their writing, their lectures or public speeches, and the contractions in their informal talk. Others use *will* and *would* for all occasions. There is no particular uniformity.

Those to whom distinctions between *shall* and *will* are important observe, in general, the following uses: for simple future, *shall* with the first person, *will* with the second and third persons; for the emphatic future, *will* with the first person, *shall* with the second and third persons. Here are a few examples taken from a series of radio talks:

I shall mention three developments. If you should pick up a lump of earth. . . .
I should like to consider this problem. I should like to describe for you. . . .
I shall mention only one example. We shall find out some more about comets. . . .
I shall close my talk with another example.

In asking questions, *shall* is ordinarily used with the first and third persons and *will* with the second person when a request for permission is implied: *Shall* I wrap it up for you? *Shall* he take you home? *Will* you do it? A note of formality may be implied to a question if the speaker uses the form that he anticipates in the answer: *Shall* you be at the meeting? I *shall.*

To express habitual or customary action, *would* is used in all three persons.

Examples:

He *would* read in the library instead of playing baseball with the boys.
She *would* sit in her rocker and knit all day long.

Should is often used in the sense of *ought,* although in some sentences *ought* may imply a slightly stronger sense of obligation.

Examples:

I really *should eat* less. [I really *ought to eat* less.]
His papers *should have been returned* to him. [His papers *ought to have been returned* to him.]

Sequence of Tenses. Use the tenses which show the correct relation of time between the main verb and the subordinate verbs.

Examples:

Yesterday I told my teacher that I *had written* my essay. [Not *have written.*]
We started for home so that our parents would not suspect that anything out of the ordinary *had taken* place. [Not *took.*]

Be careful to use the correct tense of infinitives and participles. Notice in the following examples that the time indicated by the verbal is always in relation to the time expressed by the main verb.

Examples:

I was delighted *to receive* your invitation. [Not *to have received.*]
She would have liked *to talk* with you about your garden. [Not *to have talked.*]
He probably meant *to lock* the garage door, but he forgot. [Not *to have locked.*]
Having played tennis all day, Mr. Blow was in no mood for dancing in the evening. [Not *playing.*]

Careless Shift in Tense. In telling a story, it is undesirable to shift from the past to the present and from the present to the past unless there is a real change in time. (See also section 34.) For this reason the use of the **historical present** must be undertaken warily.

Bad tense shifts:

We were speeding through the rain and the spray at eighty miles an hour. Visibility was none too good. The pavement was dotted with slick places. On a long, straight stretch we started to pass a slow moving car. Suddenly an old farm truck barged in from a side lane. Our driver *jams* on the power brakes. The car *crouches* for a second, then *swings* wildly to the left. The right-side wheels *leave* the pavement. There *is* a moment of sickening swaying, and then the car righted itself, and we were on our way again.

Careless Omission of Endings -s, -ed. Be careful not to leave off the ending *-s* of the third person singular of the present tense, or the *-ed* of the past tense of the regular verb.

Wrong:

We *use* to go there every spring to fish for trout.
He *insist* that he is ill, but I do not believe him.
I *ask* him last night to lend me his notebook.

Right:

We *used* to go there every spring to fish for trout.
He *insists* that he is ill, but I do not believe him.
I *asked* him last night to lend me his notebook.

THE SUBJUNCTIVE

6b. *The subjunctive mood is still used in a number of special situations in literary English.*

The following is a simplification of a very complex subject. As far as the form of the verb is concerned, we can say that for most verbs the subjunctive form of the verb differs from the indicative in only the third person singular of the present tense.

Indicative		*Subjunctive*	
I take	we take	if I take	if we take
you take	you take	if you take	if you take
he takes	they take	if he take	if they take

Example:

We recommend that he *take* the entrance examinations.

The verb *to be* is a special problem. The problem may be simplified by saying that the subjunctive of *to be* uses:

1. *Be* in all forms of the present tense
2. *Were* in all forms of the past tense
3. *Have been* in all forms of the present perfect tense

The only uses of the subjunctive with which a student need concern himself in his speech and writing are:

1. In *if*-clauses expressing doubt or impossibility of the condition (usually referred to as "condition contrary to fact").

Examples:

If he *were* heavier, he would be more useful to the team.
When I entered, I could hear him shouting at his secretary, and I could not help wondering if that *were* his usual manner.
Were he alive, he would be proud of his son.

2. In *that*-clauses expressing a wish, request, or command.

Examples:

The colonel requested that the delegates *be* treated with all military courtesy.
The committee demanded that he *come* to a decision immediately.

3. In main clauses to express hope, wish, or prayer, in more or less traditional and stereotyped patterns.

Examples:

Heaven *help* the working girl.
Long *live* the King!
"The subjunctive *be* hanged!" exclaimed the weary student.
The peace of quiet gardens *be* with you.

VOICE

6c. *The passive voice of the verb should not be overused.*

In narrative and descriptive writing especially, the active verb form is more direct, more vivid, and more emphatic than the passive.

The passive voice, however, has its legitimate uses. It is indispensable when the action of the verb is more important than the doer, when the doer of action may not be known, or when the writer may wish to place the emphasis on the recipient of the action rather than on the doer. It is not the passive voice that is objectionable—it is the *overuse* or the *misuse* of it.

Examples:

A sum of ten thousand dollars was collected by the committee.
In the resulting fire the building was completely gutted.
Another filling station was held up last night.

Poor:

A good time was had by all. [Better: *Everybody had a good time.*]
Your kind letter was received by me. [This is the passive of false modesty, the attempt to avoid using the personal pronoun.]
A fishing trip was suggested by my father. [More direct: *My father suggested a fishing trip.*]

The passive voice becomes the scapegoat if not the actual culprit when there is a shift in point of view in a group of sentences. Notice what happens in the following sentences:

Confused:

One girl may be writing a letter; a book absorbs the attention of another. As usual someone sat in her chair sound asleep. Constant whispers could have been heard by the lecturer.

Consistent:

During the lecture, one girl is writing a letter; another is reading a book. As usual someone sits sound asleep. Several girls are whispering constantly.

The passive voice, on the other hand, may be useful in that it enables a writer to maintain his point of view through several sentences.

Shift in point of view:

She sat absorbed over her book. A frown could be seen on her face. Then a long whistle from outside interrupted her thoughts. She glanced in annoyance toward the window. Then she smiled as if what she saw there amused her.

Consistent point of view:

As she sat there frowning, absorbed over her book, her thoughts were interrupted by a long whistle from outside. Annoyed, she glanced through the open window. Then she smiled in amusement at what she saw there.

Exercises

Exercise 1, Principal parts. With the help of your dictionary find the principal parts of the following verbs. List the form given, the past tense, the past participle, and the present participle or gerund: for example, *begin, began, begun, beginning.*

blow	drag	know	raise	slay
break	drink	lay	ride	smite
bring	drive	lead	ring	spring
burst	eat	leave	rise	sting
choose	fly	lend	set	swim
come	get	lie	shake	take
dive	go	lose	sink	throw
do	grow	prove	sit	write

Construct sentences in which you use (1) the past tense form, (2) the present perfect tense form, and (3) the past participle in the progressive form.

Exercise 2, Verb forms. In the following sentences make all corrections in verb forms that you think are necessary.

1. One morning last summer while I was still laying in bed, Uncle Toby burst into the room, and raised the window shades.
2. I raised up in bed to see where the fire was.
3. A quick glance proved to me that there was no fire.
4. "Get up," said my uncle. "The gas main has broke near Salem, and we need a man to drive a supply truck."
5. I drug myself out of bed and reached for the levis and logger boots that were laying on the floor.
6. After I had ate my breakfast, I throwed some tools into the pickup and started to get in.
7. Just then Uncle Toby bounced up, strutting like an elderly bantam, determination wrote all over him.
8. I made room for him, and as I drove I just let him set there and talk.
9. Before the day was over, I had reason to be thankful that I had brung him with me, for he was a cheerful companion during a long day's work.

10. It wasn't hard work, but it was a full eighteen hours before I had a chance to pull off my clothes and lie down again.
11. The gas main that had blowed up during the night had served several communities to the south.
12. I loaded supplies, ate sandwiches and drunk coffee, run errands, and dozed on the seat of the pickup while I waited.
13. The gas was shut off, and slowly the break was repaired late at night, with searchlights shining into our eyes from every direction.
14. I did not have time to realize how tired I had became, until I saw my uncle Toby setting up in the truck, sound asleep.
15. I put a folded coat under his head, and covered him up with some old blankets, and let him sit and snore happily.

Exercise 3, Tenses. If you find any mistakes in tenses in the following sentences, make the necessary corrections.

1. Knowing very little French, I could not follow his explanations.
2. Losing his money in gambling, he returned to his family in England.
3. I should have liked to have stayed longer in Italy.
4. The summer before, we had driven through Michigan so that we could have spent a little time with our daughter.
5. We were delighted to have received your invitation.

Exercise 4, The subjunctive. In the following sentences select the correct forms from those given in parenthesis.

1. The first man we picked asked that his name (is, was, be) withdrawn.
2. Mother insisted that he (wears, wear) his raincoat.
3. Father suggested that he (take, takes) his umbrella.
4. The next speaker moved that the resolution (is, be, was) tabled.
5. I wish I (was, were) in Florida right now.
6. If that (was, were) my dog, I (should, would) teach him better manners.
7. Someone is sure to ask that the rule (is, be) amended.
8. She certainly looks as if she (was, were) ill, but she is quite well.
9. He talks as if he (were, was) ready to make a few concessions.
10. May I ask that further study of their offer (be, is) postponed?

MECHANICS

MANUSCRIPT: FORM AND REVISION

7. Manuscripts should be carefully prepared and revised.

7a. In the preparation of manuscript follow standard procedures and any special instructions given you by your English teacher.

1. **Use standard typewriter paper or, for handwritten papers, the 8½ x 11 ruled theme paper.** Most English departments require composition students to use regulation typewriter paper, unruled if the themes are typewritten, ruled if the themes are handwritten. Notebook paper, if its use is permitted, should not be ripped out of its notebook.

But no instructor will warm up to a student who uses narrow-lined notebook paper for his themes. Writing on that sort of paper is extremely hard to read.

2. **Write legibly.** If you write by hand, make your writing easy to read. Write with a good pen and use black or dark blue ink. Do not use red, violet, or green ink. Form all letters distinctly, especially those that might be confused with other letters. Dot your *i's* and cross your *t's*. Do not decorate your letters with unnecessary loops and flourishes.

3. **Type legibly.** If you use a typewriter, see that the ribbon is fresh and the type clean. Adjust your margin properly. Always double-space your writing. Space five spaces for paragraph indentations, one space between words, and two spaces after the

end punctuation of a sentence. If you must delete material in typing, type over it with a capital "M." If you must cross out any considerable portion of your material, type your page over again. Never begin a line with a punctuation mark, such as a comma, a period, a question mark, or an exclamation point, which belongs at the end of the preceding line.

4. Label your themes correctly. Use the method of labeling papers that is recommended by your instructor. Follow his instructions exactly. If themes are to be handed in on flat, unfolded sheets of paper (the method preferred by all publishers), the right place for the name, the page number, and the theme number is the upper-right hand corner of each page. Of course you should never write on the back of the paper. To a printer, paper has only one side.

5. Be careful about the correct placing and capitalization of the title. Write the title on the first line of the first page only, or about two inches from the top of the sheet. Center the title on the page. Capitalize the first word and all important words in the title. The usual practice is to capitalize all nouns, pronouns, verbs, adverbs, adjectives, and prepositions that stand last or contain more than five letters. Do not underline the title or enclose it in quotation marks. Of course when the title is a quotation, and for some reason you wish to emphasize the fact that it is quoted, you enclose it in quotation marks. Do not use a period after it, but you may use a question mark or an exclamation point if the sense of the title calls for either of these marks. Leave a space of about an inch between the title and the first line of your theme. Do not repeat the title on succeeding pages.

6. Margins. Leave margins of an inch at the top and at the left of each page. Do not crowd your words at the right or at the bottom of the page. Some instructors like a wide margin at the right as well as at the left of the page so as to have room for comments and corrections. After the first page, begin writing on the first line.

7. Indent properly to indicate paragraphs. Indent five typewriter spaces for the first line of a paragraph.

WHY I CAME

12 Why did I come to college. That is a hard question,
2 it cannot be answered in a few words. From one point of
20 view, it seems abserd that I should be here without
15/20 knowing why I am here. Its true my parents allways wanted
me to go to college. They probably never quite analyzed
their reasons for wanting me to go. They wanted me to
1 better myself. To learn a profession or a trade. They
11 felt that a well educated man would be able to lead an
6/32 easier life than they lived. Knowing the hard life they
6/13 lived their attitude seems reasonable to me. From another
13 point of view however, it seems logical to me that I should
come to college to find out why I came to college. I am
not sure that I can find all the answers. My college work
1 may give me one answer to my question. Or maybe several
44 of the many possible answers. While I do not expect to
find all the answers, after four years here I may know
20 more definately what the question means.

29 I have talked with other freshmen about their
20
22 reasons for comeing to college. They have many solutions.
1 Most of them talk about economic security. Which of course
is a legitimate objective. Others talk about a life of
33 service to others. If you talk long enough about the subject,
you will hear mention of cultivation of the mind and the
emotions. These are ideas I will try to discuss here.

WHY I CAME

12 Why did I come to college/? That is a hard question,
2 ~~it~~ which cannot be answered in a few words. From one point of
20 view, it seems ~~absered~~ absurd that I should be here without
15/20 knowing why I am here. It's true my parents ~~allways~~ always wanted
me to go to college. They probably never quite analyzed
their reasons for wanting me to go. They wanted me to
1 better myself/ ~~To learn~~ by learning a profession or a trade. They
11 felt that a well-educated man would be able to lead an
6/32 easier life than they ^have lived. ~~Knowing~~ Because I know the hard life they
6/13 ^have lived, their attitude seems reasonable to me. From another
13 point of view, however, it seems logical to me that I should
come to college to find out why I came to college. I am
not sure that I can find all the answers. My college work
1 may give me one answer to my question/ ~~Or~~ or maybe several
44 of the many possible answers. ~~While~~ Although I do not expect to
find all the answers, after four years here I may know
20 more ~~definately~~ definitely what the question means.
29 ~~I have talked~~ As I talk with other freshmen about their
20/22 reasons for ~~comeing~~ coming to college/, ~~They have many solutions.~~ I encounter many ideas.
1 Most of them talk about economic security/, ~~Which~~ which of course
is a legitimate objective. Others talk about a life of
33 service to ~~others.~~ humanity. If you talk long enough about the subject,
you will hear mention of cultivation of the mind and the
emotions. These are ideas I will try to discuss here.

If you are quoting verse—a fairly uncommon occurrence in composition—center your quotation on the page and follow the line arrangement of the poem from which you are quoting. No quotation marks are needed. If the quotation does not end a paragraph, begin the next line of your composition flush with the left margin.

8. Deletions and corrections. Parentheses and brackets are never used to delete or cancel a word. These marks have other uses.

To delete material, draw a horizontal line through it. In typing, material may be deleted by typing a capital "M" over it—if the section to be crossed out is not too extensive.

If you wish to insert a correction in your text, mark the point of insertion with a caret (∧) and write the inserted material above the caret.

7b. Revise your manuscript carefully, both before you hand it in and after it has been returned to you.

1. Go over your paper carefully in first draft and copy it for final submission. As an aid in revising your first draft, you should consider the following checklist:

a. Has the paper an objective, a central idea, a direction?
b. Is the content made interesting by facts and examples?
c. Is the organization, in the whole paper and in the separate paragraphs, as logical as I can make it?
d. Have I corrected obvious errors in sentence structure, such as the period fault, the comma splice, failure of verbs and subjects to agree?
e. Have I checked the punctuation and spelling?

There are other things to check for, of course, but if you keep these in mind as you revise, your paper will gain in clarity and force and correctness.

2. Revise your paper carefully after the instructor has returned it to you. Make every correction indicated or suggested by your instructor. If he refers you to a handbook section, first study the section carefully to see how it applies to your error. Then, in red ink, draw a horizontal line through the word or words you wish to cancel, and in the space above, between the lines, write the revised version.

If your instructor indicates by a note or a comment in the margin that some part of your paper is confused, undeveloped, poorly phrased, inadequate in detail or evidence, or illogical, rewrite the section criticized. Whenever the revision is short, you may write between the lines. When you rewrite a number of sentences or paragraphs, however, you should first make your corrections in red ink on the face of your manuscript, and then recopy the entire page.

If you rewrite or recopy a page or an entire theme, be sure to return both versions to your instructor.

CAPITALS

One of the best rules of capitalization for the student to use is, *Do not capitalize without some definite reason. Do not overcapitalize.*

In general, the conventions of strictly formal writing require the capitalization of a number of words not capitalized in informal or journalistic writing.

8a. Capitalize the first word of every sentence, of a group of words understood as a sentence, of a direct quotation within a sentence even if quotation marks are not used, and of a line of poetry.

Examples:

I had as lief have their room as their company.
Are you making a mountain out of a molehill?
More coffee? Not now. Later, perhaps.
He replied, "The best guesser is the best prophet."
The key question of this philosophy is, Will it work?

> God's in his Heaven—
> All's right with the world!

Do *not* capitalize the first word of (a) an indirect quotation, (b) a direct quotation that is fragmentary or structurally a part of the sentence in which it stands, (c) the part of a direct quotation which follows dialogue tags like *he said* unless this begins a new sentence.

Examples:

The professor admitted that no one can know everything. [Indirect quotation]
It is always risky to speak of a philosophy as being "the wave of the future." [Fragmentary]
"Success in love," he said sadly, "does not always go to the most deserving."

For the proper capitalization of the title of a book, a story, an essay, or a student paper, see section 7a, 5.

8b. *Proper nouns and adjectives are capitalized.*

A proper noun names some particular person, place, or object; a common noun names one of a class of persons, places, or objects.

Capitalize:

1. Names of persons and places: Harry, Belinda, Kierkegaard, Jean-Paul Sartre, Cleveland, Benton County, Texas, France, Glacier Park.
2. Names of political and geographic divisions if they are part of a proper name: Dominion of Canada, Union of South Africa, the Middle West, the Orient. [But *not:* a union of states, a dominion, a republic, a county.]
3. Names of historic events or epochs: the Dark Ages, World War II, Armistice Day, the Renaissance, the Middle Ages, the Restoration.
4. Names of races and languages: English, French, Indian, Negro, Latin, Jewish, Japanese.
5. Derivatives of proper names: Roman, Miltonic, Macedonian. [But many words derived from proper nouns, such as *roman* or *italic* type, are now considered common.]
6. Names of organizations: Elks, Masons, the Beavers, Bureau of Engraving and Printing, Red Cross.
7. Religious terms: Bible, Old Testament, Catholic, Protestant, the Almighty, Christianity, Apostles' Creed.
8. Days of the week and months: Sunday, Monday, March, December, etc.

See also section 8d for distinctions between a word used as a proper noun and the same word used as a common noun.

8c. *Any title used preceding a name or as a substitute for the name is capitalized.*

A title following a name is capitalized only when it is intended to show high respect or distinction.

Examples:

President Taft, Queen Victoria, Cardinal Newman, Professor James Bentley; the President, the Speaker of the House; Cordell Hull, Secretary of State; R. W. Barfoot, professor of mathematics; D. H. Jones, the chairman of the committee.

But notice that these words are *not* capitalized when they are not part of a title.

Examples:

The country has a new queen. This year we elect a president. He became a cardinal at the age of sixty. He is now a professor.

Abbreviations after a name, such as Esq., M.A., Ph.D., LL.D., D.D., F.R.S., are usually capitalized. The following are correct either with or without capitals: Jr., jr., Sr., sr., No., no., A.M., a.m., P.M., p.m.

8d. *Common nouns are not capitalized unless they are used in the proper sense.*

1. Capitalize *North, East, South, West, Northwest, Middle West, Near East* only when these words refer to geographical divisions. Do not capitalize these words when they refer to directions.

Examples:

The Near East is in turmoil again. She is from the South. He went south for the winter. That place is east of here.

2. Capitalize the words *college, university, high school,* etc., only when they are a part of some name, but not when they are used as common nouns.

Examples:

She is now at the University of Georgia.
He is now president of a university.

The college that I attended is Pasadena College.
I graduated from Fairview High School.
After I graduated from high school I enlisted in the Marines.

3. Capitalize the names of particular studies or courses, such as *Mathematics 35, Contemporary Literature 271.*

Do not capitalize the names of studies when they do not refer to specific courses, as *geology, history, engineering, forestry, home economics, law, educational psychology.* Remember, however, that names of races and languages are always capitalized, as *English literature, French history, Latin words, Indian songs.*

4. Capitalize words denoting family relationships, as *mother, father, brother, sister, uncle,* etc., only when these words stand for the name of some individual. Note that when these words are preceded by a possessive, that is an indication that the words are common nouns.

Examples:

I knew that Mother would object. My mother never objects. I wondered what Uncle Toby would say. My uncle Toby never says much.

When no rule seems to apply, it is always well to turn to your dictionary for guidance.

Exercises

Exercise 1. Copy the following, supplying capitals where they are necessary. Give your reason for using each capital.

1. My roommate, carl lauersen, was sent by our college as a delegate to the young america convention in new york.
2. The delegates were particularly interested in the sessions of the united nations.
3. They left here monday for portland, where they boarded a united air lines plane.
4. Delegates from reed college and the university of idaho were on the same plane.
5. Carl lauersen, whose father came to this country from denmark years ago, is especially interested in meeting people from different parts of america.

6. He talked with delegates from the south, the east, and the middle west.
7. His experiences included a number of trips to such places of interest as rockefeller plaza, greenwich village, and the statue of liberty on bedloe's island.
8. Carl returned on friday, just in time to study for his final examinations in sociology 347, international law 401, and modern european history 302.

Exercise 2. Copy the following sentences, supplying capitals where necessary.

1. When I went to register at benton hall, I met a young man from lincoln high school.
2. He and I had worked together at yellowstone park during the summer.
3. He had graduated from high school three years before I did, but instead of going to college he had enlisted in the navy.
4. Now we were here at the university of california at berkeley, california, both trying to enter as freshmen.
5. I was going to take a liberal arts course, but he had his heart set on engineering.
6. His adviser, professor brown, suggested that he take a general course first, with emphasis on physics, chemistry, and, of course, mathematics.
7. He had already checked mathematics 201 and physics 301 as possible courses.
8. "I am trying to find room for modern european history 110 also," he said.
9. We had coffee together and then went to see professor bowen again.
10. We managed to get into the same section in english composition, which meets at eight on monday, wednesday, and friday.

ABBREVIATIONS AND NUMBERS

9. *In ordinary writing, abbreviations are usually avoided (with a few standard exceptions), and numbers are written out whenever they can be simply expressed in one or two words.*

9a. *In ordinary writing, the following abbreviations are customary and appropriate. All others are usually written out.*

1. Titles before proper names: Dr., Mr., Mrs., M., Messrs., Mme., Mlle.
2. Certain designations after names: Jr., jr., Sr., sr., D.D., M.A.

3. With dates only when necessary for clearness: A.D. [written before the date], B.C. [written after the date].
4. Certain expressions usually abbreviated in informal and in technical writing, though written out when a more formal effect is desired: i.e., e.g., viz., etc. [written out: *that is, for example, namely, and so forth*].
5. Names of government agencies and certain other well-known organizations: TVA, CARE, NATO, WAVES. Note that the last three of these are pronounced as single words (called *acronyms*), rather than as a series of letters.

The following are usually written out, although in footnotes, bibliographies, tabulations, and addresses they may be abbreviated to conserve space:

1. Names of countries and states: West Virginia, *not* W. Va.; Canada, *not* Can.
2. Names of the months and days of the week: September, *not* Sept.; Monday, *not* Mon.
3. Christian names: Charles, *not* Chas.; Robert, *not* Robt.
4. Names of college courses, titles of professors, and other words frequently abbreviated in campus conversation: professor, *not* prof.; library, *not* libe; political science, *not* polly sci.
5. The titles *Reverend* (not *Rev.*) and *Honorable* (not *Hon.*), at least in formal situations. These titles are used with the person's whole name, not with just the last name.
6. The following words: number, volume, chapter, page, and (*not* &), street, avenue, manufacturing, company, mountain, Christmas.

Undesirable:

I'm looking forward to Xmas vacation next Dec.
This class meets on Tue., Thurs., and Sat.
He said he worked in N.Y. for the Cohoes Man. Co.
Some day she hopes to be a prof. of home ec.
Wm. lives on Jerome Ave., near Dilmore St.

Better:

I'm looking forward to Christmas vacation next December.
This class meets on Tuesday, Thursday, and Saturday.
He said he worked in New York for the Cohoes Manufacturing Company.
Some day she hopes to be a professor of home economics.
William lives on Jerome Avenue, near Dilmore Street.

9b. ***In ordinary writing, numbers are written out whenever they can be expressed in one or two words, or in a simple phrase.***

For the use of the hyphen with compound numbers see section 11.

Examples:

Elizabeth is about *twenty-five* years old.
She earned nearly *eight thousand* dollars last year.
She was able to buy *three and a half* acres of land.

A number beginning a sentence is usually spelled out. If it cannot easily be written out, change the sentence so that the number does not stand at the beginning.

Right:

Thirty-five people attended the ceremony. [*not:* 35 people. . . .]
She paid a price of $4,550 for the property. [*not:* $4,550 was. . . .]

9c. ***Figures are used for the following:***

1. Dates: March 17, 1960; *not* March seventeenth, nineteen hundred and sixty.
2. Street and room numbers: 415 State Street, *not* four hundred fifteen State Street; University Hall 216, *not* University Hall two sixteen.
3. Page numbers: page 45, *not* page forty-five.
4. Decimals, percentages, mathematical and technical statistics.
5. Several numbers occurring in the same paragraph or section.

Example:

These systems are at distances ranging from 100,000 to 1,500,000 light years, their diameters range from 4,000 to 45,000 light years, and the total luminosities from 20 to 500 million times the luminosity of the sun.

Notice in the last example that commas are used to separate the figures into groups, for clearness and convenience in reading. Commas are not used, however, in dates, serial numbers, page numbers, or telephone numbers.

Examples:

ORegon 5-2898, *not* 52,898. [Note the use of hyphens to divide certain complex numbers into convenient groups.]

Social Security Number 35-463-8205.
The population of the town now stands at 14,364.

Exercises

Exercise 1. Correct the errors in the use of abbreviations in the following sentences.

1. Mr. Jones and Doctor Landry came over from the City Hosp.
2. The profs. at the U. are all properly trained.
3. The lab in Chem 45 was very rigorous.
4. L. A. is a great town, but all of Southern Cal. is pleasant.
5. Rev. Lindsay gave the sermon at the Episc. Church.
6. Edwin Gorbaty, Junior, worked for CARE.
7. The dance at Thompsonville Hi was a great affair.
8. I like English Lit., but Classical Civ. is too much for me.
9. I was born in 1943, A.D.
10. I think Ore. is one of the finest states in the whole U.S.A.

Exercise 2. Identify the following abbreviations. Consult your dictionary for a list of abbreviations.

1. FM
2. CIO
3. r.p.m.
4. S.J.
5. S.P.C.A.
6. f.o.b.
7. UNRRA
8. USAF
9. Sc.D.
10. op. cit.
11. colloq.
12. ff.
13. q.v.
14. TNT
15. B.T.U.

Exercise 3. In the following sentences place a circle around the numbers which should have been written out in words.

1. We had a bad storm in 1950, near the 1st of December.
2. I had to pay 21 hundred dollars for my new car.
3. Actually I paid $2,145.50.
4. On his 10th birthday he received a $10 bill.
5. Out of my bank balance of about $400, I had to pay $225 for tuition, $30 for transportation, and $18 for books.
6. The city's population is now over the 1,000,000 mark.
7. The stadium will hold exactly 45,325, plus 2,500 standees.
8. They beat us under the boards, because they were a good 3 inches taller than we were on the average.
9. I marked off 30 paces, then 3 more, then 5 more, and finally 15 more, making 53 in all.
10. His final 4-year average was 84.53.

ITALICS

10. *The word italics refers to print. In handwriting or in typing, if the writer wishes to direct the printer to set a word in italic type, he underlines it.*

Typewritten:

```
In the March, 1959, issue of Harper's Magazine
there is a review of Robert Payne's The Gold of
Troy.
```

Print:

In the March, 1959, issue of *Harper's Magazine* there is a review of Robert Payne's *The Gold of Troy.*

In business letters, instead of being underlined, the words are usually typed in capitals, as: HARPER'S MAGAZINE, THE GOLD OF TROY.

Usage varies greatly in regard to the use of italics. The principles or statements of usage in this section refer to more or less formal usage. Newspapers, as a rule, do not use italic type. The *New York Times Book Review* uses quotation marks for titles of books. The *Saturday Review* does the same thing, both for books and for musical compositions. *Harper's Magazine* italicizes the titles of books, magazines, and newspapers, but uses quotation marks for title of musical compositions. *Time* uses italics for the titles of newspapers, magazines, books, motion pictures, and musical compositions. If you are writing for publication, the only sure guide is the style sheet of the magazine you are aiming at.

The following rules are usually observed in college papers of a formal nature.

10a. *When referred to in formal writing, titles of books, plays, newspapers, magazines, musical compositions, works of art, and names of ships and aircraft are usually underlined in manuscript and printed in italics.*

Examples:

the Portland *Oregonian*
Harper's Magazine
Harry Golden's *Only in America*
Beethoven's *Fidelio*
Titian's *Holy Family*
the *Zeppelin*
the *Queen Mary*

Quotation marks are generally used for chapters or subdivisions of books, for titles of short stories, magazine articles, newspaper articles, and short poems.

As one indication of formal usage, we note that the *MLA Style Sheet*[1] demands that its contributors underline "titles of published books, plays, pamphlets, periodicals, and classical works . . . " and poems if separately published. Titles of articles and essays, chapters and sections of books, and unpublished dissertations are to be enclosed in quotation marks.

Examples:

The short stories I like best in Maugham's *East and West* are "Rain," "The Letter," and "The Force of Circumstance."

The definite article "the" and the name of the city before the title of a newspaper are usually not italicized. There are, however, a few exceptions to this rule.

10b. *Foreign words and phrases that are still not Anglicized are italicized (underlined) when used in writing.*

A dictionary will tell you whether or not a certain foreign word or phrase has been Anglicized. Different dictionaries use different symbols for this purpose.

Webster's New World Dictionary: ‡*bon voyage;* ‡*fait accompli* [double dagger before the word.]
Webster's New Collegiate: ‖*bon voyage;* ‖*Dei gratia* [parallel bars before word.]
American College Dictionary: bon voyage. French. [italicized name of language after the word.]

The following illustrates the use of italics for foreign phrases as well as the use of single and double quotation marks with italics, commas, and exclamation points:

[1] Revised ed., p. 7.

For some U.S. schoolboys, making history is often a good deal easier than mastering it. Last week, as a case in point, the *English Record,* a quarterly put out by the New York State English Council, happily published the following high-school composition:

"On a beautiful evening in August, 1582, Queen Elizabeth entered the ancient town of Coventry, and divesting herself of her clothing, mounted a snow-white stallion and rode through the principal streets of the city. On her way she met Sir Walter Raleigh, who, observing her naked condition, threw his cloak about her, crying, '*Honi soit qui mal y pense!*', which, being translated, means: 'Thy need is greater than mine!' The Queen graciously responded, '*Dieu et mon droit!*', which translated means, 'My God, you are right!' This incident is called Magna Charta."

—*Time,* Feb. 16, 1953. Courtesy of *Time.* Copyright Time Inc. 1953. Quoted from *The English Record,* Vol. III, No. 2, Winter, 1953. Used by permission.

10c. In formal writing, words, letters, and figures, when they are referred to as such, are usually italicized.

In informal writing, quotation marks are commonly used for this purpose.

In definitions, the word to be defined is commonly set in italics (underlined) and the definition is enclosed in quotation marks.

Formal style:

We realize the humorous intention when somebody invents from the noun *swashbuckler* a verb to *swashbuckle*, or to *buttle* and *cuttle* from *butler* and *cutler,* but it is not so well known that the same process (probably with the same humorous intent behind it) gave us such sober words as *burgle, sidle, edit, grovel, beg,* and *greed.*

—Owen Barfield, *History in English Words.*

Thus words like *sapolio, oleomargarine, brillo,* a name for steel wool used in polishing, *fermillac,* fermented milk, *sozodont,* the name of a tooth powder, and dozens of others like these betray at least a moderate degree of familiarity with the classical languages.

—George P. Krapp, *The Knowledge of English.*

A nasturtium is a pretty flower, but the word *nasturtium* actually means "a nose twister." Few persons remember that *sabotage* means "throwing your wooden shoes into the machinery."

Informal style:

I was amazed when I learned that "flair" came from a word that meant "to give off an odor."
He used "infect" in place of "inflict."
Your "3's" and "8's" are alike.

10d. *Italics may be used to give special emphasis to a word or phrase.*

The use of underlining for emphasis is not popular in modern style. It was once the fashion for an author to shout and scream at the reader in capitals and italics. At present it is permissible to use italics for emphasis only when the sentence would not be immediately clear without italics. The following sentences are not examples of bad writing; they are merely illustrations of an older fashion.

Great is the combined voice of men; the utterance of their *instincts,* which are truer than their *thoughts:* it is the greatest a man encounters, among the sounds and shadows which make up this World of Time. He who can resist that, has his footing somewhere *beyond* Time.—Thomas Carlyle.

But, as *you* draw near, the woman raises her wasted features. Would Domrémy know them again for the features of her child? Ah, but *you* know them, bishop, well! Oh, mercy! what a groan was *that* which the servants, waiting outside the bishop's dream at his bedside, heard from his labouring heart, as at this moment he turned away from the fountain and the woman, seeking rest in the forests afar off. Yet not *so* to escape the woman, whom once again he must behold before he dies.—Thomas De Quincey.

Exercises

Exercise 1, Italics. Copy the following sentences, underlining for italics where necessary.

1. Fenwick had just finished glancing through some articles in Holiday, Fortune, and the National Geographic Magazine.
2. Before him lay a copy of Harry Golden's Only in America, which he intended to leaf through before he got down to serious study.
3. He started to put a new recording of Tchaikovsky's Symphonie Pathétique in the player, for he could always study better to music.

4. Perhaps, he thought, something from Gershwin's Porgy and Bess would be better.
5. Finally he started to read The Meaning of Meaning, by Ogden and Richards, a book so profound that only great music was a proper accompaniment.

Exercise 2, Italics. In the following quoted selections, point out the words that should be italicized (underlined).

But the fact that the year 1894 saw the publication of Anthony Hope's The Prisoner of Zenda, Stanley J. Weyman's Under the Red Robe, George W. Cable's John March, Southerner, and Captain Charles King's Waring's Peril is nothing very surprising, and certainly does not mark that year as the beginning of a "new romantic era."

—Frank Luther Mott, *Golden Multitudes,* 1947. Courtesy The Macmillan Company.

A convenient way of testing whether one has a definite understanding of an elaborate word is to translate the word into simple language, observing whether in the process it has lost any of its content. Does congregate mean anything more than crowd together, commiserate than feel sorry for, meticulous than careful about small things, impervious than impassable? Does sternutation mean more than snoring, nigritude than blackness, protuberance than bump?

—George Philip Krapp, *The Knowledge of English,* 1927. Courtesy Henry Holt and Company.

SYLLABICATION AND HYPHENS

11a. The awkward division of a word at the end of a line of handwritten or typewritten manuscript should be avoided.

In printed matter, where a perfectly even right-hand margin is mandatory, we have become accustomed to a number of word divisions at the ends of lines. In handwritten or typewritten papers, however, it is usually unnecessary to divide many words. An uneven right-hand margin is preferable to a large number of split words. For clearness and ease in reading, it is well to observe the following cautions about dividing words at the end of a line:

1. Never divide words of one syllable, such as *thought, reigned, rhythm, signed.* Note that the *-ed* ending in the past tense form must not be split off as a syllable when it is not pronounced as a syllable.

2. Never divide a word so that a single letter is allowed to stand by itself, either at the end of a line or at the beginning of the next line, as in *a-round, e-lope, greed-y, read-y.*

3. Try to avoid dividing proper names.

4. Try not to separate a name and the initials that go with it.

5. Try to avoid dividing the last word of a paragraph or a page. In print such a division is often necessary, but in manuscript it can be easily avoided.

11b. *If a division of a word is necessary, the division should be made between syllables and a hyphen placed at the end of the line.*

It may be helpful to assume that your reader is pronouncing your sentence aloud. Divide words so that both parts are pronounceable. Furthermore, you must divide correctly between syllables, and your best resource in doing so is your dictionary, where syllables are clearly indicated. The following cautions should be of additional help:

1. Divide compound words on the hyphen, and try to avoid a second hyphen: self-evident, *not* self-evid-ent; ante-bellum, *not* ante-bel-lum.

2. In words with prefixes, divide on the prefix: non-sensical, pre-caution, ante-diluvian. Note that these words are ordinarily written solid; they are not hyphenated compounds.

3. In words with suffixes, divide on the suffix: friend-ship, yell-ing.

4. As a rule, when a word contains double consonants, divide between the two consonants: acom-modate, inter-ruption. Note, however, as in the example of yell-ing, that when the rule about double consonants conflicts with the rule about suffixes, it is the rule about suffixes that you should follow.

11c. *Two or more words forming a compound adjective before a noun are hyphenated.*

Examples:

A rough-looking fellow, a red-hot stove, a twin-screw engine, in up-to-date condition, a well-traveled highway, an off-the-shoulder dress, a two-thirds majority, a straight-from-the-shoulder remark, an old-fashioned house, a pitch-dark night

When a compound modifier consists of two or more words with a common beginning, the following style is used: A three- or four-room addition, Anglo- and Franco-American.

The following are usually not hyphenated: compound modifiers that follow the noun, compounds made up of two proper nouns, and compounds in which an adverb ending in *-ly* is used.

Examples:

The man was well known for thievery.
I found most of his information up to date.
It was a loosely worded statement.
He is a United States marshal.

11d. *Compound numbers from twenty-one to ninety-nine are hyphenated.*

Examples:

forty-five dollars
three hundred and fifty-six yards

Fractions, when used as modifiers, are hyphenated. When one of the terms of the fraction is already a compound, however, no additional hyphen is used, as in *four twenty-fifths, twenty-one fortieths.* Such simple fractions as *one half, two thirds,* etc., are often written without a hyphen.

Examples:

The bill was finally passed by a two-thirds majority.
One half of the pie was already eaten.

11e. *Hyphens are used with the following classes of words:*

1. With the prefixes *ex-* and *self-,* but rarely with other prefixes: ex-president, ex-minister, self-regard, self-denial.
2. When two functions that are usually distinct are united in one person or thing: cleaner-polisher, secretary-treasurer, publisher-editor.
3. To avoid doubling a vowel letter or tripling a consonant letter: re-echo, pre-enrollment, semi-invalid, bell-like, co-operative (also coöperative).
4. With groups making or containing prepositional phrases: son-in-law, man-of-war, Jack-of-all-trades.
5. To prevent confusion with similar words: re-form (*cf.* reform), re-cover (*cf.* recover), re-creation (*cf.* recreation).

When in doubt as to the correct form of a compound, consult *Webster's New Collegiate,* the *American College Dictionary,* or *Webster's New World Dictionary.* See also, for a general discussion of compound words, Bergen and Cornelia Evans, *A Dictionary of Contemporary American Usage,* Random House, 1957, pp. 108–110.

Exercises

Exercise 1. Indicate which of the following words you should *not* split at the end of the line. Show how you would split the others. Give your reason in each case.

1. talked
2. prearrangement
3. through
4. thorough
5. thought
6. abide
7. fellowship
8. bankbook
9. self-esteem
10. tricky
11. speedy
12. superlative
13. might
14. roamed
15. review

Exercise 2. With the aid of a dictionary determine which of the following should be written solid, which with a hyphen, and which as separate words.

1. air base
2. air cooled engine
3. all American halfback
4. all right
5. anti Communist
6. anti toxin
7. any body
8. any how
9. any more
10. any time
11. base ball
12. book store
13. by law
14. by pass

15. dining room
16. drug store
17. every body
18. every thing
19. every time
20. every where
21. eye opener
22. eye shade
23. filing cabinet
24. foot ball
25. full grown
26. good by
27. half cousin
28. half crazed lion
29. half finished house
30. in as much as
31. infra red
32. north east
33. note book
34. one armed paper hanger
35. out doors
36. post office
37. quarter back
38. re written paper
39. score board
40. score card
41. some body
42. some one
43. some thing
44. sharp tempered
45. text book
46. truck gardener
47. under graduate
48. upper class man
49. week end trip
50. well designed jacket

PUNCTUATION

The purpose of punctuation is to help make clear the meaning of printed or written language.

Correct punctuation is based, in varying degrees, on three things: (1) thought or meaning, (2) the structural patterns of the sentence, (3) the conventions of the age. Punctuation is used to make meaning clear; hence any punctuation that makes it easier for the reader to understand the meaning of a sentence is good punctuation, and any punctuation that interferes with the communication of meaning is bad punctuation. The structural pattern of sentences is also used primarily to convey meaning. It follows, then, that meaning and structure—and especially structure, since that is the visible member of the team—both use punctuation for the same purposes. In addition, punctuation is governed by a set of conventions, the familiar and customary ways of doing things, which, like the conventions of social etiquette, of play, of business, make communication between people easy and natural.

The practice of writers may be codified into a number of rules or principles. These rules or principles govern a very large number of typical situations in writing. At times, certain marks are optional, depending on the decisions of publishers or on levels of usage; on the whole, however, a college student can get along pretty well if he follows codified usage. When he is in doubt, he can always resort to common sense.

END PUNCTUATION

THE PERIOD

12a. *A period is used after a declarative or an imperative sentence, or after an indirect question.*

Examples:

No man has a good enough memory to make a successful liar. [declarative]
Never refuse a good offer. Pay no attention to what critics say. [imperative]
Mother asked where we had been. The woman asked us if we enjoyed the play. [indirect questions]
Mother asked, "Where have you been?" The woman asked, "Did you enjoy the play?" [Direct questions end with a question mark.]

12b. *Most of the common abbreviations require a period.*

Examples:

Mr., Mrs., Dr., St., Ave., Jr., Sr., a.m., p.m., A.D., B.C.

The period is not used after certain groups of letters standing for organizations or governmental agencies.

Examples:

UN, UNRA, USSR, UNESCO, TVA, FCC, NAM, NAACP.

Usage is divided in regard to some of the older abbreviations consisting of the initial letters of words. It is a good practice to consult the dictionary.

Examples:

Y.M.C.A. or YMCA, r.p.m. or rpm, A.M.A. or AMA, B.P.O.E. or BPOE.

12c. *Periods (ellipsis marks or suspension points, usually three within a sentence, four at the end of a declarative sentence) are used to indicate the omission of words from a quoted passage, or pauses or hesitation in dialogue.*

Examples:

No freeman shall be . . . imprisoned . . . save by the lawful judgment of his peers or by the law of the land.—*Magna Carta,* 1215.

The souls of emperors and cobblers are cast in the same mould. . . . The same reason that makes us wrangle with a neighbor causes a war betwixt princes.—Montaigne.

"You think I go about staring at nothing," she remarked. . . . "Not a bit of it! I have been planning all sorts of things . . . I have been thinking how I could get to Germany. . . . Or one might catch them in Switzerland. . . . I've had all sorts of plans. They can't go guarded for ever. . . ." —From H. G. Wells, *Mr. Britling Sees It Through.*

THE QUESTION MARK

12d. *A question mark is used after a direct question but not after an indirect question.*

Examples:

Can we have an Age of the Common Man without making it an Age of the Common Denominator? Do any dangers lie ahead?—Joseph Wood Krutch.

What will I do if Miss Byrne is there? What will I say to her? she asked herself, but did not wait for an answer.—Michael McLaverty, *School for Hope.* [Quotation marks are sometimes omitted when unspoken thoughts are quoted.]

Was it not Plato himself who said that he would never write a treatise on philosophy, that the latter must be acquired by conversation, the flame leaping from speaker to speaker "until the soul itself caught fire"?—Irwin Edman, "Fashions in Ideas." [Note relation of question mark to quotation marks when part of a phrase is quoted in a question.]

After we landed we learned, with a tremendous surge of pride, that as the waters rose around them, those green troops, soldiers from far northwestern states mostly, stood in ranks on the canted decks singing a popular song of the war, "Where Do We Go from Here, Boys?"—Irvin S. Cobb. [A question mark ends the sentence if the last part is a quoted question.]

Instead of asking "What would a good education consist of?" many professors of education are asking "What do most college students want?"; instead of asking "What books are wisest and best and most beautiful?" they conduct polls to determine which the largest number of students have read with least pain.—Joseph Wood Krutch, "Is Our Common Man Too Common?" [Some writers would have put commas after each *asking*. Note that a question mark is used with a title if it is a question.]

A single question mark is used after a double question, that is, a quoted question following a question. (See also section 16.)

Examples:

Did he say, "How many?"
Who said, "When do we eat?"

A question mark within parentheses may be used to indicate doubt or uncertainty as to the preceding figure or fact.

Example:

Lucien Botha was born in 1779 (?) and died in 1859.

The use of a question mark to indicate irony is not sanctioned by reputable practice. It should be avoided in serious writing.

Poor:

We returned from a most enjoyable (?) hunting trip.

A question mark is often used after commands or requests phrased as questions if a formal effect is desired, but a period for a less formal effect.

Formal:

Will the staff please assemble in the auditorium at four o'clock this afternoon?

Less formal:

Will you return the proof at your earliest convenience.

THE EXCLAMATION POINT

12e. *An exclamation point is customary after an expression of strong feeling.*

It is well for the student to use the exclamation point with some caution and discretion. His tendency will be to use it too often. Words like *yes, no, oh, well, alas, surely,* and the like, when beginning a sentence, are usually followed by a comma. If *oh* introduces an expression of strong feeling, put the exclamation point at the end of the expression. Never use more than one exclamation point after an exclamation.

Examples:

"Great guns!" he shouted in consternation.
He actually said that!
Oh, this is unspeakable!

The days wore on, and yet got nowhere. . . . Time had simply come to a standstill! He had never seen the like; this was worse than the deadest lay-up in Lofoten!—O. E. Rölvaag, *Giants in the Earth.*

"I know a lady who was told by a Jesuit that it might be her vocation to be the best-dressed woman in every room she walked into as long as she did it to the greater glory of God, so boo!" Elvira said.—Bruce Marshall.

Exercise

Exercise 1. In the following sentences supply commas, periods, question marks, and exclamation points where they are necessary.

1. "Well how many fish did you catch" asked Mr Godfrey
2. Did Dr Williams ask you "Is it time to plant dahlias"
3. "Oh fudge" she answered, "he is always rushing the season"
4. "Can you tell me" asked Blanche "why he is out in the garden now"
5. "No Dulcie" said Prof Penwick "RIP does not mean 'please reply' "
6. "Hooray" shouted Dulcie. "Then I had it right I wrote 'RSVP' "
7. The sergeant shouted, "Down Hit the dirt" just as the mortars opened up on us
8. "How many times have you told this story Mr Brown" he asked
9. Did he ask Mr Brown how many times he had told this story
10. He asked if anyone had heard the story before
11. Will you please turn in your papers now
12. "You can't fool all of the people all of the time" said Lincoln—but it isn't necessary
13. "Oh yes" he said "That's true But not many people know it"
14. Do you know who said "No gentleman can be without three copies of a book: one for show, one for use, and one for borrowers"
15. "Which one of the three" asked Belinda sweetly, "would Prof Mortimer J Adler have you mark up"

THE COMMA

Of all the marks of punctuation, the comma has the widest variety of uses. Probably because the comma is used in so many situations, any attempt to codify the practice of writers and to state usage in terms of definite principles must give due weight to the exceptions. Yet, however important the differences of practice are, to the student the most important thing is that there is such a large area of agreement. Most of the uses of the comma can be stated in terms of principles, principles which reflect what most writers are doing.

The student should always remember, however, that these descriptions of usage must be interpreted with a little common sense. It is true, for instance, that writers place a comma after an introductory clause or phrase if they feel that this sentence element is not an integral part of the main clause—that is, if it is not closely restrictive—but no rule, only common sense, can tell him when this clause stops being restrictive and becomes not restrictive.

In a general way, punctuation tends to be *close* (that is, using more commas) in serious or formal writing, where precision is vital. It tends to be *open* (that is, using a minimum of punctuation) in informal description and narration and in journalistic writing.

Although the primary function of punctuation is to help make meaning clear, punctuation has another function, a rhetorical one. The comma—and to a certain extent the semicolon—may be used to indicate degrees of pause or emphasis or rhetorical balance or contrast of ideas. The important fact still remains, however, that before a writer can make punctuation an artistic resource he must first become familiar with the general practices of writers.

Because of its wide variety of uses, the comma may appear to some as a subject of puzzling complexity, although at times it is hard to see why eager young men of eighteen, who speak familiarly of isotopes and engage to pilot Comet jets, should be bowled over by so simple a thing as a comma. At any rate, it is possible to simplify a simple subject further by grouping all comma uses into two groups. In one group we have the "**to separate**" uses; in the other group we have the "**to enclose**" uses. A picture of the whole thing makes it still simpler and clearer.

A TABLE OF COMMA USES

USUALLY TO SEPARATE	USUALLY TO ENCLOSE
13a main clauses	13h nonrestrictive clauses
13b elements in series	13i parenthetical elements
13c co-ordinate adjectives	13j absolute phrases
13d words that may be misread	13k appositives
13e introductory modifiers	13l words in direct address
13f transposed elements	13m dialogue guides
13g mild exclamations, etc.	13n dates and addresses

13a. A comma is ordinarily used to separate co-ordinate clauses joined by and, but, for, nor, or, except when the clauses are short and closely related in meaning.

A writer is safe to apply this rule rather strictly in formal writing and to relax its application progressively as the level of writing becomes more and more informal. If he does so, he will not be wrong. At the same time, he must know that there is so much divergence in practice among writers that the use of a comma to separate main clauses has become almost optional. Journalistic writing discards the comma in this situation except to prevent misreading. At the formal level, the general practice is to omit the comma when the subject of the clause does not change. If there is any other clearly defined practice to help the beginning student, it is that the comma is obligatory before *for* (to prevent confusion with the preposition *for*) and recommended before *but*.

Examples:

After a time a farmer offered to help us, and we went into the machine shed to get a chain. [The subject changes.]

A psychologist objects to what he calls "herd thinking," but what a majority of people think is always what they've heard. [With *but*]

For the boundary between sea and land is the most fleeting and transitory feature of the earth, and the sea is forever repeating its encroachments upon the continents.—Rachel Carson, *The Sea Around Us.*

I have never had more than two English lessons in my life, for though I wrote essays at school, I do not remember that I ever received any instruction on how to put sentences together.—W. Somerset Maugham, *The Summing Up*. [With *for*]

For the use of a semicolon to separate main clauses, see section 14.

13b. *Commas are used to separate words, phrases, or clauses in a series.*

A series must have at least three members; usually the last two are joined by *and* or *or*. It is at this point, the point of the conjunction, that usage differs. Although the comma is generally used here in most formal writing,[1] some writers do omit it. In informal writing there is a progressive tendency to discard the comma before the conjunction, except for clearness, as the writing grows less formal. In journalistic writing, the comma is regularly omitted.

Examples:

A university is not made up of a stadium, a library, science laboratories, and recitation halls. [Nouns]

Memory may well arise to say that he [Stephen A. Douglas] was a builder of railroads, a true servant of civilization in the West, an orator of surpassing power, the founder of Chicago University, and a man who strove for the peace of his country.—Edgar Lee Masters, *The Sangamon*. [Series of nouns with modifiers.]

They spent a month getting their outfit together—three ten-gallon hats, checkered shirts, flowing bow ties, overalls, bright gloves, and high-heeled cowboy boots. They looked just the way New Yorkers think cowboys look. —Ernie Pyle, *Home Country*. [Note the use of a dash to introduce a series.]

But notice the following from quite serious writing:

To be courageous, these stories make clear, requires no exceptional qualifications, no magic formula, no special combinations of time, place and circumstance.—John F. Kennedy, *Profiles in Courage*.

[1] In the *MLA Style Sheet*, the only comment on commas is: "Use them before 'and' and 'or' in a series of three or more." P. 9.

An unstable society, with extremes of poverty and wealth, but with easy access to riches and a quick turnover in the composition of the aristocracy, might produce a brief, frenetic and opportunistic radicalism; but it was not likely to produce radicalism which was serious, unbribable and consistent. —Arthur M. Schlesinger, Jr., *The Age of Jackson.* [Note here the use of a semicolon between main clauses.]

13c. *Commas are used to separate consecutive adjectives preceding the noun they modify when the adjectives are co-ordinate in meaning.*

The comma is correct only when the adjectives are co-ordinate —that is, when each of the adjectives refers directly to the noun. When an adjective modifies the whole idea that follows it, it is not separated from it by a comma. If you can substitute *and* for the comma, the comma is correct. Note that in the following examples, it would be natural and correct to say "a surly and treacherous and cruel fellow," but it would be unnatural to say "a lazy and old fellow."

Examples:

Bones was a surly, treacherous, cruel fellow.
Henry was a lazy old fellow.
It was a raw, blustery night. [Raw *and* blustery]
The smithy stood under the spreading chestnut tree. [*Spreading* modifies *chestnut tree,* not *tree*]

A safe practice is to omit the comma with numerals and with the common adjectives of size and age.

Examples:

The little old lady, a large red-haired girl, four tiny black dots

13d. *The comma is used to separate words and phrases that might be incorrectly joined in reading.*

This rule applies to the following types of situations:

1. When the conjunctions *for* and *but* might be mistaken for prepositions.

Confusing:

The coyote must have turned for the dog seemed to hesitate a moment. [Must have turned for the dog?]
The men slid down the ropes but one sailor seemed to be caught in the rigging. [Slid down the ropes but one sailor?]

Right:

The coyote must have turned, for the dog seemed to hesitate a moment.
The men slid down the ropes, but one sailor seemed to be caught in the rigging.

2. When a noun might be mistaken for the object of a verb, verbal, or preposition before it.

Confusing:

After washing the men filed into the dining tent.
Before starting to eat Father bowed his head in prayer.
Above the sun burned a dull red; below the sand radiated heat like a furnace.

Right:

After washing, the men filed into the dining tent. [*Not:* After washing the men]
Before starting to eat, Father bowed his head in prayer. [*Not:* Before starting to eat Father]
Above, the sun burned a dull red; below, the sand radiated heat like a furnace. [*Not:* Above the sun . . . or below the sand]

13e. Ordinarily, a comma is used to set off a modifier which precedes a main clause, especially when the introductory element is long and not closely connected with the main clause in meaning.

In punctuating modifiers that precede the main clause you must depend on your good sense as well as on rules. You must decide whether or not the sentence will be clearer with the introductory modifier set off. Length of clause alone will not tell you when to use a comma and when not to use it. Frequently very short clauses are set off for emphasis. In general, if you feel that the introductory element is nonrestrictive, put a comma after it. The following distinctions will help you.

1. Use a comma when you begin with a fairly long nonrestrictive adverbial clause.

Examples:

If a language is spoken by at least two people, then there are always some differences of usage which an observer can detect if he looks closely enough. —Charles F. Hockett, *A Course in Modern Linguistics.*

Until our communities are ready to undertake the sort of community planning that leads to garden cities, it will be empty eloquence to talk about the future of American architecture.—Lewis Mumford.

If, as I have said, the things already listed were all we had had to contribute, America would have made no distinctive and unique gift to mankind.—James Truslow Adams.

2. Use a comma to set off a beginning participial phrase modifying the subject or an absolute phrase before the subject.

Examples:

Having listened to his story, the judge nodded and then dismissed the case. [Phrase modifies *judge.*]
The excitement being over, the students returned to the classroom. [Absolute phrase]

3. Set off short introductory prepositional phrases only when they are definitely nonrestrictive, such as transitional phrases.

Examples:

In the first place, he is usually the last man to leave the office.
About three years ago his father decided to move to England.
During the concert a little dog kept howling dolefully.
In many American colleges it is possible for a boy to win twelve letters without learning how to write one.—Robert M. Hutchins.

Long introductory prepositional phrases are set off if the punctuation is an aid to clearness.

Example:

In the biological and physical as well as the sociological sciences, statistics have become, as they never were before, the most important tool of investigation.—Joseph Wood Krutch.

4. A short introductory clause is usually not followed by a comma. It may, however, be set off for greater emphasis or for clearness.

Examples:

When he gives us a test he usually leaves the room. [Informal]
If the boy comes I shall tell him to look for you in your shop. [Informal]

13f. *A comma, or commas, may be used to indicate transposed or contrasting sentence elements.*

Examples:

She will pick up a book, not any special book, but just to feel a book in her hand.
Inequality, by arousing jealousy and envy, provokes discontent.
He [Shakespeare] knew that Hamlet's dilemma, between the flesh and the spirit, was at the heart of every human being's private tragedy, and he made Hamlet so terrifyingly real, with his courtesy and his violence, his intelligence and his self-hatred, his inconsistencies and his terrors, that every generation since has been able to recognize in him its own image.—Marchette Chute, *Shakespeare of London.* [Note here how commas set off balanced elements.]

13g. *Commas are used to set off mild exclamations, sentence adverbs, and the responsives yes and no when they begin a sentence.*

Examples:

Unfortunately, the third transport ship received a direct hit.
Yes, the second essay is due tomorrow.
No, I shall not go to the game this afternoon.
Mary said, "Well, I can't think of anything to say to him."
"Oh, it does not matter," replied her mother.
"Certainly, I will have my report in on time," said Penwick.

13h. *Commas are used to set off nonrestrictive clauses. They are not used to set off restrictive clauses.*

If the distinction between restrictive and nonrestrictive clauses is not already clear to you, think of restrictive clauses as "identifying" or "pointing-out" clauses. A restrictive clause helps to locate or identify its antecedent. It says to the reader, "I mean this particular person, object, or thing, and no other." It is close to its antecedent in meaning, so close that it cannot be separated from it by a comma. A nonrestrictive clause does not identify or point out. It merely gives additional information about its antecedent.

Restrictive:

We have decided to hire a woman *who knows how to cook.* [The clause says that we have decided to hire a particular kind of women, one with ability to cook, and no other kind.]

Nonrestrictive:

We have decided to hire Mrs. Williams, *who knows how to cook.* [The name identifies the woman. The clause merely adds information.]

Restrictive:

The boy *who has a hobby* will never be lonely. [Not any boy, but that particular kind of boy]
Please bring me the book *which you see lying on my desk.* [That particular book and no other]

Nonrestrictive:

We were introduced to Mike Bradley, *who asked us to go salmon fishing with him.* [The name identifies the person; the clause does not need to identify or point out.]
Astronomy, *which is the study of heavenly bodies,* is a fascinating subject. [*Astronomy* identifies itself. It does not need a clause to tell which particular astronomy.]
My father, *who had not heard the question,* shook his head in silence. [A person has only one father. The clause cannot help to identify him.]

The same rule applies to adverbial clauses, with the added proviso that adverbial clauses opening a sentence tend to be felt as nonrestrictive, and that adverbial clauses closing a sentence tend to be restrictive. (See section 13e.)

Restrictive:

He had spent the money *before his father died.*
Our navy will not be scrapped *when peace is declared.*
I studied engineering *because I wanted to help Father in his work.*

Nonrestrictive:

Although fruit flies are a nuisance in a cherry orchard, they are useful to a geneticist.
If that was not an apology, I do not know what it was.

Participial phrases may be either restrictive or nonrestrictive, depending on the meaning intended.

Restrictive:

The boy *standing near the door* is waiting to register. [That particular boy]
A book *written by that author* is sure to be interesting. [Phrase points to particular kind of book.]

Nonrestrictive:

Tom Nolan, *standing there by the door,* is waiting to register. [Name identifies him.]
Raising his rifle quickly, he fired at the moving object. [Nothing in the phrase helps to identify the person.]

13i. *Commas are used to set off parenthetical elements (interrupters), or words, phrases, and clauses used to explain, to qualify, or to emphasize.*

Three types of punctuation are used with parenthetical elements. Parentheses are used for the most distant interrupters, dashes for something a little less distant, and commas for interrupters most closely related to the rest of the sentence. See sections 17 and 18.

Examples:

It is not only decent—in terms of our American ethics—to give every other country a chance at the game, but—the reliable old puritan ethic again—it is also efficient to do so.—Margaret Mead, *And Keep Your Powder Dry.*

Of course we were to be educated: enlightenment and virtue (again a Greek notion) were closely allied.—George Santayana, *Persons and Places.*

In a sense, several of the sentence elements discussed under other rules are "interrupters" in that they tend to break or interrupt the normal flow of a sentence, but strict classification is not here important. The parenthetical elements dealt with here may be classified as follows:

1. Conjunctive adverbs such as *however, therefore, moreover, furthermore,* when they are used within the clause. These words are more appropriate in a formal than in a colloquial style. And in any style, an epidemic of *moreover's* and *furthermore's* is as bad as a plague of *and's* and *but's.*

Examples:

An institution, *therefore,* may fail because its standards are too high.
In truth, *however,* it was probably not known until after the French Revolution.

2. Directive and qualifying words and phrases. Some of the most common of these, such as *also, perhaps, indeed, too, at least,* may, in informal writing, be considered as close modifiers and therefore not set off by commas. Others are usually set off.

Examples:

My theory, *unluckily,* was disproved by the events that followed.
He would become, *in short,* a problem child of the worst kind.
He will, *by so doing,* bring greater happiness to himself and his family.
Indeed, two of them actually did escape from the island.

3. Parenthetical clauses. Most of these are parenthetical comments, but some are adverbial clauses which break into the sentence flow.

Examples:

This, *I suppose,* is the essence of morality.
No teacher can give you an education; he can only, *as it were,* point in the direction of it.
Our interpretation of his motives is, *I think,* totally unfair.
If you must take risks on the lake, see to it that, *whenever storm warnings are up,* you at least have a life preserver with you.
These men, *if they are not subjected to the authority of political institutions,* will lead us into disaster.—Alexander Meiklejohn.

13j. *Commas are used to set off absolute phrases when they occur within the sentence.*

Examples:

A great dam came into view, *water boiling* from its curved rank of spill-ways.—Andrew H. Brown, *National Geographic.*
She stood there, her damp *face glowing* with happiness, and asked us all to be seated.

13k. *Commas are used to set off appositives.*

An appositive, or a word in apposition, is used to limit or qualify the meaning of another word, to add to its meaning, or to emphasize it. Most appositives are nonrestrictive and should therefore be set off by commas.

Examples:

Mr. Walker, *the grocer,* has just sold his business. [Simple appositive]
Her language, a terrifying *mixture* of bad grammar and slang, irritated and fascinated her teachers. [Appositive with modifiers]
The three boys made the hazardous journey down the Snake River canyon, an *exploit* which called for unusual courage and resourcefulness. [An appositive to a whole idea]

As he neared Fourth Street, another man, *a new one*, sprang up suddenly before him, *a short, heavy-set fellow*, stepping out of the shadows and striding directly toward him.—Robert M. Coates. [Notice how the use of appositives may add to sentence variety.]

Cooper, *an aristocrat in temper*, was a stickler for his social rights, *the rights to consideration, privacy, respect*, and he was often at war with himself, for his tastes and prejudices were by no means in harmony with his conscience and convictions.—Van Wyck Brooks.

But do *not* use commas with many common expressions in which the appositive and its substantive are so close that they are felt as a unit.

Examples:

My brother John, Henry the Eighth, the word *appositive*, your son James, my Aunt Caroline, William the Conqueror, the novelist Hawthorne.

Participles and occasionally adjectives may be placed for greater emphasis after the words they modify. When so placed they are said to be in the appositive position and are therefore set off by commas.

Examples:

Our plan, *sound in principle and proved in practice*, will bring greater prosperity to our community.
They were like a ballet of spinsters, *elderly but flippant*, standing in affected attitudes with the simpering graces of a bygone age.

A growl, *low and distant like the roll of a train on a faraway bridge*, began to stir in his throat.—Wolcott Gibbs.

This style, *so elegant and so simple*, was to mark all of Irving's work, *the sign of his cheerful good nature and transparent good taste. . . .* —Van Wyck Brooks. [Adjectives in the appositive position and then a substantive appositive]

Appositives may also be enclosed in parentheses or set off by dashes to indicate a greater degree of separation, if such a distinction is desired. (See sections 17 and 18.) Sometimes dashes are used because of the presence of several commas.

Examples:

Undoubtedly the greatest single source of the standard foreign image of the United States is the caricaturist's figure of Uncle Sam—the tall, spare, chin-whiskered personage in tall hat, striped trousers and star-decked vest so ingratiatingly presented on this side of the water, but so easily given ludicrous or sinister features abroad.—Allan Nevins, *The New York Times Magazine,* March 1, 1959.

The citizens of the United States are assured, under the Constitution, of the rights to personal security, liberty, equality before the law, trial by jury and "due process of law" (that is, the accused has the right to know of what he is accused), and freedom of worship, press, speech, and assembly. —Barnes and Ruedi, *The American Way of Life.*

Former bank clerks, plumbers, farmers, insurance salesmen, boxers, auto mechanics, sailors—all have found their way, for one reason or another, into New York's police force.—Wayne Phillips, *The New York Times Magazine,* March 1, 1959. [Note the use of the summarizing "all."]

Appositives are often introduced by such words as *that is, namely, such as, for instance, for example,* and the like. In long, formal sentences these words may be preceded by a colon or a semicolon. In ordinary writing, both formal and informal, *namely, that is, for example,* and *for instance* are usually preceded and followed by commas. *Such as* is not followed by a comma.

Examples:

Short prepositions, such as *in*, *on*, *to*, *for*, are not capitalized in titles.
There is only one proper thing for a driver to do when the army mule dies, namely, cut the harness and pull the cart himself.

13l. Commas are used to set off substantives used in direct address.

Examples:

George, let me tell you what I did last night. [To begin a sentence]
Come here, *my child*, and talk to me. [Within the sentence]
"Please change places with me, *Helen*," I requested. [With quotation marks]

13m. An explanatory clause like he said *(a dialogue guide), when it breaks into a sentence of dialogue, is set off by commas. See also section 16.*

Examples:

"All the same," replied Dulcinea, "a diamond is a girl's best friend."
The man answered, "You'll have trouble finding it, I think." [Dialogue guide begins the sentence.]
"It's a rough trail," explained the guide. "Walk slowly and watch out for falling rocks." [Dialogue guide at end of one sentence and before the second quoted sentence]
"I'm sorry, sir," replied Baker; "I did not mean to be rude." [With semicolon in compound sentence of dialogue]

13n. Geographical names, dates, and addresses are set off by commas.

Examples:

Barbara Lee, who was born on Friday, September 13, 1908, has never been superstitious about the number thirteen.

If you will address the package to Harry Tweed, 67 Stark Street, Yorktown, Nevada, the orderly will leave it at the post office.

Granville Stanley Hall was born in Ashfield, Massachusetts, on February 1, 1844, a farm boy who attended the district school, the local academies, and finally was graduated from Williams College, in 1867, with the conviction that he belonged in the ministry.—Oscar Cargill.

Son of James O'Neill, the actor who "cleared fifty thousand" season after season in *Monte Cristo,* Eugene O'Neill was born in the Barrett House, on Broadway at Forty-Third Street, New York, on October 16, 1888.—Oscar Cargill.

The standard form for dates is "March 20, 1959," but there is a growing tendency among many people to write "20 March 1959." Both forms must be considered correct. Some publications also omit the comma when the day of the month is not used, as "March 1959."

Exercises

Exercise 1. Punctuate each nonrestrictive clause in the following sentences.

1. Jason Boyer who presides at the college coffee shop is a friend of all the students.
2. A student whose check from home is a little late can usually get help from him.
3. My uncle Toby whom I had invited to visit me during Dads' Week End met Jason.
4. We drank the coffee which I had ordered and gossiped over old times.
5. A boy who played on the football team came in and sat down near us.
6. He was Rollo Penwick with whom I had worked at Bryce Canyon one summer.
7. Uncle Toby to whom college life was strange invited him to have coffee with us.
8. Uncle Toby and Jason who had many things in common were becoming good friends.
9. I pulled out my wallet which looked terribly flat to me and offered to pay for the coffees.
10. I am happy to have an uncle whose generosity is proverbial.

Exercise 2. Punctuate each of the following sentences. Decide whether to use a comma, a semicolon, or no mark at all. Be able to justify your decision.

1. I have considered going into social work but my mother has tried to discourage me.
2. My mother is a practical person and she thinks that I am too young to know my mind.
3. I know something about the work for I have studied sociology and made trips to the state institutions.
4. During the summer I worked in the social insurance offices and I enjoyed the work.
5. A friend of mine Irma Wells is a social case worker and I have occasionally gone with her on her trips.
6. Her work is very interesting for it introduces her to all sorts of people.
7. She visits needy families but she does not actually take them baskets of food.
8. Sometimes she comes home very angry for she has no patience with drunken husbands.
9. She makes a careful study of each client and then she recommends the most suitable kind of assistance.
10. At times the Red Cross gives immediate help and then the happiness of the needy family is a welcome reward to the case worker.

Exercise 3, Words in series. In the following sentences insert commas where they are necessary.

1. We grew up in an old-fashioned rambling house of ten rooms, surrounded by trees gardens farm buildings and wheat fields.
2. It is only as we become older mellower less violent and more tolerant than we begin to value the art of conversation.
3. The battle raged all over the bathroom until Moppet was finally washed dried brushed and perfumed.
4. All her life she had been petted humored and spoiled; she did not know the meaning of unselfishness or co-operation.
5. She gloried in her reputation of being the most untamable unpredictable and generally impossible girl in Bennington.
6. With a sigh she dropped the package into the cold murky swirling waters.
7. They regretted the colorful pageantry of football contests the festive evenings in fraternity houses and the stimulation of human contacts which they had learned to enjoy in college days.
8. A tall gaunt moody-looking man at the door bared his teeth in a mechanical grin.
9. Their scientific knowledge was devoted to making guns poison gas bombing planes and submarines for the purpose of killing their fellow men.
10. No one could understand how this motley group of third-rate artists

futile poets and frustrated esthetes had accepted him so completely as one of their kind.

Exercise 4, Introductory elements. In each of the following sentences decide whether the introductory element is to be followed by a comma or not.

1. After the surrender of the Axis armies in Africa the Allies decided to invade Sicily.
2. Having air superiority in that area they bombed the Sicilian ports and air fields.
3. Before the attack a strategic island near Sicily surrendered to avoid further destruction.
4. After the airborne troops had been dropped the rest of the invasion army attacked the beaches.
5. Protected by vast numbers of aircraft and a large fleet of warships the invading forces made several landings on the coast.

Exercise 5, Dates and addresses. Copy the following sentences. Insert commas where they are needed.

1. My father says that he was inducted into the service at Columbus Barracks Columbus Ohio on Friday May 13 1918.
2. All manuscripts must be sent to the editorial offices at 60 Fifth Avenue New York 11 New York.
3. The famous astronomer Mikolaj Kopernik was born 1473 in Torun Poland; he studied astronomy at Krakow Poland and Bologna Italy canon law at Ferrara and medicine at Padua.
4. Stephen Crane was born in Newark New Jersey on November 1 1871 and died twenty-nine years later on June 5 1900 at Badenweiler in the Black Forest.
5. They used to live at 312 Ramona Street Chico California, but they moved to 327 Hill Drive Waldport Oregon.

Exercise 6. Copy the following sentences. Supply every missing comma and tell what rule of usage applies.

1. A Welsh terrier has small dark-hazel eyes a wiry hard abundant coat of hair straight muscular legs and a long thick neck.
2. Mr. Brown who is our next-door neighbor is very ill.
3. Although the boy could neither read nor write English his diction was surprisingly cultured and dignified.
4. Of all the Smiths in the city we were trying to find the Mr. Smith whose first name was John.
5. My aunt lives at 230 University Avenue Southeast Minneapolis Minnesota.

6. We knew that the game had started for the students were cheering wildly.
7. Tall slender girls should not seek the company of short fat men.
8. Before starting to work Father carefully removed his coat folded it and laid it on a stump.
9. Lillian Foster the girl with the red hair spoke to me just as we left the room.
10. Becoming tired of fighting the boys suddenly found a victim in Styx a big white cat who belonged to our neighbor.

Exercise 7, All uses of the comma. Punctuate the following sentences. Tell what rule or principle of usage applies to each comma that you use.

1. At the desk sat a girl who gave us more cards to fill out.
2. The men were all hungry tired and resentful.
3. According to the proverb the best things are the most difficult.
4. The robins have returned but there is still snow on the ground.
5. Be not careless in deeds nor confused in words nor rambling in thought.
6. Having devoured the cookies and ice cream the boys bashfully shuffled out eager to engage in affairs more important to boys.
7. At noon we camped where a full-grown river bubbled out of the lava rock.
8. Before putting the dog inside Father gave him a bone to comfort him.
9. A tall stately lady approached our booth and smiled at us.
10. The president of our class George Baker called me that same afternoon.
11. Jane gathered the flowers for her mother was busy making an apple pie for dinner.
12. Oswald who could not remain quiet for more than two minutes finally slipped from his chair and ran out of the room.
13. Before starting to clean the maid shook out the dust mop.
14. Privates corporals and sergeants must arise and remain standing when an officer enters the barracks.
15. He seemed a harmless old fellow but the excited red-faced woman pointed a monitory finger at him.
16. Universal's stupendous colossal million-dollar four-star production was a complete failure.
17. He swam rode and hunted but his vacation was still not a success.
18. Part of his nervousness I dare say arises out of his feeling of superiority to us.
19. If I should be asked for examples of short-sighted policy I should mention these three.
20. After the game the students tore down the goal posts broke them into small pieces and took the pieces home for souvenirs.

THE SEMICOLON

14a. A semicolon is used between the main clauses of a compound sentence when they are not joined by one of the co-ordinating conjunctions.

In weight, a semicolon is more than a comma and less than a period. The period separates sentences. The semicolon separates main clauses within a sentence. Its frequent use marks a dignified, formal style, and for this reason the presence of many semicolons in a light, informal paper should be viewed with suspicion.

Ordinarily a semicolon should not be used to cut off a phrase or a dependent clause from the main clause.

Examples of correct use:

Plants and trees live a complete life without a nervous system; they breathe without lungs; they distribute sap without a heart; and they are the only living things that can convert lifeless inorganic materials into the substances which all animals require for life.—William C. Vergara, *Science in Everyday Things.*

Most of today's youngsters never seem to lose their heads; even when they let themselves go, an alarm clock seems to be ticking away at the back of their minds; it goes off sooner or later, and sends them back to school, to work, or to war.—"The Younger Generation," *Time Magazine.*

When the busman takes his proverbial holiday he takes a bus; when a sailor gets a holiday he hires a rowboat; when an anthologist has a holiday he thinks of another anthology.—Louis Untermeyer.

The college is primarily not a place of the body, nor of the feelings, nor even of the will; it is, first of all, a place of the mind.—Alexander Meiklejohn.

14b. A semicolon is used between the co-ordinate clauses of a compound sentence with one of the following conjunctive adverbs: therefore, however, hence, accordingly, furthermore, nevertheless, and consequently.

The student should be cautioned, however, that in modern prose not many such sentences are written. The one connective in this list that is likely to begin a second or third clause in a sentence is *hence.* The other connectives are almost invariably tucked away within the sentence and enclosed in commas.

14c. A semicolon is used between the clauses of a compound sentence joined by a co-ordinating conjunction when the clauses are long and when they contain other punctuation, or when a more distinct pause than the comma would give is desirable.

You should interpret this rule in terms of sentences written by professional writers. The presence of two or three commas in a short compound sentence does not justify a semicolon. Neither should you assume that you can cut off a dependent clause by a semicolon merely because you desire "a more distinct pause." Use commas with subordinate clauses if any punctuation is necessary.

Examples:

When he [Bob Hope] was playing in England, six hundred men once tramped across ten miles of moors to hear him at a neighboring camp; but when they reached the great outdoor auditorium where he was showing, they could not get within earshot. So they had to turn around and start back. When Hope finished his show, he was told about the disappointment of the six hundred; he immediately loaded his troupers into jeeps and set out after the soldiers, and when he overtook them he clowned for them through forty minutes in a pouring rain.—Frank Luther Mott, *Golden Multitudes,* The Macmillan Company, 1947. Used by permission.

Occasionally a writer will use semicolons to show balance or contrast between sentence elements, or to emphasize the parts of a series, or just to experiment with an unusual sentence. When a writer experiments with semicolons, he is usually working on a "show piece." Now, of course, it is great fun to try these exhibition sentences once in a while. You might try to imitate the following examples.

Even the Arthurian poems do not compel us to revise our judgment, despite the vividness of our recollections—the blue-black hair and violet eyes of Isolt of Ireland; the white hands, white face, and gray eyes of Isolt of Brittany;

the gold hair, fair complexion, and blue eyes of Guinevere.—Ellsworth Barnard, *Edwin Arlington Robinson*, The Macmillan Company 1952.

The sights and sounds and sensations of horse-and-carriage life were part of the universal American experience: the clop-clop of horses' hoofs; the stiff jolting of an iron-tired carriage on a stony road; the grinding noise of the brake being applied to ease the horse on a downhill stretch; the necessity of holding one's breath when the horse sneezed; the sight of sand, carried up on the tires and wooden spokes of a carriage wheel, spilling off in little cascades as the wheel revolved; the look of a country road overgrown by grass, with three tracks in it instead of two, the middle one made by horses' hoofs; the special male ordeal of getting out of the carriage and walking up the steeper hills to lighten the load; and the more severe ordeal, for the unpracticed, of harnessing a horse which could recognize inexperience at one scornful glance.—From Frederick Lewis Allen, *The Big Change*. Copyright 1952 by Frederick Lewis Allen. Reprinted by permission of Harper & Brothers.

Exercises

Exercise 1. In one of your textbooks (where the formal style would make frequent use of semicolons appropriate) find ten sentences with semicolons. Copy them and bring them to class. Try to determine the reason for each semicolon.

Exercise 2. Assume that the following sentences are from an informal autobiographical sketch. Determine the punctuation you should use in the places marked by brackets. Would you use commas, semicolons, or no marks at all?

1. I have lived on a Wisconsin farm for eighteen years [ ] and I cannot imagine a more normal or a more average American life.
2. My father and mother are average middle-class Americans [ ] we live in an average sort of house [ ] and we have average ideas and interests.
3. My father was born and reared in a little town in Norway [ ] now he is an important man in a little Norwegian town in Wisconsin.
4. Father still speaks English with a strong Norwegian accent [ ] his children [ ] however [ ] speak an American English which is the same in California or Wisconsin or New Jersey.
5. What education I got [ ] I took without question from average teachers in an average American high school [ ] fortunately [ ] however [ ] my teachers knew enough to insist that lessons had to be learned [ ] and duties had to be done.

6. They were probably good teachers [ ] in spite of their lack of "progressive" ideas [ ] for among the graduates of our high school there are a number of doctors, scientists, college professors, and even a much-decorated war hero or two.
7. We have no big industries in our little town [ ] neither do we have tenements or slums or gangs of criminals.
8. In the summer the boys played baseball, went swimming in the creek, rode bicycles into the country, or hunted and fished [ ] we had no country club set, no organized playground, and few dances and parties.
9. My father was the local dealer in Chrysler-made cars [ ] my present interest in mechanical engineering was [ ] consequently [ ] developed early through my attempt to remake wrecks into ambulatory jalopies.
10. My home town is not the best in America [ ] but I am sure it is far from being the worst [ ] in it, as in countless other American towns, one may find happy and useful citizens.

THE APOSTROPHE

15a. An apostrophe and -s are used to form the possessive of a noun, singular or plural, which does not end in -s.

Examples:

A bird's nest, women's hats, children's toys, a day's work, a horse's neck, Meier and Frank's store, Belinda's jewels, my mother-in-law's car

But when two or more names joined by *and* are represented as joint owners of something, the last name alone takes the possessive with the apostrophe.

Examples:

Look for it at Swensen and Carmody's machine shop.
Nancy and Sally's mother is in town today.
Will you please stop at Larson, Jones, and Marshall's antique shop on Fifth Avenue?

Usage sanctions such group possessives as *the Queen of England's hats,* but sometimes it is better to dodge an awkward construction by rewriting it. For instance, instead of writing *Mr. Snell, the Governor of Oregon's hat,* write it *the hat which belongs to Mr. Snell, the Governor of Oregon.*

15b. The apostrophe alone is used to form the possessive of a plural noun ending in -s.

Examples:

Ladies' hats, three months' wages, girls' dresses, the Smiths' house, foxes' tails

15c. The apostrophe with -s is used to form the possessive of singular nouns ending in -s, if the resultant form is not unpleasant or difficult to pronounce; otherwise the apostrophe alone is used.

Examples:

James's hat, Keats's poems, Jones's office, for goodness' sake, for conscience' sake, Demosthenes' orations [But note that *James'* hat or *Keats'* poems or *Jones'* office are also used.]

15d. An apostrophe with -s is used to form the possessive of certain indefinite pronouns.

Examples:

Anybody's game, someone's hat, everybody's business, one's opinions, somebody's purse, another's turn

The apostrophe should not be used with personal pronouns.

Examples:

If this coat isn't yours (not *your's*), it's probably hers (not *her's*).
The decision is ours (not *our's*). The invitation is theirs (not *their's*).
The possessive of the pronoun *it* is *its*. *It's* means "*it is.*"

15e. An apostrophe is used to indicate the omission of letters or figures.

Examples:

Doesn't, isn't, o'clock, the class of '62, I'll, it's

15f. An apostrophe and -s are used to form the plurals of figures, letters, and words referred to as words.

Examples:

You have not dotted your *i's* or crossed your *t's*.
Your *m's*, *n's*, and *u's* look alike.

He used too many *and's* and *but's* in his paper.
Be careful not to make your *3's* look like *8's*.

Some publications omit the apostrophe in these situations, but there may be confusion in a sentence like this: In his handwriting the *is* and *us* are but a wavy line!

15g. The apostrophe is often omitted in titles.

Examples:

Eastern Washington State Teachers College, Home Economics Teachers Association, The Authors League, Farmers Market

Exercises

Exercise 1. Copy the following sentences. Insert an apostrophe wherever it is correct.

1. She spent a weeks wages for a hat she saw in Smith and Fords department store.
2. At three oclock he was awakened by the sergeants voice.
3. Its said that the womens dormitory at Teachers College will have a heated swimming pool.
4. At ten oclock we stopped at Clinton and Webleys department store, where Marys sister works at the hosiery counter.
5. As I didnt get Professor Carlins history assignment, I stopped at Harrys house to ask him about it.
6. The Brandeses cat spends most of his time at Helen and Trudys house.
7. "Arent you going to call this a days work?" asked the masons assistant.
8. "Theyre having a sale of womens and childrens shoes at Nolans," she said.
9. "Its still anybodys game," yelled the announcer.
10. Isnt it true that everybodys business is usually nobodys business?

Exercise 2. Point out the words in which the apostrophe is omitted or incorrectly used. Make the necessary corrections.

1. Mr. Andrews neighbor was formerly the manager of Tom Allens ranch.
2. If this umbrella is'nt your's, it is probably theirs.
3. Its probable that somebodys going to see us out here on the rocks, isnt it?
4. Keat's poems are very beautiful, arent they?
5. Isn't it almost time for your ten-oclock lecture?

Exercise 3. Write the possessive singular and the possessive plural of each of the following:

[*Example: child child's children's*]

1. baby
2. goose
3. Williams
4. woman
5. publisher
6. wife
7. attorney
8. Powers
9. wolf
10. motorman

QUOTATION MARKS

16a. Double quotation marks are used to enclose a direct quotation in dialogue.

Examples:

"Give me a soda," said the young man to the clerk, "without flavor, please."
"Without what flavor?" asked the clerk politely.
"Without strawberry," said the young man.
"But I can't," said the clerk. "We haven't any strawberry flavor."
The young man meditated deeply. "Make it without vanilla, please," he said.

A writer should be careful not to leave out one set of quotation marks. Quotation marks come in pairs, one set at the beginning and one set at the end of every quoted part.

Wrong:

"I have no relish for the country, said Sydney Smith. It is a kind of healthy grave."
"Be awful nice to 'em goin' up, Jimmy Durante is reported to have said, because you're gonna meet 'em all comin' down."

Right:

"I have no relish for the country," said Sydney Smith. "It is a kind of healthy grave."
"Be awful nice to 'em goin' up," Jimmy Durante is reported to have said, "because you're gonna meet 'em all comin' down."

If a quotation consists of several sentences, the quotation marks are placed at the beginning and at the end of the entire quotation, not at the beginning and end of each separate sentence in that section.

"You'd have had your stomach full of fighting, young man," added Colonel Williams, "if Squire Sedgwick had not taken them just as he did. Squire," he added, "my wife shall thank you that she's not a widow when we get back to Stockbridge. I honor your courage, sir. The credit of this day is yours."—Edward Bellamy, *The Duke of Stockbridge.*

If a quotation consists of several paragraphs, quotation marks are placed before each paragraph but at the end of the last paragraph only. This convention applies to a continued speech by one speaker. If the speaker changes, his words are placed in a new paragraph or paragraphs. Short descriptive, narrative, or explanatory passages may be paragraphed with dialogue, especially if they are placed between sentences of dialogue spoken by the same person.

A quoted passage of several lines of prose or poetry—not a part of dialogue—may be indicated by indention. In typing it is often typed single-spaced. In print it may be set in smaller type than the rest of the text. No quotation marks are needed when indention is used.

No quotation marks are used with an indirect quotation.

Direct:

"How many of you have your papers ready?" asked the teacher.
The teacher said, "I am going to Cuba on my vacation."

Indirect:

The teacher asked us how many of us had our papers ready.
The teacher said she was going to Cuba on her vacation.

16b. Single quotation marks are used to enclose a quotation within a quotation.

Examples:

Mary replied, "The dean said to me, 'No report has reached this office.' "

Since then he [Adlai Stevenson] has laughingly referred to the label, as he did in his first Godkin Lecture at Harvard by saying, "I am uncomfortably reminded of the abiding truth of those classic words that never occurred to Horace: '*Via ovicipitum dura est,*' or, for the benefit of the engineers among you: 'The way of the egghead is hard.' "—John Mason Brown, *Through These Men*. [Note the position of the quotation marks in relation to other marks.]

"If the good Lord should tell me that I had only five minutes to live," said Justice Oliver Wendell Holmes, "I would say to him, 'All right, Lord, but I'm sorry you can't make it ten.' "—Quoted in Catherine Drinker Bowen's *Yankee from Olympus*.

16c. *Quotation marks are used to enclose quoted titles of stories, poems, chapters, and other subdivisions of books, and, in newspaper style, the titles of books.* *See section 10.*

16d. *Quotations marks are used to enclose words spoken of as words.*

Italics are used for this purpose, however, when the style is formal. In informal writing, quotation marks are more common.

Example:

Slang makes constant use of metaphor and simile: "sticking his neck out," "to rubberneck," "out like a light," "baloney," "shutterbug," "punch-drunk," "weasel puss," "keep your shirt on."—S. I. Hayakawa, *Language in Thought and Action*.

16e. *Quotation marks are used to enclose words used in a special sense or slang expressions in formal writing.*

Examples:

National greed has disguised itself in mandates to govern "inferior" races. [To indicate that he is using somebody else's word and that he does not think these races are inferior]

Need leads the "small fry" to rob and steal, in the same way that greed causes the "big shots" to go in for organized crime and racketeering.—Barnes and Ruedi, *The American Way of Life*. [Slang used in formal writing]

16f. *Quotation marks are used to enclose the definitions or meanings of words spoken of as words.*

Example:

Miscellaneous further illustrations of elevation are *pretty* from an early meaning "sly," through "clever," to something approaching "beautiful"; *nice* from an etymological meaning "ignorant," through its earliest English sense "foolish," and later ones like "particular," to its present broad and vague colloquial meaning of "pleasant" or "acceptable"; and *fond* from "foolish" to "affectionate."—Stuart Robertson, *The Development of Modern English.*

16g. *Commas and periods are always placed inside quotation marks.*

This rule is a printers' convention. The period and the comma are the two marks that occupy the lower half of a line of print; all other marks—the colon, the semicolon, the question mark, and the exclamation point—stand the full height of the line. To have a comma or a period trail out beyond quotation marks looks bad. Remember the convention: periods and commas *always* placed inside quotation marks. See section 16b for examples.

16h. *The question mark, the semicolon, and the exclamation point go inside quotation marks if they belong to the quoted part. They go outside if they do not belong to the quoted part.*

Examples:

Did you hear him say, "I won't go"? [The question mark belongs to the main clause, or the entire sentence. Hence it stands at the end. But notice that no period is used in addition to the end punctuation.]

"Well, I like that!" she exclaimed in anger.

"It is as much of a trade," says La Bruyère, "to make a book as it is to make a clock"; in short, literature is largely a matter of technique.—Irving Babbitt. [Note that the semicolon is not a part of the quotation. It belongs to the whole sentence.]

16i. *For dialogue guides (like he said) with quoted dialogue, use the punctuation which the structure of the sentence calls for.*

Examples:

"Sister," she replied sweetly, "did you ever hear of Cleopatra?"
"Howard!" a voice called from the garden.

She continued breathlessly: "They are going to fight. I heard them shouting and cursing at each other. Please do something, Father. . . ." [The colon introduces several sentences of dialogue. A comma is often used for the same purpose.]

"The price is not a matter of profit," he said, stiffly; "it is a matter of principle." [Notice the semicolon to separate co-ordinate clauses in a compound sentence of dialogue. Most writers use a period and a following capital letter instead of a semicolon in this sort of construction.]

The general practice is not to use a comma before a quoted part that is woven into the sentence or before a quoted title.

Examples:

Communism, he remarked, was not "in the American grain,"—a fine phrase of William Carlos Williams; for, as he continued, "There is an American grain, and I wish to live with it, and I will not live against it knowingly." —Van Wyck Brooks, *Opinions of Oliver Allston.*

It is doubtful if adolescents since the time of Byron have repeated any poems (without compulsion) as frequently or as enthusiastically as the youth of the 'twenties recited "My candle burns at both ends" and "Safe upon the solid rock . . . ."—Oscar Cargill, *Intellectual America.*

Exercises

Exercise 1. Find an essay about language or words. The bibliography at the end of the first chapter of this book will help you find one. Bring to class five sentences containing words referred to as words, or slang expressions, or definitions of words. Does the author always use italics, always quotation marks, or does he use both?

Exercise 2. Look through a collection of readings, or through a copy of a recent magazine of the more serious variety, and copy five examples of unusual uses of quotation marks, like this one by Van Wyck Brooks: Most of Allston's friends were on the "left;" they were "on the side of the heart, not on the side of the liver," and this was a matter of constitution with them.

Exercise 3. Copy the following. Punctuate it and paragraph it correctly.

1. Through the smoky air of the coffee shop one could hear little snatches of conversation: He always gives objective finals, but this time—, I have one more today and then my last on Saturday, I haven't slept for two whole days!

2. The girl at Belinda's table was saying, In our final in entomology we had to name a hundred and twenty insects . . . .
3. Belinda interrupted her: All of one kind or different?
4. Oh, Belinda, how can you make jokes at a time like this? she said. Different, of course.
5. Well, you might have answered, A hundred nineteen fleas and one black widow, explained Belinda.
6. Professor Blow, who was standing with coffee cup in his hand, looking for a place to sit down, remarked, Final week makes you lightheaded, doesn't it?
7. Oh, do sit down. Please do. Belinda's invitation was cordial.
8. We were just discussing a hundred twenty fleas and a black widow, she explained.
9. Ugh! she shivered daintily as she spoke. Makes you feel somewhat—you know—creepy!
10. A black widow is an arachnid said the other girl and an arachnid is not an insect.
11. With a sigh of relief, Professor Blow set his coffee cup on the table and pulled back a chair.
12. Fleas are not my field of major concentration, he remarked, but I heard a story about them.
13. It seems that three fleas met by chance near Rockefeller Center and made a date for lunch in an alley near Greenwich Village, where dogs are abundant.
14. Two of them met at the appointed time under the arch in Washington Square.
15. The third one did not appear until almost three o'clock.
16. What kept you? asked the first flea. Did you get snarled up in the traffic?
17. Well, you see, said the tardy flea, my friend here caught an Airedale almost immediately, but it was such a beautiful spring day that I decided to walk.

COLON AND DASH

THE COLON

17a. *The colon is used to introduce a long and formal quotation, an enumeration or a list of particulars, or a formal explanation.*

The colon is a formal mark. It should not be used before a series introduced informally. In ordinary formal context, writers usually hold to the rule that what precedes the colon must be a complete sentence, but in lists and tabulations the colon is used after the verb introducing the list. In other words, a comma or no mark at all is used before a series if the series is part of a sentence.

Poor:

My favorite amusements are: dancing, golfing, and attending movies.

Right:

My favorite amusements are dancing, golfing, and attending motion pictures.

After a colon it is customary to use a capital letter when the list that follows consists of a complete sentence or of several sentences; a small letter is used when what follows the colon is a part of the same sentence.

Examples:

Clearing his throat, the speaker began as follows: "We look before and after, and we see, through the half-drawn folds of time. . . ."

His faults are these: an uncontrollable temper, inexperience, and a lack of interest in his work.

Moreover, this author was somehow reassuring; he told the Province what it longed to hear: that its most fervent protests against Parliament were no new thing, no shocking innovation.—Catherine Drinker Bowen, *John Adams and the American Revolution.*

There are, by the way, three sorts of created beings who are sentimentally supposed to be able to judge individuals at the first glance: women, children, and dogs.—Arnold Bennett.

He must, we are sure, feel and know the steady progress of the morning: a crosstown car establishing its characteristic crescendo, a hose being played in a doorway after a hot summer night, the eight-o'clock greeting of a saw in a picture-framer's shop nearby.—"City Rhythms," from the *New Yorker.*

17b. *A colon may be used between main clauses when the second clause amplifies and interprets the first.*

Some writers use the colon in this way where others would use a semicolon.

Examples:

Lewis Carroll's "You are old, Father William" is enjoyed by multitudes of people who do not realize that it is a parody of Southey: there is a ludicrous seriousness about it which is humorous in its own right.—David Daiches, *A Study of Literature.*

But now, in "The Waste Land," he [T. S. Eliot] carries this tendency to what one must suppose its extreme possible limit: here, in a poem of only four hundred and three lines (to which are added, however, seven pages of notes), he manages to include quotations from, allusions to, or imitations of, at least thirty-five different writers (some of them, such as Shakespeare and Dante, laid under contribution several times)—as well as several popular songs; and to introduce passages in six foreign languages, including Sanskrit.—Edmund Wilson, *Axel's Castle.* Charles Scribner's Sons, 1931.

THE DASH

17c. The dash is used to indicate a sudden, abrupt break in thought or structure.

On the typewriter use two hyphens, without a space between them and the word before and after, to indicate a dash.

Examples:

This song—how many remember it?—once swept the country.
He asked me—but I cannot repeat his words.
"I wish—I wish you'd let him know—please do—it was an accident." [In dialogue to give the effect of hesitation]
"I don't know whether she would like—" [Speech abruptly broken off]

17d. The dash is used for an explanatory or parenthetical phrase or clause that breaks into the normal flow of the sentence.

Three kinds of marks may indicate parentheses—the comma, the dash, and marks of parenthesis. The degree of separation indicated by these marks varies from the lightest, for which commas are used, to the most definite and most formal, for which marks of parenthesis are used.

Examples:

At any time in their history, in expanding days or days of retrenchment, in war or in peace—or in that state towards which we hope to work now, where there will be neither war, nor the absence of war, but a world that is not war-oriented at all—the way in which people handle the problem of aggression is important.—Margaret Mead, *And Keep Your Powder Dry.*

Directly we go wrong—directly, that is to say, we cease to act in a way of which society approves—conscience begins to nag.—C. E. M. Joad.

And New Orleans—or rather the Creole quarter of New Orleans, for the rest of the city is commonplace—is delicious, suggesting old France and Spain, yet a France and Spain strangely transmuted in this new clime.—James Bryce.

17e. The dash is used to introduce or to set off a long, formal appositive or a summary.

Examples:

Before it was sand, it was rock—splintered by the chisels of the frost, crushed under advancing glaciers and carried forward with the ice in its slow advance, then ground and polished in the mill of the surf.—Rachel Carson, *The Edge of the Sea.*

That train of reasoning is what logicians call a syllogism, and has all its various parts and terms—its major premise, its minor premise, and its conclusion.—Thomas Henry Huxley. [A series of appositives]

The dash may occasionally be found before such words as *namely* and *that is* introducing an appositive. See also section 13k.

Example:

Also you find out about the queer fade-away, the slow curve, the fast in- and out-shoots that seemed to be timed almost as delicately as shrapnel, to burst, or rather break, just when they will do the most harm—namely, at the moment when the batter is swinging.—Paul Gallico.

A dash may be used before such words as *all* and *these* introducing a summary, or summarizing appositive, after a series.

Examples:

Teas, dances, new clothes, blind dates—all these should be part of your freshman year.

Regional survey and regional service—these are the chief ingredients for a responsible citizenship. . . .—Lewis Mumford.

Caution: The dash must not be used indiscriminately for all the other marks of punctuation. It should be saved for its special function, so that it will be intelligible when it is used.

PARENTHESES AND BRACKETS

PARENTHESES

18a. *Parentheses are used to enclose material that is supplementary, explanatory, or interpretive.*

The general principle to follow in the use of parenthetical marks is that commas set off material that is fairly close to the thought of the sentence (see section 13i); dashes set off material that is more distant in meaning (see section 17e); and marks of parenthesis are used to indicate the most distant parenthetical relation. This principle is not always observed by all writers. A study of a group of modern essays or serious books will probably reveal that some writers seldom use parentheses, others use them frequently but logically, and still others use them when the mood comes upon them. But the privilege of being moody and irrational in punctuation is denied to young writers.

Examples:

"I am delightfully situated," Elizabeth wrote, dwelling upon the occasional use of the Rice horse and chaise, Mr. Rice's enjoyment of her "society and conversation" at breakfast (his wife was a semi-invalid who never rose before noon), his satisfaction at seeing his children made to behave properly for the first time in their lives.—Louise Hall Tharp, *The Peabody Sisters of Salem.*

The boy smugly said he wasn't ashamed of his face and Montgomery (old enough to know better, for he was bald as an egg) hit him a glancing blow which did not even knock him down.—Esther Forbes, *Paul Revere and the World He Lived In.*

A gentleman from Carolina (where challenges are taken in one's stride) gladly explains the situation, and Underhill finally and in great trepidation accepts.—Alexander Cowie, *The Rise of the American Novel.*

If other marks of punctuation are necessary with parentheses, it is customary to place the comma, the semicolon, and the period after the second parenthesis. The question mark or the exclamation point is placed inside the parentheses if the mark belongs to the parenthetical element; otherwise outside.

Examples:

Bronson Alcott assumed that this child was joking (although that was something he never did himself).—Louise Hall Tharp.

These old doctors, on their "rhubarb colored horses," their saddle bags stuffed with drugs, or walking the street so pompously with gold-headed canes (as Oliver Wendell Holmes remembered), did kill a good many patients.—Esther Forbes.

But these promptings are not obeyed, these things not said, not done. (Would it be better if they were, sometimes?)—Wilson Follett.

Most modern nations are compositions of this kind: France, for instance; Germany (which was built of twenty-five states, integrated in turn from about 1,800 principalities); Italy, the U.S.S.R., Australia, Canada, and the U. S.—From *Fortune.*

Parentheses must not be used to cancel or cross out words that the writer intends to leave out. See section 7.

To use parentheses with the intention of crossing out words misleads the reader, who will assume, with good reason, that these words are to be read as part of the sentence. To delete, draw a straight line through the part to be deleted.

Wrong:

Public utilities are (monopolies) industries which serve the public.

Right:

Public utilities are ~~monopolies~~ industries which serve the public.

BRACKETS

18b. Brackets are used to enclose corrections, interpolations, and supplied omissions added to a quotation by the person quoting.

Examples:

Santayana says, "Religion lay on him [Dickens] like the weight of the atmosphere, sixteen pounds to the square inch, yet never noticed nor mentioned."

Exercises

Exercise 1, The colon. Go to your library and look through a copy of *Harper's Magazine* or the *Atlantic Monthly.* Copy five sentences in which colons are used. Try to determine why the colon was used in each case. Could semicolons have been used for some of the colons?

Exercise 2, The colon. In the following sentences decide whether or not the colon is used correctly.

1. The human tongue has a sweet-tasting area at the tip: a bitter-tasting area at the back: and a sour-tasting area at the sides.
2. Emotions which will upset your digestion are: worry, fear, pain, and anger.
3. The list of securities on which he paid taxes includes: Standard Oil of New Jersey and International Harvester.
4. The twenty stocks which he listed on his income tax report are the following: (A list follows.)
5. All classes meeting at 4:50 today will be canceled.

Exercise 3, Parentheses and brackets. From one of your textbooks copy five sentences in which parentheses or brackets are used. Try to determine the exact reason for each of these marks.

Exercise 4. Write five sentences of your own in which you use parentheses correctly.

TOO MUCH PUNCTUATION

19a. Superfluous commas should be avoided.

Fundamentally, the purpose of punctuation is to facilitate the communication of thoughts, ideas, or information by means of the printed or written language. But what writers—and readers—

think is necessary to achieve clear and quick communication depends on the conventions or practices of a certain age. Many years ago, writers used much punctuation; at present we use as little punctuation as possible, especially in informal writing.

Journalism may have gone too far in eliminating punctuation marks, as many an irritated reader of inadequately punctuated newspaper writing can testify. There is a middle ground that we must take—always enough punctuation for clearness, no matter what the general tendency of the time is.

The following are typical situations in which unnecessary commas should not be used in short, simple sentences that would be clear without the commas:

1. Commas should not be used between a subject and its verb, a verb and its object, a preposition and its object, an adjective and its noun.

Wrong:

My father's investments and savings, provided for my college education.

Right:

My father's investments and savings provided for my college education. [Subject and verb]

Wrong:

He had been told, that American industry would prosper again.

Right:

He had been told that American industry would prosper again. [Clause as object of verb]

Wrong:

The Co-operative Association keeps large stocks of, flour, packaged cereals, canned vegetables, dried fruit, and other foods.

Right:

The Co-operative Association keeps large stocks of flour, packaged cereals, canned vegetables, dried fruit, and other foods. [Preposition and objects]

Wrong:

He was a tall, lanky, shy, awkward, boy of fourteen.

Right:

He was a tall, lanky, shy, awkward boy of fourteen. [Adjective in a series and the noun it modifies]

2. No comma should be used after a co-ordinating conjunction joining two clauses.

Wrong:

A war to save democracy was fought years ago, but, democracy is still in danger.

Right:

A war to save democracy was fought years ago, but democracy is still in danger.

No comma is used after a co-ordinating conjunction that *begins* a main clause.

Wrong:

But, his income dwindled to nothing during the depression.

Right:

But his income dwindled to nothing during the depression.

3. No comma is used before a co-ordinating conjunction joining two words, two simple phrases, two subjects, or two predicates.

Wrong:

From his pocket he fished out an old pipe, and a pouch of tobacco.

Right:

From his pocket he fished out an old pipe and a pouch of tobacco.

Wrong:

Before she left the room she stopped to powder her nose, and to pat her hair.

Right:

Before she left the room she stopped to powder her nose and to pat her hair.

Exception: Compound elements of a sentence, such as compound subject, compound predicate, compound direct object, etc., if long and variously modified, may be separated by a comma for the sake of clearness.

Example:

A man walked into the lobby of the hotel that stands on the corner of Main Street and Seventh Avenue at four o'clock last Thursday afternoon, and with an air of secrecy approached a group of men who were sitting in the corner around a table that was covered with books and papers.

4. No comma is used to set off short introductory phrases or clauses that are not clearly parenthetical.

Unnecessary:

When the wind blows, we stake down our tents.
Every half hour, we take a new reading.

Better:

When the wind blows we stake down our tents.
Every half hour we take a new reading.

5. Commas are not used to set off closely restrictive elements, such as clauses, appositives, and phrases.

Unnecessary or wrong:

Any boy, who tries, can master this subject.
My uncle, Toby, lives on a ranch.
A man, worried about debt, cannot do his best work.

Better:

Any boy who tries can master this subject.
My uncle Toby lives on a ranch.
A man worried about debt cannot do his best work.

19b. *Periods are not used after common contractions, with abbreviations standing for governmental or international agencies, or with another terminal mark to end a sentence.*

Contractions:

I'll, wouldn't, 2nd, 10th, 3rd

Abbreviations:

CARE, UNESCO, TVA

End punctuation:

Did she say, "Stop writing"? [*not* Did she say, "Stop writing."?]

19c. Question marks are not used after indirect questions or to indicate irony or sarcasm.

Wrong:

He asked me how many fish I had caught? [Use a period.]
We enjoyed a comfortable(?) night in our tents. [Omit the mark. If the irony cannot stand on its own feet, don't prod it.]

19d. A double or triple exclamation point should not be used for greater emphasis.

Poor:

"Remember," she said. "This is the last time!! Positively!!!" [This, too, is an undesirable prodding of a statement. Use only one exclamation point at a time.]

19e. Quotation marks should not be overused.

Quotation marks should not be used for literary allusions that have become common property or for proverbs—even for clichés. In informal writing there is little need for enclosing slang in quotation marks, but in formal writing you are ordinarily expected to do so. Quotation marks with slang are a form of apology. But if you have too many occasions to say, "Excuse it, please," perhaps you should stop doing that for which you must apologize.

19f. Dashes are not used to replace all other marks of punctuation, not even in familiar letters.

SPELLING

20. The spelling problem.

The lack of correlation between English spelling and English pronunciation is well known to all. The two are often not even on speaking terms with each other. Consider the difficulties of the foreigner who runs up against the various pronunciations of only one innocent-looking little group of letters *-ough* in such words as *cough*, *dough*, *rough*, *slough*, *bough*, *sough*. The disparity between spelling and pronunciation is illustrated by the story of the exchange student from France, coming to America eager to improve his English accent, who on landing in New York saw a banner headline on the front page of a newspaper: "EXHIBITION PRONOUNCED SUCCESS." "Ah, this fantastic language!" he exclaimed in utter discouragement.

There was a time, several centuries ago, when a writer hot on the trail of an idea, gave little thought to the right letters in his words. Some writers, we know, even spelled their own names in several different ways without a twinge of remorse. The present attitude toward standardized spelling, however, is very different. There is no blinking the fact that spelling is now one of our major problems. Nor can we minimize the economic importance of trying to learn how to spell; employers everywhere assume that poor spelling is a sign of stupidity or illiteracy. Perhaps they reason, rightly or not, that carelessness in spelling is a visible, measurable sign of carelessness in other more important things. Bad spelling is something that shows—like a run in a stocking. And because it does show, because it can be easily seen and easily judged, it has become the first test of a person's education and his fitness for a job.

How Spelling Got to Be a Problem. For what it is worth to the student in spelling troubles, we can rapidly summarize what happened to our English words in the long race between spelling and pronunciation. For one thing, spelling has lost the race. It began to jell much sooner than did pronunciation. Printing helped to standardize it. A word in print, sent from one part of England to another, looked the same and stayed the same; pronunciation of that word was affected by regional differences, and it kept on changing with the passing of time. Then, of course, we inherited many of our troubles when we got words from different languages, or even from different dialects of our own language, and our troubles were not lessened when foreign visitors, like the Norman French, began to remake the home language according to their lights. And finally to perpetuate our troubles, we simply do not have enough letters in our alphabet for the number of vowel sounds and consonant sounds in our language. Some of our letters will always have to stand for several different sounds.

How the Student Got to Be a Problem. Spelling is not a problem for everyone. Some young people master spelling easily, almost unconsciously, by the time they reach college, just as they learn table manners, or driving a car, or dancing. Some of our spelling difficulties may be traced to the way we read. We read by words instead of by letters; we scarcely notice the arrangement of letters in a word. Our minds have never been trained to focus on letters. In a way that is good, and in a way that is bad. Then there are some whose minds—often very good minds—work in ways not particularly adapted to learning spelling. We say that some of us are eye-minded; that is, we learn easier by seeing a thing than by hearing it. Some college teachers, for instance, after twenty years or so of learning from books, have to write out a name or a street address to remember it. Others of us are ear-minded, and some are even motor-minded. We learn by hearing, and we learn by the muscular motion of writing out a word. It would be convenient if a psychologist could lift up the tops of our skulls, like a mechanic lifting the hood of a car, find out what is wrong, and then reach down and rewire us. But since that is not possible, we have to study ourselves and adapt our learning methods to our kind of wiring. And finally, some fail to learn how to spell simply because in our youth there never was sufficient motivation for doing so. We were just as successful in the things that mattered to us, and life was just as interesting without our knowing how to spell as it would have been with it.

What to Do about the Problem. There are almost as many schemes for teaching spelling as there are teachers. Some college teachers say, "So you never could spell! Well, it's important to learn here and now. So you just buckle down and learn it, just as you learn anything else in college." Much success has come out of this method. College men, with the amazing resiliency of youth, adapt themselves to this regime as some of them have adapted themselves to top sergeants, Korean mud, and crawling under barbed wire, because all that was necessary for survival. Any scheme that manages to catch the active co-operation and interest of students is a good scheme.

Analyzing words helps. It increases the student's awareness of words if he knows something about prefixes and suffixes and roots and stems. A study of word derivations helps a little. Dividing a word into syllables helps. Any scheme that makes a student focus on the letters of a word helps.

Systematic study of words in spelling lists, daily spelling drills, and keeping a record of misspelled words all help a great deal. The spelling list *does* contain many of the words usually misspelled; its chief value, however, is that through its use the student is made aware of words as composed of letters. Spelling rules help, too, in that they introduce some system into the seemingly hopeless snarl of English spelling.

The Value of Proofreading. And finally, even if a student finds it impossible to remember how all the words he uses are spelled, he can always proofread his written work. The college student can use his dictionary. He can check every word he is not sure of. That is what many college teachers, stenographers, editors of newspapers—in fact, anyone who writes or deals with words for a living

—have to do. To proofread a theme before it is handed in is an obligation. For a stenographer to send out a letter with a misspelled word in it is a major crime.

20a. *The following list of words often misspelled by college students is to be used as the instructor thinks necessary.*[1]

1. abbreviate
2. absence
3. absorption
4. absurd
5. accidentally
6. accommodate *
7. accompanying
8. accomplish
9. accumulate
10. accustom
11. achievement *
12. acknowledge
13. acquaintance
14. acquire *
15. acquitted
16. across
17. additionally
18. address
19. aggravate
20. all right
21. always
22. almost
23. although
24. altogether
25. amateur

26. among *
27. analysis
28. analyze
29. annual
30. answer
31. apartment
32. apology
33. apparatus
34. apparently *
35. appearance
36. appropriate
37. arctic
38. argument *
39. arising
40. arrangement
41. ascend
42. association
43. athlete
44. athletics
45. attendance
46. audience
47. auxiliary
48. awkward
49. bachelor
50. balance

51. barbarous
52. becoming
53. beginning *
54. benefited *
55. biscuit
56. boundaries
57. brilliant
58. bureau

[1] Please pay particular attention to the words marked *. Dean Thomas Clark Pollock of Washington Square College of Arts and Science of New York University has made a study of over 30,000 misspellings in the writing of college students. The words starred here are the words, or belong to the word-groups, which he found misspelled most often. The authors are grateful to Dean Pollock for permission to use his findings.

59. business *
60. cafeteria
61. calendar
62. candidate
63. career
64. carburetor
65. category *
66. certain
67. changeable
68. changing
69. characteristic
70. chosen *
71. commission
72. committed
73. committee
74. comparative *
75. competitive

76. compulsory
77. conceivable
78. conference
79. conferred
80. conqueror
81. conscience *
82. conscientious *
83. conscious *
84. continuous
85. convenient
86. courteous
87. criticism *
88. criticize *
89. curiosity
90. cylinder
91. dealt
92. decision
93. definitely *
94. describe *
95. description *
96. despair
97. desperate
98. dictionary
99. dilapidated
100. disagree
101. disappear
102. disappoint
103. disastrous *
104. discipline
105. dissatisfied
106. dissipate
107. doctor
108. dormitory
109. eighth
110. eligible
111. eliminate
112. embarrass
113. eminent
114. environment *
115. enthusiastic
116. equipment
117. equivalent
118. erroneous
119. especially
120. exaggerated
121. exceptionally
122. exhaust
123. exhilarate
124. existence *
125. experience *

126. explanation *
127. extraordinary
128. extremely
129. familiar
130. fascinate *
131. February
132. foreign
133. frantically
134. fraternities
135. generally
136. government
137. grammar *
138. guard
139. guidance
140. height *
141. hindrance
142. humorous

143. illiterate
144. imaginary *
145. imagination *
146. immediately *
147. impromptu
148. incidentally
149. incredible
150. indefinitely

151. indispensable
152. inevitable
153. infinite
154. intellectual
155. intelligence *
156. intentionally
157. interesting *
158. irrelevant
159. irresistible
160. knowledge
161. laboratory
162. legitimate
163. lightning
164. literature
165. loneliness *
166. maintenance
167. maneuver
168. marriage
169. mathematics
170. miniature
171. mischievous
172. necessary *
173. nevertheless
174. noticeable *
175. nowadays

176. oblige
177. obstacle
178. occasion
179. occasionally *
180. occurred *
181. occurrence *
182. opportunity
183. optimistic
184. original *
185. outrageous
186. pamphlet
187. parallel
188. particularly
189. pastime
190. permissible
191. perseverance
192. perspiration
193. physically
194. picnicking
195. politics
196. practically
197. precedence
198. preference
199. preferred
200. prejudice *

201. preparation
202. prevalent *
203. privilege *
204. probably *
205. professor *
206. prominent *
207. pronunciation
208. prove
209. quantity
210. recognize
211. recommend
212. reference
213. referred *
214. repetition *
215. regard
216. representative
217. restaurant
218. rhythm *
219. rhythmical
220. ridiculous
221. sandwich
222. schedule
223. secretary
224. separate *
225. siege

226. similar *
227. simultaneous
228. soliloquy
229. sophomore
230. specifically
231. specimen
232. speech
233. strictly
234. surprise *
235. temperament
236. temperature
237. thorough *
238. throughout
239. tragedy
240. tries *
241. truly
242. Tuesday
243. unanimous
244. undoubtedly
245. unnecessarily
246. village
247. villain
248. weird
249. whether *
250. writing *

20b. ***The following spelling rules will help you to remember how certain words are spelled.***

a. A word ending in silent *-e* generally drops the *-e* before a suffix beginning with a vowel letter . . .

Drop -e

admire	+ ation	= admiration	desire	+ ous	= desirous
admire	+ able	= admirable	dine	+ ing	= dining
allure	+ ing	= alluring	explore	+ ation	= exploration
arrange	+ ing	= arranging	fame	+ ous	= famous
arrive	+ ing	= arriving	imagine	+ ary	= imaginary
believe	+ ing	= believing	imagine	+ able	= imaginable
care	+ ing	= caring	love	+ able	= lovable
come	+ ing	= coming	lose	+ ing	= losing
deplore	+ able	= deplorable	move	+ able	= movable

but it retains the *-e* before a suffix beginning with a consonant letter.

Retain -e

arrange	+ ment	= arrangement
care	+ ful	= careful
force	+ ful	= forceful
hate	+ ful	= hateful
like	+ ness	= likeness
move	+ ment	= movement

But after *c* or *g*, if the suffix begins with *a* or *o*, the *e* is retained to indicate the soft sound of *c* or *g*.

Retain -e

advantage	+ ous	=	advantageous
change	+ able	=	changeable
courage	+ ous	=	courageous
notice	+ able	=	noticeable
outrage	+ ous	=	outrageous
peace	+ able	=	peaceable
service	+ able	=	serviceable

b. In words with *ie* or *ei* when the sound is long *ee*, use *i* before *e* except after *c*.

i before e

achieve	cashier	piece	shriek
apiece	field	pierce	siege
belief	fierce	priest	thief
believe	frieze	relieve	wield
brief	grief	retrieve	yield
besiege	niece	reprieve	
chief	pier	shield	

except after c

ceiling	conceive	deceive	receipt
conceit	deceit	perceive	receive

Exceptions: either, neither, financier, weird, species, seize, leisure.

These may be remembered by arranging the words in a sentence: "Neither financier seized either species of weird leisure."

The so-called "seed" words can be easily remembered. For those who cannot memorize, a careful scrutiny of the list will suffice:

1. Only one word ends in "sede": supersede
2. Three words end in "ceed": exceed
proceed
succeed

3. The rest end in "cede":

accede
cede
concede
intercede
precede
recede
secede

c. In words of one syllable and words accented on the last syllable, ending in a single consonant letter preceded by a single vowel letter, double the final consonant letter before a suffix beginning with a vowel letter.

Now this looks like a formidable rule to unravel. Let us see what it involves. In the first place, it applies to short words like *get, swim, drop, drip.* In the second place, it applies to longer words in which the accent is on the final syllable, like *refer, begin, equip.* Examine the illustrations below to see what happens:

drop [word of one syllable] + ed [suffix beginning with a vowel] = dropped.
control [accented on the last syllable] + ed [suffix] = controlled.
benefit [not accented on last syllable] + ed [suffix] = benefited.
confer [accented on last syllable] + ed [suffix] = conferred.
confer [notice the shift in accent] + ence [suffix] = conference.
defer [accented on last syllable] + ed [suffix] = deferred.
defer [notice the shift in accent] + ence [suffix] = deference.

Suffix begins with a vowel

(One syllable)

brag	—bragging	man	—mannish
cram	—cramming	plan	—planning
drag	—dragging	snap	—snapped
din	—dinning	sin	—sinning
drop	—dropped	stop	—stopped
cut	—cutting	quit	—quitting
bid	—bidding	rob	—robbed
flag	—flagged	stab	—stabbed
get	—getting	whip	—whipped
clan	—clannish	glad	—gladdest

(Accent on last syllable)

admit′	—admitted	equip′	—equipped
begin′	—beginning	commit′	—committee
commit′	—committed	occur′	—occurrence
concur′	—concurring	submit′	—submitted
confer′	—conferring	compel′	—compelled

(Not accented on last syllable)

prefer	—preference	benefit	—benefited
refer	—reference	profit	—profitable
happen	—happened	marvel	—marvelous

Suffix begins with a consonant

glad	—gladness	sin	—sinful
fat	—fatness	equip	—equipment
man	—manhood	profit	—profitless

d. A noun ending in *-y* preceded by a consonant forms the plural in *-ies;* a verb ending in *-y* preceded by a consonant forms its present tense, third person singular, in *-ies.*

(Ending in -y preceded by a consonant)

baby, babies	sky, skies	fairy, fairies
marry, marries	copy, copies	fly, flies

(Ending in -y preceded by a vowel)

attorney, attorneys	valley, valleys	delay, delays
destroy, destroys	enjoy, enjoys	chimney, chimneys

Note: Some other rules for forming plurals are:

1. For most nouns, add *-s:* boys, girls, houses, ideas, aches, pains.
2. For nouns ending with a sound similar to *s,* add *-es:* birches, foxes, boxes, classes.
3. For nouns ending in *-f, -fe, -ff,* use *-s* or *-ves:* chief, chiefs; staff, staffs, staves; wife, wives; sheriff, sheriffs; elf, elves.
4. For nouns ending in *-o,* add *-s* or *-es:* solo, solos; echo, echoes; potato, potatoes; motto, mottos, mottoes; tomato, tomatoes; alto, altos.
5. Some nouns have irregular plurals: foot, feet; mouse, mice; goose, geese; ox, oxen; woman, women; axis, axes; basis, bases; datum, data; locus, loci; formula, formulas, formulae.

6. But Mr. and Mrs. Berry are *not* "the Berries," but "the Berrys"; and Mr. and Mrs. Wolf are *not* "the Wolves," but "the Wolfs."

SIMILAR FORMS

21. *A study of the following list of words similar or identical in sound but different in meaning may help you.*

Some of these are diction problems rather than spelling problems, it is true, but the presence of these words in this list will do no harm and might conceivably do some good. Please note that this is merely a check list for quick reference. It will not take the place of a dictionary.

accent: emphasis or stress; to stress.
ascent: climbing; a way sloping up.
assent: to agree; agreement.

accept: to take something offered; to agree to; to approve; to believe.
except: to leave out; to exclude.

admittance: permission to enter a place. [*W.D.S.* 23.][1]
admission: admitting to rights and privileges; the price of being allowed to enter.

affect: to influence; to pretend; to assume. [*W.D.S.* 30–31.]
effect: to perform; make happen. "They effected an escape."

all ready: everyone is ready. "They were all ready."
already: by this time. "They had already eaten breakfast."

altar: a place of worship. "They knelt before the altar."
alter: to change. "Do not alter a single word in my report."

ante: before. "antebellum"
anti: against, opposed to. "anti-aircraft; antifreeze; antitoxin"

bole: trunk of a tree.
boll: the pod of a plant.
bowl: a hollow dish.

[1] All references to *Webster's Dictionary of Synonyms.*

breath: air drawn into lungs. "We need a breath of fresh air."
breathe: to take a breath. "We cannot breathe in this room."

capital: chief; important; leading city; resources.
capitol: the State building.

censure: blame; condemn; criticize severely.
censor: to oversee morals and conduct; to examine and make changes.

charted: mapped or diagramed. "The Arctic is still not fully charted."
chartered: hired; granted certain rights. "We chartered a boat."

choose: to pick out, select. "Do you think he will choose me?"
chose: past tense of *choose.* "They chose a new secretary."

cite: to quote or use as an example. "Can you cite another instance?"
site: location. "This is a good site for our new church."
sight: vision; to see. "At last we sighted land."

coarse: rough; crude. "coarse food; coarse manners; coarse sand"
course: direction; path; series; order. "a course of study; of course"

complement: that which completes. "subjective complement"
compliment: praise; a polite and flattering lie. "He paid her a compliment."

consul: government official appointed to look after foreign business interests.
council: a group; an assembly. "the city council"
counsel: advice; one who advises; a lawyer. "Give her good counsel."

continually: frequently repeated. [*W.D.S.* 195–196.]
continuously: with an unbroken flow.

detract: take away. "Her hair detracts from her beauty."
distract: draw away; disturb. "Do not distract my attention."

device: a contrivance, machine; a trick.
devise: to invent; to plan or work out. "to devise a scheme"

eminent: distinguished. "the eminent statesman"
imminent: about to happen. "War is imminent."

fain: eager; willingly; pleased.
feign: pretend. "She feigned complete surprise."

farther: distance in space. "We shall go on farther." [*W.D.S.* 331.]
further: in addition to; progress in time, quantity, degree. See Sec. 44.

formally: in a formal manner. "He was formally installed in office."
formerly: in the past. "Formerly, he had been a sailor."

healthy: possessing health. "He looks like a healthy boy." [*W.D.S.* 406.]
healthful: giving health. "We live in a healthful climate."

hoards: stores; collections. "The police found hoards of stolen jewels."
hordes: crowds; groups of nomads. "The barbarian hordes were attacking again."

imaginary: existing in the imagination. "Her life is full of imaginary troubles."
imaginative: having imagination; able to imagine. "She wrote an imaginative poem."

implicit: absolute; implied. "implicit obedience to orders; an implicit displeasure."
explicit: distinctly stated; definite. "He gave us explicit directions."

incredible: unbelievable. "Your story is incredible."
incredulous: unwilling to believe. "He was incredulous when I told my story."

informant: one who gives information.
informer: one who accuses or complains.

intrinsic: essential; inherent. "its intrinsic value"
extrinsic: not essential; external.

irrelevant: not to the point. "His question is irrelevant."
irreverent: lacking reverence or respect. "His actions are irreverent."

per cent: part of a hundred. "fifty per cent"
percentage: rate or proportion. "A large percentage of automobiles have faulty brakes."

principal: chief; most important; chief teacher. "the principal occupation; the principal of the school"
principle: a truth; a belief; a scientific rule. "He is a man of high principles."

rend: to tear apart; to disturb. (rend, rent, rent, rending)
rendered: make; give; represent; play or sing. "She rendered a selection."

respectfully: with respect. "Speak to your teacher respectfully."
respectively: each in turn or in order.

stationary: not movable; not changing. "a stationary engine; a stationary enrollment."
stationery: writing materials.

straight: not curved; upright; continuous; direct. "Come straight to the point."
strait: narrow; strict; restricting. "a strait jacket; a strait passage."

Those who are interested in phonetic spelling may find pleasure in translating the following Latin verses:

Civile: derigo
Fortibus in ero.
Nobile: deus trux.
Vadis indem?
Causem dux.

WORDS AND PHRASES

EXACTNESS AND USE OF THE DICTIONARY

EXACTNESS

Words are tricky things; and that is half of our problem when we read, write, and speak. People who use words are often trickier; and that is the other half of our problem.

If a word always stood for only one thing or only one idea, communication would be simple indeed. But words have a habit of acquiring many meanings. Some of the words of everyday living, such as *run, get, take, hard, read, stand,* and others, have dozens of meanings each. Some words have even reversed themselves since they came into the language. Other words seem to live perpetually in a fog, because there is nothing touchable or visible for which they stand, to which you can point with your finger and say, "This is it. This is what I mean." When you say *dog* or *horse* or *chair* or *book,* you can, if it is important enough, find some dog or horse or chair or book to point to and say, "This is it." But when words stand for ideas, such as *temperance* or *democracy* or *security,* your problem is much harder. Then all you can do is to qualify and define, or point to a person who is temperate, a state that is democratic, a system that provides security. That is not a very satisfactory state of affairs, but when we do not define, when we do not point to examples, we may be talking about one thing and our listeners may be thinking another thing. And that is a worse state of affairs.

People may be tricky in their use of words in a multitude of ways. Some do it honestly. They commit their villainy—if villainy it is—always from a noble motive. Some do it for reasons we find hard to understand. When half the world speaks what a British statesman called "this strange, upside-down language," we need not look far for examples. Such words as *democratic peoples, freedom of speech, peace-loving, free elections, aggression* mean one thing to one group of people and just the opposite to another group. Some people use words to reveal their thoughts. Others use them to conceal thought. A difference of opinion as to what a word means, however, does not always imply dishonesty or evil intent. Profoundly honest people may differ in their understanding of words, depending on differences in their background, their training, their temperament, and so on. In the minds of some honest persons, the meaning of a word changes under the stress of emotion, or even under the stress of political campaigns and elections. Such words as *creeping socialism, free enterprise, extravagance, bureaucracy* mean one thing to members of a political party when it is in office and another thing when it is out of office.

22a. Key words that may be understood in more than one sense should be carefully defined.

Most of the words that you use in your writing or speaking will do well enough without being defined. If you write, for instance, "The man rode a white horse," it does not matter much whether you are thinking of a gentle old mare by the name of Nelly that your father once owned, and your reader is thinking of a mean, unpredictable nag by the name of Satan that he once knew. Nothing of vast importance is lost through this lack of exact communication. But something of vast importance *is* involved when people use such terms as *radicals, education, American, liberals, realistic, sincerity,* and the like. These words, as we have noted earlier, are tricky, variable words. A writer's first duty is to pin them down, to define them, to tell his readers exactly in what sense he is using them. Failure to do that results in confusion, not in communication of ideas.

The foregoing points to only one of several vital problems in the exact use of words. When a student uses a general or abstract word, he is not actually using a word in a wrong sense. He has committed a "sin of omission," it is true, by not defining the word, but if he is asked he can probably do so. To correct his omission the student needs first the friendly help of someone who notices his omission and points it out to him. The type of inexactness discussed next, however, is a positive error, not merely a failure to define.

22b. *Words used in an inexact sense should be checked and restudied with the help of a good dictionary.*

The point of this statement can be understood if we first take a quick look at the ways in which we usually acquire our stock of words. Most of the common ones grew up with us; very few of those will ever bother us much. Some of the more difficult ones we got in connection with our high-school studies, through our general reading, through listening to such things as radio talks, lectures, or the talk of others, and, when curiosity or necessity led us there, by looking up unfamiliar words in a dictionary. Most of us got new words as we needed them, without much help from vocabulary improvement schemes. All of us have depended very much and very often on the context, on approximations, for meanings. Here and there we missed the point—sometimes by a narrow margin, sometimes by a mile. So here and there someone catches us up.

The word you have used—the one marked by your instructor—is a good word in its place, but it does not mean quite what you think it means. Maybe it is a word that you have picked up recently and are trying out. Maybe it is a word you did not quite hear when it was spoken or did not quite see when you read it. Now you confuse it with another word that sounds like it but which means something else. See what help the dictionary can give you.

Examples:

The owner of the estate had two special officers *patrolling* (not *paroling*) the grounds.

The Constitution *implies* (not *infers*) that the states have control of education.

The diagram or picture of our family descent is often *compared* (not *referred*) to a tree.

Proper study methods will *insure* (not *induce*) good grades in college.

When he started his business, he was deliberately setting out upon an *uncharted* (not *unchartered*) ocean.

The rest of the men went deep-sea fishing in a *chartered* (not *charted*) launch.

22c. *Vague, blanket words should be replaced with more precise words.*

This statement refers primarily to such words as *deal, factor, line, majority, point of view, proposition,* and so on. It refers also to any word that you have used not because it expresses your thought precisely and cleanly, but because you were in a hurry and it was easier to use a vague word than to think of a more exact one.

Poor:

He is interested in an occupation *in the line* of engineering.

Let us first find out what his *angle* is.

From the *point of view* of economy of operation, the small car is superior to a big car.

Better:

He is interested in engineering. He is interested in any occupation that involves engineering.

First let us find out what his idea is. (or *decision,* or *suggestion*)

A small car is more economical to operate than a big car.

22d. *A writer should guard against the right word taking an unintended meaning in the context.*

A serious writer, that is, should guard against unintentional humor or boners. Boners, either the natural or the synthetic variety, are of course the stock in trade of the gag writer or the television comedian.

Poor:

The writer made the poem more effective by the use of metaphors and illusions.
Finally, at midnight, I sat down to learn my history.
A college teacher should not at all times be a sober person, but he should wear a smile and occasionally tell a joke.

Exercise

Exercise 1. Point out every instance of inexact use of words in the following sentences and suggest a revision.

1. The long arm of television permeates all of the civilized world.
2. In this poem the author tells about England's downfall from a leading country.
3. The most common fault I have found in children is the disability to amuse themselves.
4. The effect of the poem depends on what the reader divulges from it.
5. In order to solve their curiosity, they must read the story to the end.
6. He describes in a realistic way about the things he has experienced in the slums of a big city.
7. My problems are more of an uncertainty, like being able to place a comma in this place or a semicolon in that place.
8. I still remember the joy that came to me every spring when at last I could disperse with my shoes and go barefoot.
9. My hobby includes time, work, and expense.
10. Baby-sitting teaches patience, responsibility, the art of diversion, and numerable other traits.

USE OF THE DICTIONARY

22e. *Information found in a dictionary will help a student use words and phrases more exactly.*

A dictionary lists the words of a language, in alphabetical order, and gives information about their meaning, their spelling, their use, their pronunciation, their history, and so on; the degree of completeness of this information depends on the size and purpose of the dictionary. The information found in a dictionary is based on a very extensive study of the language in action; for every word listed, a great mass of information has been collected, classified, filed, and studied by a trained staff and, where necessary, by consultants from special fields in which the word is used. All information in a good dictionary is based on a study of usage. A dictionary reflects usage; it does not prescribe it. It is an authority only in so far as it accurately reflects usage.

The various dictionaries of the English language fall into the following classes:

1. The monumentally complete ones, in which a word gets full historical treatment, with quotations illustrating its use, from the time of its birth to the date of completion of the dictionary.

a. The *New English Dictionary,* in 10 vols. and a supplement, 1888–1928, reissued in corrected edition as *Oxford English Dictionary,* 12 vols., 1933 (also known as *N.E.D., O.E.D.,* the *Oxford,* and *Murray's*). In the *N.E.D.* there are 1,827,306 quotations of usage.
b. The *Century Dictionary*, 10 vols., 1901, vols. 11 and 12 added in 1909; the *New Century,* in 3 vols., 1948. This new edition has 160,000 entries and 12,000 illustrative quotations.

2. The one-volume unabridged dictionaries, which you find in schoolrooms and libraries for reference use. These are usually kept up to date by spot revisions and by "New Word Sections."

a. *Webster's New International Dictionary*, 2nd ed. Springfield, Massachusetts: G. & C. Merriam Company.
b. *New Standard Dictionary.* New York: Funk & Wagnalls Company.

3. The one-volume, desk-size dictionaries, one of which almost every college student buys as a part of his working equipment. Each one of these listed here is well worth the cost; the choice is usually governed by the recommendation of the student's English instructor.

a. *Webster's New World Dictionary.* Cleveland, Ohio: World Publishing Co.
b. *Webster's New Collegiate Dictionary.* Springfield, Massachusetts: G. & C. Merriam Co.
c. *American College Dictionary,* text ed. New York: Harper & Brothers.

d. *New College Standard.* New York: Funk & Wagnalls Co.
e. Thorndike-Barnhart *Comprehensive Desk Dictionary.* Garden City: Doubleday & Co.

The following kind of information may be secured from a desk-size dictionary.

1. The meaning of a word. As you can see on page 341 in the specimen from the *American College Dictionary* (*ACD*), a dictionary uses several methods for clarifying the meaning of a word. It uses phrases of definition, and it sometimes follows the definition with illustrative examples, as: **10.** prompt to perceive: *a quick eye.* It uses synonyms, and when practicable it compares and contrasts a group of synonyms. It classifies the different meanings of a word, numbers them, and if a word has special technical uses, it labels these uses and explains them. Some dictionaries list the oldest meaning first; others list the most commonly used meaning first. A student must know what scheme his dictionary uses. He must, moreover, read *all* the definitions of a word in order to decide, on the basis of his own sentence, whether his use of the word is correct and appropriate.

2. The spelling of a word. If you do not know how to spell a word, you can always look it up in your dictionary—well, *almost* always. A story is told about a famous politician, who once telephoned from a hunting resort to his secretary, directing her to send him his gun. The connection was bad, and the secretary could not understand what he wanted. "Spell it out, please," she directed. "Gun," replied the politician. " 'G' as in 'Jerusalem,' 'u' as in 'Europe,' and 'n' as in 'pneumonia.' " Usually the student knows the first letter of his word. When two spellings are listed, as *canyon, cañon,* both are in good standing, although at times there may be an explanatory note to show why there is a variant, as for instance that *color* is American usage, *colour* is British.

3. The pronunciation of a word. Pronunciation of words in a dictionary may be indicated by (1) a set of symbols without respelling; (2) respelling the word with diacritical marks and symbols; and (3) respelling the word in a phonetic alphabet. The second method is the one most commonly used. Since every dic-

quick (kwĭk), *adj.* **1.** done, proceeding, or occurring with promptness or rapidity, as an action, process, etc.; prompt; immediate: *a quick answer.* **2.** that is over or completed within a short space of time. **3.** moving with speed. **4.** swift or rapid, as motion. **5.** hasty; impatient: *a quick temper.* **6.** lively or keen, as feelings. **7.** having a high degree of vigor, energy, or activity. **8.** prompt in action; acting with swiftness or rapidity. **9.** prompt or swift (to do something): *quick to respond.* **10.** prompt to perceive: *a quick eye.* **11.** prompt to understand, learn, etc.; of ready intelligence. **12.** consisting of living plants: *a quick hedge.* **13.** brisk, as fire, flames, heat, etc. **14.** *Finance.* readily convertible into cash; liquid, as assets. **15.** *Mining.* containing ore, or productive, as veins. **16.** *Archaic or Dial.* endowed with life. **17.** *Archaic or Dial.* living, as persons, animals, plants, etc. —*n.* **18.** living persons: *the quick and the dead.* **19.** *Chiefly Brit.* living plants (esp. hawthorn) as set to form a hedge. **20.** a single such plant. **21.** the tender sensitive flesh of the living body, esp. that under the nails: *nails bitten down to the quick.* **22.** the vital or most important part. —*adv.* **23.** quickly. [ME; OE *cwic, cwicu* living, c. OS *quik*, G *queck, keck,* Icel. *kvikr;* akin to L *vīvus* living] —**quick′ness,** *n.*

—**Syn. 3.** QUICK, FAST, SWIFT, RAPID describe speedy tempo. QUICK applies particularly to something practically instantaneous, an action or reaction, perhaps, of very brief duration: *to give a quick look around, to make a quick change of clothes.* FAST and SWIFT refer to actions, movements, etc., which continue for a time, and usually to those which are uninterrupted; when used of communication, transportation, and the like, they suggest a definite goal and a continuous trip. SWIFT, the more formal—even poetic—word suggests the greater speed: *a fast train, a swift message.* RAPID, less speedy than the others, applies to a rate or movement or action, and usually to a series of actions of movements, related or unrelated: *rapid calculation, a rapid walker.* **11.** See **sharp.**

Reprinted by courtesy of the publishers from *the American College Dictionary, Copyright,* 1959, by Random House, Inc.

tionary uses a slightly different scheme, it is obviously a matter of common sense for the owner of a desk-size dictionary to get acquainted with the scheme used in his dictionary. A study of the preface and the discussion of pronunciation and the various "Pronunciation Keys" will be time well spent. As in everything else, the editors of a dictionary try to record, as accurately as is humanly possible, the pronunciation or pronunciations used among the educated, and whenever there are regional or national differences in pronunciation to note and explain these differences. Every desk-size dictionary has a section on pronunciation: page xxii in the *ACD,* page ix in *Webster's New Collegiate.* Then there is always the *Webster's New International,* 2nd ed., with its excellent discussion of pronunciation on page xxvi, especially section 5, "The Meaning of Correctness in Pronunciation," section 6, "Treatment of Standard Pronunciation in This Dictionary," and section 8, "Styles of Speech Suited to Various Occasions." In the desk-size *Webster's New World Dictionary* the student can find an excellent brief account of pronunciation written by Harold Whitehall, pages xv–xxi. If a special study of pronunciation is made in the class, students may be interested to refer to *A Pronouncing Dictionary of American English,* by John S. Kenyon and Thomas A. Knott, published by G. & C. Merriam in 1944. Excursions to this book are best made with the advice and help of the instructor.

4. Labels: subject, geographical, usage. If you will turn to pages 344–345 and examine the specimen pages from *Webster's New Collegiate,* you will see certain labels, in italics, between the word and the definitions. See, for example: John Doe, *Law;* joint, 6. *Geol.;* jointer, 2. *Agric. Mach.;* Jonathan, *Hort.* These labels show that the words so indicated, or in the senses or meanings so indicated, belong to law, to geology, to agricultural machinery, to horticulture. Then note these: jointweed, *U.S.;* jollity, 2. *Brit.;* jornada, *Southwest U.S. & Mexico.* These geographical labels are used to show that a word is found most commonly in these regions. And finally there are the usage labels: joint, 5. *Slang;* joker, 2.a. *Political Cant;* jolly, 4. *Colloq.;* josh, *Slang, U.S.* If you will look up the word *colloquial* in the same dictionary, you will find that it means the word or expression so marked is "acceptable and correct in ordinary conversation, friendly letters, or informal speeches, but unsuited to formal speeches or writing."

5. Derivation of a word. As you know, our words have come from many languages, and during their long journey from the time they passed the linguistic Ellis Island to the present, some have undergone many changes in form and meaning. Would you believe, for instance, that our word *emerald* had an ancestor who in Latin was once *smaragdus* and in Greek *smaragdos?* Puzzle over that one for a while! The Roman Emperor Nero once used a polished *smaragdus* as a lens in front of his near-sighted eye. The Bowery was once the home of a Dutch *bouwer,* or farmer, in New York City. The derivations of words are interesting in themselves, and they might conceivably enrich your understanding of a word.

The following words have unusually interesting origins: *bedlam, boycott, broker, calico, curfew, daisy, dollar, exhume, lunacy, panic, sandwich, sinister, saxophone, tawdry, thug, vandal.*

6. Grammatical information. A desk-size dictionary gives adequate information about the plurals of nouns and the principal parts of verbs. Inflectional forms are usually given only when they are irregular or when they present difficulties of spelling or pronunciation. For example, no plurals are given for *book, chair, handkerchief* because it is assumed that these words, and all like them, form their plural in the usual way. But after *index* you find two plurals, *indexes, indices;* after *deer* you find the information that the plural is also *deer* (occasionally *deers*)*;* after *ox* you find the plural is *oxen* (rarely *ox*). Similarly, no principal parts are given after regular verbs, especially when no special problems are involved: see *talk, walk,* but note that *study* is followed by *studied, studying* to show what happens to the ending in the formation of the past tense and the present participle and gerund.

7. Idiomatic phrases. The unabridged dictionary lists a large number of idiomatic phrases; the desk-size dictionaries list only a few, but still enough to interest any student. Here are a few samples: *get even with, get across, fight shy of, hang together, lay by the heels, lay hold of, take stock, take the floor, give rise to.*

8. Synonyms and antonyms. Two words that have exactly the same meaning are none too common in the English language, but words may have approximately the same meaning, or approximately the same meaning in certain uses. These are called synonyms. If you will refer to the specimen from the *ACD*, you will see that some synonyms are used in the phrases of definition after the word "quick," and that below the definitions there are four synonyms differentiated: *quick, fast, swift, rapid.* Antonyms are less commonly listed. For instance under "reproach" in the *ACD*, the synonyms are *chide, abuse, reprimand, condemn, criticize, rebuke, scold, reprove;* the antonym is *praise.*

Exercises

Exercise 1. Look up the meanings of each of the following words. List at least two very different meanings for each.

aggravate	fellow	nice	homely
criticize	irony	hobby	curious

John the Baptist. (2) John the Apostle, whose name is attached to the Fourth Gospel, three Epistles, and the Book of Revelation. **b** (1) The Gospel of John. (2) One of the three Epistles of John. See BIBLE.

John Bull (bo͝ol). The English nation personified; the English people; also, the, or a, typical Englishman.

John Doe (dō). *Law.* The fictitious lessee acting as plaintiff in the common-law action of ejectment. Hence, a fictitious name for a party, real or fictitious, to any transaction, action, or proceeding.

John Do′ry (dō′rĭ; 70); *pl.* JOHN DORYS (-rĭz). Also **John Do′ree** (-rē). [*John* + *doree, dory,* the fish.] A marine fish of the family Zeidae; specif., a common yellow to olive European food fish (*Zeus faber*), or an allied Australian fish (*Zeus australis*).

John Han′cock (hăn′kŏk). An autograph signature; — from the legibility of the handwriting of John Hancock.

john′ny·cake′ (jŏn′ĭ·kāk′), *n.* [For *journey cake.*] *U.S.* A bread made of Indian meal, flour, eggs, milk, etc.

John′ny–jump′–up′, *n.* Also **Johnny jumper. a** Any of several American violets, as the bird's-foot violet. **b** *U.S.* The wild pansy.

John′son·ese′ (jŏn′sŭn·ēz′; -ēs′), *n.* The diction or literary style of Dr. Samuel Johnson, or one formed in imitation of it; — used derogatorily of stilted or pompous style.

John′son grass (jŏn′s′n). [After W. *Johnson* of Alabama, who planted it about 1840–45.] A tall perennial European grass (*Sorghum halepense*) valuable in southern and western U. S. for pasture and hay.

John·so′ni·an (jŏn·sō′nĭ·ăn; 58), *adj.* Pertaining to, or resembling, Dr. Samuel Johnson or his style; derogatorily, pompous; inflated. — *n.* A follower or copier of Dr. Johnson. — **John·so′ni·an·ism** (-ĭz′m), *n.*

‖**joie de vi′vre** (zhwȧ′ dẽ vē′vr′). [F.] Literally, joy in living; hence, zest; keen enjoyment of the pleasures of life.

join (join), *v. t.* [OF. *joindre*, fr. L. *jungere* to yoke, join.] **1.** To connect physically; to fasten or put together; to couple. **2.** To unite in association, specif., in marriage; to associate oneself with; as, to *join* the church. **3.** To unite in time, effort, action, consideration, or other immaterial manner; as, to *join* prayers. **4.** To assemble in a group; as, to *join* forces. **5.** To accept, or engage in, as a contest; as, to *join* battle. **6.** *Colloq.* To be adjacent to; adjoin. **7.** *Geom.* To connect by a line, esp. by a straight line. — *v. i.* **1.** To come together so as to be connected; to unite. **2.** To engage; to join battle.

Syn. Join, combine, unite, connect, link, associate, relate mean to attach or fasten two or more things to each other or to become so attached or fastened. **Join** presupposes prior detachment and the bringing of them into contact or conjunction; **combine** usually implies a mingling or merging, often suggesting the loss of identity of each unit; **unite** implies a oneness that results from a joining or combining; **connect** implies a loose or obvious attachment without loss of any unit's identity; **link** implies the strength of the connection; **associate**, referring more often to persons than to things, suggests a connection based upon companionship or the like; **relate**, if used of persons, suggests a connection by blood, or if used of things, a connection based on some logical principle, such as cause of an effect, effect of a cause, subordination, etc. (as, to *join* hands; to *combine* ingredients; to *unite* churches; to *connect* railway coaches; to *link* persons in marriage; to *associate* ideas; to *relate* one event to another).

— *n.* Act of joining; place or point of junction.

join′der (join′dẽr), *n.* [F. *joindre*, inf. as n.] **1.** Act of joining; a

articulata) of the buckwheat family, with jointed, almost leafless stems, and spikelike racemes of small white flowers.

joint′worm′ (-wûrm′), *n.* The larva of any of several small chalcid flies (genus *Harmolita*, family Eurytomidae), which attack the stems of grain and cause gall-like swellings.

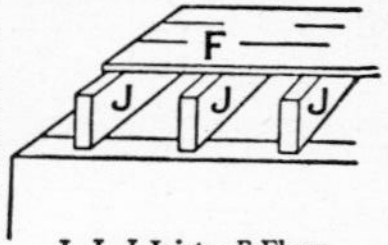

J, J, J Joists; *F* Floor.

joist (joist), *n.* [OF. *giste*, fr. L. *jacēre* to lie.] **a** Any of the small timbers or beams ranged parallelwise from wall to wall in a building to support the floor, or to support the laths or furring strips of a ceiling. **b** *U.S.* A stud or scantling about 3 by 4 inches in section. — *v. t.* To furnish with joists.

joke (jōk), *n.* [L. *jocus* joke, jest, game.] **1.** Something said or done to excite a laugh; something witty or sportive; jest; witticism. **2.** Something said or done in sport and not seriously. **3.** A laughingstock; as, he is a *joke* — **Syn.** See JEST. — *v. i.* To do something as a joke; to be merry; to jest. — *v. t.* To make merry with; to rally; banter; as, to *joke* a comrade. — **jok′ing·ly** (jōk′ĭng·lĭ), *adv.*

jok′er (jōk′ẽr), *n.* **1.** One who jokes; a jester. **2. a** *Political Cant.* An apparently harmless clause inserted in a legislative bill to render it inoperative or uncertain in some respect without arousing opposition at the time of its passage. **b** Hence, an unsuspected clause in a document, or the like, which in effect nullifies or greatly alters its apparent terms. **3.** *Card Playing.* An extra card now usually made to accompany the regulation pack. When used, it has special privileges; thus, in euchre it is the best trump.

jole (jōl). Var. of JOWL.

jol′li·er (jŏl′ĭ·ẽr), *n.* *Colloq.* One who jollies, flatters, etc.

jol′li·fi·ca′tion (jŏl′ĭ·fĭ·kā′shŭn), *n.* [*jolly* + *-fication.*] *Colloq.* A merrymaking; jovial festivity.

jol′li·fy (jŏl′ĭ·fī), *v. t. & i.*; -FIED (-fīd); -FY′ING. *Colloq.* To make, or to be, jolly.

jol′li·ty (jŏl′ĭ·tĭ), *n.*; *pl.* -TIES (-tĭz). **1.** State or quality of being jolly; gaiety. **2.** *Brit.* A festive gathering. — **Syn.** See MIRTH.

jol′ly (jŏl′ĭ), *adj.*; JOL′LI·ER (-ĭ·ẽr); JOL′LI·EST. [OF. *joli, jolif*, joyful, merry.] **1.** Full of spirits; joyful. **2.** Full of life and mirth; jovial; merry. **3.** Expressing or inspiring mirth. **4.** *Colloq.* Splendid; pleasant; also, large; strong. — **Syn.** See MERRY. — *n.*; *pl.* JOLLIES (-ĭz). **1.** *Brit. Sailors' Slang.* A marine. **2.** *Colloq.* Something said or done to keep a person or people in good humor or quiet. **3.** *Slang, Eng.* A social meeting for mirth and good cheer. — *v. t.*; JOL′LIED (-ĭd); JOL′LY·ING. *Colloq.* To encourage to feel pleasant or cheerful; — often implying a bantering spirit; hence, to poke fun at; rally. — *v. i.* **1.** To be or act jolly. **2.** *Colloq.* To jolly a person or people. — **jol′li·ly**, *adv.* — **jol′li·ness**, *n.*

jolly boat. *Naut.* A boat of medium size belonging to a ship, used for general rough or small work.

Jolly Roger. See ROGER, 2.

jolt (jōlt), *v. i. & t.* **1.** To shake with short, abrupt risings and fallings, as a carriage moving on rough ground; to jar. **2.** *Boxing.* To jar with a hard blow. — *n.* A butt, knock, or blow; a sudden shock or jerk; in boxing, a jarring blow. — **jolt′er**, *n.*

Jo′nah (jō′nȧ), *n.* [Heb. *Yōnāh*, lit., dove.] **1.** *Bib.* A Hebrew prophet, who, during a tempest sent by God because of his disobedience, was cast overboard from his ship, swallowed by a great fish, and

join'er (join'ĕr), *n.* **1.** One who or that which joins. **2.** One whose occupation is to construct articles by joining pieces of wood; a skilled woodworker who does the woodwork (as doors, stairs, etc.) necessary for the finishing of buildings.

join'er·y (-ĭ), *n.* Also **joiner work.** Art or trade of a joiner; the work of a joiner; also, things made by a joiner.

joint (joint), *n.* [OF. *joint, jointe,* fr. L. *junctus,* past part. of *jungere, junctum,* to join.] **1.** The part, or the arrangement of the part, where two bones of an animal's body, or parts of an invertebrate's body, are joined, esp. so as to admit of motion; hence, a part in a plant where branches give off. **2.** The part or space included between two articulations, knots, or nodes. **3.** Specif., any of the large pieces of meat as cut for roasting. **4.** The place or part where two things or parts are joined or united; junction; as, a *joint* in a pipe; a *joint* between two pieces of timber. **5.** *Slang.* A gathering place; loosely, any establishment, resort, etc. **6.** *Geol.* A fracture in rock, smaller than a fault and not accompanied by dislocation.
— *adj.* [OF., past part. of *joindre.*] **1.** Joined; combined; specif., *Law,* of the lives of two or more persons, united in time; concurrent. **2.** Common to two or more; as: **a** Involving the united activity of two or more. **b** Shared by, or affecting, two or more; as, a *joint* account; a *joint* fine; specif., in diplomacy, designating an action or expression in which two or more governments unite (dist. from *identic*). **3.** United, joined, or sharing with another or with others; acting together; as, *joint* creditor; *joint* debtor. **4.** *Parl. Practice.* Of or pertaining to the two branches of a legislative body; as, a *joint* committee.
— *v. t.* **1.** To unite by a joint or joints; to fit together. **2.** To separate the joints of; cut up into joints, as meat. **3.** To provide with a joint or joints; to articulate.

joint'ed (join'tĕd; -tĭd), *adj.* Having joints.

joint'er (join'tĕr), *n.* **1.** One that joints; esp., any various tools used in making joints. **2.** *Agric. Mach.* A triangular-shaped edged attachment to a plow beam for covering trash in plowing. See PLOW, *Illust.*

joint'ly, *adv.* In a joint manner; together; unitedly.

joint resolution. A resolution adopted jointly by the two branches of a legislative body.

joint'ress (join'trĕs; -trĭs), *n.* *Law.* A woman who has a jointure.

joint stock. Stock or capital held in company; capital held as a common stock or fund.

joint'-stock' com'pa·ny. *Law.* A company or association, consisting of a number of individuals organized to conduct a business for gain, with a joint stock, the shares owned by any member being transferable without the consent of the rest.

join'ture (join'tŭr), *n.* [OF., fr. L. *junctura,* fr. *jungere* to join.] **1.** *Obs.* A joining; union. **2.** *Law.* The joint tenancy of an estate, or the estate so held. *Obs.,* except specif., an estate settled on a wife to be taken by her in lieu of dower.

joint'weed' (joint'wēd'), *n.* *U. S.* An American herb (*Polygonella*

Jo'nas (-năs), *n.* *Douay Bib.* Jonah.

Jon'a·than (jŏn'ȧ·thăn), *n.* [Heb. *Yōnāthān.*] *Bib.* Son of Saul, and friend of David.

Jon'a·than, *n.* *Hort.* A late autumn variety of red apple.

jon'gleur' (zhôɴ'glûr'; jŏng'glĕr), *n.* [F. See JUGGLER.] In medieval France and Norman England, an itinerant minstrel who recited or sang by way of entertainment, as at courts.

jon'quil (jŏng'kwĭl; jŏn'-; *still by some,* jŭng'kwĭl), *n.* [F. *jonquille,* fr. Sp. *junquillo* jonquil, reed, dim. of *junco* a rush, fr. L. *juncus.*] A bulbous plant (*Narcissus jonquilla*) of southern Europe and Algeria, with long, rushlike leaves, and yellow or white, single or double fragrant flowers resembling those of the daffodil; also, a bulb or flower of the plant. See CORONA, *Illust.*

jook joint (jo͝ok; jo͝ok). See JUKE JOINT.

jor'dan (jôr'd'n), **jor'den,** *n.* *Obs. exc. Dial.* A chamber pot.

Jor'dan al'monds (jôr'd'n). [ME. *jardyne almaunde* (*jardyne,* fr. OF. *jardin* garden); hence, prop., a cultivated almond.] Almonds imported from Málaga, used in confectionery.

‖**jor·na'da** (hôr·nä'thä), *n.* [Sp.] The toil, travel, or the like, of a day; hence, *Southwest U. S. & Mexico,* a long stretch of desert region.

jo'rum (jō'rŭm; 70), *n.* [Prob. from *Joram,* in 2 Sam. viii. 10, who brought vessels of silver, etc.] *Colloq.* A large drinking vessel, or its contents.

Jo'seph (jō'zĕf; -zĭf), *n.* [L. *Joseph, Josephus,* fr. Gr. *Iōsēph,* fr. Heb. *Yōsēph.*] **1.** *Bib.* **a** A Hebrew patriarch, son of Jacob, who gave him a "coat of many colors." See JACOB. **b** The husband of Mary, mother of Jesus. **c** The rich councilor of Arimathea, ***Joseph of Arimathea,*** who placed the body of Jesus in his tomb. **2.** [*not cap.*] An 18th-century cloak, esp. a woman's riding coat.

josh (jŏsh), *v. t. & i.* *Slang, U. S.* To make fun (of); to chaff; banter. — *n.* *Slang, U. S.* A bantering joke. — **josh'er** (-ĕr), *n.*

Josh'u·a (jŏsh'ū·ȧ), *n.* [Heb. *Yĕhōshūa'.*] *Bib.* **a** The successor of Moses, who led the Israelites into Canaan. **b** A book of the Old Testament. See BIBLE.

Joshua tree. A branched treelike yucca (*Yucca brevifolia*) of the southwestern U. S., often 25 feet high, with short leaves and clustered greenish-white flowers.

jos'kin (jŏs'kĭn), *n.* *Slang.* A bumpkin; a boor.

joss (jŏs), *n.* [Pidgin English, fr. Pg. *deos, deus,* a god, fr. L. *deus.*] *Pidgin English.* A Chinese household divinity; also, a cult image.

joss house. *Pidgin English.* A Chinese temple.

joss stick. A reed covered with, or a cylinder of, paste made of the dust of odoriferous woods. The Chinese burn joss sticks as incense.

jos'tle (jŏs''l), *v. t. & i.;* JOS'TLED (-'ld); JOS'TLING (-lĭng). [Dim. of *joust, just,* v. See JOUST.] To run against and shake; to elbow; to hustle; to crowd. — *n.* A crowding or bumping together; interference. — **jos'tler** (-lĕr), *n.*

Exercise 2. Look up each of the following words. Decide whether both spellings are in use in your locality, or whether one is more common than the other.

honor, honour	sulfur, sulphur	color, colour
theater, theatre	adviser, advisor	night, nite

Exercise 3. Look up the pronunciation of the following words. Notice where the accent is placed in each word. Where more than one pronunciation is listed in your dictionary, try pronouncing the word in each way. Which pronunciation do you use in your own conversation?

acumen	decade	finance	irreparable
aspirant	decadence	formidable	lamentable
combatant	despicable	gondola	preferable
culinary	exquisite	inquiry	superfluous

APPROPRIATENESS

23. ***The skilled writer uses words that are in keeping with the subject of his paper, with the occasion, and with the readers he is addressing.***

Some of the papers that you write are formal; some are informal. When you write a serious discussion of a serious subject, you should use language that is dignified though not pretentious or affected. If your occasion is informal, you write in an informal, easy manner. We have mentioned before (Chapter 1), the analogy of levels of usage with manners or dress. Every intelligent person has different styles of writing at his command just as he has clothes appropriate for different occasions. You do not attend a formal dinner in sweater and slacks, or a football game in a tuxedo, unless you are determined to make a spectacular and probably unfavorable impression. There *are* rules and conventions in the use of language, just as there are conventions and decencies governing human intercourse everywhere else—at a dinner table, at a football game, on a street corner, anywhere. A writer's good sense, wide awake to the situation around him, is his best rule of conduct.

Here are a few examples of failure in appropriateness:

Inappropriate in formal writing:

The college selects its students on the basis of their demonstrated ability to accomplish high-level academic work, their personal and social maturity, and their potentiality *for getting a lot out of it.* [The "occasion" of this sentence is a college catalogue, and the original phrasing was "potentiality for further intellectual and social growth and development."]

The State Department's difficulty was that it had failed to find any device for ensuring that the press would *keep mum* on the new international agreement. [remain silent]

Inappropriate in informal writing:

I certainly hope you are having a good time at college this year and *realizing your potentiality for intellectual growth and development.* [This time the "occasion" is an informal letter, and an appropriate phrasing would be "getting a lot out of it."]
He told me what to do and I accomplished the operation. [I did it]

23a. The inappropriate use of slang should be avoided in serious writing.

Slang has been defined as a kind of made-to-order language, characterized by extravagant or grotesque fancy or humor. Some examples are *hep, beat, savvy, take the rap, gripe, jalopy, jive, snide, baloney, scram, vamoose.* The last three examples also show what often happens to slang: it gets pretty *corny.* *Webster's New World Dictionary* points out that slang is "generally short-lived but may survive and become part of the colloquial or informal vocabulary." Slang is usually inappropriate in serious or formal writing, but some writers use it with telling effects. Actually, most students are less likely to get into trouble by using slang in college papers than by using stilted, general, vague, and pompously bookish words under the impression that a simple and direct style is not good enough for important ideas.

23b. A mixture of the colloquial and the formal styles is usually inappropriate in serious writing.

Most dictionaries use *colloq.* as a usage label for certain words and phrases. The editors of these dictionaries are careful to point out that the label implies no condemnation of the word or phrase.

Colloquial means informal, or characteristic of a conversational style, as opposed to a formal, literary style. Now of course, as everyone knows, there are thousands upon thousands of other words, not so labeled in any dictionary, that are also appropriate in conversation, in informal writing, in familiar letters, in all the situations of everyday living in which language is used. Every educated person uses colloquial English, and, what is very important to remember, he uses it correctly if he uses it appropriately. In the writing of college students the importance of the problem of colloquialism has been much overrated. If a student suspects some word or phrase in his more formal papers, he can easily check it through his dictionary. If it is marked *colloq.* there, he should question its appropriateness. The dictionary will usually supply a formal equivalent.

Exercises

Exercise 1. The following sentences contain expressions inappropriate in a formal context. Revise each sentence.

1. The prime minister explained patiently that the nations of the West did not ever scheme to gang up on the Soviet Union.
2. He lost a fortune in the stock-market game.
3. As the session was nearing adjournment, the President asked Congress to shake a leg.
4. When Father spoke sternly to me, I found it wisest to make like a rabbit.
5. There was a man who was obviously looking for trouble, but he was run in by the police before he could do any damage.

Exercise 2. Half of the following italicized expressions are appropriate in formal writing; half are not. With the help of your dictionary, decide which are more appropriate in colloquial than in formal usage.

1. The girl said that she was driving at an excessive speed so that she would not *run out* of gas before she reached home.
2. When the professor was irritated, he would *take it out on* his students.
3. The dean was slightly *under the weather.*
4. One of the boys was unruly, and the teacher *gave him the works.*
5. I believe that he *had had words* with him before this.
6. He was readmitted to class after he had promised *to make good.*
7. After that the teacher made him work *to beat the Dutch.*
8. No boy likes *to eat his own words* even if he knows he is wrong.

9. It is poor sportsmanship *to jump on* a boy for every trifling offense.
10. Adults should not try *to squelch* a boy's spirit and imagination.

IDIOMS

24a. *Idiomatic English should be cultivated in preference to formal, bookish English.*

An idiom is an expression peculiar to a language. An idiom may be (it is not always so) irrational, untranslatable, even ungrammatical. How can one, literally, *pick a quarrel* with a person who is *beside himself with anxiety?* How can one translate "How do you do?" into French or German? Because idioms are created out of the day-to-day living of ordinary men and women, they are themselves alive, pungent, racy. They are truly the heart of the language. But it is highly misleading to say, as has often been said, that idiomatic speech is that used by cultivated Englishmen. Many idioms border on slang; many of the idioms now accepted as part of the language were roundly denounced by cultivated but squeamish English gentlemen of a former day.

You must not think that the study of English idiom concerns itself with a few illogical phrases like those just mentioned, or with a score or so of verbs that must always be used with certain prepositions. Vizetelly and De Bekker in *Idioms and Idiomatic Phrases* list 498 pages of idioms. You cannot memorize all the idioms in the English language. Idiomatic speech will come naturally to you if you have grown up with the language; if you haven't, you have something of a problem on your hands.

Many idiomatic phrases have grown up around the verbs of everyday living—to go, to do, to catch, to get, to make, to take, and so on. Notice the following examples. Some of these phrases are more appropriate in speech and informal writing; others are appropriate on all occasions.

To catch:

The pile of rags *caught fire.* [ignited]
You'll *catch it!* [be punished]
They *caught sight of* a plane. [saw]

To do:

I am *done for.* [vanquished, ruined]
We shall *do away with* poverty. [abolish]
He *did* himself *proud.* [distinguished]

To make:

She *made faces* at her mother. [grimaced]
He *made free* with my money. [squandered]
He *made good.* [succeeded]
He *made off* with the jewels. [escaped]
I cannot *make out* what he is saying. [understand]
Please *make sure* of it. [be certain]

Webster's New International lists a very large number of idiomatic phrases. The desk-size dictionaries list fewer, of course. Here is a comparison of what three of the dictionaries list under *hang:*

WNWD	*WNCD*	*ACD*
hang around	hang fire	hang back
hang fire	hang together	hang in the balance
hang it	hang out	hang out
hang on	hang up	hang together
hang out		hang up
hang together		
hang up		

24b. *Observe the idiomatic use of prepositions after certain verbs, participles, adjectives, and nouns.*

The following list will not take the place of an unabridged dictionary. It will serve merely as a check list to put you on your guard. Consult the dictionary for more complete information.

abstain from
accede to
acquiesce in
acquit of
addicted to
adept in
adhere to
agree to (a thing)
agree with (a person)
agreeable to
angry at (a thing)
angry with (a person)
averse to
capable of

characteristic of
compare to (for illustration)
compare with (to examine qualities)
concern in (be interested)
concerned for (troubled)
concerned with (involved)
concur in (an opinion)
concur with (a person)
desire for
desirous of
desist from
devoid of
differ about
differ from (things)
differ with (a person)
different from
disagree with
disdain for
dissent from
distaste for
empty of
envious of
expert in
foreign to
guard against
hint at
identical with
independent of
infer from
initiate into
inseparable from
jealous of
obedient to
oblivious of
preparatory to
prerequisite to
prior to
proficient in
profit by
prohibit from
protest against
reason with
regret for
repugnant to
sensitive to
separate from
substitute for
superior to
sympathize with
tamper with
unmindful of
vie with

Exercises

Exercise 1. In your desk dictionary find the idioms listed under several of the following words. You will find idiomatic phrases printed in boldface type, usually after the synonyms. Bring to class a number of these for class discussion. Try to decide why some are marked *colloq.* and some are without a label.

eat	go	head	mouth	stand
foot	hand	heart	pick	take
get	have	horse	run	word

Exercise 2. Supply the idiomatic preposition in the space indicated by parentheses in each of the following sentences.

1. When she smiles, who can be angry ( ) her?
2. I must differ ( ) you in my interpretation of this poem.
3. It is obvious that Mother was concerned ( ) our safety.

4. Surely he will profit ( ) your advice.
5. Tonight the Bears will vie ( ) the Gophers for first place.

Exercise 3. Point out and correct the errors in idiom in the following sentences.

1. He was acquitted from the charge of nepotism.
2. There is no substitute to victory.
3. She is adept about misinterpreting whatever you say.
4. My aunt had become sensitive against drafts and noises.
5. The new refrigerator is much superior than the old one.

CONCRETENESS

25. *The concrete or specific or homely word is more likely to touch the reader's imagination than its abstract or general or bookish counterpart.*

General words name classes or groups; specific words name the individual objects, actions, or qualities which compose the group. The terms are to some extent relative: *furniture* is a class of things; *chair* is more specific than *furniture,* more general than *armchair. Weapon* is a general noun. When you say, "She assaulted him with a deadly weapon," just what control do you have over what goes on in your reader's mind? What picture do your words call up? Did she stab him with a hatpin, club him with a brass book end, slash him with a safety razor blade that she had picked out of her sewing basket, or shoot him with a 22 target pistol? You say that the police found an ornament that she had dropped in the scuffle. It was probably a piece of jewelry—which is more specific than "ornament"—but it would have been more specific and more effective to say "a green jade earring."

The verb *move* is general; *stride, amble, creep, glide, fly, lope* are all more specific ways of moving. The adjective *large* is general; when you try to make it more specific, you discover that different varieties of largeness are associated with different nouns. For instance, *bulky, towering, brawny, monstrous, fat, spacious, hulking* are applicable to which of these—a building, a man, a child, a room?

A concrete noun names something that can be perceived through any of the senses, such as *pencil, robin, cloud, smoke, shoe, hair, clatter.* Abstract words name ideas, or qualities, more or less detached from any particular thing bearing those qualities, as *beauty*, *empiricism*, *whiteness*, *truth*, *devotion*, *weariness.* Now of course you can seldom give a concrete equivalent of an abstract word, but you can—and should—spell out your concept of the abstraction that you use. To say "Father is both stubborn and easygoing" is not enough; bring him out on the stage for us to see, and show him in a typical action.

Homely words are those associated with the objects and activities of everyday living; bookish words are those associated with literary formality.

The following pairs of words and expressions will help to make the distinctions clearer:

Specific words	*General words*
An armchair, a smock, a carving knife, a frying pan, murder, a welder, a violet, our old black cat	Furniture, apparel, cutlery, kitchen utensil, a crime, an industrial worker, a flower, an animal
Concrete words	*Abstract words*
She served him like a dog; my mother hummed a lullaby; a splinter of shrapnel ripped open his right arm; he was drunk as a lord	The faithfulness of an animal, the harmony of music, a misfortune of battle, extreme intoxication
Homely words	*Bookish words*
Marriage, a bed, breakfast, my son, our church, a lie, to eat, to dig, to plow	Matrimony, a couch, the matutinal meal, a male descendant, a religious organization, prevarication, to devour, to delve, to cultivate

Let us hasten to say at this point that these are by no means scientific classifications of all words in the language. We are merely picking out handfuls of words as samples, and saying in effect:

"Look at these. This type seems to do something more to your imagination than that one." Abstract and general words are not bad words; they are necessary for the expression of abstract qualities and general ideas. But in the writing of the average student abstract and general words are used too often where concrete and specific words would do a better job.

The following examples will help to make the idea clearer:

General and ineffective:

The inconvenience of taking a bath in these old English homes is hard to realize.

Concrete and specific:

I do not mind taking sectional baths with two pints of water in the country, where it seems unexceptional and goes along with fresh air, old clothes and being sleepy by nine o'clock in the evening. But segmented bathing in this weary, constricted, suburban household has nothing of rural simplicity about it, only skimpiness and inadequacy, and it makes you feel when you finish like a postage stamp that has been licked and then not used.

—Margaret Halsey, *With Malice Toward Some*, Simon & Schuster 1938. Reprinted by permission of the publisher.

General and effective:

When we returned to America, we found renewed pleasure in the sights and smells of springtime.

Concrete and specific:

From out of war, from out of death, we three came home to the North American continent. Here in spring we watched the yellow and the purple crocuses appear, the purple polyanthus and violets, the pussy willows, plum blossoms, and forsythia. The trees that were dead swelled with life, and the plants that had withered turned green. The rain smelled of new life, and new earth; death and decay seemed far removed.

—Agnes Newton Keith, *Three Came Home*. Copyright 1946, 1947 by Agnes Newton Keith. Courtesy of Little, Brown & Company and the Atlantic Monthly Press.

Ineffective:

He removed his shoes and walked more comfortably in his bare feet.

More vivid:

He leaned down and untied the laces, slipped off first one shoe and then the other. And he worked his damp feet comfortably in the hot dry dust until little spurts of it came up between his toes, and until the skin on his feet tightened with dryness.

—John Steinbeck, *The Grapes of Wrath.*

Ineffective:

We drove happily through the countryside, admiring the beautiful scenery along the road.

More vivid:

As the horse's back rose and fell gently, like a ship, between the shafts, the countryside slipped past—misted woods, glimpses of park land, a grey mansion with tall chimneys, terraces and glasshouses, amongst the steaming trees.

—A. J. Cronin, *The Green Years.*

Ineffective:

We noticed a girl sitting in a chair and crying.

More vivid:

She was sitting deep down in the chair, with her knees high up and pressed together, while her head was cast down on her lap and her two hands held a handkerchief to her eyes. And her body heaved spasmodically as she sobbed.

—Liam O'Flaherty, *Spring Sowing.*

General and vague:

The repulsiveness of the man impressed me most. I noted the fatness of his body and features and the oily quality of his gestures.

Specific and concrete:

On gazing for the first time directly at him I experienced a feeling of nausea. A figure inclined to corpulence, dressed with care, remarkable only above the neck—and then what a head! It was large, and had a copious mop of limp hair combed back from the high forehead—hair of a disagreeable blonde tint, dutch-cut behind, falling over the pinkish soft neck almost to the shoulders. In his pianist's or artist's hair, which shook *en masse* when the owner walked, two large and outstanding and altogether brutal white ears tried to hide themselves. The face, a cross between Greek and Jew, had a Reynard expression, something distinctly wily and perfectly disagreeable. And equally with the hair blonde moustache—or rather moustachios projectingly important—waved beneath the prominent nostrils, and served to partially conceal the pallid mouth, weak and large, whose lips assumed from time to time a smile which had something almost foetal about it. Over the even weaker chin was disposed a blonde goatee. The cheeks were fatty. The continually perspiring forehead exhibited innumerable pinkish pockmarks. In conversing with a companion this being emitted a disgusting smoothness, his very gestures were oily like his skin. He wore a pair of bloated wristless hands, the knuckles lost in fat, with which he smoothed the air from time to time. He was speaking low and effortless French, completely absorbed in the developing ideas which issued fluently from his moustachios. About him there clung an aura of cringing. His hair, whiskers and neck looked as if they were trick neck, whiskers and hair, as if they might at any moment suddenly disintegrate, as if the smoothness of his eloquence alone kept them in place.

—E. E. Cummings, *The Enormous Room.* Copyright renewed E. E. Cummings, 1949.

Exercises

Exercise 1. Find several specific words for each of the following general words.

animal	grass	tree	vehicle	to play
ship	bird	flower	to laugh	to hit
building	road	furniture	to clean	to fasten

Exercise 2. Construct sentences in which you give concrete examples of each of the following abstract terms.

stubbornness	thoroughness	dullness
efficiency	fear	humility

Exercise 3. Rewrite the following sentences, making them more specific and concrete.

1. Two high-school girls were studying in their room.
2. In front of the theater a long line waited for the ticket window to open.
3. The little boy had been playing in the back yard.
4. The professor became irritated by the questions.
5. The sounds at midnight are interesting to hear.

CONCISENESS

26. *Avoid using more words than are necessary for the adequate expression of your thought.*

The stylistic fault of *wordiness* has been a concern of writers and rhetoricians for many centuries. Wordiness has been called by many names—verbosity, pleonasm, redundancy, prolixity, diffuseness, circumlocution, periphrasis. By whatever name, wordiness simply means the use of more words than you need in a particular situation. To achieve the goal of conciseness, the student must ask himself whether every word he writes is doing its work, carrying its proper load of meaning, and helping its neighbors with their loads. Busy editorial officers have a favorite phrase: "Boil it down!" This may be an unconscious metaphor borrowed from the process of boiling down maple sugar. Perhaps you can use this metaphor as a helpful way to self-criticism. Is your writing still watery and flat, like the sap fresh from a maple tree? Or have you "boiled it down" so that what remains is pure sugar?

Do not mistake brevity for conciseness. A sentence is not concise if it lacks the words necessary not only for the adequate expression of the idea but also for the effective communication of the idea to the reader. Cutting out words will not always result in conciseness. You may summarize *The Brothers Karamazov* or *Gone with the Wind* in five hundred words, but can you persuade three million persons to read your five-hundred word summary? Cutting out words in a good essay might also cut out of it those qualities which make it good—strength, variety, maturity, grace, cleverness, even accuracy.

Study the difference in the effect produced by the following pairs of sentences. Notice that the first, although longer, is always clearer, stronger, and richer.

1. Objects, on our first acquaintance with them, have that singleness and integrity of impression that it seems as if nothing could destroy or obliterate them, so firmly are they stamped and riveted on the brain.
2. Our first impressions of objects are the most lasting.

1. The ant and the moth have cells for each of their young, but our little ones lie in festering heaps, in homes that consume them like graves; and night by night, from the corners of our streets, rises up the cry of the homeless—"I was a stranger, and ye took me not in."
2. Insects are more careful about their young than are human beings.

1. When we had done all this, there fell upon us the beneficent and deliberate evening; so that as we sat a little while together near the rakes, we saw the valley more solemn and dim around us and all the trees and hedgerows quite still, and held by a complete silence.—Hilaire Belloc.
2. When we had finished, it was evening; so that we sat a little while near the rakes and looked out upon the quiet valley.

Now study the following sets of sentences. Do you see what is meant by conciseness?

1. Whenever anyone called for someone to help him do some certain thing, Jim was always the first to volunteer and lend his help for the cause.
2. Whenever anyone called for help, Jim was always the first to volunteer.

1. This spirit of co-operation is essential and necessary for anyone to have in order to get along with other people, and this is a quality that Jim had what it took.
2. Jim had the spirit of co-operation which is necessary if one wishes to get along with people.

1. Jim was one of those people of whom there are few in this world like him.
2. There are few people like Jim.

1. Lumbering is placed in the upper ten industries in the United States from the standpoint of importance.
2. Lumbering is one of the ten most important industries in the United States.

This section will concern itself with several kinds of wordiness which are to be avoided by the writer who hopes to be concise, direct, and to the point.

26a. Repetition of the same word.

A word carelessly repeated weakens the effectiveness of a sentence. Careless repetition is frequently associated with wordiness, as may be seen in the following examples. The fault may be corrected by using synonyms, by using pronouns, or by completely rewriting the sentence.

Poor:

I have been asked to write on a subject that has been the subject of controversy among sports commentators for years. That subject, as you have probably guessed, is none other than the question of which is the most interesting, basketball or football.

Better:

I shall try to determine which is more interesting to watch—basketball or football.

Poor:

A person who has seen each game for the first time would probably prefer the basketball game to the football game because this game is easy to comprehend and can be understood much more quickly.

Better:

A person seeing each game for the first time might prefer basketball to football because of its greater simplicity.

The importance of avoiding awkward repetition must not distract the writer from the possibilities of repetition for emphasis—a tried and true device for securing certain kinds of attention from the reader. It is perhaps especially appropriate in persuasion and oratory, as the famous selection from Winston Churchill below suggests, and it is used sparingly by most contemporary writers.

Wycliffe was, no doubt, a *learned* man. But the *learning* of his day would have *burned* him, had it dared, as it did *burn* his dead body afterwards. —Wendell Phillips.

The nation has been deeply *stirred*, *stirred* by a solemn passion, *stirred* by the knowledge of wrong, of ideals lost, of government too often debauched and made an instrument of evil.—Woodrow Wilson.

It was as *scholars* that you were here; it is to the feeling and life of *scholars* that you return.—George William Curtis.

We shall go on to the end, *we shall fight* in France, *we shall fight* on the seas and oceans, *we shall fight* with *growing* confidence and *growing* strength in the air, *we shall defend* our Island, whatever the cost may be, *we shall fight* on the beaches, *we shall fight* on the landing grounds, *we shall fight* in the fields and in the streets, *we shall fight* in the hills; we shall never surrender, and even if, which I do not for a moment believe, this Island or a large part of it were subjugated and starving, then our Empire beyond the seas, armed and guarded by the British Fleet, would carry on the struggle, until, in God's good time, the New World, with all its power and might, steps forth to the rescue and the liberation of the old.

—Winston Churchill, *Blood, Sweat, and Tears*, G. P. Putnam's Sons, 1941. Reprinted by permission of the publisher.

The effectiveness of a sentence, or of a series of sentences, may be strengthened by repeating the same form of construction.

To differ is grotesque and eccentric. To protest is preposterous. To defy is incendiary and revolutionary.—George William Curtis.

Made drunk with the freedom of ideas, college students should charge destructively against all the institutions of a faulty world and all the conventions of a silly one.—Bernard DeVoto.

The life of Man is a long march through the night,
|| surrounded by invisible foes,
|| tortured by weariness and pain, towards a goal that
|| few can hope to reach, and where
|| none may tarry long.
—Bertrand Russell.

To make parallels clearer, such signal words as prepositions, conjunctions, articles, and auxiliaries may be repeated:

When he was at the beach, he longed
|| *for* his humid office in the city,
|| *for* the sweltering crowds on the subways,
|| *for* the hurried noonday snack at the drug store.

They left the world || *as* wicked and
|| *as* ignorant as they found it.

26b. *Repetition of words with the same meaning (tautology).*

Wordy:

The analysis was *thoroughly and wholly complete.*
All the requirements of *frank* and *honest candor* made his speech popular.

The *basic fundamental essentials* of a college education are *simply* and *briefly* these.
He woke up at six *a.m. this morning.*

26c. The double that before a clause (pleonasm).

Wordy:

I was very glad that when I came in to the house that I found everything in order. [Omit the second *that.*]

26d. Roundabout expressions (circumlocution or periphrasis).

Wordy:

The reason why I was so upset was because she seemed so angry with me. [reason—why—because] [*Revise:* I was upset because she seemed so angry with me.]

26e. Puffers.

A college professor once prefaced the giving out of final examination questions with this story: "I am reminded of an interesting marine animal, the squid, which when closely pursued by an enemy releases a flood of ink and usually manages to escape in the cloudy murk." The following samples illustrate what is meant by puffing up a simple idea by means of words. Despite the fact that one who can write like this will often qualify for a political career, it is still bad writing.

Wordy:

Most people will agree, if they give the situation their careful consideration, that the commodity which is most plentiful in this world and which usually is most thoughtlessly wasted is the exact equivalent of currency, coin of the realm, or by whatever name it is legal tender. [Time is money.]

It has been observed by those who possess a wide familiarity with streams, rivers, and so forth, that water which presents a deceptive surface appearance of placidity usually conceals a great depth. [Still waters flow deep.]

26f. Intensives and other modifiers.

It is a wise idea to question critically all modifiers (adjectives and adverbs), because it is often here that wordiness gets a foothold. The so-called "intensives"—*very, much,* etc.—are especially likely to weaken a sentence.

Wordy:

I certainly was very much pleased when they told me they were so much interested. [I was very pleased when they told me they were interested.]

He was absolutely and completely surprised by the very great size of the impressively beautiful church. [He was astounded by the size of the beautiful church.]

26g. Repetition of similar sounds.

The awkward repetition of similar sounds in prose may seriously distract your reader from what you are trying to communicate. Consider the following warning on the subject, and note the examples:

Bad prose is bad business, even if the badness be nothing worse than discord. Let the ear then have its way as the phrases are conned; rougher rhythms and inharmonious sounds will drag; as we read we resent something wrong, so that we hesitate, and look back to see where was the jar or the limp. *E.g.* "A more ac*commo*dating den*omin*ation is *commonly* given to it." "*Gratitude* for his *rectitude*"; "an organisational centre of crystallisation"; "necessar*ily* tempor*ary*"; "very near*ly* entir*ely*"; "so that it at once commenced"; "the native rulers were as a rule," etc. . . . "Of all I have kn*own* he could at least hold his *own*," is not only an untimely assonance but imparts the alien rhythm of verse.

—From *Notes on the Composition of Scientific Papers,* by Sir T. Clifford Allbutt, 3rd ed. (London: Macmillan & Co., Ltd., 1923).

26h. "Fine writing."

"Fine writing" is not, as the phrase seems to indicate, good writing. It is flowery, artificial, overblown writing. In an effort to be literary, the writer loads his style with too many adjectives and adverbs, with big words, awkward repetitions of high-sounding phrases, and trite figures of speech. (See also Section 27c.) "Fine writing" is often the result of an over-complicated sentence structure. Its effect is a voice that sounds pompous and stuffy, and no sensitive reader will listen to such a voice for very long. In exercise 2 below you will find five examples of "fine writing." See what you can do with them.

Exercises

Exercise 1. In the following sentences, underline the awkward repetitions and examples of wordiness. Make the sentences more concise by cutting or by other revision.

1. There are many elements in the problem. One of the elements is the element of politics. Of all of them, politics is the most significant element.
2. We were absolutely positive that if he had gone home that he would have said goodbye first.
3. In regard to this check, is it perfectly all right to endorse the check on the back?
4. Naturally the very large amount of time and money that is virtually wasted by college students and undergraduates amounts to a very great deal indeed.
5. She had a set rule for almost everything that she did and for anything on which she had made up her mind it was very hard to convince her otherwise.
6. The main reason for the domestic troubles in my family is on account of money and financial troubles.
7. Jones is chiefly interested in the line of mathematics, physics, chemistry, and etc.
8. My grandmother she didn't think I should ought to study English.
9. She had got along perfectly all right and she couldn't hardly read a word.
10. I thought that if I could not take chemistry that I would not have the necessary prerequisites for pharmacology.

Exercise 2. Simplify and strengthen the following sentences:

1. At the tender age of fourteen he left his paternal hearth to espouse the wandering life of the wayfarer over the briny deep.
2. In the case of friendship, before a person can accomplish these other factors that are mentioned, he must commit himself first to the right point of view psychologically and mentally.
3. The modern young lass of today is steadily ascending rung by rung to the status formerly held by the sterner sex in the business world.
4. After the war, youths who had forsaken the shady walks of their Alma Mater to engage in strife on far-flung battlefields around the world came

trooping back to seek knowledge and wisdom in the cloistered seclusion of the campus.

5. In recognition of the historical fruition of this great nation, which all of us should be proud to be citizens of, it certainly would help, without any doubt, if we were always in a state of readiness and preparation to defend it.

VIVIDNESS AND METAPHOR

27. A writer should use words and phrases that give life and freshness to his style.

There are of course dozens of ways to make a style "vivid." Some of them were discussed in previous sections under the headings of "concreteness" and "conciseness." In this section we consider some other devices available to the writer who wishes to produce fresher, livelier language. Such a writer, first, should be aware of the possibilities for freshness in the various parts of speech—nouns, modifiers, verbs. Second, the writer should be aware of the possibilities in figurative language, or metaphor. Then he must also be aware of the dangers of metaphor, particularly since so much figurative language has been used before and has lost its freshness. Finally, he must recognize the related problem of overused language generally: the problem of triteness and clichés.

27a. Use the parts of speech with awareness of their different possibilities for lively, specific language.

The various parts of speech offer to the careful writer different problems, different advantages and dangers, in achieving freshness. Here we will consider very briefly some of the issues at stake when you use nouns, when you use adjectives and adverbs, and when you use verbs.

1. When you use nouns, obviously, a vivid style is more likely to be produced by specific than by general words. When you say, "I heard a bird singing," your words may call up a definite sense image in the mind of your reader—or they may not—but you do not know what that image is. If instead of "bird" you say "meadow lark" or "hermit thrush," your reader will at least make an effort to recall the song of the meadow lark or the hermit thrush. Whenever you use a specific noun, you make it easy for your reader's mind to create a specific image. You do more than suggest images by your words; you direct the picture-making that goes on in your reader's brain.

2. When you use modifiers (adjectives and adverbs), you must be aware of some special dangers. (See also section 26f.) No part of speech, generally speaking, is more likely to lie down and die than a flat, uninspired adjective or adverb. You say, "That was a *good* lecture," when you mean that it was *witty, stimulating, eloquent, instructive, entertaining,* or *informative.* You say, "She is a *nice* girl," when you mean that she is *friendly, sympathetic, generous, vivacious, modest, talented,* or *conventional.* What adjectives can you find that are more vivid than *pleasant, dull, swell, big, easy, hard?* A book of synonyms will help you find them. In the case of adverbs, note that often a weak verb-adverb group may be replaced more effectively by a single verb. Study the following examples:

He ran quickly. [He fled, sprinted, trotted, rushed, surged.]
He was breathing rapidly. [He was panting, blowing, wheezing, puffing, gasping.]
He cut through it. [He pierced it, sliced it, tore it open, split it, ripped it open.]
He threw it down violently. [He hurled it, flung it, heaved it, pitched it.]

3. When you use verbs, you should consider replacing general or abstract verbs with verbs that are more specific and descriptive. Here are some examples:

He moved toward the door. [He crept, crawled, strolled, sidled, inched, drifted, flitted toward the door.]
He spoke several words. [He whispered, roared, shouted, hissed, mumbled, muttered several words.]
We put it on the wagon. [We tossed, lifted, pitched, threw it on the wagon.]
He got on the horse. [He scrambled, leaped, jumped, vaulted on the horse.]

27b. *Metaphors are an essential technique for adding freshness to language.*

A metaphor, very simply, is a device for talking about one thing as if it were something else. "Oh, my love is like a red, red rose," says the poet, "that's newly sprung in June." Now we all know that his love is *not* a red, red rose, and she is only "like" a rose in a very limited, qualified way. This suggests the delight and the danger of metaphor. To suggest a likeness, while at the same time defining the limit of that likeness, is the delicate process of making a metaphor.

Many people speak of a metaphor as a "simile" when the likeness is directly expressed—that is, when the connectives "like" or "as" are used. Actually this distinction makes little practical difference. The point is that metaphorical language, or figurative language as it is often called, can appear in a huge variety of ways with vast differences in the effects produced.

Similes:

The water lay gray and wrinkled like an elephant's skin.—Nancy Hale.

My very thoughts were like the ghostly rustle of dead leaves.—Joseph Conrad.

She barged in with the children like a bomber escorted by fighters.—Margaret Halsey.

Sending men to that army is like shoveling fleas across a barnyard.—Lincoln.

Here the wind took on a wild dignity . . . lashing the island-dotted reaches of the Bay into waves that fled up the Hudson like a herd of gray horses with white manes swimming steadily in from the sea. . . .—Elizabeth Page.

Metaphors:

Life is a tragedy wherein we sit as spectators for a while, and then act out our part in it.—Jonathan Swift.

The burning geyser was sending out comets of flame which were igniting the dry fiber of the surrounding trees.—Caroline Mytinger.

Figures of speech are frequently used for humor, as the following examples will show:

He had a voice like a coyote with bronchitis.—O. Henry.
He was all lit up like a Christmas tree.
Her mouth opened like a folding bed.
She had a large Wagnerian mother with a voice that would shatter glass. —From *My Fair Lady*.

We must be careful, however, not to pepper a writing style with isolated figures of speech that are merely clever or cute. More useful to the student is the observance of figures of speech in context, where they look more at home, where we can see how they fit into their surroundings.

I fear chiefly lest my expression may not be *extra-vagant* enough, may not wander far enough beyond the narrow limits of my daily experience, so as to be adequate to the truth of which I have been convinced. *Extra vagance!* it depends on how you are yarded. The migrating buffalo, which seeks new pastures in another latitude, is not extravagant like the cow which kicks over the pail, leaps the cowyard fence, and runs after her calf, in milking time. I desire to speak somewhere *without* bounds; like a man in a waking moment, to men in their waking moments; for I am convinced that I cannot exaggerate enough even to lay the foundation of a true expression.

—From *Walden,* by H. D. Thoreau. First published in 1849.

Then suddenly the starlings attacked the tree behind which she had hidden. In one flock they pelted it like so many winged stones. The whole tree hummed with the whizz they made, as if each bird plucked a wire. A whizz, a buzz rose from the bird-buzzing, bird-vibrant, bird-blackened tree. The tree became a rhapsody, a quivering cacophony, a whizz and vibrant rapture, branches, leaves, birds syllabling discordantly life, life, life, without measure, without stop devouring the tree. Then up! Then off!

—From *Between the Acts* by Virginia Woolf. Copyright 1941 by Harcourt, Brace and Company, Inc.

Then the creeping murderer, the octopus, steals out, slowly, softly, moving like a gray mist, pretending now to be a bit of weed, now a rock, now a lump of decaying meat while its evil goat eyes watch coldly. It oozes and flows toward a feeding crab, and as it comes close its yellow eyes burn and its body turns rosy with the pulsing color of anticipation and rage. Then suddenly it runs lightly on the tips of its arms, as ferociously as a charging cat. It leaps savagely on the crab, there is a puff of black fluid, and the struggling mass is obscured in the sepia cloud while the octopus murders the crab. On the exposed rocks out of water, the barnacles bubble behind their closed doors and the limpets dry out.

—From *Cannery Row.* Copyright 1945 by John Steinbeck. Reprinted by permission of The Viking Press, Inc.

It was a street of uniform bald houses of four rooms and scullery. Its parlour windows bayed out to the street, without the grace of one yard of green or the gentility of a gate. Some of the houses, at that time, in a spasm of discontent with their estate, had turned themselves into shops, and had made a bad job of it, being neither good shop nor honest house; but though it was down it grinned. Always there was the noise of dogs and babies, and the cheery call of neighbor to neighbor and the occult cries of coal-man, winkle-man, milk-man, and balloon-and-flag man.

—Thomas Burke, *The Wind and the Rain.* Copyright 1924 by Doubleday, Doran and Company, Inc. Reprinted by permission of the publishers.

27c. *Metaphors and other phrases that have become trite must be avoided.*

A great deal of our everyday language is made up of phrases that were originally figures of speech, but have become so familiar to us that they have become "dead"—that is, they have lost their doubleness, and refer simply to single items of experience. Examples are *touch and go, guidepost, halcyon days, beyond the pale.* The originally metaphorical character of these words is pretty well lost, and there is no particular objection to their use if they are not overused. More dangerous for the writer, however, are the metaphors that are "dying"—that is, they still retain some slight doubleness of meaning, but the doubleness has become so watered down and weakened by time that the phrases are irritating to a reader. Examples are *budding genius, the table groaned, fit as a fiddle, the money was burning a hole in my pocket.* Such uses of language are to be avoided: they are clichés.

Many modern writers make ingenious use of the thousands of clichés in our contemporary language for purposes of comedy or irony or satire. Here is a simple example by the humorist, S. J. Perelman. Perelman takes a phrase like "burning a hole in my pocket" (a dying metaphor), and brings it back to life by pretending to take it literally.

I was strolling aimlessly down Fifth Avenue the other afternoon when several dollars which had been burning a hole in my pocket suddenly burst into flame and I found myself in Brentano's. By the time my pants had stopped smoldering I discovered I owned a profusely illustrated set of Brantome's spicy "Lives of Fair and Gallant Ladies."

—S. J. Perelman, *The Most of S. J. Perelman.* Simon & Schuster, Inc., 1958.

This of course is a very special use of trite language. The moral is clear: unless you know very well what you are doing, do not use phrases like "burning a hole in my pocket."

A full treatment of clichés could fill a big book. But the following list may help to put you on your guard:

aching void
acid test
after all has been said
all in all
all work and no play
a long-felt want
among those present
ardent admirers
arms of Morpheus
as luck would have it
at a loss for words
at one fell swoop
beat a hasty retreat
beggars description
better half
better late than never
blissfully ignorant
blushing bride
bolt from the blue
bountiful repast
breathless silence
briny deep
budding genius
busy as a bee
by leaps and bounds
caught like rats in a trap
checkered career
cheered to the echo
clear as crystal
conspicuous by his absence
course of true love
devouring element
discreet silence
doomed to disappointment
downy couch
drastic action
dull, sickening thud
each and every one
easier said than done
equal to the occasion
fair sex
familiar landmark
favor with a selection
festive occasion
few and far between
filthy lucre
goes without saying
great open spaces
gridiron warriors
grim reaper
hands across the sea
holy bonds of matrimony
in all its glory
in the last analysis
irony of fate
justice to the occasion

last but not least
lonely sentinel
long-felt want
mantle of snow
meets the eye
method in his madness
monarch of all he surveys
mother nature
motley crowd
nipped in the bud
none the worse for his experience
none the worse for wear
no sooner said than done
partake of refreshments
pleasing prospect
powers that be
presided at the piano
proud possessor
psychological moment
reigns supreme
rendered a selection
replete with interest
riot of color
ripe old age
sadder but wiser
shadow of the goal posts
silence reigned supreme
single blessedness
specimen of humanity
sumptuous repast
sweat of his brow
sweet girl graduate
table groaned
tired but happy
vale of tears
venture a suggestion
watery grave
wee small hours
wends his way
where ignorance is bliss
with bated breath
words fail to express
worked like a Trojan
wrought havoc

Exercises

Exercise 1. Here is a short paragraph of what might be called "plain statement." The language is unembellished and not particularised; there is little or no metaphor. Rewrite this passage to make it more "vivid," by giving attention to the parts of speech and to the possibilities for metaphor.

The boy walked home from school very slowly. It was April, and he observed as he went the various signs of the spring season. As he approached his own house, he paused to talk to his neighbor, who was puttering about on his lawn. Finally he turned and walked indoors, for he was hungry.

Exercise 2. Now rewrite this passage again, this time using just as many dying metaphors, clichés, and trite phrases as you can.

Exercise 3. Select a sports story from a newspaper, and underline all its clichés. Then translate the story into plain statement.

Exercise 4. Do the same for a news story about the international situation. You will observe that one of the difficulties you may encounter in performing this operation arises from the fact that when a writer is using a great many clichés, you (and he) simply cannot tell what he is talking about.

EFFECTIVE SENTENCES

SENTENCE UNITY

The problem of unity in a sentence concerns itself primarily with either "not enough" or "too much."

NOT ENOUGH

28a. ***In standard English, the structural unity of the written sentence depends on the presence of a finite verb with its subject.***

The completeness or unity of a sentence is based, in one sense, on its structure. As we shall see later, it is also based on its thought or content. The sentence, however, is not a formula or an unchangeable pattern. On the contrary, it is a unit of such variety and flexibility that no rule, only the good sense of the writer, can decide when "not enough" becomes "complete," and when "complete" becomes "too much."

Obviously, a sentence is "not enough" when it is not grammatically complete; that is, when it does not have an expressed or implied subject and verb. For a discussion of sentence fragments see section 1.

TOO MUCH

28b. ***Sentence unity may be destroyed by the inclusion of words, phrases, or clauses that have no direct bearing on the principal thought of the sentence.***

A sentence may have "too much" in several ways. First, two unrelated ideas of the same weight and importance may be thrown together to make a compound sentence. The proper cure for this sort of fault is subordination. The methods of subordination are discussed in section 29. Second, a sentence may appear bulging and baggy from having too many related minor details thrown into it. For the cure of this fault see section 28c. Finally, a sentence may lack unity because the writer tossed into it some unrelated minor detail which happened to pop into his mind while he was writing.

Unrelated details:

My uncle, short of temper and of breath, eighty years old at this time and weighing two hundred pounds, swore angrily at the tramp. [The swearing may be related to "temper" but not clearly to his weight and his age.]

The destructiveness of the termite, which is an insect with almost human instincts for social organization, is very great. [The relative clause has nothing to do with the termite's ability to do harm.]

After the Spanish Civil War, free speech, which is guaranteed to every American by our Constitution, was suppressed by the Franco regime. [If this is about Spain, the reference to America is merely thrown in.]

Unified:

My uncle, a short-tempered man, swore angrily at the tramp.

The destructiveness of the termite is very great.

After the Spanish Civil War free speech in Spain was suppressed by the Franco regime.

28c. Overloading a sentence with details obscures its unity and destroys its clearness and order.

If the details are important, they should be told in separate sentences, where they can be given proper value. If they are unimportant, they may be omitted.

Confused:

Military training teaches a person to stand up straight and walk with his head up; this helps in future life because it becomes a habit and so many people have the bad habit of walking stooped and this leads to poor health and poor appearance.

Military science teaches also common courtesies, not only to your superior officers but to everyone to whom courtesy is due; for instance when you enter offices, or the courtesies you should use when you are using firearms while hunting or shooting in the presence of another person.

If you write sentences like these, your remedy is to go back to the first principles of thought communication: say one thing at a time; say it as simply and clearly as you can; say it so that it cannot be misunderstood.

Let us try to dissect these sentences in order to discover what the writer tried to say.

Revised:

Military training teaches a person to stand erect and to walk with his head up. [That is enough for one sentence.] Good posture [Is that what the writer meant by "this" and "it"?] becomes habitual. It leads directly to better health and better appearance.

Military science also teaches common courtesy, not only to officers superior in rank but also to everyone. [Are there some persons to whom "courtesy is not due"?] For instance, it teaches one how to enter an office, or how to handle firearms with safety to others. [These two examples are so badly chosen that no sentence can make them apt or congruous.]

Exercises

Exercise 1. Determine which of the following are sentence fragments. Correct them by supplying the missing elements.

1. Being of sound mind and a ready wit, Belinda was occasionally accused of being catty.
2. Her sharp claws in their velvet sheath being harmless except in self-defense.
3. Giggling in delight, she read to them a poem about the adventures of Mehitabel.
4. The natural dignity and self-respect of cats leading some people to think that cats are two-faced.
5. The only two-faced cat on record being sacred to the Egyptian goddess Isis.
6. Arbutus, our old black cat, came in late one morning, glanced at Belinda out of his good eye, and looked about for his favorite chair.

7. His other eye having been temporarily closed during a fearful encounter in the night.
8. The astonishing thing being, as Belinda observed, that cats should have two holes cut in their coats exactly at the places where their eyes were.
9. Having dislodged me from his favorite chair, Arbutus was soon snoring happily.
10. Before drifting off into oblivion, he opened his good eye and murmured, "Wake me up in time for his funeral, will you, sir?"

Exercise 2. Reorganize and rewrite the following sentences. Discard details that do not belong.

1. Getting lost in the woods after the first snowfall, which happens to more people than you imagine, especially in the northern woods, is a horrifying experience.
2. One such experience which happened to me in northern Minnesota during the Thanksgiving Day vacation while I was a senior in high school taught me a valuable lesson.
3. I had been hunting rabbits with a 22 rifle, and these rabbits, unlike those in western states, which are often infected with tularemia, are good to eat, and suddenly everything was changed by a heavy snowfall.
4. I tried to remember what my father, who disliked to go out in the woods himself and absolutely refused to hunt, told me when he talked to our Cub Scout group once; it was to try to remember the last familiar landmark you had seen and retrace your steps to it.
5. I closed my eyes, trying to visualize a familiar scene, just as I had once seen a man do in a TV Western, and when I opened my eyes everything snapped into place because I recognized a familiar tree through the falling snow.

SUBORDINATION

Subordination of sentence elements is a device which may be used to correct two types of sentence faults: (1) putting minor ideas or facts into main clauses within the sentence and (2) putting minor ideas or facts into a succession of short, choppy sentences. See also section 28c.

The subordinate elements to which a main clause may be reduced are an appositive, a phrase, and a clause. Occasionally something which the writer has expressed in a main clause may be reduced to a single word.

29a. *Dependent or minor ideas should be placed in subordinate constructions in the sentence.*

Too much co-ordination is a sign of immaturity, in thinking as well as in writing. A child will say, "We had a birthday party, and Bobby and Jackie came to the party, and we had ice cream, and we played games." A mature person will not assume that all ideas, details, or facts are of the same importance or that they should be expressed on the same level. He knows that some thoughts are of first importance, that others are supporting or explaining details, and he will write sentences that show the proper relationship of one part of the sentence to another.

Immature:

The opening to the tunnel was covered by a grating, and this was made of iron, and it was very heavy.

Better:

The opening to the tunnel was covered by a very heavy iron grating. [Use a word in place of the clause.]

Poor:

Grasshoppers, for instance, have a keen sense of hearing, and this is centered in their front knees.

Better:

Grasshoppers have a keen sense of hearing, centered in their front knees. [Use a participial phrase.]

Weak:

The Smithsonian Institution is constantly working for a better understanding of nature for man's benefit, and it gets little or no publicity.

Better:

The Smithsonian Institution is constantly working, with little or no publicity, for a better understanding of nature for man's benefit. [Use a prepositional phrase.]

Weak:

The great god Jupiter was honored for bringing rain to the farms and vineyards, and he was the ruler of the gods.

Better:

The great Jupiter, the ruler of the gods, was also honored for bringing rain to farms and vineyards. [Use an appositive.]

Poor:

Rocky Mountain goats come to feed on this white clay, and they need it to supplement their diet.

Better:

Rocky mountain goats come down to feed on this white clay, which they need to supplement their diet. [Use an adjective clause.]

Poor:

We have given away billions of dollars, but we have not gained the friendship of many foreign peoples.

Better:

Although we have given away billions of dollars in foreign aid, we have not gained the friendship of many foreign peoples. [Use adverbial clause.]

Long, straggling sentences are often ineffective. They should be broken up into compact units. The weakness of a long sentence is not in its length. A long sentence may be highly effective because of its easy flow and rhythm. The weakness lies in its shapelessness. Notice how these sentences by E. Arnot Robertson are built on a pattern of parallel clauses, each one adding to the single effect of the whole.

Example:

London, sprawling over so many miles, was impossible to miss for the bombers: if they were not picking their targets in detail there was no need for them to come low enough for the few guns or searchlights to matter; and the people knew it. It was disturbing beyond expression, the emanation of close-packed, controlled fear from millions of human beings cowering in shelters, in cellars, keeping up a fine pretence of indifference in their own homes, nervously carrying on with gaiety or trying to sleep, if they were workers who must sleep, with vaselined cotton wool in their ears, or their bedclothes over their heads, or their windows closed in the stuffy night; striving to shut out the noise of death which was all they could shut out.

—E. Arnot Robertson, *The Signpost*. Printed by permission of The Macmillan Company.

The cure for the disease of the straggling sentence is "subordinate and divide"—subordinate what seems to be of secondary importance, and divide if you cannot subordinate.

Straggling:

When I was a little girl, I did not care for motion pictures, but as I grew into high-school age I began to go every week and now that I am out of high school I do not go so often and I am more particular about the quality of the pictures that I see.

Revised:

My taste in motion pictures has developed through three stages: a complete indifference to them in my childhood, a movie-a-week phase in my high-school days, and my present discriminating enjoyment of a few of the best.

Straggling:

In my sophomore year the teacher thought that we needed more drill in creative writing, which was the same course we had had the previous year, but in my junior year we did not have any English course but instead spent two terms studying literature.

Revised:

My high-school training in English consisted of a two-year course in creative writing, the second year a repetition of the first, and a year's study of literature.

Co-ordination and subordination are devices by which a writer may give different degrees of emphasis to different parts of his sentence. No one but the writer can know what his intentions were when he wrote a certain sentence. All that we can do is to say, "Is this what you really meant to say? Try combining your main clauses. Try subordinating one of them. There will be a difference in the emphasis that you get, but your revised sentence may be closer to what you meant to say."

The English language has evolved certain sentence patterns that often go contrary to the norms. For instance, in a sentence like this: "It is assumed that what a man displays on the walls of his living room is more important to him than what he throws into a corner," the important idea is obviously in a subordinate clause. Yet we accept that pattern. It is good English. There is wide objection, however, to putting the main idea into a "when" clause, as in: "One day I was pulling weeds in the garden when I saw two timber wolves near the corral." This sort of thing is usually called "upside-down subordination." It makes many educated people squirm. They say you should have written, "One day, as I was pulling weeds in the garden, I saw two timber wolves near the corral." Here is another instance of the necessity of making a choice. You are the one who has to make it.

There is a type of excessive subordination, often called "overlapping" or "tandem" subordination, that usually results in awkward sentences. It is best to avoid it.

Poor:

I had heard the warning so often that I was so used to hearing it that I failed to realize that it was important. [Three "that" clauses in succession]

Better:

Repeated warnings had dulled my appreciation of their importance. The warnings had been repeated so often that I failed to realize their importance.

29b. One should avoid expressing in short, choppy, co-ordinate sentences a group of ideas that can be expressed more precisely by using subordination.

Again, the reader cannot look into the writer's mind to see what his intentions were when he wrote a sentence. In the following examples, the revisions *seem* to represent more precisely what the writer meant to say.

See also the comment on the primer style under section 29a.

Poor:

The performance was over. I arose to go out. I was so nervous that I had to sit down on a chair. Soon I grew calm again.

Better:

After the performance was over, I arose to go out, but I was so nervous that I had to sit on a chair until I became calmer.

Poor:

Back of the grandstand are the stables. The stables are long, rambling, one-story barns. Each barn is divided into box stalls. Each stall is enough to accommodate one horse.

Better:

The stables, situated behind the grandstand, are long, rambling, one-story barns, each barn divided into stalls large enough to accommodate one horse apiece.

Exercises

Exercise 1. Use an appositive to subordinate one of the clauses in each of the following sentences.

1. The girl looked at the carbon smear on the back of the first letter she had typed; she was our new secretary.
2. She cast a quick, nervous glance at Mr. Ford; he was our boss.
3. The girl's name was Lorna, and it was her first job, but she wanted to make a good impression.
4. Her teacher in secretarial science had impressed upon her the importance of three virtues; these were neatness, speed, and efficiency.
5. Now, to her chagrin, she had made one good impression; it was a carbon copy, in reverse, on the back of her first typed letter.

Exercise 2. Subordinate one of the clauses in each of the following sentences by reducing it to a prepositional or verbal phrase.

1. There are many kinds of birds that winter in our back yard, and among them is the Alaska robin.
2. They spend the summers in the high altitudes, and then they come here to a warmer climate for the winter.
3. The hummingbird is small and frail, but it travels vast distances.
4. It flies from Central America to Canada, and it must have a constant supply of food as it flies north.
5. The grosbeaks come here a little later, and they feed on the green seeds of elm trees.

Exercise 3. In each of the following sentences change one of the main clauses to a subordinate clause.

1. My new boss started out as an office boy, and he believes in hard work. [Use an adjective clause.]
2. He did not have much formal education, but he advanced rapidly to a position of responsibility. [Use an adverb clause.]

3. Hard work makes up for a lack of education; that is his firm belief. [Use a noun clause.]
4. I entered his office with my head held high, and I almost tripped over a shadow on the floor. [Use an adverb clause.]
5. Mr. Ford quickly explained what my work would be; it would consist of taking dictation and typing. [Use a noun clause.]
6. I found my desk, hung up my coat, spoke to another girl in the room, and then the buzzer rang. [Use an adverb clause beginning with *after.*]
7. I had practiced taking dictation for three years, and so I was not nervous when I re-entered his office. [Use an adverb clause with *because.*]
8. I could have been in real trouble, but he was careful to spell out names and technical terms slowly. [Use an adverb clause with *if.*]
9. I started to type the first letter; this should have been the easiest part of my work. [Use an adjective clause with *which.*]
10. I reversed the first carbon; I still am wondering why. [Use a noun clause.]

REFERENCE OF PRONOUNS

30a. The antecedent of a pronoun in a sentence should be immediately clear to the reader.

As a rule, pronouns should have definite antecedents and should be placed as near their antecedents as possible. The hedging in this last sentence, represented by the phrase "as a rule," refers to two or three special situations. First, there are a number of idiomatic phrases in which a pronoun has no visible antecedent, such as: *it rained last night; it's the climate; it is time to go home.* There is no lack of clearness in these sentences. Second, the pronoun *you,* in the sense of *one,* or *a person,* has wide currency in informal written and spoken English, and occasionally in good formal writing. Third, the pronouns *which, this, that* may refer to an idea or fact expressed by a whole clause or a sentence, or by a part of a clause, if the reference is unmistakably clear.

In good writing, the meaning of a sentence should be clear to an intelligent reader on the first reading. If the reader has to hesitate, if he has to search for the substantive to which the pronoun refers, or if he has to puzzle over which of two possible antecedents it does refer to, the sentence is not as good as it should be.

And we may add here that even if you can find a bucketful of muddled sentences in the writing of great scientists, great educators, or great public servants, those sentences still are muddled and not as good as they could have been.

Indefinite:

I can remember that we met many people, but I did not enjoy *it* very much. [To what does *it* refer?]

Clear:

I can remember that we met many people, but I did not enjoy the reception very much. [Supply the word for which *it* stands.]

Indefinite:

My mother was a school teacher; therefore it is no wonder that I have chosen *that* as my profession. [The antecedent of *that* is only vaguely implied.]

Clear:

My mother was a school teacher; therefore it is no wonder that I have chosen teaching as my profession.

Misleading:

Each damaged article is marked in such a way that *it* cannot be erased. [The reader is confused because *it* seems to refer to *article.*]

Clear:

Each damaged article is marked in such a way that the mark cannot be erased.

It is usually awkward to have a pronoun refer to an antecedent in a subordinate position. The reader will instinctively associate a pronoun with the most prominent substantive in the clause he has just read. The result is confusion—possibly a momentary confusion but still an undesirable one.

Confusing:

Men have lounged and crouched around their fires; they have been the companions of their dreams and meditations. [The reader will hesitate when he comes to "they have," because he will assume that the subject of the sentence is still "men."]

Clear:

Men have lounged and crouched around their fires—the companions of their dreams and their meditations.

or:

Men have lounged and crouched around their fires, since fires have been the companions of their dreams and meditations.

30b. The reference of a pronoun should not be ambiguous.

Ambiguous:

He crossed his other leg, took out a handkerchief from a back pocket, wiped his forehead, blew his nose, and carefully and methodically folded and replaced it. [Does *it* refer to *nose?*]

Clear:

He crossed his other leg, took out a handkerchief from a back pocket, wiped his forehead, blew his nose, and then carefully and methodically folded the handkerchief and replaced it.

Ambiguous:

Almost all of the merchants know their customers and they are in the habit of calling them by name.

Clear:

In a small town everyone knows everyone else so well that even the merchants usually address their customers by name.

Ambiguous:

At the breakfast table, Dorothy told Mary that she had committed a bad social error. [Who had committed the error? Dorothy or Mary?]

Clear:

At the breakfast table, Dorothy accused Mary of committing a bad social error.

It is neither customary nor necessary to resort to an explanatory antecedent in parentheses after a pronoun.

Poor:

Father told the doctor that he (Father) did not think that the war would greatly affect his (the doctor's) profession.

Better:

Father said to the doctor, "I do not think that the war is going to affect your profession very much."

30c. *In formal and serious writing, the indefinite reference is less common than in informal writing and in speech.*

We are here referring to two particular situations: (1) the use of the indefinite *you* to mean *one, a person* and the indefinite *they* to mean *people,* and (2) the use of *this, that,* and *which* to refer to a clause, sentence, or a general idea.

1. The indefinite *you* and *they* are common in speech and in many forms of informal writing; they are less appropriate in formal writing. The student should guard against making their use a habit, especially in papers of explanation.

Formal:

First the seed is scattered evenly over the ground; then the soil is raked lightly and firmed with a roller. [Note the passive voice here.]

Colloquial:

First you scatter the seed; then you rake it in and firm the soil with a roller.

Formal:

When a soldier salutes, he must stand up straight and bring his right hand up smartly to the visor of his cap.

Colloquial:

When saluting, you must stand up straight and bring your right hand up smartly to the visor of your cap.

Formal:

Fraternities are not permitted in some colleges in the East.

Colloquial:

They (*or* You) do not have fraternities in some colleges in the East.

Formal:

In the army, a soldier does not ask; he obeys.

Colloquial:

In the army, you do not ask; you do what you are told.

2. A pronoun may have a clause or a sentence for its antecedent; it may even refer to a thought expressed by a part of the preceding sentence. As long as the reference is unmistakable, the sentence is clear. But the careless writer may fall into the habit of stringing together a series of "this," "that," and "which" clauses without troubling himself about either clearness or exactness. Whenever the writer suspects the clearness or definiteness of an antecedent, he should try to summarize the general idea of the clause referred to by using some expression like *this fact, this condition, a fact which,* and so forth. If the result is still unsatisfactory, he should rewrite the sentence.

Notice that the references are entirely clear in the following sentences.

Clear:

I have given up smoking. That should please my mother.
So you have decided to support my candidate. This is indeed a surprise.
Father suggested that I keep the money, which I did without a protest.

Now notice the vague references in the following.

Vague:

After locking the beasts in the barn, I went to bed and slept soundly, which is one of the effects of hunting cows. [The writer evidently means "sound sleep," but *which* could refer to two other things in the sentence.]

Clear:

After locking the beasts in the barn, I went to bed and slept soundly, for sound sleep is one of the effects of hunting cows.

Vague:

If a girl suspects that her roommate needs help or a friendly word of encouragement, she should do it before it is too late. [Do what?]

Clear:

If a girl suspects that her roommate needs help or a friendly word of encouragement, she should offer assistance before it is too late.

Vague:

The fish are kept alive and fresh in glass tanks, and it also attracts people, which helps the business considerably. [What do *it* and *which* refer to?]

Clear:

The fish are kept alive and fresh in glass tanks. The display of live fish helps business by attracting people to the place.

30d. *The careless use of* same, such, above, *and* said *as reference words often produces an awkward sentence.*

These words are used as reference words in legal or technical writing; in ordinary writing they should be avoided, not because they are incorrect but because they usually lead to awkwardness of expression. Use one of the common pronouns (it, them, this) or the name of the thing to which you refer.

Poor:

I stood there holding the monkey wrench and oil can in my hands. The foreman ordered me to return the same to the engine room.

Better:

I stood there holding the monkey wrench and oil can in my hands. The foreman ordered me to return the tools to the engine room.

Poor:

The significance of said decision is not yet fully comprehended.

Better:

The significance of the decision referred to is not yet fully comprehended.

Poor:

Please return same to me by bearer.

Better:

Please return it [or name the object] to me by the bearer of this note.

Poor:

The above is a complete refutation of their arguments.

Better:

These facts completely refute their arguments.

30e. A pronoun should agree with its antecedent in number, gender, and person.

For a discussion of the agreement of pronouns and antecedents see "Pronouns," section 4j. Note also that the "everybody-their" construction is common in conversational usage.

Poor:

I advise every beginner to purchase the best instruments they can afford. [*Every* is singular and therefore must be followed by a singular pronoun.]

Better:

I advise every beginner to purchase the best instruments he can afford.

Poor:

When an orchestra becomes successful, their success reflects upon the type of leadership they have had. [You must be consistent. If you begin by considering *orchestra* as singular, you must continue to refer to it as one unit.]

Better:

When an orchestra becomes successful, its success reflects the kind of leadership it has had.

30f. It is usually awkward to begin an essay with a reference to the title.

If the title is the same as the subject of the first sentence, it is better to repeat the words of the title. For instance, if your title is "Trout Fishing," do not begin your paper, "This has always been my favorite sport." Say, "Trout fishing has always been my favorite sport."

Exercise

Exercise 1. In each of the following sentences underline the pronoun or pronouns with faulty reference. Rewrite each sentence so as to correct the error.

1. The dean's duties are that of a mother.
2. Dynamite is placed on the rock, and after breaking the rock it is loaded into cars to be taken away.

3. Although one would think that he lives on excitement, they would be mistaken.
4. The soil here is sandy and loose, which makes it easy digging.
5. We often see peculiar resemblances between people and animals. Many times it is not meant to be uncomplimentary, and this is one of those instances.
6. When a person first meets her, they notice that she has a scar over her right eye.
7. We built many bridges over small swamps which kept us constantly occupied.
8. He seldom reprimands us for anything, but when he does, it is always taken seriously.
9. If I meet a person and they sit and constantly complain, it doesn't make a good impression on me.
10. I would prefer getting a job at the Medical School this year, doing odd jobs for them.

PROPER ARRANGEMENT

31. The parts of a sentence should be so arranged that the meaning of the sentence is clear at the first reading.

Since English is not a highly inflected language, the meaning of an English sentence depends largely on the arrangement of the words in it. The reader naturally assumes that the parts of a sentence which are placed next to each other are logically related to each other. You must therefore be careful to arrange words in a sentence in such a way that its meaning will be clear on the first reading. The rule which will guide you may be stated in two parts: (1) place all modifiers, whether words, phrases, or clauses, as close as possible to the words they modify; (2) avoid placing these elements near other words they might be taken to modify.

1. THE PROBLEM OF ONLY *AND* NOT.

These two adverbs are here singled out for comment because they have been problem children for a long time. Logically, an adverb should be placed near the word it modifies; idiomatically, it is often placed elsewhere. For instance, would you say, "We have room for only two more," or, "We only have room for two more"? The person with a logical mind says that "only" modifies "two"; the person who prefers the second form answers that idiom does not pay much attention to logic. He explains the position of "only" by calling it a "sentence adverb," modifying the thought of the sentence, and therefore its proper position is before the verb.

Both forms are used. The second is used generally in speech, in a great deal of informal writing, and often in formal writing. The first form is used by writers and speakers who are disturbed by the sound of the other form. No statistical study of the incidence of each form in formal writing has been made.

The same explanation applies to "not." Would you say: "Not everyone can be first," or "Everyone can't be first"? Logic sanctions the first form; idiom sanctions the second form—at least in speech and informal writing.

Only slightly less controversial is the placing of several other adverbs, such as *almost, nearly, merely, scarcely.*

Common in speech:

He *merely* said it because he did not stop to think.
He *only* took fifth place in the race.
Every student can*not* win honors in college.
The canteen *only* contained about two cups of water.
Harry *almost* weeded the whole garden this morning.

More logical and preferred by many:

He said it *merely* because he did not stop to think.
He took *only* fifth place in the race.
Not every student can win honors in college.
The canteen contained *only* about two cups of water.
Harry weeded *almost* the whole garden this morning.

2. PHRASES.

Misplaced:

He began to lose his desire to reach the summit *after a time.* [Does it refer to *to reach* or *began to lose?*]

I was dressed and ready to start climbing *within an hour.* [Does it refer to *being dressed* or to *starting to climb?*]

Every girl was really sorry to have the trip end *for more reasons than one.*

Clear:

He began *after a time* to lose his desire to reach the summit.

Within an hour I was dressed and ready to start climbing.

For more reasons than one, every girl was really sorry to have the trip end. [Refers to *being sorry,* not to *the trip ending.*]

3. CLAUSES.

Misplaced:

When you were a child do you remember all the interesting toys you had? [Does the clause refer to *remember* or to *toys you had?*]

Clear:

Do you remember all the interesting toys you had *when you were a child?*

4. SQUINTING MODIFIERS.

Modifiers so placed in a sentence that they may be understood with either the preceding or the following words are called squinting modifiers. As a rule, it is better not to try to cure the fault by means of punctuation.

Squinting:

Because we covered more ground with a tractor *in six days* we finished plowing the field.

Clear:

Because we covered more ground with a tractor, we finished plowing the field *in six days.*

Squinting:

After we had stopped at a service station *with the help of a lady attendant* we found our position on the map. [Putting a comma after *station* is not a satisfactory correction.]

Clear:

After we had stopped at a service station, a lady attendant helped us to locate our position on the map.

Squinting:

As we drove westward *every now and then* the blinding rays of the sun shone into our eyes. [Putting a comma after *westward* is a makeshift correction. It does not eliminate the confusion entirely.]

Clear:

As we drove westward, the blinding rays of the sun *frequently* shone into our eyes.

5. THE SPLIT INFINITIVE.

Placing an adverbial modifier between the sign *to* and the verb of an infinitive results in what is traditionally known as the "split infinitive." The split infinitive is no longer considered one of the seven deadly sins of college composition—if it ever was. It is not true that the parts of an infinitive are inseparable. But since a split infinitive still causes many persons discomfort, if not actual suffering, it is better for the student not to split his infinitives too rashly or promiscuously. A good rule to follow is this: place the adverbial modifier between *to* and the verb of an infinitive only when such an arrangement is necessary to avoid an awkward phrase.

Split infinitive:

A writer should remember to not carelessly split his infinitives.

Better:

A writer should remember not to split his infinitives carelessly.

6. IN GENERAL, ANY WORDS THAT NORMALLY BELONG NEAR EACH OTHER SHOULD NOT BE SEPARATED.

This statement applies particularly to subject and verb, verb and object, the parts of a verb phrase, substantives and adjective modifiers, and substantives and appositives.

Awkward:

The explorers had, after many adventures and much suffering, reached the headwaters of the Salmon River. [Verb *had reached* separated by long phrase]

Improved:

After many adventures and much suffering, the explorers had reached the headwaters of the Salmon River.

Awkward:

Before it became dark, the stragglers caught up with the main party, tired, wet, discouraged. [Adjective modifiers separated from the word they modify]

Improved:

Before it became dark, the tired, wet, and discouraged stragglers caught up with the main party.

Awkward:

Justice Holmes, in a brilliantly written interpretation of the Fourteenth Amendment, dissented. [Subject and verb split by a long phrase]

Better:

Justice Holmes dissented in a brilliantly written interpretation of the Fourteenth Amendment.

Exercise

Exercise 1. Point out the misplaced element in each of the following sentences. Correct each sentence. Do not use punctuation as a means of correcting an error.

1. Twenty years ago girls used to come to school where I was principal without any stockings on.
2. I shall attempt to explain the function of the least known, to one who does not play the game, section of the football team.
3. Their activity and progress in recent years have surprised the world.
4. At one time I remember that she had three engagement rings.
5. Masefield has many ideas about things that are different.
6. We were finally settled in seats that cost twice as much as we had paid for our tickets when the play began.
7. He usually has a lapful of food at the close of the dinner which he brushes to the floor to be stepped on by some other boarder.
8. If you should disturb her by coming in late, you will hear that she was awakened for the next three months.
9. There is a telephone at the end of the counter which is constantly in use.

10. Freshman English courses are taught by instructors who are required to have at least a master's degree in most colleges.
11. He would tell me to look up words I could not spell in the dictionary.
12. A crowd gathers to sorrowfully gaze upon the destruction of the magnificent structure.
13. He finally had to prove that his rival was a coward in order to hold his wife.
14. The pleasant, merry-faced girl seems exactly like a viola with its upturned face to the sun.
15. The woman was arrested for shoplifting by a private detective.
16. Wood can be kept for a long time without danger of rotting in the woodshed or the basement.
17. A year later I went to several classes with five or six other children conducted by our minister.
18. The freshmen only have to wear their green caps one year.
19. Why do they spend all their money, time, and effort to please a man with a new dress and a fingerwave?
20. The new laboratory at Dairen has found new uses too numerous to mention for the soy bean.

DANGLING MODIFIERS

32a. Awkward dangling modifiers should be avoided.

At present there is considerable difference of opinion among educated people over the use of what is traditionally known as the "dangling modifier." Some say that it should be called the "misrelated modifier," for instead of dangling it actually attaches itself too easily to the wrong word. When it does, especially when it results in confusion or in unintentional humor, it is bad. When it calls attention to itself and away from the intended meaning of the sentence, it is bad. One might add that it can be bad because so many educated persons have been taught to regard it as a slovenly way of writing.

Here are some examples of danglers:

While reading my morning paper, the toast burned.
When delicately browned on both sides and sizzling hot, she called to the guests to bring their plates.
Driving along the park highway, an old brown bear could be seen sitting squarely in the middle of the road.

In each of these sentences, it does not matter whether the phrase dangles because it is not attached where it should be or is misrelated because it attaches itself where it should not be. Each sentence is bad.

A dangler may be corrected in two ways: (1) by changing the phrase to a clause and (2) by providing a noun or pronoun to which the dangler can properly attach itself.

Examples:

While I was reading my morning paper, the toast burned.
While reading my morning paper, I burned my toast.
When the steak was delicately browned on both sides and sizzling hot, the hostess asked the guests to bring their plates.
Driving along the park highway, we saw an old brown bear sitting squarely in the middle of the road.

Before we list the various types of "dangling" or "misrelated" modifiers, let us look at two or three special situations.

1. The absolute phrase does not dangle. In the absolute phrase the word that the participle attaches itself to is in the phrase itself.

Examples:

The day's work being over, we returned to town.
The guests having arrived, Mother went to the door.
Three more girls, their wet hair plastered down over their eyes, stumbled into the classroom.

2. Certain idiomatic phrases, especially those that express a general action and those that serve as directive and transitional links, are always acceptable in either formal or informal situations. These are phrases like *generally speaking, looking at it from another point of view, taking everything into consideration, providing that . . . , failing . . .* , and others that are similar.

Examples:

Failing agreement, the meeting was adjourned.
Generally speaking, the worse a pun is, the better it is.

The following are types of objectionable verbal phrases:

1. THE PARTICIPLE OR GERUND.

Dangling:

Having a Chinese name, my teacher asked me to write a paper about Chinese customs. [The reader associates *having* with *teacher*. Actually the participle refers to the person represented by *me*.]

Upon asking him to explain, he told me that he was born and brought up in Seattle.

Revised:

Since I have a Chinese name, my teacher asked me to write a paper about Chinese customs.

When I asked him to explain, he told me that he was born and brought up in Seattle.

2. THE DANGLING INFINITIVE.

Awkward:

To succeed as a coach, the style of play must be adapted to fit the available material.
To appreciate this poem, it must be read aloud.
To enjoy outdoor sports, sensible clothing must be worn.

Revised:

If one is to succeed as a coach, he must be able to adapt his style of play to the material at his command.
To appreciate this poem, one must read it aloud.
This poem can be better appreciated if you read it aloud.
A person can enjoy outdoor sports better if he wears sensible clothing.

3. THE DANGLING PHRASE OF RESULT.

Awkward:

I helped my mother wash clothes this morning, thus causing me to miss my English class. [Who caused me to miss my class?]
I sold my automobile for three hundred dollars, thereby giving me enough money to pay my debts.

Revised:

I missed my English class this morning because I had to stay at home to help my mother wash clothes.
The sale of my automobile brought me three hundred dollars, enough to pay all my debts.

32b. *Misrelated elliptical clauses may produce an unintentionally ludicrous meaning.*

In an elliptical clause the subject is implied or understood. In such a construction there is sometimes a danger that the reader associates the clause with the wrong word in the rest of the sentence.

Awkward:

His foot was injured while swimming in Wild Cat Hole. [Was the foot swimming?]
When six years of age, my father took the family to a farm near Calgary. [Who was six years of age?]
While on a tour of Mexico, my expensive camera was stolen.

Revised:

His foot was injured while he was swimming in Wild Cat Hole.
When I was six years old, my father took the family to a farm near Calgary.
While we were on a tour of Mexico, my expensive camera was stolen.

32c. *A sentence with any sort of expression, like a phrase or an appositive, that is not easily understood with the rest of the sentence is awkward and usually misleading.*

Illogical:

A gentleman farmer, his wardrobe ranges from faultlessly tailored suits to four-buckle rubber boots. [The expression *a gentleman farmer* seems to be in apposition with *wardrobe.*]

After five years in a city school, a country school presents many problems in adjustment. [One naturally associates the opening phrase with a *country school.*]

Revised:

As he is a gentleman farmer, his wardrobe ranges from faultlessly tailored suits to four-buckle rubber boots.

A person who has spent five years in a city school encounters many problems in adjustment when he goes to a country school.

The dangling or misrelated modifier, it can be seen from the examples offered, is a stylistic blunder. If it causes confusion, even momentary confusion, or if it is associated with an unasked-for ludicrous image, it is undesirable. For a discussion of danglers used by many professional writers, see Pooley's *Teaching English Usage,* pp. 107–113.

Exercises

Exercise 1. Which of the following sentences contain objectionable danglers? Correct any error that you find.

1. Moving to a drier climate, her asthma improved quickly.
2. After moving to Arizona, her health improved.
3. After eating our dinners, we noticed that it had started to rain.
4. We threw sand upon the fire, thus preventing it from spreading.
5. The fire having been extinguished, everyone went to sleep again.
6. Meeting him by chance on the street, he told me he had decided to quit school.
7. Being late, my entrance made a deep impression upon the class.
8. After asking my name, the professor repeated the next day's assignment.
9. Entering the North Gate, the new chapel stands out prominently.
10. Being too small for me to sit up in, I thought the new car was not worth its price.

Exercise 2. Some of the following sentences are correct. Some contain objectionable danglers. Pick out the faulty sentences and correct them.

1. Being an enthusiastic photographer, my camera accompanies me on every trip.
2. The camera being a delicate instrument, it is never packed with the rest of the equipment.
3. After putting it on the car seat beside me, I usually cover it with a sweater.
4. Being thus exposed to the hot sun, you may discover that your film has been ruined.
5. To get an artistic picture, all the conditions must be right.
6. When taking pictures with color film, autumn foliage is a favorite subject.
7. After driving almost to the rim of Crater Lake crater, the clouds drifted away and the sun shone brilliantly.
8. Being at a high altitude, a polarizing filter is attached to the lens, thus increasing the contrast between the blues and the whites.
9. To use a polarizer successfully, the sun must be at your right or your left as you take the picture.
10. After using the polarizer, I took some more pictures with a skylight filter, thereby doubling my chances of getting some unusual pictures.

EMPHASIS IN THE SENTENCE

33. ***The relative importance of ideas in a sentence may be shown by various devices of structure. The principle used is known as "emphasis."***

"Emphasis" is a word that may be understood in more than one sense. A speaker may emphasize some of his words by shouting or screaming them; a writer may emphasize words by indicating that they be printed in italics or capitals. Some writers and speakers have used these methods. But that is not the sense in which we use the word here. By "emphasis" we mean using rhetorical devices that show the relative importance or prominence of ideas in a sentence or a paragraph. Some of these devices we have already discussed in connection with other qualities of good writing—clarity, directness, order, coherence, conciseness, directness. Two or three others will be pointed out here and in the following sections.

It may be well to restate here the various devices by which the relative importance of ideas can be shown:

1. By placing an important idea by itself in a short sentence.
2. By placing the idea in the main clause of a complex sentence.
3. By changing the usual order of a sentence. (Sympathy I did not want!)
4. By using parallel structure. (See section 35.)
5. By using the order of climax.
6. By repeating key words. (See section 26a.)
7. By using the active instead of the passive voice.
8. By giving an important idea a fuller treatment.
9. By placing important words in prominent positions.
10. By using periodic structure.

THE EMPHATIC POSITION

33a. ***The relative importance of ideas can be indicated by placing the important words in the important positions in the sentence.***

The most conspicuous positions in the sentence are the beginning and the end. These are the positions that should be used for ideas that deserve attention and emphasis. The less important details, the modifiers, the transitional phrases should be placed within the sentence.

No writer can consistently rearrange his sentences so as to begin and end them with important ideas. Many sentences are so short that the reader's mind comprehends them as units. In many others the word order is determined by the nature of the English language. For example, we write: "He is a good man." "Her son was killed in France." "The day's work is done." "The President saluted the flag." In sentences like these the question of emphatic position cannot arise.

Whenever possible without sacrificing clearness and smoothness, place explanatory phrases or minor details within the sentence.

Weak:

However, the general disclaimed any responsibility for the order.

The student who cheats in an examination is cheating only himself in the final analysis.

Public speaking should be taught in freshman English, I think.

Better:

The general, however, disclaimed any responsibility for the order.

The student who cheats in an examination is, in the final analysis, cheating only himself.

Public speaking, I think, should be taught in freshman English.

THE PERIODIC FORM

33b. Occasionally one may express a thought more effectively by changing a sentence from the loose to the periodic form.

A sentence in which the thought is not complete until the end is called a periodic sentence. The effect of the periodic sentence is one of suspense. Your reader, in other words, is forced to wait for the main idea until after he has comprehended the subordinate details upon which the main idea is based. Not all sentences in English are periodic; a large majority of them, in fact, are loose. It is precisely because of this that an occasional periodic sentence is emphatic.

Study the difference in effect produced by the following:

Loose:

Stop talking if you have nothing more to say.

It is of course impractical to legislate for those who will behave themselves while completely ignoring those who will not.

The catalytic agents of college life are athletics, forensics, musical organizations, journalism, parties, and dances.

Periodic:

If you have nothing more to say, stop talking.

To legislate for those who will behave themselves while completely ignoring those who will not is, of course, impractical.

Athletics, forensics, musical organizations, journalism, parties, dances—these are the catalytic agents of college life.

Here are two examples of long periodic sentences. Notice in each how suspense is built up by delaying the main statement until the end.

In the almost unique intimacy and good-fellowship of Oxford life, where for the moment men from every nation and every class are living together and surveying the nations of the earth in human and humorous companionship, the Rhodes Scholar, if he has in him the capacity for wisdom, learns the difference between an abstract formula and a living point of view. —Frank Aydelotte, "What the American Rhodes Scholar Gets from Oxford."

To transfer admiration from the thing possessed to its possessor; to conceive that the mere possession of material wealth makes of its possessor a proper object of worship; to feel abject before another who is wealthier—such emotions do not so much as enter the American mind.—Hilaire Belloc.

Exercises

Exercise 1. Using the principle of "emphasis by position," improve the following sentences.

1. Duty is what we expect from others, as someone has said.
2. American youth is more interested in security than in adventure, according to the writer's opinion.
3. Generally speaking, modern youth has had all the adventure it can stand.

4. The great adventures of the future will be in outer space, according to the convocation speaker.
5. The challenging new frontiers are those of the mind and the soul, the speaker pointed out.

Exercise 2. Change the following loose sentences to periodic sentences.

1. Why are not mountain tops warmer than their bases since they are closer to the sun?
2. The sun's heat rays pass right through the air at the top of a mountain because the air at such altitudes is very thin.
3. Modern, American-style motels are being built in some of the Western European countries.
4. Many American tourists will enjoy their conveniences after they had spent the day walking and driving.
5. Let the others have their quaint hotels if they value atmosphere more than comfort.

ACTIVE OR PASSIVE VOICE

33c. *The passive voice should be avoided where the active is more natural and direct.*

The use of the passive voice is not a grammatical or a stylistic fault; it is the *overuse* of it that is a fault. The passive voice is properly used when (1) the object or receiver of the action of the verb is more important than the doer, (2) the doer of the action is not known, (3) the writer wishes to place the emphasis on the receiver instead of on the doer.

Examples:

Several priceless old manuscripts were destroyed.
The wounded prisoner was dragged into the trench.

But notice the difference in the following sentences when the active voice replaces the passive.

Weak:

Other games are also played by the guests.

As the top of the stairs is approached, a quickening of the steps of the person is announced by the trembling of the floor.

The Sunday dinner is a meal at which everyone is present and is enjoyed immensely by all.

Many agonizing minutes are spent by the student in deciding on a subject for a speech.

Better:

The guests also play other games.

As the intruder approaches the top of the stairs, the trembling of the floor announces the quickening of his steps.

Sunday dinner is a meal at which everyone is present and which everyone enjoys.

The student spends many agonizing minutes deciding upon a subject for a speech.

Exercise

Exercise 1. Improve the following sentences by changing the verbs from the passive to the active.

1. But his suggestion was received by me with disdain.
2. A last puff is taken, which momentarily illuminates the boy's face, and a glowing arc is noticed when the cigarette is flicked across the lawn.
3. I had heard that the party was to be just a "kid dance," but it was soon found out that it was great fun.
4. With his help the mistake was soon corrected by us.
5. Here and there are heard whispered explanations and giggles.
6. My courses were not given much thought by me.
7. Three women came in, and the question "Are you relatives of the groom?" was asked.
8. A daily trip is made to the attic to wipe the dust from her keepsakes, and then she sheds a tear or two over them.
9. The tractor cannot be driven and the mowing machine manipulated by one man at the same time.
10. In the laboratory all available information is studied by chemists. After this extensive study, experiments are performed. The data are recorded in detail. If no satisfactory results are obtained, another study is carried out, but this time the data obtained from the first trial are included. These trials are carried on until satisfactory results are gained.

SHIFT IN POINT OF VIEW

34. Any unnecessary and illogical shift in point of view should be avoided.

The most common shifts in point of view are (1) from active to passive voice, (2) from past to present tense, (3) from *one* to *you,*

(4) from indirect to direct discourse, (5) from formal to colloquial style. Writing is more pleasing if the writer maintains his point of view unless, of course, he has some logical reason for changing to another.

34a. Unnecessary shifts from active to passive voice are undesirable.

Shift:

Every boy rolls up his sleeping bag and carries it to the truck; fires are doused with water and earth is spread over them.
We swept the room carefully, and the furniture and shelves were also dusted.

Better:

Every boy rolls his sleeping bag, carries it to the truck, douses the fires with water, and spreads earth over them.
We carefully swept the room and dusted the furniture and the shelves.

34b. Needless shifts in tense—from past to present or from present to past—are usually objectionable.

Shift:

Elsie *asked* the doctor about her mother but *receives* an evasive reply. [This sort of shift, from past to present, must be watched for in narrative accounts.]
I *begin* to get a little curious and *stuck* my head from under the blanket to see who *should be* prowling around at that time of the night. [The writer shifts from present to past to future.]

Better:

Elsie *asked* the doctor about her mother but *received* an evasive reply. [Both verbs in the past tense]
I *began* to get a little curious and *stuck* my head out from under the blanket to see who *was prowling* around at that time of the night. [All three verbs in past tense]

34c. A needless shift in number and person should be avoided.

Shift:

You must make yourself interesting to the group that *listens* to you and *are* constantly trying to detect your mistakes. [If *group* is used as a singular once, it should not be used as a plural in the same sentence.]

Better (informal style):

You must make yourself interesting to the group that *listens* to you and *is* constantly trying to detect your mistakes.

Correct in a formal context:

One must always make himself interesting to the group that *listens* to him and *is* constantly trying to detect his mistakes.

Shift:

If one's mouth is dry, eat a lump of sugar or chew gum. [Shift from *one* to *you.*]

Better:

If one's mouth is dry, one should eat a lump of sugar or chew gum. [It is doubtful, however, if any person who used *one* with such formal precision would chew gum.]

34d. An unnecessary shift in subject or perspective is usually awkward.

Shift:

Miller was a great athlete, but studying was not his strong point.
I am taking a course in forestry, though life in the woods does not greatly appeal to me.

Better:

Miller was a great athlete but a poor student.
I am taking a course in forestry, although I am not especially fond of a life in the woods.

34e. A needless shift from indirect to direct discourse is awkward.

Illogical:

The girls wonder, "Is my hair combed? Will this dress suit my figure?"
He asked us would we find him a room.

Consistent:

The girls wonder, "Is my hair combed? Will this dress suit my figure?"
He asked us to find him a room. He asked us, "Will you find me a room?"

34f. A shift from the formal to the colloquial style in serious writing is usually inappropriate.

Inappropriate:

The main fault of the League of Nations was that the big shots would not gang up on any large nation that was breaking the peace.
The Russian authorities seemed to be steamed up about another attack upon their merchant ships in the Mediterranean.

Formal style:

The main fault of the League of Nations was that the great powers refused to combine against any one of their group that was breaking the peace.
The Russian authorities seemed to be angered by another attack upon their merchant ships in the Mediterranean.

34g. A writer should guard against mixing two distinctly separate constructions in a sentence.

A "mixed construction" is usually the result of hasty and careless writing. The writer begins one construction, and immediately, without troubling himself to look back on what he has written, continues with another construction.

Mixed:

In our basement we found a small wood stove, which upon removing the front, made it resemble a fireplace. [*Which* refers to *stove*. The stove cannot remove its own front, nor can the stove make itself resemble anything.]

Clear:

In our basement we found a small wood stove, which we made into a fireplace by removing its front.
In our basement we found a small wood stove. By removing its front, we made it resemble a fireplace.

Mixed:

She did not say a word, but took me to the back yard in what seemed to me a bit hurriedly. [The writer has forgotten his original intention. He could say either *took me in what seemed a hurried manner* or *took me a bit hurriedly*.]

Occasionally a writer will run an independent clause into a sentence in such a way that it appears to stand as the subject of a verb.

Mixed:

I had no money was the reason I did not buy it.
Elsie was disliked by her stepmother was the reason why she left London.

Clear:

I did not buy it because I had no money.
Elsie left London because she was disliked by her stepmother.

34h. *A writer should be on his guard against unintentional humor or absurdity in serious writing.*

Poor:

In my case I apply golf to myself as others apply stamps or antiques to themselves.
I saw a spout of water and I thought it was a whale, but I don't know what kind of fish it was.
To build a good model takes time and patience to have a good model when you are finished.

34i. *Mixed figures of speech are inappropriate in serious writing.*

In the teaching of writing, warnings against scrambled metaphors may have been given an undeserved and an unfortunate prominence. A mixed metaphor is often a sign of mental vitality. It is surely a lesser literary crime than page after page of dull and uninspired prose. If you scramble two incongruous images, you probably need little more than a hint to show you that your metaphors are inappropriate. It is manifestly absurd to speak of "watering the spark of originality," or "blazing a trail over the sea of knowledge," or of "being blinded by a thirst for revenge." Even Shakespeare spoke of taking up arms against a sea of troubles. If your instructor points out a mixed figure of speech in your writing, laugh over it. He will laugh with you and then "encourage the spark of imagination which the mixed metaphor foreshadows, water it with drops of kindness and fertilize it with praise, so that the springs of originality may blossom forth like a tree and shed their light over many arid pages of prose writing!"

The following samples illustrate what is meant by "mixed imagery."

Many high-school athletes think they can ride on their high-school laurels right into a position on the college team. [How can one ride on a laurel?]
The future of jazz was at its lowest ebb. [Even were the future not transported to the past, a rare feat in itself, how could a future ebb?]
Instead of narrowly pursuing the mechanics of grammar, the clever teacher will often digress into anecdotes which will make the class fairly rock with laughter. [Can "mechanics" be pursued, either narrowly or broadly?]
A college education enables the graduate to meet the snares and pitfalls of life with a broader point of view.

Exercises

Exercise 1. The following are sections from student papers. Rewrite each in the past tense.

1. The door closed with its customary protest, and we stand in the darkness.

   "Hey, quit jiggling my bed. Can't you see I'm trying to sleep?" complained a plaintive voice.

   Then at last with groping hands I find my bed. I ease myself into the blankets, but the bed groaned and squeaked its nightly protestation. With the covers pulled snugly around me I prepare to sleep. Then the door admitted another freshman, who in passing, gives my bed another jiggling.
2. A tall, well-groomed man wearing a black pin-striped suit entered the room. He greets the students with a warm smile that made them feel he is a friend as well as an instructor. His deep voice reassured them. His brown sparkling eyes were cheerful and mischievous, and his jet black mustache gave him the air of a comic-opera villain. There isn't a bit of curl in his straight black hair. It is neat and always has the look of just having been combed and brushed.

Exercise 2. In each of the following sentences specify the type of illogical shift that you find—in tense, voice, subject, number, or person. Then make the necessary corrections.

1. The train was two hours late, so Mrs. Smith and I decide to wait in the car.
2. Never before had I operated an elevator, but it surely must be simple because all you had to do was to press a button, which I did.
3. There was just one short half hour of work left. The clerks in the sports department, where I am working, are busy bustling around trying to get rid of the last shoppers.
4. In some cases, when the person was released from prison he committed another crime, and from then on usually leads a life of crime.
5. Many girls who live in the poor sections of the town would profit by becoming a member of a Camp Fire Girls group.

6. We filled out our registration blanks and attended several lectures; also placement tests in English and mathematics were taken.
7. I do not mean that the whole day should be spent on one assignment, but do it carefully and thoroughly.
8. The target was kept moving while the men try to demolish it with a well-placed shot.
9. The twins were not identical; one is larger than the other.
10. There is little enthusiasm shown by the students. However, why should they?

Exercise 3, Mixed constructions. Rewrite the following sentences. Do not be afraid to break them up if they can be improved in that manner.

1. There are today possibly two ways of evaluating the Alcan Highway either as a merchant in Canada or Alaska who sees in it as a source of income or a tourist.
2. Concentration upon what I have been doing has been a bad point because my mind is always wandering about thinking of other things.
3. The dust storms had blown the topsoil off the farms was the reason they had become uneconomical to operate.
4. When parents hand out the money whenever their child wants it, is contributing to the future unhappiness of their son.
5. The reason movies are so popular is due to their low cost and quality.
6. You may notice an old hound dog lying on the ground and looks as if he were asleep.
7. We were constantly giving parties that we never asked anyone outside our little group to come.
8. The ladies of a century ago thought it necessary to lead a life of leisure and a disgrace to work.
9. Is it true what they are saying about her?
10. The more advanced one goes into a subject, the more interesting it becomes.

PARALLEL STRUCTURE

35a. Ideas of equal value in a sentence should be expressed in parallel structure.

It is true that we do not always need strict structural parallelism, but when it can be used, it is a handy device by which the sentence gains in clearness as well as in force. In its simplest form, the device can be explained as a balancing of noun with noun, an infinitive with another infinitive, a phrase with another phrase, and a clause with another clause. Let us first look at a few examples from the work of skilled writers:

You are || the rulers and the ruled,
the lawgivers and the law-abiding,
the beginning and the end.

—Adlai Stevenson

As she passed through the wards in her plain dress,
|| so quiet,
so unassuming,
she struck || the casual observer simply as the pattern of a perfect lady; but the keener eye perceived something more than that—
|| the serenity of high deliberation in the scope of the capacious brow,
the sign of power in the dominating curve of the thin nose, and
the traces of a harsh and dangerous temper—
|| something peevish,
something mocking, and yet
something precise—in the small and delicate mouth.

—from *Eminent Victorians* by Lytton Strachey. Reprinted by permission of Harcourt, Brace & Co., Inc.

In this land the citizens are still invited
|| to write their plays and books,
to paint their pictures,
to meet for discussion,
to dissent as well as to agree,
to mount soapboxes in the public square,
to enjoy education in all subjects without censorship,
to hold court and judge one another,
to compose music,
to talk politics with their neighbors without wondering whether the secret police are listening,
to exchange ideas as well as goods,
to kid the government when it needs kidding, and
to read || real news of
real events instead of
phony news manufactured by a paid agent of the state.

—E. B. White, "Freedom," *One Man's Meat,* Harper & Brothers. Copyright 1942 by E. B. White. Reproduced by permission of the publisher.

These sentences are written in the grand manner, it is true, but they do show what a skilled writer can do with parallel structure. The device is usable at the student level also, as the following examples show:

Awkward:

Sororities teach a girl to be a lady and courteous. [Noun paralleled with an adjective]
Our English instructor asked us to close our books, to take pen and paper, and that we were to write a short theme. [Two infinitives and a clause]
Few of the leaders anticipated the bitterness of the strike or how long it would last. [A noun and a clause]

Parallel in form:

Sororities teach a girl to be	*ladylike* and *courteous.* [adjective // adjective]
Our English instructor asked us	*to close* our books, *to take* pen and paper, and *to write* a short theme.
Few of the leaders anticipated	the *bitterness* or the *duration* of the strike. [noun // noun]

35b. ***A subordinate*** **which or who** ***clause should not be carelessly joined to a main clause by*** **and.**

The "and which" or "and who" fault, as it is called, consists of using "and which" or "and who" in a sentence that does not have a preceding "which" or "who" clause.

Faulty:

He is a man of wide experience *and who* is also very popular with the farmers.
I am interested in electronics, because it is a new field *and which* offers interesting opportunities to one who knows science.

Parallel:

He is a man of	wide experience and great popularity among the farmers.
I am interested in electronics	which is a new field and which offers interesting opportunities . . . .

35c. *The false parallel—that is, using parallel structure for ideas that are not parallel—should be avoided.*

Illogical and awkward:

I finally realized that my daydreaming was not making me beautiful, slender, or friends. [The three words seem to depend on *making me,* but two of them are adjectives and one is a noun. They are not logically parallel.]
She has black hair, blue eyes, and is very fair.
She has black hair, blue eyes, and wears glasses.

Revised:

I finally realized that my daydreaming was not making me beautiful and slender or bringing me friends.
She has black hair, blue eyes, and a very fair complexion. [Series of three nouns]
She has black hair and blue eyes, and she wears glasses. [Put the *and* between the two which are similar. Put the third into a separate clause.]

Parallel forms may be used with the correlative conjunctions *both . . . and, either . . . or, neither . . . nor, not only . . . but also.* Care should be taken in placing these correlatives so that the intended meaning of the sentence is not obscured.

Exercise

Exercise 1. In the following sentences underline the parts that should be expressed in parallel form. Then rewrite each sentence.

1. Vern is a large boy, blonde hair, very large nose, deep-set blue eyes, and his white teeth flash when he smiles.
2. After I graduated from high school I debated whether to go on to college or if I should enlist at once.
3. It is important to analyze these three types of radio broadcasts with a view to purpose, presentation, and how they are sponsored.
4. We try to teach them how to get along with people, table manners, good habits, and how to get the most from life.
5. Chipmunk burrows have two openings, one for general use and there is also another one that can be used in case of emergency.
6. In the evening we would play baseball, pitch horseshoes, or some other type of outdoor game.
7. My work in his office consisted of typing addresses and to answer the telephone.

8. His students are still wondering whether his advice was meant to be taken seriously or if he was merely joking.
9. The natives are both afraid and they are suspicious also.
10. They do not know whether to hide or if they should co-operate with us.

COMPARISONS

36a. In standard formal English, comparisons should be logical and complete.

Written English, especially formal written English, requires a logic and a precision in expressing comparisons that is often lacking in loose, informal speech. In informal speech certain elliptical or illogical comparisons have become idiomatic. Some of these shortened comparisons, or illogical comparisons, are becoming more and more common in writing, both formal and informal; as in other cases of divided usage, the choice made by the student should be based on an understanding of the facts of usage.

1. In informal writing do not omit *than* or *as* in a double comparison.

Usually inappropriate in formal usage:

Agriculture is now as important, if not more important than mining. [as important than mining?]
Clark is as fast if not faster than Harrison. [as fast than Harrison?]
The salaries earned by college graduates vary as much if not more than those earned by high-school graduates.

Logical but awkward:

Agriculture is now as important as, if not more important than mining.
Clark is as fast as, if not faster than Harrison.
The salaries earned by college graduates vary as much as, if not more than those earned by high-school graduates.

The last three examples illustrate what is often called the "suspended construction." Some writers use it; others object to it on the score of awkwardness. It can be easily avoided.

Logical and smooth:

Agriculture is now as important as mining, if not more so.
Clark is as fast as Harrison, if not faster.
The salaries of college graduates vary as much as those of high-school graduates, if not more.

2. Do not omit one term of a comparison.

Misleading:

I admire him more than Scott.
The United States helped Russia more than England.

Clear:

I admire him more than I admire Scott (*or* more than Scott does).
The United States helped Russia more than England did (*or* more than we helped England).

3. Do not omit *other* after *than* or *as* in comparing two members of the same group or class.

Misleading:

Kowalski is heavier than any man on the team. [If Kowalski is not on the team, the sentence is clear. If he *is* a member of the team, he cannot be heavier than himself.]

Clear:

Kowalski is heavier than any other man on the team.
Kowalski is the heaviest man on the team.

4. Finish your comparisons so that you will not seem to be comparing something that you do not intend to compare.

Misleading:

The salary of an English teacher is lower than a lawyer. [Are you comparing salaries, or are you comparing salary and lawyer?]
The duties and responsibilities of a traffic officer are more complex than a game warden.

Clear:

The salary of an English teacher is lower than that of a lawyer. [In your desire to escape awkwardness you should not say, "An English teacher earns less than a lawyer." If you want to be accurate in fact as well as logical in expression, you could say, "An English teacher earns more than does a lawyer, but he gets less."]

The duties and responsibilities of a traffic officer are more complex than those of a game warden. [Name the second term of the comparison.]

36b. *In standard English, comparisons are completed except when the missing term of the comparison can be easily supplied by the reader.*

Not clear:

It is easier to remain silent when attacks are made upon the things one loves. [Easier than what?]

Students who live in a dormitory do better work. [Better than students who live where?]

Clear:

It is easier to remain silent when attacks are made upon the things one loves than to risk criticism by defending them.

Students who live in a dormitory do better work than those who room in private homes (*or* who live in fraternity houses).

There are, however, many idiomatic expressions in which an unfinished comparison is easily understood, such as: "It is always better to tell the truth"; "her explanation is simpler"; "we thought it wiser to agree." No misunderstanding is possible in statements like these. The uncompleted superlative is also used, especially in speech, and its sense is not that of a comparison but of an intensive, as in: "She is the most unselfish woman," "he is a most peculiar man."

We must also add here that although in general a comparative refers to two and a superlative refers to three or more, idiomatically the superlative is often used with two persons or objects.[1] This use of the superlative is undoubtedly more common in speech than in formal writing.

[1] George O. Curme, *Syntax,* p. 504; Robert C. Pooley, *Teaching English Usage,* pp. 119–123; Bergen Evans and Cornelia Evans, *A Dictionary of Contemporary American Usage,* pp. 105–107.

Exercise

Exercise 1. Revise the comparisons in the following sentences. Use the forms appropriate in standard written English.

1. When you compare the father's and mother's influence on a child, that of the mother is always strongest and most lasting.
2. The terms which McVey recommended were as liberal if not more liberal than those originally asked for by the unions.
3. It is supposed to be one of, if not the hardest course in the university.
4. Morry, their captain, is as fast, if not faster than any man on their team.
5. On Saturday night more men study their lessons than girls.
6. He is scorned by the intellectuals, but his poems are better known than any poet in America.
7. Girls are probably better in flattering their teachers than the best of the male effort.
8. His step was as light as many middle-aged men.
9. They have raised their standard of living to a point higher than any place on earth.
10. Our new professor is the darlingest man; he is such a dear about late themes, and he is so liberal with his grades.

WORDS LEFT OUT

37. Words necessary for clearness should not be left out.

Two kinds of omissions need be considered here. One is the result of carelessness. The cure for that type is more careful proofreading. The second is the omission that results from the carrying over of speech habits into writing. We often speak in a more clipped or telegraphic manner than is permissible in writing, especially serious and dignified writing on serious subjects.

The following are some of the omissions that need to be guarded against:

1. MISLEADING OMISSION OF THAT.

Misleading:

I soon observed nearly all the women, especially the young and pretty ones, were carrying strange little baskets. [Did he "observe the women, especially the young and pretty ones," or did he observe *that* the women were carrying baskets?]

He told me his story in its original version had been rejected by thirteen publishers. [Supply *that.* He told me *that* his story . . . . The confusion is undesirable even if it is but momentary.]

2. OMISSION OF A PART OF A VERB OR VERB PHRASE.

Misleading:

The patient was given an anesthetic and the instruments made ready. [It is better to say *were made ready,* because *patient* is singular, and the verb following it cannot be understood with *instruments made ready. Instruments* is plural.]

His ideas were progressive and adopted without debate. [Repeat *were.* The two verbs are not parallel. The first *were* is used as a main verb; the second *were* is an auxiliary verb, or a part of the verb phrase *were adopted.*]

3. OMISSION OF WORDS WHICH WOULD MAKE A PARALLEL SERIES INTELLIGIBLE.

Confused:

He is about fifty-nine years old, gray hair, and very distinctive features. [He *is* gray hair?]

Improved:

He is about fifty-nine years old. He has gray hair and very distinctive features. [Supply the necessary verb.]

4. NOUNS OR VERBS UNDERSTOOD IN A DOUBLE CAPACITY.

Illogical:

A Raisin in the Sun is one of the best, if not the best play I have ever seen. [This sort of construction is very common in speech; in written English, however, many people object to it. Some writers have used it.]

Improved:

A Raisin in the Sun is one of the best plays that I have ever seen, if not the best.

5. OMISSION OF IDIOMATIC PREPOSITIONS.

Incomplete:

Winter term a new course in chemistry will be offered. [Say *During the winter term . . .*]

This is a good time to show your faith and devotion to your country. [Say *faith in.*]
Customers have neither respect nor faith in a merchant who cheats. [Say *respect for.*]

For a more complex sentence in which idiomatic prepositions are used with precise care, examine the following sentence taken from Galsworthy's essay on drama.

This third method requires a certain detachment; it requires a sympathy with, a love of, and a curiosity as to, things for their own sake; it requires a far view, together with patient industry, for no immediately practical results.

Exercise

Exercise 1. Supply the missing words in the following sentences. Rearrange the wording wherever it is necessary.

1. Being able to write well may mean the difference between obtaining and being turned down a job.
2. Some men never have and never will understand generosity.
3. He was one of the first, if not the first man taught by the Wright brothers how to fly a plane.
4. The prisoner protested tearfully that he was innocent and he was being mistaken for someone else.
5. A fraternity house or a dormitory is a question which many freshmen have to answer.

VARIETY

38. *Variety in the length and the structure of sentences usually makes writing more effective.*

A writer may avoid monotony of sentence structure by avoiding the following:

1. Beginning a series of sentences with the same word or the same subject;
2. Beginning a series of sentences with participial phrases;
3. Using the same sentence pattern in a group of sentences;
4. Beginning each of a series of sentences with the same kind of subordinate clause.

Notice the monotony of the sentence patterns in the following excerpts from student papers:

Short sentences beginning with a participial phrase:

After cleaning up, we lay down and went to sleep. Upon awakening, we heard a mocking bird singing beautifully. Looking out the window, we could see it perched on a limb of a magnolia tree. Feeling much better by this time, we decided to dress and go out in search of adventure.

Short sentences, all beginning with the subject:

My roommate has some very good traits. She spends most of her study time in the library. She always has her work done, for she is quite studious. She is very good at giving good advice. She keeps me well informed as to the college rules and regulations. She, being a sophomore, knows the students and the professors quite well. She knows each member of the football team personally. She is what is termed a campus "big shot."

The principle may be expressed in positive form:

1. Mix simple sentences with complex or compound sentences;
2. Put a short sentence in the midst of several long ones;
3. Occasionally begin a sentence with modifiers instead of with the subject;
4. Occasionally begin with a conjunction instead of with the subject.

Observe the pleasing variety of sentences in the following paragraph from a freshman paper.

During the scorching summer of 1959 I was invited by Russell Towboat and Mooring Company to work in their confectionary at the ferry boat depot. [prepositional phrase] I was thrilled at the thought. [short sentence] Therefore I asked not what my salary would be, what hours I would work, or what my little task would be—I accepted. [begins with conjunction] My salary was an enormous fifty cents an hour; I worked a split shift, from six to eight in the morning and from three to five in the afternoon; and my task, not at all little, was selling everything from steaming cups of Maxwell House to trip tickets—three for a quarter, nine cents apiece. [long compound sentence] Worse yet was the fact that I pedaled daily to and from work on an old, broken-down single-tired Champion. [begins with adjective] More appropriately should I have been called the champion, for I not only traveled three hilly miles each trip but also lugged along Dad's bulky tire pump for the frequent times that the brittle tires sneezed out their air. [Note the beginning adverbial modifier and the reversed subject-verb order.]

It is not exactly cricket to set beside a competent freshman paper a bit of expert writing by a professional. And yet we can learn and do learn by competing against players who are better than we are. In the first selection observe that variety comes from an *occasional* departure from the usual, that writing is smooth and easy and rich because the variety in patterns seems natural. Too many sentences beginning with "something beside the subject" create a feeling of monotony as quickly as too many sentences beginning with the subject. In the second selection observe how richness and variety are achieved by weaving various details, in phrases, clauses, appositives, into the sentences themselves.

Often enough—and often justifiably—your ordinary lover of Nature has been accused of sentimentality. He prattles, so his condemners say, of the sweet twitter of birds and of the flowers that bloom in the spring. He disregards the seamy side of things and sees the world in greeting-card terms. The cute kitten and the Easter bunny are his symbols. He never asks of the tiger: "Did He who made the lamb make thee?" But since about the middle of the nineteenth century another kind of sentimentality has been at least as prevalent and a good deal more respectable—what might be called, I mean, the sentimentality of violence. If to feel a false emotion based upon a deliberately incomplete view of the facts is to be guilty of sentimentalism, then the view that Nature is consistently violent and cruel is as sentimental as its opposite. She is no more characteristically red in tooth and claw than she is characteristically a kind mother. She is both, or neither, or something that includes and transcends the two. What is commonly called the realistic view is as sentimental as what is commonly called sentimental.

No doubt it is human to insist upon the adequacy of a simple "either or." No doubt it is not only human, but laudably so, to distinguish throughout the animal—even throughout the vegetable and inanimate—world between what, in us, would be kindliness on the one hand and cruelty on the other. Even a storm we call "fierce," and a spring sun "caressing." If Nature is neutral, we are not. The ability to set up dichotomies is one of the most fateful of the abilities that man has discovered in himself. But though we cannot and should not live permanently in what may or may not actually be the valueless world Nature sometimes appears, it is nevertheless our privilege to enjoy the dizzy pleasure of occasional moments when we seem almost to have left humanity behind and to survey the world—from some high, more than Himalayan peak—*sub specie aeternitatis.*

This rain, for instance, which has been falling, falling, falling. If it interferes with our plans we call it "hateful," but that is only a turn of speech and few people are naive enough to suppose that the rain actually intended to spoil the picnic they had planned. Some few more—but no longer, I suppose—are capable of believing that it comes in answer to some farmer's prayer, or, if it lasts too long, as punishment for some sin of the community. Yet we are no more than one step removed from so simple a philosophy when we assume in a more general way that Nature's intentions are somehow benevolent or the opposite; that she "means" well or ill for us or her other children. Their needs and their desires are too various for her to be able to favor them all. She could not, even if she would, be good to each and every one. She is cruel to the rabbit put into the mouth of a fox but kind to the fox's cubs to whom she has given a dinner. The child who wept over the picture of the Christian martyrs in the arena because she was sorry for "that poor lion over there who hasn't got any Christian" was a true philosopher.

—Joseph Wood Krutch, *The Twelve Seasons.* Copyright by William Sloane Associates, Inc., 1949. Reprinted by permission of the publisher.

Very different was dapper Mr. Groce, our teacher of English composition and literature, a little plump man, with a keen, dry, cheerful, yet irritable disposition, a sparkling bird-like eye, and a little black mustache and diminutive chin-beard. I suspect that he was too intelligent to put up patiently with all the conventions. Had he not been a public-school teacher, dependent on the democratic hypocrisies of a government committee, he might have said unconventional things. This inner rebellion kept him from being sentimental, moralistic, or religious in respect to poetry; yet he *understood* perfectly the penumbra of emotion that good and bad poetry alike may drag after them in an untrained mind. He knew how to rescue the structural and rational beauties of a poem from the bog of private feeling. To me this was a timely lesson, for it was precisely sadness and religiosity and grandiloquence that first attached me in poetry; and perhaps I owe to Mr. Groce the beginnings of a capacity to distinguish the musical and expressive charm of poetry from its moral appeal. At any rate, at sixteen, I composed my first longish poem, in Spenser's measure, after *Childe Harold* and *Adonais,* full of pessimistic, languid, Byronic sentiments, describing the various kinds of superiority that Night has over Day. It got the prize.

—George Santayana, *Persons and Places,* Charles Scribner's Sons, New York, 1944. Reprinted by permission.

AWKWARDNESS AND OBSCURITY

39. Sentences that are confused, awkward, illogical, or obscure should be rewritten.

An awkward and confused sentence may occasionally be a sign of slovenly thinking, but it is probably more often a result of haste and carelessness in writing. A confused sentence may have several faults: the central thought may be lost in a tangle of modifiers; the thoughts may not be arranged properly; the words used may be inexact, ambiguous, or inappropriate; several constructions may be telescoped into one. See also section 34.

If the fault in the sentence can be diagnosed and identified, the instructor will refer you to the right section in this handbook, where you can learn the principle involved and find out how sentences like the one you wrote can be repaired. But sometimes a sentence is so bad that it isn't worth saving. You can do better if you chuck it into the waste basket and start over again. Get your mind focused on what you are trying to say, and then say it as simply and directly as you can. If you cannot say it in one sentence use two or three—but make your thought clear.

Confused:

My belief is that if more emphasis was stressed in college on extemporary speaking, the graduating student would be better prepared to face people of social prominence and college professors.

Revised:

I believe that colleges should stress courses in extemporary speaking in order to give their graduates more confidence and social ease.

Confused:

The word "laureate" comes from the Greeks when they used laurels to crown certain people.

Revised:

The word "laureate" comes from the language of the ancient Greeks, who used a laurel crown as a mark of special honor.

Confused:

In high school not much need for correct punctuation and principles is stressed, but in college punctuation and correct forms are closely criticized.

Revised:

Correct punctuation and the principles of good writing are stressed more in college courses than in high-school courses.

Confused:

Muskrats work on the dikes before we get to them by burrowing through between two ponds and thus connect them when their contents are supposed to be kept separate.

Revised:

Muskrats burrow tunnels through the dikes between the ponds. Through these openings the water flows from one pond to another.

Exercise

Exercise 1. Revise the following sentences.

1. He describes in a realistic way about the things he has experienced in the slums of a big city.
2. Many people have sacrificed wonderful professions because of simple misconceptions of their judgment.
3. The next day you climb out of bed, dead tired, joints stiff, and the horrible memory of having only four hours sleep.
4. Privacy hindered my studying while in high school because living in a house where there are many children it is very hard to secure privacy.
5. We can't always receive the best end of the deal because if everyone was perfect what kind of world would this be?
6. In the race for longevity of life among plants and animals it is possible that a few trees may hold the championship.
7. College can also equip me with reasons that I can succeed in any vocation I undertake.
8. The courage to go forward and sticking to your own conviction, in spite of other people's opinion, is a thing that is the hardest to do but a point that you should always think about.
9. My parents are very conservative, although my mother has a broader view on the modern generation of today.
10. Having never attended college before gives me the opportunity to develop to the fullest extent my study habits and idle time.

THE PARAGRAPH

ADEQUATE DEVELOPMENT

40a. Effective presentation of ideas requires paragraphs of suitable length.

Rarely do college freshmen write paragraphs that are too long; their chief difficulty is finding enough to say so that their paragraphs will not resemble a series of stunted sentences.

If a writer has three or four paragraphs on every page of his theme paper, his paragraphs are too short. If he splits up a five-hundred-word essay into ten or twelve paragraphs, his paragraphs are too short. The paragraphs of a newspaper story are short, it is true; so are the paragraphs of a business letter. But we are not speaking of those special types of writing when we say "expository" writing. In expository writing it is customary to develop ideas more fully, or to group ideas into larger units than in news stories or in letters. In expository writing, a series of very short paragraphs is an indication of malnutrition; the paragraphs need to be fed details to make them effective.

If your instructor refers you to this section, rewrite your paper. Start with a plan, or an outline, which calls for a limited number of facts or ideas. Your trouble may be too ambitious a subject. Cut it down to fit your space. Then write a thesis sentence stating your central idea. Write a topic sentence for each paragraph. With these as your guide, proceed to make your paper interesting by means of details, concrete examples, illustrations, comparisons, specific instances, reasons—all those things which transform a skeleton into writing that is alive.

An analysis of paragraphs taken from student papers will make the principle clearer.

Undeveloped paragraph:

The biggest problem that has arisen from this war is the loss of earning power for some individuals who have sacrificed legs, arms. and hands for their country, but some steps have been taken to find a solution for this problem. [This is vague, undeveloped, and unconvincing.]

Rewritten paragraph:

One of the biggest post-war problems, what to do for the veterans whose earning power has been curtailed through loss of arms, hands, or legs, is being solved. One G.I. Joe thought his useful life was ended when he lost an arm from an explosion at Hickam Field. Who would ever want a one-armed mechanic? But the Briggs Clarifier Company hired him upon his discharge from the hospital. His employer said it took five weeks to get the wounded look out of his eyes. Soon his untiring efforts and hard work brought him an adequate income. He became a clerk, later a draftsman, and now he is a service engineer. Another man lost both his hands on Tarawa. Now, equipped with two plastic hands, he is studying to become a hardware salesman.

Undeveloped paragraph:

Happiness cannot be expressed in words. It is something which must be felt to be understood. It cannot be told to someone else. It may consist of various things which mean one thing to one person but nothing to another person. [This is vague and general. It is unconvincing.]

Rewritten paragraph:

Happiness is too intangible a thing to put into words and confine on paper; I can only give examples of the moments when I find it. [Notice how the topic sentence prepares the reader for development by examples.] Happiness may begin on a clear, cold morning, when we burst from the house with shivering and screams about the weather. Then the lawns are fields of white spears; the rooftops are white slopes smothered in fog as the first slanting rays of the sun strike them. Shrill notes of a clarinet being practised sound on the cold air; the lesser sounds blend in—the tramp of uniformed students marching and swearing and singing, the laughter of girls. On these cold mornings happiness comes to sing and purr beneath some radiant warmth inside me, and only meanness can drive it away. Another kind of happiness may come when I dance to one of the Count's wonderful dirges. My body, with that of my partner, is lost in movement and rhythm. My partner is right too, that one with black hair and broad shoulders who sings tenor. Then I feel a gaiety and lightness, and I have a misty satisfaction that I am wearing my new suit, and the bass fiddler is a jolly fat fellow.

Some scrappy paragraphs are the result of the student's failure to think in larger units. The writer fails to determine his central idea, and he fails to recognize his miniature paragraphs as merely parts of his topic idea.

Scrappy paragraphs:

Father and Mother marveled at the way my sister Lois and I got along; they still do in fact. They are proud of the family unity we show.

When Lois married, I was as thrilled and happy as she, I am sure. I think I knew better than anyone else what a wonderful wife she would be. Her marriage is an example to me.

Although my sister never attended college, she has encouraged me greatly. I am working to live up to the high standards she set for me, and I am constantly hoping that some day I can in some way repay her.

[Try combining under a topic sentence like this: *My sister Lois has been a companion and an example to me.*]

The buzzard usually glides over wooded areas in search for food because a domestic animal is more likely to meet a mishap in the forest than out in a plain pasture. Also one will find buzzards around the sloughs in the summer because the water is drying up and the buzzard will feed on the dead fish.

The buzzard lives in a nest on top of high cliffs and in tree tops.

It is against the law to shoot buzzards because they salvage the animals that have died in the woods through an accident.

[Try combining these three paragraphs under a topic sentence which makes a statement about the feeding and nesting habits of buzzards.]

I suppose any mother is happy and proud when her daughters surprise her by cooking a meal. I know that my mother always is. This is one way in which we like to make her happy.

Mother always remembers kindness, whether it be in thoughts and actions, and always forgets the unkindness of others. She appreciates having us cook for her.

[Try constructing a topic sentence about Mother's appreciation of a kind act.]

40b. *Concrete details help to make a paragraph interesting and effective.*

The tendency of beginners is to write in generalizations and abstractions. In picturing a scene—"The closing hour at the cafe is always a scene of great confusion." What actually is going on? Why not make us see—hear and smell, too—the various details of that confusion? In criticism—"I like this poem." Why do you like it? Because it makes you think, or because it repeats what you have always believed? Because it irritates you? or because it soothes you? In presentation of character—"My father is an honest man." How is he honest? What does he do that shows honesty? Drag him out on the stage and let us watch him being honest. In discussions of college problems—"College men are more conventional and conservative than college women." Give us examples—many of them. Let us see these college men and women in situations that require choice; let us see how they act and what they think in relation to political questions, to books, to art, to social morality. Give the reader proof. Give him the evidence you have observed.

Here are several excerpts from freshman papers to show how the writers have used details.

Before:

A little old woman came out of the house and slowly made her way down the hill to the water's edge.

After:

An old woman with a face like a crumpled leaf crept out of the grey, weather-worn house that frowned down on the sea from beneath two ragged pines. She was dressed in black, and she carried a small pillow, a book, a red plaid blanket, and a black cotton umbrella under one arm. Leaning heavily on a silver-headed cane while she pricked her quavering way along the slippery, grass-grown path that squirmed over the bluff and down to the sea, she looked like a fairy-tale cricket, a lame one.

Before:

The closing hour at the cafe where I work is always a scene of great confusion. The juke-box is playing, the customers are shouting their orders, everyone is impatient and in a hurry.

After:

The air is blue and suffocating with smoke. Everyone screeches orders at once, and someone wants me to turn up the juke-box because the crowd cannot hear the music. He will probably play either "Minnie the Moocher," which isn't musical or soothing to the nerves, or "'Take It Easy," advice which under the circumstances is highly ironic. One of the soldiers, who must have been on the campus for several weeks, wants to know where the Pi Phi house is; another, who is obviously exaggerating, says that he has waited ten minutes for his hamburger. Some helpful soul says, "Just give me anything; I don't care what," or "What do you have that's good?" Someone wonders what kinds of shakes we have, and after I have named all fourteen flavors, says, "I'll take vanilla." At 9:30 we are out of glasses, silverware, and ice cream, and someone has spilled a cup of coffee on the floor. Then the carbonator freezes, and while I am concentrating on defrosting it, a mathematical genius shoves a handful of coins at me and drones, "I want five cents out of this, fifteen out of this, forty out of this, with two nickles change, a hamburger out of this, three shakes from this, and change this bill to three ones, two fifty-cent pieces, two quarters, four dimes, a nickle, and five pennies—have you got that?" A girl who has been lounging in a booth all evening elbows her way to the counter and shouts, "I have to be in by ten. Will you get me six hamburgers to go right away? One with lettuce and no mayonnaise, one with mayonnaise and no lettuce, one with both and mustard, one with nothing but meat, and onions in the other two. I don't know what else they want besides onions. Hurry, please!" Some shrewd thinker will corner me, demanding to know if we don't have some cigarettes hidden under the counter. And then—as suddenly as it came, the mob has vanished, leaving stacks of dirty dishes, whatever silverware could not be used at home, and a quaint little professor to tell us fish stories until long after order has been restored.

UNITY IN PARAGRAPH

41a. Effective paragraphs of exposition observe the principle of unity.

A paragraph of exposition is a unit of structure. It deals with one idea, or with one phase of a larger idea. Its unity is destroyed by digressions from the main thought, by the addition of irrelevant details, or by afterthoughts that should have been disposed of earlier in the composition.

If your instructor refers you to this section, you may do one of two things. If the detail which destroys the unity of your paragraph is a minor digression, you may cross it out. If your paragraph is a muddle of two or more major ideas, you may select the one idea which you intend to develop and rewrite the entire paragraph. See section 40 for help in building up and presenting an idea in paragraph form.

The following are examples of paragraphs that violate unity. Some people object to studying other people's mistakes; most people learn in that way more easily than by making mistakes of their own. Most of us, however, are fated to learn in both ways.

Well-built and comfortable houses can be built for a small amount of money. Any family with small means may build a well-equipped home a short distance from the city limits for less than they could live on in a run-down apartment. Materials for building are also important. Houses are more and more being built with steel frames. The windows are usually steel sashes. The outside may be almost any type—brick, stone, wood, or stucco. [This paragraph breaks in half after the second sentence, since the writer seems to have forgotten his original idea, that families of small means can build inexpensive houses.]

Little is known about McGuffey's early theories of education because he failed to write down his sermons and lectures. It is known, however, that he felt the need of a systematic education and textbooks. He liked to do his teaching outside. He would seat his children on logs. He had a log for each subject. The best students would sit at the head of the log and the poorest at the foot. He would often question his students until they could see the truth or falsity of their reasoning. By these methods he encouraged the competitive spirit among his students, and taught them to think logically and speak clearly. He established the tastes of four fifths of the nation's school children in regard to literature, morality, social development, and—next to the Bible—their religion. [The last sentence violates paragraph unity. It is about McGuffey's teaching, but it is not about the particular aspect dealt with by this paragraph. The central topic of this paragraph deals with McGuffey's early ideas about education as they can be known from his methods.]

Life on the farm is an eternal battle against nature. [Topic sentence.] There is always the rush to harvest the crops and to get next year's grain planted before the fall rains start. To get this accomplished the farmer must be out at work by daybreak. Fruits and vegetables have to be gathered before the early frost; hence everyone is bustling around from morning till night. Fall is beautiful when the leaves on the trees change color and then fall off. Winter sends its warming cover over the frozen ground. This causes the animals to hunt for something to eat. There is nothing, so the farmer has to feed them. After his day's work is done, the farmer puts on his slippers, reclines on the davenport in front of the fireplace, and spends a peaceful evening reading. Within a few months spring begins with its beautiful flowers and green grass. The cows give more milk so the farmer has more work to do. After the first spring rain, the corn must be cultivated. As summer approaches, the farmer begins to worry for fear that the sun will come up and cook the grain before it is fully developed, or maybe a thunderstorm will come up thus causing his hay crop to rot. [You will say that this is pretty bad. It *is* bad writing. The writer of this has completely forgotten what he had started out to say. Instead of being an "eternal battle," life in this paragraph becomes a pleasant and exciting experience—which it probably is, but that is not what the writer set out to prove. The cure for this sort of muddled writing is a going back to first principles: keep your eye on your main purpose; say one thing at a time.]

41b. *The topic sentence is a useful device for securing unity in a paragraph of exposition.*

When your instructor refers you to this section, you should underline the topic sentence of your paragraph or write a topic sentence if it is implied in your paragraph. It is quite probable that your instructor is trying to make you see that your paragraph lacks unity, or a close-knit structure, faults which your attention to a topic sentence would help to correct.

Not all expository paragraphs, of course, begin with a topic sentence. In some paragraphs the summary is left to be made by the reader; the paragraph details do aim at one central idea, but they are not conveniently tied together by a topic sentence. In some paragraphs, however, it seems as if all that held the ideas together was a mutual friendship, or a common interest in the same subject. Such paragraphs are hard to write—successfully—and even harder to teach! The fact remains that the most common, the most typical paragraph of exposition has a topic sentence, usually expressed somewhere near the beginning, either after the transitional phrases or combined with them.

What has been said here, and on pages 79–96, about the topic sentence applies primarily to fully developed paragraphs of exposition, not to special paragraphs, nor to paragraphs of narration or description.

In the following selections from papers written by college freshmen, observe how much the supplied topic sentence adds to the clearness and effectiveness of each paragraph.

[The facts surrounding James Smithson and his connection with scientific work are interesting.] Never in his life did Smithson visit the United States. He was born in France in 1765 and was educated at Pembroke College, Oxford, where he received his M.A. degree in chemistry and mineralogy. Later his work as an analytical chemist won him a membership in the Royal Society. His mineralogical specimens, numbering more than 10,000, became the property of the Institution after its founding. He willed his property to his nephew, Henry James Hungerford, and in default of Hungerford's direct heirs, Smithson bequeathed it to the United States for the founding of an institution to bear his name. He died in Genoa in 1829; his body now lies interred in the institution which he hoped would make his name live in unforgotten glory.

[Termites are widely distributed throughout the world.] Living species occur in all the regions except the Arctic and the Antarctic. The African or Ethiopian region is richest in number of species. Termites also occur in the temperate regions of Europe and North America. Certain species have been found as far north as the Quesnal Lake region in British Columbia. Others have been found in Ontario, Canada. These same species have been found at high altitudes in the Rocky Mountains and the Pacific Coast range. To the south, Patagonia seems to be the limit of their distribution.

Refer also to pages 79–96 for examples of various types of paragraphs with expressed topic sentences.

COHERENCE IN PARAGRAPHS

42a. A skillful arrangement of details in a paragraph helps to produce effective paragraphs.

Study the section on "The Paragraph," pages 96–99, for an understanding of the various ways in which material may be arranged in expository writing. If your instructor refers you to this section, he may wish to suggest one of the following methods as being better than the one you have used. Rewrite the paragraph in conformity with his suggestion.

1. Try presenting your material from "the general to the particular." Most paragraphs of exposition follow this order. The writer states his general idea first in a topic sentence, and then he presents the reasons, details, examples, illustrations, and so on, which make his general statement understandable and convincing.

2. Try the "order of enumeration." In your topic sentence state that your idea may be seen from two points of view, that it has three important aspects, that you are going to use four illustrations, that you have two excellent reasons for believing it, and so on. You can see various uses for this method. You should also see that this order may help you to write a clear, compact, and well-organized paragraph.

The following topic sentences from the works of professional writers demonstrate how this method is used:

All social organization is of two forms.
There were also three less desirable results of the Peace Conference.
There are two uses of knowledge.
Among the leading purposes of law today we may list three.

Remember, however, that this sort of beginning gives a formal tone to your writing. Use the device occasionally, when the material of your paragraph is adapted to classification and enumeration.

3. Try the "time order." If details can be arranged in the order of happening, there is no particular advantage to be gained by trying any other arrangement. The order of time (often called the "chronological" order), or happening, produces a clear and orderly paragraph. It is inherently simple, perhaps elementary—but it has the unquestioned virtue of being almost foolproof. It may be used with material that at first glance does not arrange itself in the order of time. For instance, "How to Train a Horse" can become "How I Trained My Horse"; "Academic Freedom" can become "The Historical Development of the Concept of Academic Freedom"; "The Right to Work" can become "How the Notion Grew Up that a Job Is Property."

4. Try using the "inductive order." It may be that your paragraph idea should not be stated bluntly in the first sentence. The reader may not be ready for it. Prepare him for it by using your details, your examples and instances, to guide his thoughts, so that when you are ready to use your summarizing topic sentence he will also be ready to accept it.

42b. *Paragraphs are made more effective by the skillful use of connectives and transitions.*

If your instructor refers you to this section, read also the section on transitions, pages 97–98, and study the examples given here.

There are five main ways of linking ideas—by using conjunctions and transitional words and phrases, by using pronouns, by repeating key words, by using a summarizing word, and by expressing similar thoughts in parallel structure.

1. *CONJUNCTIONS AND TRANSITIONAL EXPRESSIONS*

The following is a brief list of transitional words and phrases. You must not think that this list is complete; neither should you assume that the natural, spontaneous phrases of transition that occur to you as you write are either incorrect or unliterary.

on the other hand	conversely	finally
in the second place	of course	after all
on the contrary	in conclusion	I mean
at the same time	to sum up	indeed
in particular	moreover	next
in spite of this	in addition	similarly
in like manner	for example	again
and so again	for instance	I repeat
as I have said	furthermore	and truly
in contrast to this	accordingly	meanwhile

Examples of transitions:

In like manner, all kinds of deficient and impolitic usages are referred to the national love of trade; though, *oddly enough,* it would be a weighty charge against a foreigner that he regarded the Americans as a trading people.—Charles Dickens.

I am not blaming or excusing anyone here. . . . I find, *for instance,* that prejudice, essentially, is worse on the prejudiced than on their targets.—Louis Adamic.

There were then very few regular troops in the kingdom. A town, *therefore,* which could send forth, at an hour's notice, twenty thousand men . . . —Thomas Babington Macaulay.

Their [the immigrants'] children, *however*, follow the general increase which is found in the American population. *Furthermore*, the form of the body of immigrants' children undergoes certain changes. . . .—Franz Boas.

2. PRONOUNS REFERRING TO ANTECEDENTS IN THE PRECEDING SENTENCES

Examples:

In the summer, Father had his usual two or three weeks of vacation. *These* were spent usually at our cabin in the mountains.

I know a writer of newspaper editorials. *Himself* a liberal, *he* has to grind out a thousand words daily which reflect the ultra conservative policy of the paper for which *he* works. *He* keeps a record like a batting chart. . . . —Stuart Chase.

3. KEY WORDS REPEATED

Examples:

Nothing in the way of civilization is inborn, as are the forms and workings of our bodies. Everything that goes to make up civilization must be acquired anew in infancy and childhood, by each and all of us.—James Harvey Robinson.

This is all true, of course, but I am unregenerate enough to think that the purpose in studying any language is to speak it and read it. I know from experience that you cannot read a language unless you can speak it. I know that our students are not taught to speak Latin or Greek. I am therefore not surprised that they can read neither language.—John Erskine, "An Education To Be Used." *New York Times Magazine,* Jan. 20, 1939. By permission of the author.

4. USING A SUMMARIZING WORD LIKE ALL

Example:

A popularity among millions, a facile agreement with readers whom the author pretends to lead, but whom in reality he anxiously follows, an erroneous judgment that little interests of your moment are permanent human interests—*all these* come under the test of time.—Hilaire Belloc.

In the light of this equality, we know that the virtues most cherished by free people—love of truth, pride of work, devotion to country—*all* are treasures equally precious in the lives of the most humble and of the most exalted. The men who mine coal and fire furnaces and balance ledgers and turn lathes and pick cotton and heal the sick and plant corn—*all* serve as proudly, and as profitably, for America as the statesmen who draft treaties or the legislators who enact laws.—President Eisenhower's Inaugural Address, January, 1953.

5. *PARALLEL STRUCTURE (See also section 35 and pages 67–71 in Chapter II, "The Sentence.")*

Examples:

We had hated the physical suffering and horror of war. . . . We had hated the febrile emotionalism, the propaganda lies and exaggerations. . . . We had hated the intellectual suppressions of war. . . . We had hated war's release of the most primitive passions. . . . We had hated, or thought we had hated, war's complete overriding of the individual. . . .—Walter Millis, *Zero Hour.*

POINT OF VIEW

43. *Maintain a consistent point of view.*

The issues involved in this section may be said to include everything you have learned about writing in this book. To maintain a consistent point of view is to be sensitive to all the principles our handbook has outlined. Sentence structure and grammar, appropriateness of vocabulary, even mechanics and spelling—all these have a direct bearing on your central problem as a writer: that of producing a consistent, controlled prose style.

43a. *Maintain a consistent point of view in time and space.*

One way to understand the phrase "point of view" is to think of it quite literally, as a "point" from which one "views" one's subject. In section 34 we spoke of some dangers of shifting point of view within sentences. The same principles apply here to larger units: paragraphs and whole papers. Having chosen a particular "point" from which the material is to be "viewed," the writer owes it to his reader to maintain his position, and not to skip around unless he does so for a very good reason. This injunction applies to points in *time* as well as in *space*. At its simplest, it means that a paragraph in the present tense should be followed by a paragraph in the past tense only if the break in point of view is deliberate and desirable. Similarly, if a scene is to be described from the vantage point of one particular spot, or through the eyes of one particular person, then an abrupt removal to another spot or another person, simply to suit the author's whim or convenience, is sure to disturb a careful reader.

Here are some passages from a brief anecdote, written by a college student, that will help us to define some of these difficulties.

> The small gray Chevrolet pulled up to the side of the road and halted as the hitchhiker dropped his solicitous thumb and moved to the car. He looked inquiringly at the driver, his companion, and the back seat, and opened the door.
>
> "Going to Baker?"
>
> The driver, decked out in blue denims and with a short peaked cap covering a head of silver hair brushed down on the sides, gave a nod and replied, "Sure am. Hop in back."
>
> The stranger got in and found the back seat already taken by a large German police dog, stretched out full length on the seat. His surprised grunt came just as the farmer's companion, apparently his wife, turned around and rasped, "Don't worry about him, son, he's pretty friendly. Get down, Boss."
>
> The object of her order gave a perturbed gesture with his front paws and jumped to the floor as the new rider took over the back seat. He glanced at the backs of his two benefactors.

The *point* from which we are asked to *view* this scene is, of course, the physical position occupied by the hitchhiker. Notice how we follow him about, and when he is in the car, we too see the car from the back seat where he is situated. This is logical and proper enough. The woman in the front seat is "apparently" the farmer's wife; we know no more about her than the hitchhiker does. But note too that we are not so placed as to know what's going on in the hitchhiker's mind. The speaker refers to him as "the stranger" and "the new rider." We are observing the situation from outside any one person's consciousness, and this too is part of our point of view. The writer has placed us in a certain position of distance from "the stranger," and he must be careful to maintain that distance unless he has a good reason for changing it.

The story goes on:

> The dog was resting, head on his paws, with his eyes fixed on the new rider. He was a massive beast, and the result of good care showed in a well-filled body that rested firm under a sleek gray coat. The stranger passed his eyes from the dog's rump along the line of his back to his head, and noticing the canine gaze still upon him, glanced briefly at the long, angular jaws.
>
> The gaze prompts a sudden thought, and half to himself he comments, "That dog must have been raised in the Arctic."

Here a change in point of view has taken place—a change that is probably too abrupt, though it is not absolutely drastic. We have moved closer to the "stranger": first we are aware that he notices "the canine gaze"; then, with a curious and awkward change of tense, we are told that a "sudden thought" is prompted inside him. A few sentences later, however, as the author describes a conversation taking place in the car, we find this sentence:

> "Just what breed of dog is this?" came from the back seat.

Can you see what has happened? We have suddenly been catapulted, in our point of view, from the back seat to the front seat, right over the upholstery! The scene that we saw from one point in space, we now see—for no good reason—from quite another point. And a few sentences later, the writer slips even further from his original place next to the hitchhiker as he tells us:

> The woman was intent on continuing the discussion, but then the idea of some new plan faded from her mind and she turned full around to face the front and the road unwinding ahead of them.

As you can easily see, we have now come almost full circle, for when we know what is going on inside the woman's mind, we have been shunted about inside that automobile in a pretty thoroughgoing fashion. (Only the farmer has remained inscrutable!) In the hands of a skilled professional writer, such shifts might be meaningful and desirable, but for most beginning writers a shift in point of view is perilous. Though the problem is most obviously demanding in fiction, as in this example, it is vital in all writing and must be watched carefully.

43b. *Maintain a consistent tone toward your reader.*

You will recall from our discussion in Chapter 1 that when a writer selects language to express what he has to say, he inevitably manufacturers as he does so a particular speaking "voice," a kind of personality through which he projects his meaning. This dramatic identity, this mouthpiece, is a crucial aspect of a point of view. The voice must suggest by its language a certain relation to the reader—informal or formal, intimate, friendly, hostile. It is this relation with the reader that we call *tone.*

By leafing through any daily newspaper, you can discover a number of different voices that make their appeal to you with many different tones. Some of them, as in the more formal news articles or editorials, hold you at arm's length, or they orate to you as if from a pulpit:

A strong possibility has arisen that the artistic administration of the new center will be taken over by the Metropolitan Opera Company.

A stern repudiation of these irresponsible and even un-American tactics is recommended to every thinking citizen.

Note the use of passive verbs in these sentences—a device that usually leads to a formal tone. On the other hand, you can be slapped on the back by other voices as they assume an intimacy with you which may indeed be quite unwelcome.

Remember that heat in October? Sure burned us! You should see the huge stock of suits and coats we *didn't* sell!

Sometimes, in other passages, the voice that addresses you may be so extremely detached and formal as hardly to exist at all, except as something dry, crisp, and impersonal:

Pursuant to the provisions of the amended Certificate of Incorporation, notice is hereby given that the Board of Directors will dispose of said property on Wednesday, 16 May, at ten o'clock in the forenoon.

These examples will suggest the enormous range of possibilities in manipulating tone. The problem of consistency, of course, is simply not to change personalities as you move from paragraph to paragraph.

43c. Maintain a consistent attitude toward your subject matter.

A familiar use of the phrase "point of view" occurs in a question like "What is his point of view on that?"—meaning, What is his attitude, his value judgment, his opinion? This aspect of the problem is also part of the character or voice you are creating with your language. Consistency in attitude is simply a matter of taking a stand and sticking to it, without wavering or contradictory statements. If you have expressed appreciation for the United States foreign policy in your first paragraph, do not deride it in your fourth unless the intervening sentences demonstrate and defend the change in attitude. The part of speech to watch with particular care in expressing attitude is, of course, the adjective. A great many adjectives state by definition a speaker's approval of the modified noun; examples are *attractive, beautiful, industrious, virtuous, warm-hearted.* Such adjectives are called *honorific;* they almost always commit their users to a favorable view of the subject. On the other hand, many adjectives act by definition in just the opposite way: *unattractive, ugly, lazy, evil, cold-hearted.* Such adjectives are called *pejorative,* and they are very difficult to use without suggesting disapproval. Between these extremes, there are infinite subtle variations of approval and disapproval to be controlled by the skilled writer.

Exercises

Exercise 1. Look through the opening paragraphs of a short story, and define carefully the time and place of the narrator's point of view. Show what shifts in position there may be, and try to decide why such shifts are there.

Exercise 2. Take half a dozen paragraphs from today's newspaper to show different speaking voices in action with markedly different tones. Show what assumptions the reader is invited to adopt about his own relation to the various voices.

Exercise 3. Select one of the newspaper paragraphs that is especially informal in tone, and rewrite it formally.

Exercise 4. Find a voice in the newspaper that is particularly distant or detached from the reader; rewrite the paragraph to bring the speaker closer to the reader.

Exercise 5. Show in all these paragraphs just what words are used to express *attitude* toward what is being talked about. Rewrite two or three of these, reversing the attitude expressed by changing the adjectives and other language.

A GLOSSARY OF USAGE

44. *This section may be consulted for information about current usage.*

When you consult this glossary (a collection of notes and comments on words and expressions), please be sure to read first the section called "Levels of Usage and Functional Varieties of English," pages 13–15, so that you will better understand what is meant by some of the terms used here. From the point of view of the modern scientific observer of language in action, "correctness" and "incorrectness" in English usage are relative terms. As a matter of fact, the use of these terms is discouraged. Linguists prefer to speak of the "appropriateness" of a word or expression rather than of its "correctness." An expression is appropriate in a certain situation, on a certain occasion, in a certain locality, among certain people; it may be inappropriate in another situation, on another occasion, in another locality, among other people.[1]

No one can blame the college student for being slightly bewildered by this apparent complexity of standards. The student should keep in mind, however, the fact that out of the vast store of English words and idioms, only a relatively few are, as it were, restricted. Most of them are appropriate on any occasion, formal or informal, anywhere, under any conditions. They belong to what we call "standard English." One does not begin to use a foreign language when he stops speaking standard informal English

[1] John S. Kenyon, "Cultural Levels and Functional Varieties of English," *College English,* vol. 10, pp. 31–36 (Oct., 1948).

and begins writing standard formal English. It is still the same language. The minor differences between the two varieties we have observed and analyzed many times in this book.

In this section—the glossary—we are concerned primarily with a few words and phrases appropriate usually to informal, especially to conversational varieties of English which students inadvertently carry over into formal situations. The problem of usage is not a moral but a social one, and the penalties for sprinkling formal writing with expressions appropriate to informal speech only are largely social penalities. At times there may be no penalties; at other times social penalties may be cruel, as any girl who arrives at a party in the wrong kind of dress can testify. The penalties can be economic, too, since an applicant for a job is often judged —it may be hastily and unjustly but still judged—by the language he uses. If one were giving the student advice about certain disputed items of usage, one might quote Alexander Pope's words:

> Be not the first by whom the new are tried,
> Nor yet the last to lay the old aside.

A, an. Use *a* before a word beginning with any consonant sound except silent *h*. *Examples:* a book, a tree, a European country, a union, a utility. Use *an* before a word beginning with a vowel sound. *Examples:* an American, an elephant, an irate man, an onion, an hour, an honorable person.

Accept, except. These words are often confused because of a slight resemblance in sound. *Accept* means "to receive," "to agree to." *Except* means "to exclude," "to make an exception." *Examples:* He accepted our offer. At the last moment, she was excepted from the honor list.

Ad. This clipped form, and other like it, such as *math, prof, exam, auto,* are appropriate in informal speech. *Ad* sometimes appears in informal writing. In formal writing, *advertisement* is generally used.

Affect, effect. Confusion may result from the similarity of sound. *Affect,* as a verb, means "to influence." Its noun use is too rare to be a source of trouble. *Effect,* as a verb, means "to bring about." As a noun, *effect* means "result." *Examples:* The strike will *affect* the steel industry. The *effects* of the strike will be great. The labor board will try to *effect* a settlement.

Aggravate. *Aggravate* means "to intensify," "to increase." Colloquially it means "to irritate," "to annoy." *Colloquial:* The speaker's mannerisms aggravated everyone. *Formal:* The speaker's mannerisms annoyed everyone.

Agree to, agree with. You *agree that* something is true. You *agree to* a proposal. You *agree with* a person. One thing *agrees with* (corresponds with) another.

Ain't. Never used in standard written English.

Allow. Means "to permit." Dialectal for *assert, say, think, believe.*

All right. See *alright.*

All the farther, all the faster. Frequently used in conversational English. In formal or literary English, *as far as, as fast as* are more commonly used.

Allude, refer. *Allude* means to refer to a person or thing indirectly or by suggestion. *Example:* When the teacher spoke of "budding Swifts," every student wondered to whom he was alluding. To *refer* to something means to mention it specifically. *Example:* I shall now take time to refer to the question of smoking on the campus.

Allusion, illusion. An *allusion* is an indirect reference. (See *allude.*) An *illusion* is a deceptive appearance or false notion. The two words have nothing in common except a slight resemblance in sound.

Already, all ready. *Already,* an adverb, means "by this time," "before this time." *All ready,* two words, means "entirely ready" or that everyone is ready. *Examples:* The war had already started. The men were all ready to go.

Alright. The correct spelling is *all right. All right,* according to the editors of *Webster's New International,* is colloquial in the sense of *satisfactory, correct,* or *yes;* slang when used merely for emphasis. *Webster's New Collegiate* labels it *colloquial.* The *ACD* and *WNWD* list it without any label. But of course its hyphenated use before a noun, as in She is an *all-right* girl, is questionable.

Altogether, all together. *Altogether* (one word), an adverb, means "entirely," "completely," "on the whole." *All together* (two words) means "in a group." *Examples:* Father was altogether too generous. The brothers were all together again.

Among, between. *Among* is used with three or more things or persons, as: Among those present were the Smiths; they divided the property among six relatives; talk this over among yourselves. *Between* may refer to two things, as: Let nothing stand between you and me; much must be done between sunrise and breakfast. *Between* may also refer to more than two things when it "brings the things or persons severally and individually into the relation expressed," as: a treaty between three nations, between the leaves of a book. See Pooley, *Teaching English Usage,* pp. 135–137 or Bergen Evans and Cornelia Evans, *A Dictionary of Contemporary English Usage,* p. 60.

Amount, number. *Amount* refers to quantity; *number* refers to things that can be counted. *Examples:* The number (*not* amount) of students, the amount of trouble, the amount of coal.

A.M., P.M., a.m., p.m. Should not be used for *in the morning, in the afternoon.* Correct with name of the hour. *Examples:* I am leaving this afternoon (*not* this p.m.).

And etc. *Etc.,* for *et cetera,* means "and so forth." *And etc.* would mean "and and so forth." In ordinary writing it is better to write out the abbreviation. When you do use it, do not spell it *ect.*

Any place, anyplace. *Anyplace,* for *anywhere,* is labeled *colloquial* by the *New International Dictionary.* None of the desk dictionaries lists it. Evans (p. 36) says it is acceptable English. Most people would shy away from its use in formal writing. Similar colloquial forms are *no place* for *nowhere, everyhow* for *in every way, every place* for *everywhere, some place* for *somewhere.*

Anyway, anyways. *Anyway* is preferred in more formal situations.

Anywheres, everywheres. Dialect and colloquial forms of *anywhere, everywhere.*

Apt, likely, liable. *Apt* suggests a habitual or inherent tendency. *Likely* suggests a probability. *Liable* suggests a chance, a risk of some sort, or a danger. But in American speech all three are often used to mean a probability and nothing more. See *Webster's Dictionary of Synonyms*, p. 67. *Examples:* She is apt to be irritable because she is not well. A cheerful boy is likely to succeed in that occupation. You are liable to break your neck if you try to climb that rock.

As. (1) Dialectal when used in place of *that* or *whether.*

I do not know whether (not *as*) I shall vote this year.
I cannot say that (not *as*) I care much for his verses.

(2) *As* in the sense of *because* is frowned upon by some writers. It is, however, widely current in speech and in many kinds of writing. It seems to be more appropriate with a clause that begins a sentence than with one that follows the main clause. Fowler, in *Modern English Usage,* p. 31, says that there is no objection to causal or explanatory *as*-clauses if they are placed before the main sentence. *Because* and *since* are stronger and more explicit than *as,* which is the least formal of the causal conjunctions. See "because," in *Webster's Dictionary of Synonyms,* p. 111.

As . . . as, so . . . as. In negative statements some careful writers prefer *so . . . as* to *as . . . as.* At present, *as . . . as* seems to be established in both speech and writing for both positive and negative statements. For negative statements in a very formal style, *so . . . as* is probably preferable. *Examples:* Your promise is as good as your bond. *Formal:* A vast army is not so important as a well-equipped air force. *Informal:* A vast army is not as important as a well-equipped air force.

At. Redundant, both in speech and writing, in such sentences as: Where are we at now? Where does he live at? Where at did you stop?

Awful, awfully. Colloquially, these words and *frightful, terribly,* *shocking, horrible,* and the "frightfully" abused favorite of college students, *disgusting,* are used as mild intensives. They mean little more than an accented *very.* In formal writing, *awful* and *awfully* should be saved for their precise meaning, which is used to express something that is full of awe or awe inspiring. *Examples:* I accept the awful responsibility of carrying on the war. The destroyers were tossed about like eggshells by the awful storm.

Badly. Used colloquially for *very much* or *very greatly* with words signifying *to want* or *to need. Example:* He needs a haircut badly.

Balance. When used for the *remainder, the rest,* it is usually considered colloquial. *Colloquial uses:* The balance of the crew will be released. We listened to records the balance of the evening. *Formal:* The rest of the crew will be released.

Bank on. In the sense of *rely upon* it is a colloquial idiom.

Being as, being that. Dialectal for *since, because. Example:* Since (*not* being as) it is long past midnight, we should abandon the search.

Beside, besides. According to present usage, *beside* is used as a preposition meaning "at the side of," as in: Please sit down beside me. *Besides* is ordinarily used as an adverb, meaning "in addition to," as in: There were no casualties besides the one reported earlier.

Blame on, blame it on. Labeled *colloquial* by *Webster's Collegiate.* Listed without usage label by the *ACD* and *WNWD.* Evans and Evans (p. 64) say it is a standard idiom.

Bunch. Colloquial when used to mean "several," "a group." *Examples:* We saw a group (*not* a bunch) of boys near the entrance. It was ascertained that several (*not* a bunch) of them belonged to the Broadway gang.

Bust, busted, bursted, burst. *Bust, busted,* and *bursted* are considered dialectal, inelegant, and slangy for *burst.* But he who has occasion to say he is *going on a bust* should not make matters worse by saying he is *going on a burst! Examples:* The dam burst (*not* busted). The whole building burst (*not* bursted) into flames.

But what, but that. These have been considered colloquial, but Evans and Evans say *but that* is standard literary English (pp. 77–78) in sentences like: I don't doubt but that he is disappointed, and that *but what* is not standard when it refers to a person, as: There is no one but what prays for peace. Most educated people, however, prefer a simple *that* instead of *but that* or *but what* in written English. *Example:* There is no doubt that (*not* but that *or* but what) the prime minister hopes to avoid war.

Calculate, reckon. Both are now U.S. colloquial or dialectal when used to mean *plan, think, expect.*

Can, may. In formal usage, *may* implies permission or possibility, *can* implies ability. In informal usage, *can* is very often used in the meaning of *may. Informal:* Mother, can I go now? Can't we stay up until midnight? No, you can't. *Formal:* Sir, may I go now? The delegate can speak three languages.

Can't hardly. A double negative, objectionable in formal situations, widely used in speech. Many people object to it strongly.

Cannot help but, can't help but. These forms are widely used in speech and by some writers in formal writing. Other writers object to these forms. See George O. Curme, *Syntax,* pp. 252–253. Evans and Evans (p. 218) say that "I cannot help but think" is the preferred idiom in the United States, but "I cannot help thinking" is the only acceptable form in Great Britain. If you keep your eyes open and your ears attuned, you will find both forms used by educated speakers and writers in this country. *Examples:* We cannot help feeling proud of our boys. We cannot help but feel proud of them.

Cause of. To say that the *cause of* something was *on account of* is a muddled construction. *Examples:* The cause of my late theme was my having (*not* on account of I had) too much work to do. The cause of my late theme was the fact that I had too much work to do. Both of these sentences, however, are awkward. It may be better to avoid the *cause of* construction entirely and simply say, "My theme is late because I had too much to do."

Compare to, compare with. *Compare to* means "to represent as similar." *Compare with* means "to examine the differences and similarities of two things." *Compare* is often used without any preposition. See *Webster's Dictionary of Synonyms,* p. 175. *Examples:* One may compare some men to wolves. One may compare the novels of Dreiser with those of Zola.

Complected. Not in standard use for *complexioned.*

Considerable. Should not be used for *considerably,* as: My golf improved considerably (*not* considerable) during the summer.

Contact. In the sense of "to communicate with" it is very widely used in speech and in writing, but some people object to it strongly, probably because it is overused. Such verbs as *meet, interview, speak to* may be substituted for *contact.*

Continual, continuous. If a difference exists between the meanings of these two words, it is that *continual* implies a continued succession or recurrence, and *continuous* implies unbroken continuity. (See *Webster's Dictionary of Synonyms,* p. 195.)

Contractions. Less appropriate in formal writing, where they are occasionally found, than in speech and informal writing, where they are entirely at home. *Examples:* I'd like to go, but I'm tired. Can't he explain it to you, or doesn't he care?

Could of. Illiterate for *could have.*

Couple. Colloquial for *two, a few, several. Colloquial:* A couple of men left the theater. *Formal:* Two (*or* several) men left the theater.

Criticize. May mean "to find fault with" but may also mean "to judge," "to review." See *Webster's Dictionary of Synonyms,* p. 210.

Crowd. Colloquial for *a set, clique. Formal:* She became acquainted with the country-club set (*not* crowd).

Cunning. An American colloquialism used to describe attractive children and other small animals. There is no exact equivalent in formal English.

Cute. See *cunning.* It is descriptive of something small and dainty and attractive, such as a child. It is appropriate in informal speech, although overused, and it seldom appears in writing.

Data, strata, phenomena. These are the plurals of *datum, stratum,* and *phenomenon.* At present these words seem to be in a transitional stage, inasmuch as some good writers and speakers use them as singular forms while others believe strongly that only the correct Latin forms should be used. There is no doubt, however, that a mixture of forms is undesirable, as: Although the data collected at the laboratory are vouched for by several scientists, much of it has to be restudied.

Date. A colloquialism for everything from a casual meeting to an assignation. It seems a pity that the English language is so poor that it does not have an acceptable word for a concept so important in the life of an undergraduate. After all, a *date* is not exactly an *appointment,* nor an *engagement*—certainly not an *assignation.* Nor could a college girl who brought her "date" to her mother's home find time to speak of him as "the male person with whom I have made a social engagement." *Beau* and *escort* are faintly reminiscent of crinoline and pantalets. And speaking of needed terms, where is the budding philologist or poet who will give us an acceptable expression for "girl friend" and "boy friend"?

Deal. Used figuratively in "a square deal" or "a new deal." Informal in the sense of "a commercial transaction" or "a political bargain."

Didn't ought. Similar to *hadn't ought,* which see.

Differ from, differ with. One thing *differs from* another. One person *differs with* another when he disputes or quarrels with him. One may also *differ from* a person when he disagrees with him. See *Webster's Dictionary of Synonyms,* p. 250.

Different from, different than. Both forms have been used by good writers. At present, *different from* seems to be preferred when a single word follows it, as in: His suggestion is different from mine. When a clause follows, many speakers and writers use *than* to avoid a roundabout construction, as in: This group of engineers will use a very different method of extracting the ore than the old Quebec miners used. (Instead of *different from that which*) See Pooley, *Teaching English Usage,* pp. 166–168; Margaret Nicholson, *A Dictionary of American English Usage,* p. 129.

Doesn't, don't. The accepted contraction of *does not* is *doesn't.* The contraction of *do not* is *don't. Example:* Harry doesn't (*not* don't) live here any more.

Double negative. The so-called "double negative" is a minor trouble spot in the writing of college students. To clarify the subject, we may consider three types. One type, in which one negative nullifies the other, is entirely correct and appropriate in any type of speech or writing. This type is usually ignored in any discussion of double negatives. *Examples:* The brief rest was not unwelcome. They are not unco-operative. These people are not uneducated. The expression is really not incorrect.

A second type, in which two or more negatives are used to make the negative more emphatic, belongs to substandard speech. There is slight occasion to worry about it in the writing of college students. *Examples:* I don't know nothin'. Nobody never tells me nothing. We ain't seen nobody. Teacher, I can't write no themes!

A third type appears as a "concealed" double negative in a very small number of expressions like *can't hardly, didn't hardly, wouldn't scarcely.* These expressions are not appropriate in writing. They are heard widely in speech.

Dove. The most generally used form is *dived. Webster's New International* labels *dove* as colloquial chiefly U. S. There is no doubt that *dove* has been widely used in speech, and occasionally in writing. There is also no doubt that many educated people object to it. See Pooley, *Teaching English Usage,* p. 139.

Due to, caused by, owing to. *Due to* was originally an adjective. No one questions its adjectival use in sentences like these: His lameness was *due to* an accident. The bad spring floods, *due to* prolonged rains, did much damage to the stockyards. The adverbial use of *due to,* as in "Due to an accident, we arrived late," has been common in speech for a long time, and there is no lack of instances of this use in formal writing. (See: Fowler, *Modern English Usage,* p. 123; Curme, *Syntax,* pp. 560–561; Krapp, *A Comprehensive Guide to Good English,* p. 210; Pooley, *Teaching English Usage,* p. 140.) Many educated people, however, object to its use as an abverb or a preposition. The realistic attitude of this handbook is that it is unwise to invite the censure of people whose opinions you value by using expressions that make them squirm. *Owing to* will easily take the place of *due to.* If you ask why *owing to* is better than *due to,* the answer must be that these two just grew up differently.

Generally accepted:

The child's inability to learn may be *due to* poor eyesight.
The accident was *caused by* his carelessness.
Owing to poor sales and high costs, the shop had to close.

Informal usage, accepted by some in formal situations:

Due to an accident, we arrived late.
Due to high taxes, many industries are unable to continue.

Revisions to avoid the construction:

We arrived late because we had an accident.
Our late arrival was due to an accident.
Many industries are unable to continue because of high taxes.
The failure of the crop was caused by the rainy season.

Elegant. Means "characterized by elegance," "fastidious," "refined." Colloquial in the sense of "fine," "excellent," "superior." *Example:* She gave an excellent (*not* elegant) interpretation of Ophelia. This is a delicious (*not* elegant) salad.

Enthuse. U. S. colloquial for "to be enthusiastic" or "to show enthusiasm." Many people dislike it thoroughly. *Formal:* She never showed any enthusiasm (*not* enthused) about grand opera.

Equally as good. This may be wordy, but many educated people use the expression. It means "equally good," or "just as good." *Examples:* My composition was just as good (*not* equally as good) as his.

Etc. *Et cetera,* meaning "and so forth," "and others," "and the rest," should be avoided in literary and artistic writing. If you use it in informal or technical writing, never use *and etc.*

Exam. *See* ad.

Except. Dialectal, regional, or archaic for *unless. Dialectal:* I will not go except you go too. *Standard:* I will not go unless you go too.

Expect. Colloquial in the sense of "suppose."

Farther, further. The fine distinction between these two words, and between the superlative forms, *farthest, furthest,* is that both can be used to speak of distance, but that *further* and *furthest* have an additional meaning of "additional." See *Webster's Dictionary of Synonyms*, p. 331, and Pooley, p. 146. *Standard usage:* They could go no farther. The Johansen party penetrated furthest into the jungle. The senator promised further revelations soon.

Faze. American slang or colloquial for *disconcert, worry, disturb, bother, daunt.* It has no connection with *phase. Colloquial:* He wasn't fazed by the amount of work he had to do.

Fellow. Colloquial for *a person, a boy, a man, a beau, a sweetheart.* It is a very useful word in college, for it dodges the embarrassing necessity of distinguishing between a man and a boy.

Fewer, less. Use *fewer* when referring to numbers. Use *less* when referring to quantity or degree. (See also *amount, number.*) *Examples:* There will be fewer (*not* less) men on the campus next year. Most women are earning less than they did last year.

Fine. See *nice.* A vague word of approval, entirely proper in conversation. In exact writing a more exact word should be used. See Evans and Evans, *A Dictionary of Contemporary American Usage,* pp. 317–318.

Fix. In the sense of *a predicament, to arrange, to repair,* it is colloquial. *Formal:* The headmaster was in a predicament (*not* fix). The engineers did not have time to repair (*not* fix) the bridges. *Colloquial:* Give me a few minutes more so that I can fix my hair. Do you think you can fix my watch?

Folks. Colloquial for "relatives, family."

For to. Now archaic or illiterate. Omit *for* in such expressions as: He went for to buy a new hat.

Funny. Colloquial for *strange, queer, odd.*

Gent. Shortened form of gentleman. Now considered vulgar. Say *men's clothes* instead of *gents' clothes.*

Gentleman, lady. It is better to say *man, woman* instead of *gentleman, lady* except when there is intended distinction between persons of refinement and persons of ill breeding.

Get. Get has a large number of uses, both formal and informal. In formal or literary contexts it means *obtain, receive, procure, acquire.* In informal and conversational usage, it has a large number of meanings, figurative, idiomatic, and otherwise. Whenever you are in doubt about some expression involving *get,* consult your dictionary. In speech *have got* in the sense of *have* is very common. The form *have got to* in the sense of *must* or *have to* is felt to be more emphatic. *Get to go* for *manage to go* or *contrive to go* is labeled dialectal by *Webster's International. Got* and *gotten* are both past participles found in speech and in writing. (See A. C. Bartlett, *"Get, have got,* and *have got to," College English,* Feb., 1949.)

Guess. In the sense of *suppose, think,* it is still objectionable to many people, although many good writers have so used it for five hundred years. Avoid trouble by saying "I presume," or "I suppose," instead of "I guess."

Had of. Illiterate for *had. Standard:* I wish I had (*not* had of) written my theme yesterday.

Had better, had best, had rather. Correct idiomatic forms. So are *would rather, would best, would better.*

Had ought, hadn't ought. These are regional or dialectal or colloquial forms. It is easy to avoid criticism by saying *ought, should, should have, shouldn't have,* forms appropriate in both speech and writing.

Hanged, hung. People are *hanged;* objects are *hung. Standard:*

Carter was hanged (*not* hung) for murdering his wife. Her wet clothes were hung (*not* hanged) on a stick before the fire.

Hardly, scarcely, only. Avoid combining with another negative so as to form what is called the "double negative." Some of these double negatives are current colloquially. *Formal:* He was so weary that he could (*not* couldn't) hardly move. The little animal ventures out (*not* does not venture out) only at night. He could (*not* couldn't) scarcely see the man on the pier.

Have got. See *get.*

Healthful, Healthy. *Webster's New International* states that *healthy* and *healthful* "are interchangeable within certain limits." But in a strict sense, *heathy* means "being in a state of health"; *healthful* means "serving the promote health." People are healthy, but good food is healthful. See also *Webster's Dictionary of Synonyms,* p. 406.

If, whether. Both *if* and *whether* are used to introduce a noun clause in indirect questions after verbs like *doubt, ask, wonder. Whether* is more likely to be used if an alternative introduced by *or* is stated. There is still some feeling among teachers and writers that *whether* is more formal, but both words are used and have been used for many years to introduce noun clauses. *Examples:* I doubt if they can come. He wondered whether or not he should warn the settlers. Ask him if he has any food left.

In, into. In theory, the distinction between these words is that *in* denotes location inside something, whereas *into* denotes motion from outside to inside something. In practice, however, *in* is also used in the sense of *into. Examples:* Throw that in the waste basket. Please jump in the lake.

In back of, back of. Both forms, still considered by many to belong to informal speech, have been used in writing for some time. The more formal word is *behind.*

In regards to. The correct idiom is *in regard to.*

Invite. Should not be used for *invitation,* especially in formal situations. *Example:* We sent her an invitation (*not* an invite).

Is when, is where. In definitions, using a *when* or *where* clause after the verb *is* produces an awkward sentence. A *when* clause after the verb *is,* however, has some sanction of usage both in writing and speech. Thoreau said, "Morning is when I am most awake . . . ." Of course that is not a definition. In a definition, instead of writing "A sonnet is when a poem has fourteen lines," you can easily dodge all difficulties by writing "A sonnet is a poem of fourteen lines." See R. B. Thomas, "*When* clauses after *is* (*was*)," *College English,* April, 1949. Bergen Evans and Cornelia Evans, in *A Dictionary of Contemporary American Usage*, p. 552, state most surprisingly, "*When* cannot be used to join a clause to a noun as children sometimes do in giving a definition . . . ." and "*Where* cannot be used . . . to introduce a definition . . . ."

Its, it's. *Its* is the possessive form of *it.* *It's* is the contraction of *it is.* The two forms should not be confused.

Kind, sort. In colloquial usage, these words are often felt to be plural in constructions like this: "These kind of dogs are usually hard to train." In more formal situations, both in speech and in writing, most people prefer the singular, as: "I do not like this sort of entertainment. That kind of man is not to be trusted."

Kind of, sort of. Colloquial when used to modify a verb or an adjective. Use *somewhat, somehow, a little, in some degree, rather, for some reason* in formal contexts.

Lady. See *gentleman.*

Lay, lie. The principal parts of *lay* are: Now I *lay* it down; I *laid* it down; I have *laid* it down. The principal parts of *lie* are: I *lie* down; I *lay* down this morning; the dog *had lain* in the shade all day. Professor Pooley, in *Teaching English* Usage, pp. 163–166, points out that many educated persons have in the past confused the principal parts of these two verbs, but he does not recommend further confusion. The participles of *lie* and *lay* are *lying* and *laying.* *Standard:* He had laid (*not* lain) his bundle on the table. It had lain (*not* laid) there all morning. The dog was lying (*not* laying) in the road.

Lead, led. The past tense of *lead* (pronounced *leed*) is *led* (pronounced like the metal *lead.*)

Learn, teach. In current usage, *learn* does not mean "teach." *Standard:* My mother taught (*not* learned) me how to cook.

Leave, let. It is just as correct to say *leave him alone* as *let him alone.* These two words have several different meanings, none of which cause any difficulty in college writing.

Liable, apt, likely. See *apt.*

Like, as, as if. In written English, *as* and *as if* introduce clauses; *like* generally governs a noun or pronoun. In speech, the substitution of *like* for *as,* and less commonly for *as if,* is widespread, and, it should be noted, so is the disapproval of it. Evans and Evans (p. 276) list many authors from Shakespeare to Masefield and Maugham who have used *like* for *as.* In spite of this fact, many educated persons still disapprove of it. But *like* is used informally as a conjuction, and it is probable that sooner or later it will gain general acceptance in formal writing. It has not done so yet. *Informal:* I wish you would do like I said you should. *Formal:* The war, just as he had predicted, lasted more than five years. Few men could sway an audience as he did.

Line. Like *field, factor,* and *proposition* it should be used with care. In its most popular collegiate use, *line* is number twenty-nine of the fifty groups of meanings given in *Webster's International:* "characteristic form of glib, and often persuasive, address." In that sense it is slang. One hesitates to recommend an adequate literary substitute. In another sense, as in the following examples, it is vague and redundant. *Poor:* We bought a few things in the line of groceries. *Better:* We bought some groceries. *Poor:* Have you any interesting books in the line of fiction? *Better:* Have you any interesting novels? *Poor:* He wrote epics and other poems along that line. *Better:* He wrote epics and other narrative poems.

Locate. In the sense of *settle,* it is more appropriate in informal than in formal use.

Lot, lots of. Widely used colloquially for *many, much, a large number, a large amount, a great deal.* *Colloquial:* He has a lot to learn. (*Formal:* He has much to learn.) There are lots of exceptions to this rule. (*Formal:* There are many . . . .)

Mad. Colloquially *mad* is used in the sense of *angry.* In formal usage it means "insane."

Majority. Inaccurate when used with measures of quantity, time, distance. The appropriate word is *most. Example:* Most of the day (*not* The majority of the day) we stood in line and waited.

Might of. Illiterate for *might have.*

Most, almost. Most, in formal written English, is the superlative form of *much* or *many. Examples:* Much food, more food, most food; many men, more men, most men. *Almost* is an adverb meaning "nearly." In colloquial use *most* is often substituted for *almost. Formal:* almost (*not* most) all of our men have returned from Korea. In conversational usage, *most* is frequently used to qualify *all, everyone, everybody, anyone, anybody, always.*

Neither, nor; either, or. *Neither* should be followed by *nor; either* should be followed by *or.* Both *neither* and *either* may be used with more than two alternatives, as: Either past, present, or future . . . . See Nicholson, p. 362.

Nice. A vague word of mild approval. Use sparingly in serious writing. In informal speech it is appropriate when you mean to be vague and mild.

No good, no-good. Colloquial when used for *worthless, useless, of no value.*

Nowhere near, nowheres near. Labeled *archaic and dialectal* in *Webster's New International Dictionary.* In writing and in more or less formal speech it is better to use *not nearly. Example:* That was not nearly (*not* nowhere near) as much as he had expected.

O, Oh. *O* is used with another word, a substantive, usually in direct address. It is always capitalized and is not followed by any mark of punctuation. *Oh* is an exclamation, not capitalized except when it begins a sentence, and is followed by either a comma or an exclamation point.

Off of. The *of* is unnecessary. *Example:* Please get off (*not* off of) that ladder. He took the book off (*not* off of) the shelf.

Out loud. Labeled *colloquial* by *WNID.* Standard forms, good in both formal and informal situations, are *aloud, loud, loudly, audibly. Example:* He called aloud for help.

Outside of. Colloquial for *except, besides. Example:* When the robbery occurred, the policeman saw no one except (*not* outside of) the mailman on the street.

Over with. In the sense of *finished, ended,* it is colloquial.

Party. Except in legal and telephone usage, it is colloquial when it means "a person."

Per cent. It may be used after numbers. The sign % is not used except after figures in tabulations or in technical writing. It is not an exact synonym for *percentage. Examples:* A high percentage of the population is illiterate. Only ten per cent (or *percent*) are self-supporting. But Evans and Evans say there is no difference in meaning between the two words (p. 363).

Plenty. Colloquial when used as an adverb in such expressions as *plenty good, plenty good enough, plenty rich,* etc., or as an adjective before a noun. *Colloquial:* He was plenty rich. The room is plenty large. There is plenty wood for another fire. *Formal:* He was very rich. The room is large enough. There is enough wood for another fire. Ten dollars is plenty.

P.M. See *A.M., a.m.*

Poorly. Colloquial for *in poor health, not well, unwell.*

Practicable, practical. *Practicable* means "something possible, feasible, usable." *Practical* means "useful, not theoretical, experienced." *Practical* may apply to persons, things, ideas; *practicable* may not apply to persons. See *WDS,* page 639.

Proposition, proposal. *Proposal* implies a direct and explicit act of proposing; *proposition* implies a statement or principle for discussion. The loose use of *proposition* to mean "idea, thing, a task, a business enterprise, a problem," is disliked by many people. *Examples:* It is a poor practice (*not* proposition) to study until three in the morning. Moving the settlers out of the district was an impractical plan (*not* proposition).

Quiet, quite. Two words carelessly confused. *Quiet* has to do with stillness or calmness. In formal standard usage, *quite* means "entirely, completely." You are quite right. In informal usage it may also be used to mean "very, to a considerable degree." The dog seems quite friendly.

Raise, rise. Two verbs often confused. The principal parts are:

Raise:	*Rise:*
I *raise* my hand.	I *rise* in the morning
He *raised* the window.	They *rose* before I did.
They *have raised* the flag.	They *had risen* at sunrise.

Real. Colloquial as an adverb in the sense of *really* or *very*. *Colloquial:* His playing was real brilliant. It was a real exciting game. *Formal:* His playing was really brilliant. It was a very exciting game.

Reason is because, reason is on account of. In informal speech, such constructions as "The reason I came to college was because I wanted to study engineering" are common, and they occur occasionally in writing. Some educated persons consider the expressions established in both writing and speech; others object to them on two counts: they are wordy and repetitious, and they are slovenly. It is well to learn how to avoid them.

Awkward: The reason they were defeated was because the field was wet.
The reason he was late was because the roads were blocked.
The reason for my poor work in English is due to my poor high-school preparation.
The reason I can't spell is on account of I never learned how in high school.

Revised: They were defeated because the field was wet.
He was late because the roads were blocked.
My poor work in English is due to my poor high-school preparation.
I am a poor speller because I did not learn how to spell in high school.

Right. In the sense of *very,* it is dialectal. *Example:* He was a very (*not* right) good speaker.

Same, such. Appropriate in legal documents. In ordinary speech and writing, it is better to use *it, this, that.* *Example:* Please repair the camera and ship it (*not* same) to me tomorrow.

Seldom ever, seldom or ever. The correct idioms are *seldom, very seldom, hardly ever, seldom if ever.*

Set, sit. Two verbs often confused. Learn the principal parts: I *set* it down; I *have set* it down; now he *sits* down; I *sat* down; they *have sat* down. But of course one may speak of *a setting hen,* and *the sun sets,* not *sits.* You may set the cup on the shelf and then sit down. I sat on the stool after I had set the cup down.

Shape. Colloquial for *condition.* *Colloquial:* The athlete was in excellent shape. *Formal:* The equipment was in very good condition (*not* shape).

So. As a conjunction between main clauses, *so* is much overused in student writing. Usually the primary fault is too little subordination instead of too much use of *so.* *Examples:* The bridge was blown up during the night, and so the attack was delayed. The attack was delayed because the bridge had been blown up during the night. The Russians were not ready, so they waited until August to declare war on Japan. Since the Russians were not ready, they waited until August to declare war on Japan.

In clauses of purpose, the standard subordinating conjunction is *so that,* as in: They flew low so that they could observe the results of the bombing. But *so* is also used, especially in spoken English.

So as a "feminine intensive" can be easily overworked in speech—and it often is. It has a long literary tradition, however. *Examples:* She is so kind and so charming. The work is so hard.

Such. As an intensive, it is used like *awful* or *so.* See Pooley, *Teaching English Usage,* pp. 96–98. *Such* introducing a clause of result is followed by *that.* *Example:* There was such an explosion that it could be felt for twenty miles.

When introducing a relative clause, *such* is followed by *as*. *Example:* Such amendments as you may stipulate will be included in the contract.

Sure. Colloquial for *certainly, surely, indeed. Formal:* This is certainly (*not* sure) an interesting story.

Suspicion. Dialectal when used as a verb. The standard form is *suspect. Example:* We suspected (*not* suspicioned) that something was wrong.

Swell. Colloquial for *stylish, fashionable, smartly clothed.* Slang for *excellent, very good, interesting, enjoyable,* and a host of other words expressing approval or commendation. *Examples:* We had an enjoyable (*not* a swell) evening. It is a thrilling (*not a* swell) game.

Take stock in. Colloquial for *accept, believe, put faith in. Example:* Can we believe (*not* take stock in) his promises?

That there, this here, etc. Illiterate forms. The standard forms are *that, this, these, those.*

Their, they're. *Their* is a possessive pronoun. *They're* means "they are." *Example:* They're happy because *their* team won.

To, too, two. An elementary spelling problem. *Example:* He *too* should make *two* trips *to* the dictionary *to* learn how *to* spell. It's not *too* hard.

Try and, try to. *Webster's New International* labels *try and* as *colloq.* for *try to,* but Pooley (pp. 132–133) points out that *try and* has a long and respectable history.

Very, very much. Many educated persons object to *very* instead of *very much* or *very greatly* as a modifier of a verb or a participle in a verb phrase. Other persons point out examples of its use in the works of reputable writers. See the note under *very* in *Webster's New International. Examples:* They were very pleased. They were very much pleased. They seemed very disturbed. They seemed very greatly disturbed.

Wait on. Regional for *wait for, stay for.* Standard in the sense of *attend, perform services for,* as: It was the other girl who waited on me.

Want in, want out, want off, etc. Dialectal forms for *want to come in, want to go out, want to get off,* etc.

Way, ways. *Way* is colloquial for *condition.* *Ways* is dialectal for *distance, way.* Formal: When we saw him, he was in bad health (*not* in a bad way.) We walked a long distance (*not* ways) before we rested.

Where at. The *at* is unnecessary. *Example:* Where is he now? (*not* Where at is he now?)

While. Frequently overused as a conjunction. Usually *but, and,* or *whereas* would be more precise. It is standard in the sense of *at the same time as* or *although.* It is colloquial in the sense of *whereas.*

Without. Dialectal for *unless.*

You all. In Southern speech, *you all* is the plural form of *you.*

INDEX TO QUOTED PASSAGES

QUOTATIONS IDENTIFIED HERE BY AUTHOR ONLY ARE USUALLY VERY BRIEF.

INDEX

ALL NUMBERS REFER TO PAGES.

HANDBOOK KEY